The Rise of a Party-State in Kenya

The Rise
of a Party-State
in Kenya

From "Harambee!" to "Nyayo!"

Jennifer A. Widner

UNIVERSITY OF CALIFORNIA PRESS
Berkeley · Los Angeles · Oxford

University of California Press
Berkeley and Los Angeles, California

University of California Press, Ltd.
Oxford, England

Library of Congress Cataloging-in-Publication Data

Widner, Jennifer A.

   The rise of a party-state in Kenya : from "Harambee" to "Nyayo!" /
Jennifer A. Widner
    p.   cm.
   Includes bibliographical references and index.
   ISBN 0-520-07624-9
   1. Kenya—Politics and government—1978–   2. Kenya African
National Union.   I. Title.
DT433.584.W53   1993
967.6204—dc20   91-44328
                                                    CIP

Printed in the United States of America
9   8   7   6   5   4   3   2   1

Contents

List of Maps and Tables   ix

Acknowledgments   xi

List of Acronyms, Abbreviations,
and Foreign Terms   xv

Abbreviated Chronology of Events   xvii

1. Creating Political Order   1
   Single-Party Dominance   4
   The Rise of the Party-State in Africa   8
   The Argument   22
   The Kenyan Case   30
   Overview   37

2. Single-Party Dominance, 1964–1969   39
   "Civil Society": Class, Ethnicity, and Clientelism   41
   The Competition for Resources   47
   The Players   51
   Political Strategy and KANU as a Catchall Party   56
   Harambee and the Basis for Compromise   60
   Restriction of Opposition   66
   The Provincial Administration and the Civil
      Service   70

Party-Government Relations in Post-
Independence Kenya 72

3. The Struggle in the Rift Valley, 1970–1975 75
The Source of Competition 77
Organizing an Opposition 84
The Rise of a Populist Coalition 85
Calls for Redistribution 88
GEMA and the Bid to Rejuvenate KANU 92
The President's Strategy 94
The Battle for Political Space 98
Resolution 103
Conclusions 107

4. The Transition Period, 1976–1980 110
GEMA and the Change-the-Constitution
Movement 112
Ethnic Arithmetic and the Party Elections
of 1977 118
Distributional Coalitions and the 1979 General
Election 125
KANU at the End of the Transition Period 128

5. From "Harambee!" to "Nyayo!" 1980–1985 130
Moi's Accession to the Presidency 133
Faction and the Proscription of Ethnic Welfare
Societies 137
The New KANU Monopoly 143
The Njonjo Affair 147
Nyayo: Following in the Footsteps 150
The Party-State in 1985 154

6. Party, State, and Civil Society, 1985–1990 162
The Consolidation of Changes in Party-State
Relations 164
Changing Patterns of Participation 171
"Civil Society" and Opposition Success 178
Testing the Limits 195

7. The Kenyan Party-State in Comparative Perspective 198
The Argument in Review 199
KANU in Comparative Perspective 204

The Kenyan Holdout   214
Single-Party Rule, "Civil Society," and Patterns
   of Governance   224

Appendix: The Uses of Evidence   233

Notes   237

Bibliography   257

Index   271

Maps and Tables

MAPS

1. Ethno-Regional Boundaries in Kenya   xxi
2. Parliamentary Constituencies in Kenya, 1963–1987   xxii–iii

TABLES

1. Key Members of the "Family" Faction of KANU's
   Conservative Wing, 1965–1978   76
2. Key Figures in the 1974–1975 Rift Valley Opposition and
   Their Subsequent Careers   106
3. Distribution of Harambee Contributions from the
   President, Vice President, or Senior Officials, Proportion
   of Total by Region, 1977–1983   143
4. The Status of Multi-Party Debate in Sub-Saharan Africa,
   July 1991, Showing Participants in First Wave of Change   216

Acknowledgments

Today's political science too often inculcates a dispassionate view of politics among scholars. Somewhere in the "literature reviews," mathematical models, "event counts," and language of "transaction costs" are buried issues and incidents that have real impacts on people's lives. The research that led to this book offered the kind of political education graduate schools and secluded research centers do not provide. In the 1980s, restrictions on speech and association in Kenya chilled discussion of policy and institutional development. During the period in which the research was carried out, Kenyan civil servants became noticeably less willing to take decisions, for fear of disapproval, and government business in some ministries slowed markedly. Politics was not fit material for discussion in public places because of the proliferation of security agents in bars, clubs, and offices. The process of carrying out the study and writing successive drafts thus offered a series of object lessons about what it means to live in a political system rapidly becoming both less competitive and more uncertain. Those lessons were sometimes painful but always invaluable. My first debt is to those Kenyan citizens who tolerated my clumsy questions, took the time to discuss events in their country, and assumed the risks they did. I look forward to the day when I might acknowledge their assistance individually.

Because of the limits on information-gathering and analysis in Kenya, there are not only additional facts but also nuances and interpretations or events and statements the author may have overlooked. The task of refining and improving this understanding will necessarily lie with others. This project has underscored what we all know but often do not acknowledge: scholarship is a community endeavor. It is my hope that my Kenyan colleagues, in particular, will be able to expand and correct the analysis presented.

In that context, my second debt is to fellow students of Kenyan affairs and Africa specialists. I benefited greatly from theoretical discussions with Robert Bates and have appreciated his continuing encouragement. David Throup provided meticulous comments on an early manuscript draft—certainly some of the most detailed I received, although I did not adequately acknowledge them at the time. Angelique Haugerud, Joel Barkan, Judith Geist, Barbara Grosch, David Leonard, Susanne Mueller, Kinuthia Macharia, and Steven Orvis also contributed valuably to various aspects of the research. I recognize that not all will agree with the conclusions this book derives but hope that the argument it offers will be the basis of many fruitful conversations.

I owe a great deal to the manuscript's two press readers, Thomas Callaghy and Crawford Young, who provided the most useful written comments. I am grateful to both for the time they invested and for their willingness to reveal their identities after the review process was over, which enabled me to pursue questions further. Their breadth of knowledge, sensitivity to the problems of scholarship in African settings, and understanding of the craft offered invaluable lessons.

My third debt is to the people who made the research and writing possible. The National Science Foundation gave a Dissertation Improvement Grant to support the fieldwork. William J. Foltz provided the initial encouragement to pursue the study of African politics and shaped the analytic approach of portions of the study in the course of many discussions. He inspired by his clarity of mind and encouraged, when continuation seemed impossible, with his pragmatism. Robert Harms offered insights from the histories of other African countries, intellectual breadth, and good-natured support throughout the research phase of the study. My colleagues in the Harvard Government Department and at the Center for International Affairs at Harvard have contributed greatly to the completion of the project. Their civility, commitment, and wit made possible an exchange of ideas I have found but rarely. Special thanks are due to Jorge Dominguez, Frances Hagopian, Samuel Huntington, Stephen Haggard, Robert Keohane, and Susan Pharr. Gwen Robinson deserves much appreciation for her meticulous research assistance during the later stages of the manuscript's preparation.

Editors are often underappreciated. Without the great thoughtfulness and perseverance of the editorial team at the University of California Press, this book would not have been possible. Richard Holway, Erika Büky, Peter Dreyer, and Doug Abrams all worked very hard to ensure consistency and accuracy in the text and to push me to consider new material. Rarely is an author so lucky as to have the advice of *two* Africa-hands!

Finally, I would like to thank the members of my family, who have had to endure too many static-filled telephone calls, writing vacations, and mad dashes to airports.

Acronyms, Abbreviations, and Foreign Terms

CPK	Church of the Province of Kenya (Anglican)
FORD	Forum for the Restoration of Democracy
GEMA	Gikuyu, Embu, and Meru Association
GSU	Government Services Unit
ICJ	International Commission of Jurists
KADU	Kenya African Democratic Union
KANU	Kenya African National Union
KASA	Kenya African Socialist Alliance
KAU	Kenya African Union
KCA	Kikuyu Central Association
KCGA	Kenya Coffee Growers' Association
KIA	Kenya Institute for Administration
KLFA	Kenya Land Freedom Army
KPCU	Kenya Planters' Cooperative Union
KPU	Kenya People's Union
KTDA	Kenya Tea Development Authority

LSK	Law Society of Kenya
MVOA	Matatu Vehicle Owners Association
NCCK	National Council of Churches of Kenya
NTZDC	Nyayo Tea Zones Development Corporation
PCEA	Presbyterian Church of East Africa
KSh	Kenyan shilling (1 KSh = 100 cents)
ahoi	Kikuyu term for squatters or farming households without their own land
jua kali	"hot sun": a term for the informal sector of the economy in Kenya
harambee	Swahili for "let's pull together"; self-help development
majimboism	regionalism
matajiri	Swahili for "the wealthy" or "the rich"
matatu	a privately owned small truck converted to transport passengers commercially
nyayo	Swahili for "follow in the footsteps"
shamba	a plot of land for farming
ujamaa	Swahili for "family"; the name given to the villagization and rural development program adopted in Tanzania in 1967
wananchi	the common people

Abbreviated Chronology
of Events

1963   Kenya gains independence

1969   Kenya People's Union (KPU) banned

1972   ILO report on regional inequalities

1973   GEMA spearheads attempt to "rejuvenate" KANU

1974   General elections

1975   J. M. Kariuki assassinated

1976   Change-the-Constitution Movement sponsored by the "Family"

1977   Abortive KANU party elections

1978   Kenyatta dies in August; Daniel arap Moi becomes president

1979   General elections

1980   Proscription of ethnic welfare societies

1982   Constitutional amendment makes Kenya a de jure single-party state

1982   Coup attempt in August

1983   Ouster of Minister for Constitutional Affairs Charles Njonjo

1983   General elections

1985   KANU party elections

1986   Queuing system replaces secret ballot (March)

1986   KANU Disciplinary Committee created

1986   Constitutional Amendment Bill of 1986 eliminates provisions for security of tenure of attorney general, controller, and auditor general

1987   Redistricting creates thirty new constituencies

1987   KANU Disciplinary Committee dissolved; Ministry of National Guidance and Political Affairs created

1988   Constitutional amendment removes security of tenure of judges

1988   KANU party elections called two years early (September)

1990   Kenneth Matiba and Charles Rubia lead call for multi-party system

1990   KANU absorbs confederation of trade unions and the women's movement

1990   Charles Rubia and Kenneth Matiba detained without trial

1990   Saba Saba Day riots (July)

1990   KANU Review Committee formed to assess party procedures

1990   Oginga Odinga hints at creation of new opposition party in November

1991   Student-led protests in Nairobi in mid-November

1991   Donors' meeting in Paris at the end of November leads to suspension of most government-to-government economic assistance, pending improved respect for civil liberties and a clear reduction in levels of corruption; the International Monetary Fund halts loans in December

1991   Moi arrests Nicholas Biwott, former minister of energy, on suspicion that Biwott had personally appropriated foreign aid and participated in the murder of Robert Ouko, the late minister for foreign affairs. On December 3, Moi announces that new political parties will be allowed to register

1991   In late December, several cabinet ministers resign to protest the president's failure to call elections within KANU

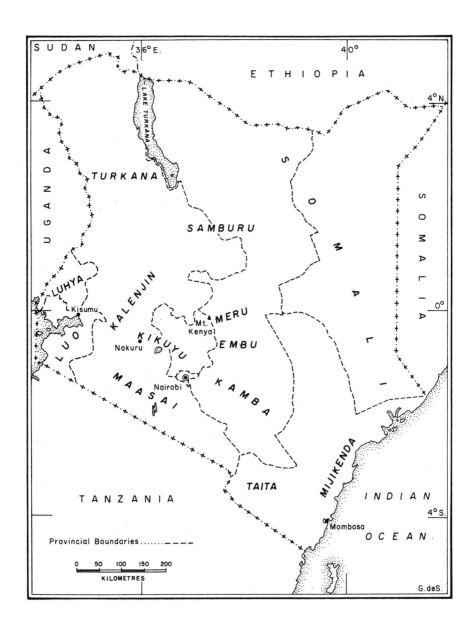

Map 1. Ethno-regional boundaries in Kenya. *Source:* David Leonard, *African Successes: The Public Management of Kenyan Rural Development* (Berkeley: University of California Press, 1991), p. xx.

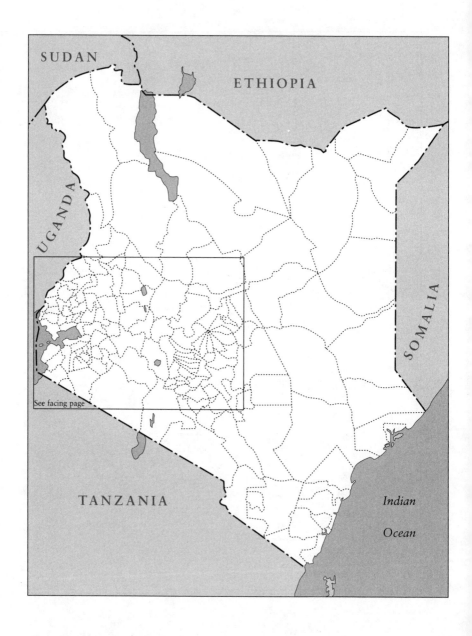

Map 2. Parliamentary constituencies in Kenya, 1963–1987.

Index to Constituencies Discussed in Text

1	Embu North	16	Kiambaa
2	Embu East	17	Kikuyu
3	Embu South	18	Limuru
4	Kangundo	19	Eldoret North
5	Nyandarua South	20	Eldoret South
6	Nyandarua North	21	Tinderet
7	Nyeri	22	Kericho
8	Mathira	23	Lurambi North
9	Othaya	24	Lurambi South
10	South Tetu (Mukurweini)	25	Mumias
11	Mbiri	26	Emukhaya
12	Kandara	27	Butere
13	Makuyu	28	Bungoma Central
14	Gatundu	29	Bungoma South
15	Githunguri	30	Bungoma East
		31	Bondo

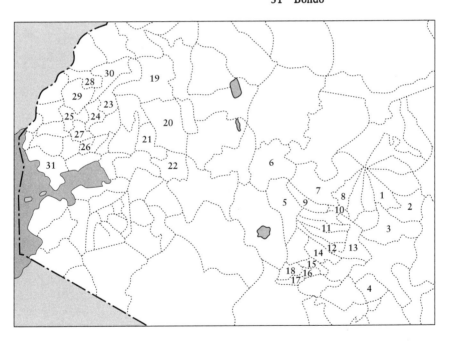

CHAPTER ONE

Creating Political Order

In December 1989, disagreement erupted between Kenya's president, Daniel arap Moi, and Professor Wangari Maathai, the leader of a Kenyan environmental group, and foreign donors. The subject of the row was a plan to construct a new sixty-story office tower to house the headquarters of the Kenya African National Union (KANU), the country's only legal political party, and a party-run media center. The design called for a large statue of the president as the centerpiece of the building's decoration. Kenya had already moved to borrow $160 million to supplement $40 million in local loans, both steps in violation of agreements with the World Bank and International Monetary Fund stipulating only limited borrowing—and borrowing only for productive purposes. Moi told Maathai and the foreign donors that they could take their complaints elsewhere.[1]

The plans were symbolic of a significant change in the character of Kenyan political life, a change that began to crystallize during the Moi era. Until Moi's efforts to modify the relationship between the party and the government, beginning in 1982, KANU had existed only as a loosely knit grouping of politicians. Under Moi's predecessor, Jomo Kenyatta, Kenya's first independence leader, the party had tolerated some internal criticism and debate over its platform, albeit to a gradually diminishing degree. It had used its loyalty pledge rarely, and its ranks harbored a number of well-organized and enduring "factional" divisions, nearly "corporate" in character.[2] The provincial administration, not the party, was Kenyatta's chosen vehicle for securing compliance with government policies and stances.

Under Moi, the relationship between the party and the government began to change. The new president was increasingly ill at ease with the existence of alternative forms of political association and moved rapidly to curtail the ethnic and regional welfare societies that had long served as a springboard for political candidates. Following the proscription of these organizations in 1980, and the move to a de jure single-party system in 1982, Moi sought to eradicate factional divisions in KANU by creating internal disciplinary committees and proposing a system of party schools (never established) to instill rules of behavior and fidelity to the positions of the new government. He moved still further away from the Kenyatta political strategy of the 1960s by seeking a more active role in the selection of party officers and by supporting, off and on, a "youth wing" with watchdog or surveillance responsibilities. In short, between 1980 and the proposal for the office tower in 1989, the party acquired a new and far stronger role in the pursuit of political order, and its boundaries began to merge with those of the Office of the President, or "State House." The proposed building, with its statue of the president, would enshrine the new order in stone and steel.

Other changes accompanied the new relationship between party and government. Immediately after the declaration of a single-party system in 1982, the government put down a coup attempt by air force officers and their allies, who allegedly sought to secure greater participation or representation in public affairs. The real reasons for the coup attempt and its collapse are not known. The "August disturbances," as the government of Kenya later called them, generated significant presidential and popular uneasiness, however. Kenyans from widely different parts of the country and walks of life spoke of the need to proceed cautiously so as not to follow the paths of their neighbors in strife-torn Uganda, Sudan, Ethiopia, and Somalia.

By the middle of the decade, the tenor of everyday Kenyan politics had changed in the view of the editor of the *Weekly Review*, Hilary Ng'weno. During the 1985 party elections in Kenya, Ng'weno apologized to his readers for his magazine's coverage of national events. He remarked that Kenyan political life, always complicated, had finally become opaque, a matter of personalities and one-on-one, closed-door negotiation instead of predictable public stands on issues and coherent, brokered alliances. Rumor and speculation were rife, inspired by the many levels of significance associated with words and actions in the absence of agreements that could stabilize meanings. Political language acquired a new "code"; where previously politicians had spoken in Parliament and with each other of "who gets what," they increasingly substituted parable and metaphor. With constraints on political association, churches and other organizations with international connections became the refuge for dissenting voices and took a more active role in debate. Rates of participation in standard political activities, such as voting, diminished. Indeed, turnout in national elections had declined to 30 percent of eligible voters by 1983. With much of the rest of the continent, Kenya had come to share a "shrinking of the political arena."[3] Although opposition among elites and some of the "popular classes" had not ceased, it had taken different forms, and, in most instances, it failed to stop presidential efforts to restrict political activity.

This book proposes one understanding of these complex political events and tries to demonstrate its utility in making sense of some of the situations that seem impenetrable even to so astute an observer as Hilary Ng'weno. It focuses on the shift in government-party relations and tries to explain the move from a single-party-dominant system in which KANU remained a loosely organized "debating society" with little policy influence toward a Kenyan "party-state" in which KANU increasingly became a vehicle for the Office of the President to control political opposition. It documents the sustained interest in democratic reforms among some segments of the political elite and tries to explain why it proved so difficult for these people to organize effectively to maintain space for political competition.

Within the universe of African politics, there is substantial variation in the degree to which single-party-dominant systems have become "party-states." Kenya long appeared to be an exception to trends detected in countries such as Ghana and Zaire. During the 1960s and 1970s, it was one of Africa's "relative successes" in the eyes of many Westerners. This reputation stemmed in large part from the country's agricultural performance, paralleled on the African continent only by South Africa, Zimbabwe, and Côte d'Ivoire, but it also derived from the perception that the country had retained key elements of the Westminster parliamentary system that had been adopted at independence. Although the Kenyatta era witnessed several political assassinations, detentions, and the proscription of the opposition Kenya People's Union (KPU), most analysts saw a qualitative difference between the political life that existed in Kenya and the systems of Ghana or Tanzania. Even when members of the KANU government periodically attempted to quash alternative political parties, debate continued between well-defined, semi-organized, and enduring factions within the ranks. Kenyatta pointedly ignored suggestions that he strengthen the organization by developing a clear platform or by providing funds through the party for local projects and events. Nor did he use the party as a vehicle for securing acceptance of policies. Party members maintained stronger ties with their local constituents than did their counterparts in comparable countries simply by virtue of having to compete in periodic elections without party financial backing. Indeed, even during the late 1980s, some Kenya-watchers still suggested that debate was more public, and that responsiveness to citizen demands was greater, than in most other African nations. In writing about this period, Joel Barkan and Frank Holmquist observed: "The Kenyan state appear[s] to be more account-able to its public than its neighbors are . . . [and to be] regarded as more legitimate by its citizens."[4] Dirk Berg-Schlosser concurred, arguing that in contrast to the situation in most of its sub-Saharan neighbors, mem-bers of Parliament in Kenya "do constitute an important link between the central political system and the public at large, at least in rural areas."[5]

Nonetheless, between 1980 and late 1991, Kenyans have witnessed a qualitative change in the role of the party in political life. The Office of the President took an ever more active role in KANU and used the or-ganization to control dissent within the country. Only late in 1990, when pressure from donors and from the "crowd" in Nairobi forced his hand, did Moi establish a KANU Review Committee and limit the ex-pansion of control by the party over the country's political life. Foreign donors again used their leverage to back the demands of some of the local opposition, precipitating the government's announcement in De-cember 1991 that Kenya would agree to register opposition parties.

It is precisely the distinctiveness of the case, the recentness of the changes, that makes Kenya especially interesting for those who seek a better understanding of the dynamics of transformation in government-party relations. By asking what altered between the early years of the Kenyatta era and the 1980s to produce the move to a party-state and by analyzing the sources of resistance to this shift, it should be possible to refine—or re-define—existing forms of explanation for the widespread growth of party-states across sub-Saharan Africa.

SINGLE-PARTY DOMINANCE

The single-party systems of sub-Saharan Africa have displayed signifi-cant variation since independence. A dominant party can tolerate a wide array of political opinions or only one. It can exercise influence over policy formation and supply decision-making elites, or it can yield those roles to a civil service. It can play a central role in enforcement of presidential decisions, or it can survive completely removed from that process. Certain characteristics often appear to go together. A party tolerant of debate is also likely to wield less influence over policy and play a more limited role in implementation than is one in which there is little difference between the "party platform" and the views of the president's office. Not all parties that limit dissent within their own ranks are vehicles for policy implementation and law enforcement, however.

The changes that took place in Kenya under Daniel arap Moi between 1980 and 1991 are especially interesting because they seem to fit a pattern that is observed elsewhere on the continent and is still poorly understood. In some countries, single parties have changed from loose and relatively powerless amalgams to vehicles through which heads of state are able to exercise social and political control. It is useful to characterize this pattern as a shift from a form of single-party dominance in which the party is a loosely organized "debating society" to a "party-state" in which the party is an adjunct of the executive or office of the president.

In using the term *party-state*, this analysis draws upon the insights of other social scientists but also modifies these. The late 1960s marked the academic discovery of "party-states" in Africa. The emergence of single-party systems in Guinea, Ghana, Zaire, Tanzania, and other countries shortly after independence forced observers to surrender their understanding of political parties as organizational vehicles for channeling and articulating the interests of different economic groups and to search for a new concept of the "political party" or party system that permitted a better account of the events unfolding on the African continent. Beginning with an investigation of the Parti démocratique de Côte d'Ivoire (PDCI), the political scientist Aristide Zolberg suggested that the day-to-day activities of most West African parties had little to do with straightforward articulation of group demands. Instead, he argued, party cells and branches spent enormous amounts of energy in the task of mobilizing participation and generating support for political incumbents. West African parties invested heavily in symbols and social events to *transmit* the points of view of government leaders to new voters and mobilize support for the regime. Other scholars amplified this analysis and likened many of the continent's parties to political machines that employed patronage to secure cooperation of local elites where central governments lacked the capacity to do so.[6] In most cases, these parties quickly eliminated their oppositions through enactment of extra-parliamentary restrictions on political meetings and absorption of leaders from other groups.[7]

In 1966, Zolberg published his classic work on party-state relations in the West African region, *Creating Political Order: The Party-States of West Africa*. On the basis of his observations of political change in the post-independence period, Zolberg posited two trends in West African politics: a trend toward single-party or single-party-dominant systems and subsequent confusion of the boundaries between the political party and the government—the emergence of the party-state. Zolberg suggested that the distinction between the incumbent party and government tended to diminish at the pinnacles of power and at the base. A high degree of governmental centralization meant that the senior officials of both government and party owed their continued tenure to a single man.

Zolberg and other analysts of the 1960s and early 1970s recognized that some of the new African parties assumed policy-making roles, and that authority for developing legislation thus came to rest in the hands of the party leadership, as did the power to appoint individuals to senior government posts. In many of the cases Zolberg describes, however, the responsibility for policy initiatives quickly passed from the party to the occupants of the president's office. Thus the concept of the "party-state" more appropriately refers to a governmental structure in which the party has lost policy influence and has assumed the role of transmitter and enforcer of policy decisions, with executive police powers. Heads of state sought to incorporate and co-opt representatives of major occupational groupings, forcing them to register as party organizations, and to institute "youth wings" or other "watchdog" agencies within the party that extended the leadership's surveillance capacity. In most cases, the party leadership impressed civil servants or police agents into service as collection agents in annual membership campaigns, making the difference between the party and the government less and less distinguishable to the average citizen. Finally, many leaders instituted schools or training programs to foster a shared point of view among party workers, candidates for office, and administrators. In Ghana, for instance, the First Republic government established the Nkrumah Ideological Institute to perform this role.

Thus, where they arose, the party-states of Africa distinguished themselves from other single-party-dominant systems, in which one party gained an overwhelming share of legislative seats, in (a) the use of the party, not just as a means of mobilizing regime support, but as an adjunct to the security forces in monitoring and controlling opposition; (b) confusion of party tasks with public tasks through use of administrative bodies to carry out party functions; and (c) the propagation of a single party platform, with little or no tolerance of internal dissent. In these cases, parties disappeared as vehicles for "interest articulation" or "aggregation," leading some observers, such as Immanuel Wallerstein, to talk about the spread of "no-party" systems.[8] Certainly, as systems of representation, parties nearly vanished, but as structures or organizations for monitoring and controlling political activity at the local level, the party persisted and had specific consequences for patterns of participation.

If one-party systems are "the product of the efforts of a political elite to organize and to legitimate rule by one social force over another in a bifurcated society,"[9] the party-state represents an effort by leaders both to exclude participation of some social groups and at the same time to shape the views held by members of weaker interest groups. The leaders of party-states seek to "organize and develop the party as an essential structural support,"[10] making the party simultaneously a vehicle for securing legitimacy and for controlling association, while at the same time subordinating its influence in policy determination. The party thus loses its function as a forum for interest-group bargaining and for interest aggregation—a function single-party-dominant systems still retain, to varying degrees—and acquires tasks performed by the executive in multi-party systems, including responsibility for socialization or public education and for certain forms of public order.

These modifications in the role of the party also altered the relationship between individual citizens and governments. Merging political party and government gave the former new tools to maintain its monopoly, even though the limited resources of these organizations and the dispersion of political power across a variety of centers of authority, some inaccessible to official influence, created the specter of a repressive political system different from the totalitarian models offered by Europe. The changes provided new instruments for controlling political activity. Repression was "rarely methodical and systematic," Zolberg pointed out;[11] it focused on individuals, not categories of citizens. By cutting off some, but not all, channels for expressing discontent, it precipitated illegal activities, whose aims became more drastic as the process of securing formal representation or participation became more difficult.

THE RISE OF THE PARTY-STATE IN AFRICA

There are five main schools of thought that seek to explain the tendency of single-party systems to become "party-states." One view, the oldest of the five, focuses on the absence of institutionalized "rules of the game" that foster civility and compromise. It suggests that several common characteristics of African social, economic, and political contexts provide incentive for leaders to make exceptional, "unlimited" or non-negotiable demands in their dealings with one another and to seek political monopoly. The "party-state" represents an attempt by those in power to prevent "all-or-nothing" demands by opposition groups.

A second school of thought locates the rise of the "party-state" principally in the structure of African societies—that is, in the organizational character of the main economic interest groups or "civil society." Limited reliance of populations on a formal market economy means that governments are not able to use market incentives to secure compliance with policies. States are thus "weak," while "societies," or social structures, are "strong" in their ability to resist policy implementation. Under these conditions, governments resort to exhortation and to use of the party as a means of obtaining support for policy implementation. Organizations originally designed to represent interests become extensions of the state's police power.

A third perspective argues that movement away from a multi-party Westminster-style parliamentary system varies with the degree to which political elites are beholden to external economic interests. Politicians seek to protect their own lucrative ties with foreign-owned enterprises, and to this end they restrict competition. Continued provision of loans by international commercial banks and bilateral or multilateral donors enables leaders to purchase support while simultaneously restricting the political space available for contesting government policies.

A fourth, less fully elaborated, view maintains that where state-led development that leaves little scope for private initiative takes place in an economy, and where economic power becomes concentrated in the office of the head of state, entrepreneurial groups attempt to defend their established points of access to bureaucratic favor and state resources against the electoral alternation of political personnel by seeking to proscribe opposition. Political "departicipation," including the conversion of party systems into vehicles for exercising "top down" control over populations, results from the efforts of entrepreneurs to render more secure the positions of public officials on whose resources they depend, when the loss of access potentially means near-total loss of livelihood. In short, the "commercial bourgeoisie" that carried liberal democratic ideas in Europe is absent in the African cases. The African "bourgeoisie" has typically taken the form of an "organizational bour-geoisie" or "politico-commercial class" that is heavily dependent on government contracts and permits for survival. Its bargaining power, including its capacity to preserve political space, is in consequence sharply limited. There is no Magna Carta in the offing.

The fifth approach suggests that the creation of what Wallerstein has called a "no-party state," and what this study calls a "party-state," is the outgrowth of a particular stage of the process of import-substitution industrialization. Students of Latin American politics have argued that "bureaucratic-authoritarianism," of which the retreat from mobiliza-tional politics is a part, is a reaction by military and technocratic groups to the difficulty of shifting resources to manufacturing of intermediate goods, often in conjunction with foreign firms. Such policies become necessary when the domestic market for consumer goods is limited and levels of international debt (and thus need for revenues and for foreign exchange are high), while workers and domestic businesses continue to make strong claims on the state for benefits.

Explanation One: Absence of Agreement on Rules of the Game   Zol-berg traces the search for electoral monopoly by incumbent parties and the merging of party and government back to six different kinds of pres-sures, which include:

1.   The perception that the opposition is led by people who chal-lenge the fundamental values of the incumbent party

2.   The perception that resource scarcity makes politics a zero-sum game, with the winners taking all and the losers receiving nothing

3.   The belief that fellow politicians have not internalized the rules of the game, and that adherence to standards of political civility that normally attend adoption of a Westminster parliamentary system can-not be assumed

4.   The absence of factors that normally limit the kinds of issues up for negotiation

5.   The record of assassinations of heads of state in Africa, which induces fear of opposition

6.   A pattern of international involvement that makes it possible for opposition groups to acquire more financial support than they could succeed in amassing from domestic constituents, and that consequently undermines the legitimacy of the electoral system.[12]

This view suggests that the rise of "party-states" has its roots in characteristics common to many African countries after independence, some social and cultural, others economic, and still others psychological.

Less a "theory" than an inventory of the circumstances that correlated with the shift to a "party-state" in the West African cases, the perspective does not try to identify necessary and sufficient conditions, leaving the observer to wonder whether "party-states" emerge when all of these circumstances, or only some of them, come together. Nonetheless, the approach offers some useful general insights that facilitate explanation. For example, the fourth reason Zolberg offers for the rise of the party-state, the absence of pressures to limit the character of the demands parties make, is most likely related to the perception that opposition groups are seeking "all-or-nothing solutions" and have failed to internalize the "rules of the game." Where communal and economic divisions coincide, as they do in many sub-Saharan countries, there is little reason for political actors to attenuate their demands or to see those of others as limited. That is, when disproportionate levels of economic benefit appear to accrue on the basis of community membership rather than of a generally recognized "fair procedure," the competition for resources will likely take on the appearance of an all-or-nothing fight for access to policy influence instead of a discussion of appropriate measures. It is not the policies themselves that are subject to constant renegotiation but rather the fundamental institutions in which policy debate takes place. The uncertainty engendered by these conditions creates an incentive for governments to use dominant party organizations to "educate" and to control opposition.

Add a shrinking resource base and the prospect of international involvement in local politics to the equation, and, as Zolberg suggests, the incumbent political leadership is likely to perceive any opposition as a potential threat, not just to its continuation in power, but to the prospect of its ever returning to a position of influence once power has been lost. Most governments try to pass out development monies as part of an effort to broaden and deepen their bases of support. Where economies are stagnant and there is less and less capital available for distribution, leaders' efforts to secure bases in communities or regions traditionally less favored by government policy can come only at the expense of those who are the existing bulwark of support. Policies thus become hotly contested. When opposition groups can enlist military assistance from foreign governments, the stakes in the competition escalate still further, to the point where incentives to limit demands and to seek compromise may disappear completely.

One version of this explanation focuses on the constraints created by severely limited public revenues and "weak" institutions. "In the absence of effectively institutionalized rules, the players are not restrained from employing coercion, violence, and other . . . [arbitrary means to monopolize power]," Robert Jackson and Carl Rosberg suggest, for example.[13] It is incomplete institutionalization, or lack of legitimacy of rules and lack of trust that laws and contracts will be upheld, that encourages resort to authoritarian measures.

The independent variables or "causes" Zolberg offers fail, however, to explain the differences between African countries. For example, to the extent that Tanzania was a party-state in the 1960s, according to Zolberg's typology, it differed from Kenya under Jomo Kenyatta. Yet both countries had similar economic bases and little prospect of foreign intervention on behalf of opposition factions. Further, it is not clear why the relationship between the party and the state in Kenya should have altered when it did.

Explanation Two: Weak States, Strong Societies   The predominant contemporary understanding of "political departicipation" in Africa, of which the shift to a party-state is a subsidiary focus, derives from studies of the difficulty of policy implementation in African settings, as analyzed, for example, by Goran Hyden and Joel Migdal.[14] Proponents of this view have argued that the difficulty of securing agreement on the "rules of the game" in African politics traces back to characteristics of economic and social structure. Dispersion of power among multiple, contending centers of authority—ethnic and religious communities or local economic strongmen, for example—creates special difficulties for policy implementation. This is especially so, Hyden argues, when most production and consumption takes place through the kinds of lineage structures that are common ways of organizing labor in Africa. And it does so particularly when the economic dependence of residents on observable, official market transactions is limited.

In this view, African leaders confront a real dilemma. To implement policies—to win cooperation—they need to have a variety of incentives and disincentives at their disposal. In the industrialized countries, control over financial resources is critical among these levers. Tax policies affect the behavior of individuals only as long as it is possible to know a person's income level and to extract payment, however. In most African countries, a variety of social and economic systems coexist. To the extent that economic transactions take place through informal, unrecorded exchanges rather than through formal markets, the use of tax policy to support other policy objectives is extremely difficult.

Moreover, the more dependent a civil servant is on sources of income other than his or her government job, the less likely he or she is to place the impersonal implementation of a policy directive above a personal favor in a conflict of interest. Limited state resources for surveillance of market transactions and personnel and inefficient management practices that make payment of salaries unreliable increase the difficulty governments face still further. They strengthen communal groups in civil society. These new claimants rapidly learn that in such an environment it is easier to secure benefits through clientage than through creation of organizations to provide sustained support for common demands.

Finally, as Crawford Young has trenchantly noted, state institutions create their own "interest groups." They generate a "patterned pluralism," tailoring the character of civil societies. "As the state's different parts acquire interests and autonomous reasons of their own and are fortified by clientage relations with groups external to the state, it becomes far more than an arena for the enactment of societal conflict; the state is a stage for ceaseless struggle among its component parts for the fleeting possession of its mythological unitary will." [15] In any society, policies and institutions generate clienteles. In sub-Saharan Africa, according to this view, these clienteles wield comparatively greater power than they do in the industrial West, however. Relatively undiversified economies and pressure on employees to support extended households with uneven income streams makes creation and maintenance of patronage relationships within the civil service or other parts of the government structure more urgent.

Under these conditions, government leaders may be tempted to resort to force. Surveillance, if not proscription, of alternative centers of political authority—opposition political parties, religious and ethnic welfare organizations and their leaders, corporate groups—is usually a first step. In most cases, creation of a single-party system and then increasing use of the party itself for surveillance purposes are the consequences. Although his own views are not identical with the "weak states, strong societies" approach, Thomas Callaghy captures the logic of this argument when he says that "to a large extent, authoritarian forms of rule result not from high levels of power and legitimacy, but from the tenuousness of authority and the search for it." [16]

Goran Hyden maintains, specifically, that the "economy of affection" is the source of the trend toward authoritarian rule so pervasive in sub-Saharan Africa. "In the absence of any advanced structural dependencies, there are few institutions in which officials and peasants share a common interest," he writes. Therefore, "the scope for the protection and development of public institutions through adherence to formal rules is very limited." [17] Leaders are left with two approaches to managing competing interests: one, the formation of loose coalitions of clan leaders who have been given the opportunity to secure benefits for their constituencies; the other, control of the political arena by the head of state. There are strict limits on the first strategy, Hyden argues, because the state can tolerate only so much participation. It has finite resources at its disposal. If "clan" groups demand an ever-growing amount of those as a quid pro quo for supporting the government, then there is a problem:

> A major reason for this "shrinking of the arena" is that there is a limit to how much participation a polity characterized by clan pressures can tolerate. Such a polity is only manageable if the number of clan leaders does not exceed what is possible for the ruler himself to control and the costs of stepping outside the boundaries of the area are very high. Thus, in order to keep access to the political arena in check it has become necessary to extend controls over rewards in the economy. [18]

As in the case of Zolberg's explanation, however, the "weak states, strong societies" approach fails to explain adequately the variations between and within countries. A researcher would expect a higher incidence of party-states in countries where (a) the economy is unstable and undiversified; and/or (b) civil servants are paid poorly or unevenly and are dependent upon other sources of income; and/or (c) many economic transactions take place through unmonitored and unmeasured parallel market activity. Where, for any of these reasons, lineage modes of production persist or have been "reinvigorated"[19] and provide important forms of social security to employees, or where financial levers are useless because of the existence of large parallel economies, governments are likely to have difficulty securing implementation of projects and programs according to impersonal, bureaucratic rules. Using these indicators, it would be reasonable to expect the development of a party-state in Zaire or Zambia, but not in Côte d'Ivoire, Kenya, or Zimbabwe, whose economies have performed more strongly and whose civil services are better managed. This form of explanation, then, cannot really account for the patterns observed.

Neither are the kinship networks that Hyden and others identify as especially disposed to the generation of clientage always salient in all societies at all times, or as ways of organizing critical economic tasks. They vary in strength and structure, and any theory that predicts patterns of behavior from their existence must both recognize the variations that exist and offer a theory sufficiently nuanced to be able to relate changes in the character of lineage social organization to changes in "formal politics," or participation in national institutions. To date, no one has done so in systematic fashion, and probably with good reason. Every country in sub-Saharan Africa includes a large number of different societies, each with its own descent system. Although it may be possible to generalize about the effects of these structures on political behavior, this form of explanation cannot easily account for changes in "state-society" relationships, particularly for the strength of the clientelism that is supposed to provide the spur to repression. To explain broad patterns of political change, these explanations must identify underlying alterations in social structure within the group of principal political actors.

The "weak states, strong societies" approach is too clumsy an analytic strategy. It does not explain the differences in political outcomes apparent in Africa, including variations in the character of political authoritarianism.

Explanation Three: The "Underdevelopment" Perspective   A third group of scholars, including Colin Leys, Ngugi wa Thiong'o, Peter Anyang' Nyong'o, and James Karioki have identified the economic dependence of African elites on foreign enterprises and foreign governments as the source of African political authoritarianism. Local political elites who manage subsidiaries of multinational corporations or who sit on the boards of these businesses depend on the survival and success of their foreign patrons and try to influence domestic policy making to protect these interests. Rafael Kaplinsky analyzed the magnitude of foreign equity in Kenyan firms as a proportion of total equity, as well as the extent of foreign participation in firms chaired by some of the country's elites, and found that in 1976, half of the capital of Kenya's larger industrial firms and tourist enterprises was foreign-owned.[20] According to this line of argument, government policies, inasmuch as they are responsive to foreign imperatives, prove inappropriate for generating economic growth. They benefit only local elites allied with multinational enterprises. Independent governments thus preside over the impoverishment of local majorities and have "to be strong enough to master the tensions and conflicts generated among the mass of the people by the process of underdevelopment."[21] That means heavy reliance on police and armed forces.

These states resemble the "Bonapartist" state of France in the 1850s. In *Underdevelopment in Kenya*, Colin Leys wrote: "There are never quite enough spoils to go round, and the weakness of the new would-be bourgeoisie reveals itself in all sorts of conflicts, which threaten to engulf the rest of society as individuals seek to enlist ethnic and regional support on behalf of their interests. To avoid this the 'national bourgeoisie' discovers the need for a 'popular leader to whom will fall the dual role of stabilizing the regime and of perpetuating the domination of the bourgeoisie.'"[22] As part of this process, the head of state eliminates many opportunities for these groups to gain influence over policy. It concentrates power in the hands of the president, and "the party becomes a mere shell."

Bilateral and multilateral aid programs have fostered the persistence of these weak, authoritarian states by removing the government's need to rely on domestically generated financial resources, in this view.[23] Aid, especially military assistance, has functioned as a "windfall," absolving leaders of the need to tax farmers or reduce tax evasion by elites. For example, Anyang' Nyong'o has written that the Moi campaign to stop the populist Luo politician Oginga Odinga stemmed from "a force more powerful than the dramatis personae on the political stage" and suggests that "this alliance of forces can be traced to the conservative former white settlers (still resident in Kenya), the opportunistic Asian business community, apartheid capital in Kenya, Israeli intelligence, the U.S. military-financial complex, and conservative Tory capital from Great Britain."[24] Of these, Anyang' Nyong'o argues that U.S. military interests exercised most influence over governance in Kenya, and characterizes the American government's attitude as willingness to tolerate an "Ivan the Terrible" if that proved the best way to preserve U.S. interests.

Some underdevelopment theorists have suggested the need to modify this approach slightly. Nicola Swainson has argued, for example, that in his initial study of Kenya, Leys overstressed the degree to which the government acted on behalf of foreign interests. The struggle between parts of the new bourgeoisie has been the primary source of government policy, she suggests. "The main concern of the ruling group at the political level has been the integration of different sectors of the bourgeoisie," she writes. "The party in some respects epitomizes the failure of the bourgeoisie to integrate at a national level, and it was not surprising to find the new party derived most of its support from the petty bourgeoisie (school teachers, traders, middle peasants)."[25]

Leys himself later modified his original explanation, suggesting that the "national bourgeoisie" in Kenya was not wholly a creature of foreign capital, and that it had succeeded in gaining control of the state and using that power to buy out foreign enterprises. Indeed, he subsequently argued against the underdevelopment perspective on several grounds. "A more plausible explanation of Kenyan economic growth since the 1940s lies, rather, in the specific social relations of production developed before, during, and since the colonial period, and particularly . . . in the key role of the class formed out of the process of indigenous capital accumulation," he suggests.[26] Breaking the inevitability of the sequence he originally outlined—which "dependency" theories took as gospel—Leys observes that Kenyan entrepreneurs replaced foreign participation in many sectors of the economy, with the exception of manufacturing and tourism, and that even in these two sectors, they held a larger share of equity in 1976 than they had in 1966.[27]

Leys also points out that it is not easy to identify "high levels of inequality" other than in comparative perspective, and he reiterates Bill Warren's warning that dependency theorists often employ an idealized, counterfactual model of capitalism without inequalities against which to evaluate the presence of the dependency syndrome. Because no society is without inequalities and economic cycles, this standard effectively renders these analyses useless.[28] By this criterion, any country might appear "dependent."

Others have pointed out that the correlations the underdevelopment perspective predicts are not always evident. As the Kenyan scholar Michael Chege has noted, "Dependency fails to explain why a country like Somalia, hardly a haven for multinational corporations, . . . developed such an autocratic militarist regime in contrast to, say, Nigeria or Brazil."[29] There is no clear relationship between the share of manufacturing, agriculture, or services under foreign control and the extent or form of political repression. The level of official development assistance as a proportion of gross domestic product is an equally poor predictor of tolerance for political competition,[30] suggesting that aid "windfalls" are not key determinants of regime type.

Further, not all aid is automatically forthcoming to authoritarian governments; some forms of external assistance are linked to political liberalization or go to nongovernmental organizations whose activities are useful to oppositions. In the case of Kenya, the United States has played a particularly ambiguous role, channeling some small assistance, during the period of this study, to the Kenyan Public Law Institute for defense of civil liberties and harboring defenders of political competition, but releasing military assistance held in escrow when the Moi government's cooperation was needed on an international security problem.[31] In 1991, the U.S. government released only a small portion of the $47 million intended for Kenya, pending signs of greater respect for civil liberties by the Moi government.

Most important for this study, the "underdevelopment" perspective, even in its modified form, fails to explain preferences for specific strategies, institutions, or forms of authoritarian rule, and therefore supplies little intellectual leverage in understanding the rise of "party-states." It operates at too high a level of generality. Sholto Cross has noted that it is "useful to be able to discuss the link between étatism and presidentialism without necessarily thereby inferring a class role for the presidency."[32] This book suggests that there are indeed reasons for the behavior of heads of state other than class interest. It probes the significance of political institutions in generating the outcomes observed, including not just "étatism" but also the particular character of party-state relations.

Explanation Four: Concentration of Power and Political "Departicipation"   Yet a fourth explanation focuses attention on the behavior of entrepreneurs. Many scholars of European political history have argued that an independent class of capitalist entrepreneurs or aristocrats-turned-businesspeople was indispensable for the emergence of competitive politics in the West. In many parts of Africa, where state-led development takes place in an economy that leaves little scope for private initiative, and where economic power becomes concentrated in the office of the head of state, entrepreneurial logic varies from this norm, however. Dependence on government officials for licenses, capital, infrastructure, foreign exchange, police protection, and protection against competition leads local businesspeople to invest in the careers of the bureaucrats on whose services or favor they depend, whether through appointment of officials to boards of trustees, hiring of relatives, or outright payment. Once these transactions have taken place, the private-sector entrepreneurs, many of whom hold civil service jobs they use to accumulate capital, seek to defend their investments. They do so in direct proportion to the difficulty of maintaining their standards of living through occupations independent of government control. That is, the fewer the opportunities to earn an income in agriculture or other private-sector activities, the more vigorous the efforts of the entrepreneurial elite to secure the careers of those bureaucrats with whom they have developed close ties. They try to protect their "favored bureaucratic routes of access" against the electoral alternation of political personnel by seeking to proscribe opposition to those in power, in whose careers they have invested so much. Political "departicipation," including the conversion of party systems into vehicles for exercising "top down" control over populations, results from the efforts of entrepreneurs to secure the positions of favored public officials, when the loss of access potentially means near-total loss of livelihood.[33]

As Richard Sandbrook and Irving Leonard Markovitz have pointed out, in some cases civil servants use their privileged access to information and resources to construct "semi-private" enterprises.[34] This "organizational bourgeoisie" acquires a stake in continued tenure in government and moves to limit political opposition. Essentially, it privatizes the state and then tries to defend its class interests by constraining the role and openness of elections.

This view contributes to understanding the rise of single-party-dominant systems and authoritarianism in Africa. It usefully elaborates Zolberg's analysis of why opposition demands are often unlimited and political competitors so often see themselves as participants in a zero-sum game. That is, when entrepreneurs are wholly dependent on government for the routine operation of their businesses, whoever controls discretion over contracts and licenses controls the ability of elites to maintain their standards of living. Rather than competing within the rules to influence policy, they try instead to change the rules of competition. This analysis thus contributes significantly to explaining why governments attempt to limit public debate about policy and to proscribe opposition.

Like the other views cited, however, this analytical approach is too broad to explain the shift from single-party-dominant systems to party-states, or the variations between countries in the manner in which this change has taken place. Although control over jobs, printing presses, and the "commanding heights" of the economy undoubtedly vested great power in African chief executives and limited the accountability of their governments to citizens' demands, this does not explain differences in the strategies presidents and heads of state pursued—why, for example, Kenyatta favored a loosely organized dominant party, whereas Moi opted to eliminate competition and strengthen party discipline. To be useful, this approach must pursue the relationship between particular kinds of economic policies and the character and strength of the interest groups they spawn. It is important to ask what conditions give rise to groups with countervailing power—groups that are simultaneously independent of the government for their incomes but sufficiently affected by government actions to have a stake in the quality of public management and thus in the preservation of the "political space" necessary to contest policy choices.

Explanation Five: Bureaucratic Authoritarianism   Students of Latin American politics have puzzled over the rise of a "new authoritarianism" or "bureaucratic authoritarianism" in which high-level technocrats restrict electoral competition and the influence of electoral outcomes on policy choice. Unlike earlier forms of authoritarian rule in Latin America and Europe, "bureaucratic authoritarianism" seeks, not to mobilize followers, but to promote apathy on the part of citizens. It eschews cultivation of corporatist links between groups in the society. Instead, "the links between civil society and the bureaucratic-authoritarian regime are achieved through the co-optation of individuals and private interests into the system." [35]

In this view, the transformation to the "new authoritarianism" comes about in response to the economic pressures generated at the end of the consumer-goods phase of import-substitution industrialization. Initially, as a country industrializes, its entrepreneurs produce consumer goods and goods for export, with an emphasis on the former in cases where governments have decided to favor import-substitution policies. Expansion of the domestic market for these goods requires that workers receive sufficient pay to buy the new products. Industrialists and workers frequently join forces in a populist coalition:

> The broadening functions of the state, entailed by the abandonment of free trade and laissez-faire policies, provided employment for many middle class

empleados and téchnicos; the nationalism cum industrialization argument had direct appeal for the military; the expansion of industry and government, together with the growth of the economy, benefitted urban workers, created more jobs, fostered migration to the urban-industrial centers, extended the market economy, raised consumption levels, and increased unionization; in the agrarian sector, the producers of non-exportable goods benefitted greatly from the expansion of the domestic market.[36]

Because the economy is growing, there are financial reserves to meet a significant portion of the new demands workers and other elements of the "popular sector" make. Later, as basic consumer demand stabilizes or subsides, businesses seek profits through other sorts of entrepreneurial activity but principally through investment in production of intermediate and capital goods—investment that requires high levels of technology and capital available only through joint ventures with foreign firms and through diversion of public resources to the kinds of economic development these new activities require. As states divert resources to business during this "deepening" period, the "popular sector" sees its share of resources decline, given the insistence of foreign actors that the government not run a budget deficit and that it pursue orthodox macroeconomic policies. Its members become increasingly active in politics in an effort to defend their shares of resources. Professionals and technocrats in the civil service and the military find performance of their roles frustrated by the demands of the public, and eventually they join forces to limit popular influence over policy and constrain further politicization of workers and small producers.[37]

The argument as it applies to the Latin American cases has its critics. Albert Hirschman has suggested that the "deepening" phase is not clearly defined in most countries, and that it in any event does not correlate with the onset of increasingly authoritarian rule. He suggests that transition to more orthodox, market-oriented policies may produce the effects Guillermo O'Donnell and David Collier have described and sought to explain, but he sees nothing inevitable about the relationship. The case of Colombia, he argues, does not fit. Fernando Cardoso suggests that the analysis applies only to military regimes that foster the advance of capitalist development and are constituted in reaction to left-wing political movements.[38]

Some of those who use this form of analysis have suggested its extension to African cases. "African countries are generally pre-industrial, oriented around agricultural and mineral exports, with relatively low levels of popular sector activation," David Collier notes.[39] He suggests that the countries of sub-Saharan Africa experience an array of economic difficulties similar to those of the Latin American cases. These problems are associated with their position in the international economic system: high levels of foreign debt, balance of payments problems, overvalued currencies, and inflation.

The extension of the "bureaucratic authoritarianism" model to African cases at first appears to capture a dimension of political life that few Africa specialists have studied: the tendency for political parties in some countries to become arms of the presidency and a means of limiting politicization rather than mobilizing support. This type of explanation suffers from several difficulties, however. First, as Crawford Young has noted, "neither the military nor the bureaucratic establishments in Africa exhibited the [same] self-confident claim to technical mastery, much less the ideological commitment to a national capitalist development strategy, as, say, their Brazilian counterparts."[40] Although civil servants and military officers do sit on the boards of foreign companies and sometimes act to secure the economic interests of their foreign partners, there is a significant difference between the pursuit of individual benefit in these cases and fostering the long-term development of capitalism or even of particular kinds of enterprises. Second, "popular sectors" display little programmatic political organization in Africa and are insufficiently strong to press repeatedly for platforms antagonistic to the interests of business. Indeed, research by Henry Bienen suggests that "urban" or "popular" groups have moved into the streets to contest the allocation of resources or the introduction of orthodox economic policies only in relatively few cases.[41] Third, the tactics used to generate "apathy" among the popular classes by some Latin American governments differ substantially from those favored by African heads of state. Except in a few extreme cases, military or police "death squads" are not part of the tactical repertoire in most African authoritarian systems. Detentions without trial and petty harassment are more common. Although the bureaucratic-authoritarian model explains why leaders may seek not to mobilize a populace but to engender apathy, it contributes little to our understanding of the institutions and practices favored.

The conditions all five approaches posit for the rise of single-party systems and for the merging of party and government correspond well with the public and private statements of African leaders during the 1960s and 1970s. Certainly, these men worried about the threats to their rule and to their lives that communal conflict, international intervention, poverty, and the concentration of wealth created. Nonetheless, all five approaches lack the capacity to help us understand the dramatic differences between the West African cases and either the case of Kenya from independence through 1978 or other cases beyond the shores of the continent. In the cases of both Kenya and Zaire, for instance, economic dependence on observable transactions in official markets was far from complete, resources were scarce, communal groups occasionally pursued interests that ignored the religious or ethnic claims of other citizens, practice of democratic "civility" was tentative at best, and the specter of external intervention or political assassination posed a clear threat. What inspired some political leaders to react to these conditions by seeking an electoral monopoly and by subsuming the party under the central government while others chose to tolerate some level of association outside the dominant party and a degree of debate about policy among these groups?

THE ARGUMENT

Although this study builds on elements of the views outlined, it departs from existing explanations by focusing on the importance of institutional design for political behavior, and particularly on the incentives that institutions create for the content and character of bargaining between political elites. What the Kenyan case shows is the critical importance of variables that have nothing to do with the persistence of kinship-based systems of social and economic organization—or with choice of economic policy per se.

Anyang' Nyong'o argues persuasively that in the case of Kenya, "it was largely the disintegration of the nationalist coalition that enabled a strong authoritarian president to emerge." He suggests that "a section of the nationalist coalition favoured this rise, seeing in it an opportunity to have access to states apparatuses and thereby acquire avenues for capital accumulation and personal enrichment." The dominant faction maintained the party when it suited its interests to do so, and then allowed it to "atrophy to deny any other organized faction . . . from using it politically to attain its objectives within the bounds of law." [42] This element of the coalition was able to exploit these opportunities and to become the core of a new bourgeoisie. The willingness to cede power to a single party in order to gain short-term economic benefits ultimately worked to the disadvantage of this new group. It began to lose control over the presidency and access to the state.

Anyang' Nyong'o's explanation stops short of a full account, however. It does not distinguish between the authoritarianisms (plural) that have governed Kenyan society during the first thirty years of the country's independence. It notes quite correctly that elements of the nationalist coalition used state resources to accumulate resources and to move themselves into the upper reaches of the petite bourgeoisie or the *matajiri* ("wealthy") class, dividing into factions as they competed for access to opportunities to acquire new assets. But Anyang' Nyong'o offers few explanations for the difficulty these groups experienced in creating a unified front and in opposing the president when he trampled on their interests. Why could they not control the authoritarian system whose creation they had sanctioned?

Answering this question requires an excursion into the ways in which political institutions shape interest-group formation and behavior. I propose that the shift from single-party dominance to the party-state, as it is defined here, depends on the concurrence of three main conditions.

1. In countries where ethnic, regional, and economic divisions coincide, as they do in most of sub-Saharan Africa, a shift from single-party dominance to a party-state is likely unless electoral rules or informal, extra-parliamentary institutions force elites to bargain across boundaries in their efforts to secure winning coalitions.

The tendency of political elites to make unlimited claims in the public arena varies with the perception that other elites' demands are efforts to propel the interests of a single community ahead of those of others on a continuing basis. Where demands for economic redistribution to disadvantaged regions or for improvement of the competitiveness of a particular sector of the economy appear to be demands for communal advantage, the "rules of the game" Zolberg identifies are shattered and the likelihood that those in power will seek to limit opposition through use of the party as a vehicle for social control rises. Only where formal or informal institutions of government—electoral rules, for example—force bargaining across ethnic, regional, and economic boundaries will compromise appear individually as well as collectively rational.

It is important to distinguish ethnic and religious lines of division as understood in this proposition from the lineage-based social organization that figures prominently in the "weak states, strong societies" argument. In most parts of sub-Saharan Africa, the larger ethnic divisions that have become politically salient in recent years are new forms of organization—political machines that employ ethnic idioms designed to draw members of different lineages and clan units into a political bloc, whether or not their members speak the same language and share the same systems of social organization.

These ethnic welfare societies or machines are often springboards for political careers. Where members occupy the same positions in the economy or a specific geographic area, the languages of class and community often intermingle, giving demands a cast of exclusivity. Where members occupy different regions or different positions in the economy, candidates may try to appeal to shared community membership as a way of distracting voters from the economic differences between them, creating a kind of "smoke screen."[43] Whether these kinds of bases and divisions promote political division along communal lines depends entirely on the incentives for bargaining a party system creates.

2. The shift to a party-state occurs when factions within the dominant party cannot constitute strong opposition to ascendant factions, whose members attempt to curtail political association or other civil liberties, because of the difficulty of organizing constituents around issues that generate no divisible benefits but improve collective welfare generally. Most civil-liberties issues are of this type. It is especially difficult for members of opposition factions to organize against the fusion of government and party in most African settings (a) because single-party or single-party-dominant systems decrease the likelihood that citizens will cast their votes for politicians who promise general policy changes rather than discrete projects, and (b) either because there are few people who have a disproportionate stake in these questions or there are few who can bear the exceptional costs entailed in organizing citizens in support of changes in government. Where one or more of the opposition factions have significant sources of money and compensate lawyers or public-interest groups for their efforts in fighting changes in government-party relations in court or in the international arena, the shift from single-party dominance to a party-state is likely to take place more slowly and possibly less completely than in countries where opposition factions are fragmented and financially weak.[44]

There are three parts to this observation. First, the argument centers on the difference between "maintaining the competitiveness of politics" as a campaign issue in contrast to pork-barrel politics, or demands that deliver divisible benefits. Some kinds of policy choices generate rewards for the particular individuals who lobby for them. For example, programs to build dispensaries or hospitals, irrigation schemes or market centers, sewer systems or access roads can be designed to benefit those who sought their passage in the legislature or who voted for candidates who incorporated these projects into their platforms. Because the benefits of these policies are divisible, it may pay members of Parliament to organize voting blocs to secure the required policy changes—to lobby their fellow representatives or political elites—provided the costs of the individual effort required are lower than the present discounted value of the possible gain. One might call these "type 1" issues.

Not all policy issues have this character, however. Many kinds of political reforms have the character of public goods; that is, once enacted, they benefit large numbers of people without regard for the level of individual contribution to the effort to secure their passage and implementation. They permit "free riding." Because of this characteristic, individual voters and the politicians who claim to speak for them have relatively little incentive to invest their efforts in overcoming opposition and in pushing reforms through the legislature. Specifically, because it is difficult for those who have expended time and money or accepted exceptional risks to exclude those who did not contribute from the benefits of reform and to procure the benefits for themselves and their constituents, special incentive is required to impel a politician to stand up for such measures. In the absence of such incentives, each individual will simply wait for another to move first to make the investment required to generate the reform—and in many cases nothing will happen. This kind of behavior may occur even when the anticipated individual benefits generated by the policy or reform exceed the costs of participation. One might call these kinds of policies and reforms "type 2" issues.

Under most circumstances, efforts to defend the level of public contestation in a political system are efforts to pursue "type 2" issues. Creation or protection of the legal ability to associate and to speak at public gatherings, to travel within and outside of the country, and so on, are public goods in the technical sense of that term.

Differences in institutional settings account for much of the variation in the willingness of political actors to accept the burdens of general reforms that affect the entire country and that potentially create large numbers of winners but a few powerful losers. That is, the structures of formal and informal representative systems can create special incentives for the provision of such policies and help overcome the "free-rider problem" political economists so often see as an obstacle to organization.

Elected elites can be assumed to act so as to preserve or extend their access to resources they can use for "constituency service" or local projects. These increase candidate visibility with constituents. In competitive political systems, where parties may alternate in power, political elites have an incentive to defend their "political space," their freedom to speak, associate, campaign, and otherwise contest public policy vigilantly. If they allow their ability to participate to be curbed, they stand to lose control over resources, either in the short run or when their party loses power.

The character of the party system makes a difference for political outcomes in three ways. First, competitive party systems help provide incentives for politicians to bear the costs of organizing reform platforms. Parties are different from factions in that they have independent organizational bases and personnel to carry out administrative tasks. The party leadership has a stake in the continued existence of the organization. That stake defines an interest in maintaining the "political space" the system of representation accords the opposition. Furthermore, the leadership can turn around and demand that candidates carrying the party banner contribute to the effort to pursue the watchdog and reform activities implied by that interest. That is, they can demand that candidates claiming affiliation with the party take time out from the pursuit of purely local interests or even attenuate local demands and devote themselves to more general, "type 2" issues as a quid pro quo of membership,[45] as V. O. Key noted in his study of the "single-party states" of the Old South in the United States.

Second, competitive party systems and single-party systems differ in the kinds of costs they create for those who try to organize to increase the level of public contestation within a political system. Although it is the free-rider problem created by general political reform as a "type 2" good that is central to the analysis offered here, it is also the case that single-party systems change the cost structure associated with organizing reform. In single-party systems, members of factions must tread lightly in defending their political space for fear of losing favor with the party leadership; absent a credible threat to defect to an opposition party, a candidate is likely to find that access to patronage during election periods diminishes; or the leadership may launch proceedings to expel a fractious candidate from the party altogether. Although faction members have an incentive to defend their political space in single-party systems, they face risks in doing so that candidates in competitive party systems do not encounter.

Third, the factions that proliferate in most single-party systems also provide a poor base for pursuit of policy changes at the national level in another respect.[46] In some one-party systems, a dominant faction is able to secure the patronage to construct and operate a political machine. This analysis is often used to understand African single-party systems.[47] Not all African single-party systems operate in this way, however. Many display high degrees of factional division—to which leaders often point as evidence of pluralistic competition. Factional division is especially common where mobilization across political divisions is difficult as a result of legal restrictions, geographic constraints, or significant differences in economic activities, and where the public treasury is so poor that patronage resources are few.[48] Indeed, it could be argued that such systems are increasingly the dominant form of one-party system in Africa. Where there is a high degree of factional competition and no clear and enduring organizational base for any subgroup, candidates are less likely to take a stand on a reform issue than they are simply to break with one ad hoc group and move to another. They have little incentive to demand changes in the positions held by other faction members. To do so would take investment of time, if not of money, and the creation from scratch of channels for articulating and discussing demands. Unless there is some additional factor that limits their ability to move between factions or otherwise encourages politicians to acquire a stake in the policy positions promulgated by one group and in the defense of the group's ability to participate, it will prove extremely difficult to constitute any sort of "watchdog" activities to make sure that those in power respect the desire of others to participate.[49] In general, "exit" will be preferred to "voice."

The observation made in point two also suggests that there is an endogenous element to the explanation of the shift to a party-state from a single-party system. That is, when a country moves from a multi-party system to a single-party system, it sets in motion a process in which, under the socioeconomic conditions that prevail in most sub-Saharan cases, the reduced incentives for political elites to support high levels of public contestation lead to passage of legislation that further weakens the ability of politicians to defend their political space. Whatever the pattern of factionalism that evolves within the party—a two-way split in which one faction monopolizes patronage resources or a high degree of fragmentation—once legislation that reduces opportunities for contesting policies goes into effect, the fusion of party functions with the administrative responsibilities of the state becomes increasingly difficult to resist. Increasing political "departicipation" and disfranchisement are an inevitable result of the incentive pattern created.[50]

In this way, the creation of single-party states can contribute to or precipitate the weakening and even disappearance of the social groups that are major claimants to state resources in other parts of the world. Although it does not necessarily affect the positions of "predatory elites," the creation of such a state may make it more difficult for the elements of a "civil society" to coalesce. It may thus contribute to what Thomas Callaghy has called sociopolitical "shredding" and may make it easier for a head of state to initiate and secure acceptance of legislation of whatever type or content.[51]

Political repression also makes resort to this form of party-state much more likely, however. If political scientists can speak of legislative and bureaucratic structures enacting their environment or shaping interest-group structure and behavior, it is also the case that the party-state shapes civil society (by destroying it) and creates its own rationale. When a government has already moved to proscribe some forms of participation, opposition goes underground and becomes more difficult to monitor, save by resorting to obtrusive methods of surveillance and control. The organizational structure of the party, with its network of village representatives and local cells, becomes much more efficient as an instrument for gathering information during these periods than does the administration, with its less extensive network. For example, it is possible to mobilize youth wings to listen in marketplaces for rumors of political meetings. Further, the party-state provides a vehicle for indoctrinating potential opposition supporters and for communicating to them the high cost of deviation from the party line.

3. Finally, this argument explains variations between the African cases and other countries and variations among the African cases as a consequence of differences in the array and economic power of different social groups. Where opposition faction leaders can bolster their bargaining power with the spokespeople for the "in" faction by drawing on private resources for campaigns and for patronage, or where they can defend themselves against persecution by acquiring allies in an international forum, the shift to a party-state is likely to occur more slowly and less completely than in other situations.

Thus, *movement toward a party-state form of governance is less likely when there are extra-parliamentary interest groups that have independent financial bases or occupy critical positions in the economy that they may translate into bargaining power. The rise of a party-state is more likely (a) when the absence of private business or professional opportunities endangers the ability of opposition politicians to bring court cases contesting restriction of their political space, and (b) when either the absence of a free press or the absence of access to international ties by opposition figures makes it difficult to bring pressure on governments that restrict political space despite judicial decisions against them.*

The construction of a party-state requires modifications to a country's constitution and usually to the constitution of the dominant political party as well. Although the modifications are likely to take place without open amendment of the documents concerned, these steps can be challenged by opposition leaders as long as these men and women have independent economic bases and so are not vulnerable to efforts by the incumbents to retaliate in economic terms, and as long as they can take their appeals to an independent judiciary, similarly protected. Furthermore, judicial decisions and requests must be binding, so that incumbents are forced to pay attention to them. In most cases, that assumes either a free local press to publicize violations or ties between opposition leaders and an international community capable of denying the incumbents critical resources unless they adhere to the letter and spirit of rulings.

To protest a restriction of civil liberties in court is to risk losing, and where the defendants, the government's managers, control most economic opportunities as well as civil service jobs, to lose is to lose big. Even where associational life has largely disappeared because of political repression, a public-spirited individual might be willing to challenge an administrative ruling or a law that blocked pursuit of personal livelihood. After all, in every society there are individuals who generate "public goods" for reasons of their own. If defeat in court would jeopardize the ability of an individual to provide for a household or ruin the future life chances of children, the probability of protest through the judicial system is much lower. Where the state plays a substantial role as an investor and manager of enterprises, or where it maintains substantial power over private employment through extensive licensing regulations, a country's governors can wield devastating power over plaintiffs. The size of the "private sector," the degree of concentration of holdings within that sector, and the level of economic diversification can thus strongly influence the willingness of citizens to press judicial challenges. That should come as little surprise. Historically, democratic political structures have always arisen in countries with "capitalist" economic systems, or, more accurately, with substantial private economic activity.[52] (Not all capitalist systems or mixed economies are accompanied by democratic systems of representation, however.) African countries vary greatly in the degree to which they permit private economic activity without state intervention.

The existence of groups in civil society with economic "gatekeeping" powers, or the ability to diminish the state's capacity to function if a head of state tries to circumscribe political space, is important too. Only protest by independent domestic interest groups or critical elements of the international community that has clear material consequences is likely to discourage a head of state from passing new legislation to evade court rulings in cases individual plaintiffs have brought. Barrington Moore's analysis of the different political paths taken by industrializing countries makes clear the importance for "democratic outcomes" of groups in civil society, usually a commercial bourgeoisie or independent aristocracy with sufficient economic clout to be able to bargain with government leaders and counter the exercise of military or police powers.[53]

Although Kenya is shorter of land than most other sub-Saharan countries, it has generally offered greater latitude to private-sector economic activity than have most. That a party-state was in the making there in the 1980s is one of the puzzles this study seeks to solve.

THE KENYAN CASE

At the root of the shift from a multi-party to a single-party system lies a concern for securing short-run political order where community and economic divisions coincide. The aim is to win the adherence of elites and social groups (communal, class, or clientelistic) to government policies. Once in place, the single-party system creates an incentive structure that precipitates the rise of a "party-state." The presence of interest groups with financial bases and organizations independent of the people who inhabit the office of the president or the chief executive may slow or alter this process. Thus, both structural and institutional variables exercise critical influence over the character of "authoritarianism," and specifically over the relationship between party and state.

In Kenya, the rise of the party-state has occurred more slowly than in the other sub-Saharan countries where it has appeared, and the tendency has occasionally reversed itself, but it has taken place, nonetheless. Kenya came to independence with a multi-party parliamentary system and two major political parties, the Kenya African National Union (KANU) and the Kenya African Democratic Union (KADU). It departed rapidly from the independence formula, as did most African countries, moving to a republican system of government with a strong president and to a noncompetitive party system.

In the early years of the Kenyatta government, the Kenya African National Union (KANU) was a weak party in which several semi-corporate groups competed for influence. Of the two main groups, one was a cross-ethnic coalition that championed the interests of the landless, those engaged in small-scale farming, and low-skilled workers. Opposed to this "radical" or "populist" group was another cross-ethnic coalition that sought to expand opportunities for large-scale farming, for business, and, to some degree, for skilled labor. A third, less cohesive group made up of former KADU members, sought agricultural policies that benefited larger farming operations but limited free exchange of land between residents of different regions. Kenyatta kept party and administrative affairs separate from one another by maintaining KANU as a forum for debate between groups and using the administration to carry out education functions and tasks associated with the maintenance of public order.

Until Kenyatta fell ill in the mid 1970s, most efforts on the part of politicians to try to strengthen the party and enforce a particular point of view or program met with failure. Although Kenyatta was not a champion of multi-party competition and believed firmly that Kenya could thrive only if there were a single political party, he favored a system tolerant of diverse points of view—within limits. For example, in 1965, members of the populist wing of the party tried to establish a training institute for KANU officials. Allegedly financed with funds from Communist bloc countries, Oginga Odinga, one of Kenyatta's vice presidents, and Bildad Kaggia, a former leader of the struggle for independence, laid the groundwork for a Lumumba Institute.[54] The effort lasted only four months, however. Opposition came partly from the members of the Kenya African Democratic Union (KADU), KANU's competitor in the independence elections, then rapidly disappearing because of defections of its membership to KANU. Opposition came also from Daniel arap Moi, most likely at the instigation of Kenyatta, who, in his role as father of the country, had earlier allowed the radical wing some leeway.

Why Kenyatta departed from the strategies of control many other African leaders pursued and favored a loosely organized, nonmobilizational party is not entirely clear. Some have speculated that the decision reflected Kenyatta's personal predilections. Another argument is that he had been in jail during the party's first year of existence and may have wanted to avoid rewriting the party's founding documents to meet his own tastes.[55] Kenyatta was a shrewd politician and probably realized that fragmentation and political instability would result from any effort to force competing interests, released by the triumph of the nationalist cause, into a single mold through a detailed program. Instead, he could foster national unity by diverting the attention of politicians to debate over the platform of a penniless political party while he himself maintained contact with all sides and cultivated the role implicit in his honorific title of Mzee, the "old man." He chose to reign rather than to rule.[56]

By the early 1970s, the pattern of the immediate post-independence period had started to change. The late 1960s had witnessed first the censure of the "radicals" within KANU, then the elimination of the splinter party formed to carry the populist program forward by a change in the electoral rules. The remaining semicorporate groups that had earlier debated one another at party functions and in Parliament began to give way to factions organized around high officials or elites with access to the Office of the President. The defense of the political space that politicians needed to build platforms and electoral support became increasingly difficult. With the fragmentation of earlier coalitions, there were few individuals or groups willing and able to bear the costs of defending the right of association. The ability to contest policy diminished, although not without short-term reverses when the individuals surrounding the ailing president found that it was in their own interest to maintain civil liberties. The division of functions between party and administration that had prevailed earlier continued.

By 1982, the old internal divisions within KANU had given way almost completely to a fragmented and shifting array of factions, and the implementation of restrictions on political space began to occur rapidly, with little objection from members of Parliament. Under the new president, Daniel arap Moi, the administration and the party began to trade functions. Increasingly, the leaders of the party owed their offices to the president and, by 1989, half the members elected to Parliament occupied ministerial positions. The distinction between the personnel attached to the State House and those attached to the management of the party eroded in practice, as did the distinction between the holders of elective office and the administration. The middle- and lower-level KANU officers and politicians lost most of their role in national policy making, although they maintained their ability to seek local projects and to quiz ministers on the performance of their programs. The party became dependent upon the provincial service for collection of membership fees, and the service, in turn, became more heavily involved in determining which citizens had to be able to produce party membership cards. The party acquired some new roles, too, although some of these elicited discontent from members. Beginning in the early 1980s, party branches acquired surveillance functions through the creation of youth wings and disciplinary committees, for example, as well as responsibility for helping the administration maintain public order.

These changes in the character of the party and in the allocation of functions between the government and the party correlated with change in three independent variables. First, the incentives for interregional and interethnic bargaining diminished steadily from the early 1970s on, slowly undermining the informal "rules of the game" that had long promoted trust and compromise in Kenya's divided society. Second, within the party, the replacement of organized interests by multiple, ad hoc factional groupings made it increasingly difficult to protect the political space of opposition politicians against encroachment by the Office of the President. Third, the rate at which the country moved toward a party-state from a loose, single-party system varied depending on the ability of opposition groups to acquire either financial bases or international attention independently of the State House.

At no time, whether under Kenyatta or under Moi, did the State House rely exclusively on one strategy for securing political order. The Kenyatta government was well acquainted with techniques of political intimidation, including use of detention laws and violence.[57] Nonetheless, it distinguished itself from governments in comparable African countries and from its successor government in its willingness to live with a weak, faction-ridden governing party, some toleration for political competition or association outside the governing party, greater reliance on the efforts of civil servants in place of party officials to persuade farmers and other citizens to adhere to chosen policies, and its creation of a semi-institutionalized form of patronage or compensation. This strategy made possible the operation of a proportionality rule in the allocation of many types of development resources and in the allocation of ministerial positions and senior party posts, where some groups, such as the well-organized Kikuyu, accepted losses in relation to their past strength, in return for positions at the helm of new public enterprises or for contributions to their local communities.

It was the particular design of the compensation system, however, that permitted Kenyatta to eschew the use of KANU as a vehicle for social and political control. The primary element of this strategy was the inauguration of a form of "self-help development" called *harambee* ("Let's pull together" in Swahili). Harambee was an innovative strategy for promoting development and for ensuring that at least some projects were consonant with local perceptions of need. It also had political objectives, however. At a self-help development fund-raiser, the local member of Parliament (MP) was expected to make a substantial contribution or gift. Indeed, failure to do so sharply diminished one's chances of reelection. As Kenyatta anticipated, however, harambee contributions constituted a significant financial burden for an MP, and an enterprising politician would almost certainly have to bargain for assistance from other, senior politicians, regardless of ethnic or regional background, and with the president in his capacity as a fellow politician. The politician's dilemma constituted a new means of creating political order. First, it provided group spokesmen with a material incentive to limit the claims they made against one another's communities; bids for disproportional benefit in the distribution of public resources would meet with an end to harambee contributions from politicians in other districts or regions. Second, it enabled the president, as a fellow party member, to compensate those MPs who compromised and accepted the State House's policy proposals from his own purse and from the private pockets of the country's leaders. Harambee contributions by the president, vice president, senior ministers, and spokesmen for ethnic groups provided the currency to build coalitions and compensate groups for losses in representation or share of resources. These private contributions to school construction projects, financing of cattle dips, purchase of choir robes, and so on, in return for smaller donations from community members, could improve the electoral chances of a member of Parliament who had relinquished a claim to continued Treasury support for an unsuccessful irrigation scheme, for example, or to continued high levels of expenditure on road construction in his or her constituency.

Beginning in 1978, the locus of political power and the locus of economic power began to diverge, and at precisely the same time economic conditions made perceived losses higher and "adequate" compensation more difficult. Under Kenyatta, the interests of the Kikuyu business community, the only real source of capital formation other than the state, however small, corresponded substantially with those of the head of state.

Upon accepting the presidency, Moi faced a different situation. Moi, the man who managed the ruling coalition, was not a member of its largest subgroup. It was necessary to remunerate his Kalenjin support while maintaining the allegiance of other major groups, negotiating with greater numbers of key spokesmen, in consequence, and thus raising the costs of the Kenyatta style of governance. Absent these, the only access to resources was through the Treasury or through bribes and "shakedowns" on international business contracts. Emergence of a new opposition party seemed likely.

The disjunction upped the ante in two other ways as well. In the first place, the Kikuyu business community had deep pockets. The Gikuyu, Embu, and Meru Association (GEMA), a cultural society or "welfare union," was banned, along with other ethnic welfare societies, in 1980. It had previously amassed substantial reserves, however, and merely went underground, assuming the guise of Agricultural and Industrial Holdings, Ltd. The money remained to "bid up" any efforts by Moi to pursue Kenyatta's strategy. Second, economic problems and a burgeoning population changed the nature of the stakes involved. Whereas under Kenyatta the distributional issues confronting spokesmen for ethnic groups had primarily been about distribution of material benefits, such as roads or water facilities, under Moi they increasingly concerned the distribution of opportunity: access to education first, and then to land and employment. It is far more difficult to compensate for losses that affect long-term competitiveness, or social mobility, than it is to buy support for reducing funding of roads.

The second source of the shift to a "party-state" in Kenya was located in the incentive structure created by factionalism in a single-party system. The existence of multiple, shifting factions within KANU, the dominant party by 1967, made it more, not less, difficult to champion policies that affected the nation as a whole. Beginning in the mid 1970s, as Kenyatta became ill and devoted less attention to the trading of harambee contributions and other political capital for policy support, bids by one faction or another to strengthen the party by enforcing a single point of view became more frequent. At first, the tentative victor in this struggle was the "conservative" wing, led by one of the party's founders, James Gichuru. What his opponent, Oginga Odinga, had failed to do in trying to create a Lumumba Institute, Gichuru attempted once again, seeking "revitalization" of the party. He met with the president's weakened but still significant opposition. The relationship between KANU and the State House remained unchanged, despite Gichuru's efforts, but the Gichuru faction succeeded in curtailing its strongest opposition within the party, a populist coalition led by J. M. Kariuki, who in 1975 became a martyr to his cause and to his campaign to defend the openness of the political system.

By the mid 1970s, the rights to associate and to travel had suffered several legal setbacks, which either failed to elicit a reaction from members of Parliament or encountered only the weak opposition of individuals unable to constitute organized bases of action. Resistance to the Office of the President and its efforts to restrict levels of political challenge in Kenyan society became increasingly difficult as factions multiplied and replaced the semicorporate groups of the post-independence period. The popular recognition of a difference between KANU A, the "old-timers" involved in the party since the independence negotiations, and KANU B, the political elite who had joined later, ignored a plethora of groupings that formed around individual men and women and came and went with the rapidly changing fortunes of their leaders. For most politicians, it appeared to make more sense to gravitate toward the particular "insider" who promised to secure a passport or a harambee license than to accept the risks and invest in the coalition-building necessary to oppose policies that permitted the selective issuance of passports to members of Parliament. If one insider failed to "deliver," then one turned to another.

Upon Kenyatta's death in 1978, Daniel arap Moi promoted faction as part of a strategy for limiting organized opposition and maintaining control. He used his constitutional power to nominate twelve members of Parliament to advance the political fortunes of allies or of individuals he believed posed little threat to his rule. He rotated politicians in and out of important positions, ensuring that factions would constantly form and re-form. Thus, major restrictions on the ability of Kenyans to associate and to debate policy passed through Parliament with relatively little opposition, ranging from the proscription of opposition political parties in 1982 to 1989 legislation that made "rumor-mongering" a crime.

By comparison with many African countries, the rise of the "party-state" in Kenya took place slowly and haltingly. That it did so reflected the ability of some interest groups or elements of civil society to mobilize opposition to restriction of political freedoms and fusion of governmental and party functions outside of Parliament. In sub-Saharan countries such as Zaire, there is no such thing as a commercial class independent of government, and restrictions on political space arose before opposition groups were able to secure international ties that might enhance their bargaining power with their own governments.[58] In Kenya, although the business elite first developed its resources by cultivating very close ties with government, it became less dependent on the state than did the equivalent elites in most African countries. It has nonetheless lacked full control over any one sector of the economy. Further, those outside of politics who sought to protect civil liberties were quick to begin to cultivate international ties through churches, press organizations, bar associations, and even environmental groups. These groups have helped provide a check on the fusion of administrative and party powers or functions—sometimes more effectively so, sometimes less. They account for the rate at which the single-party system has evolved into a party-state and the way it did so. Eventually, aid donors intervened and used the leverage of control over loans to force Moi to legalize political opposition.

OVERVIEW

This book is about the rise of the party-state in Kenya and what this case can tell us about the source of variations in patterns of governance on the African continent. Because of the character of the evidence used in the study, the presentation necessarily includes a fair amount of historical detail. To simplify the reader's task, chapters 2 through 5 are organized chronologically, each detailing the dominant strategies the State House used to maintain order, the relationship between KANU and the State House within that strategy, and the reasons for changes in these. Chapter 2 provides a more complete discussion of the Kenyatta era than was offered in the introduction. Chapter 3 shows the pressures to which the Kenyatta strategy was subject between 1972 and 1978, the period of the founder's illness, and the consequences of the changes made at this time. Chapter 4 analyzes the early years of the Moi government, including the grounds for initial expectations that Moi would repeal some of the more repressive aspects of the Kenyatta state. Chapter 5 charts the shift in political strategies that took place under Moi, the reconfiguration of KANU, and the subsequent effects of these changes on patterns of debate and association. Chapter 6 discusses the 1985–90 period of consolidation and charts the struggles of some Kenyans to oppose KANU's new role. The final chapter offers a summary of the study, places the Kenyan case in comparative perspective, and discusses the specific contributions of its findings to current discussions of "governance" in Africa.

To one actively engaged in current Kenyan politics, this account is likely to seem incomplete. The intention is to identify the key elements and processes taking place. The many subplots and subthemes that make Kenyan politics so fascinating are not part of this account, partly because of the difficulty of such research in the current climate and partly because of the need to protect the identities of those who have contributed to this case study.[59] The task of refining and improving this understanding will necessarily lie with others.

CHAPTER TWO

Single-Party Dominance, 1964-1969

Party systems are important elements of strategies for securing political order. That is, whether organized as systems of representation or as vehicles for surveillance, they are designed to help obtain compliance with the particular allocation of resources and responsibilities, benefits and burdens a government imposes or negotiates. The details of how they operate make a big difference for the character of political life, however. It is possible for these systems to generate incentives for patterns of participation not imagined or intended by their creators.

In its first years of independence, Kenya had a very distinctive single-party-dominant system. Unlike many of its sub-Saharan neighbors, the country had laws permitting opposition political parties. Moreover, the dominant party, the Kenya African National Union (KANU), remained relatively weak. It possessed no internal structures for resolving differences between members and forging a common party platform and thus had little role in interest articulation and aggregation—functions parties in multiple-party and single-party systems often perform. These tasks were carried out informally through the harambee system. Furthermore, KANU exercised little control over policy. Most legislative initiatives originated in the Office of the President, or the executive, and then appeared on Parliament's agenda for discussion and adoption.

KANU was weak for two main reasons. First, at independence, Kenya included citizens with diverse economic interests, some of them already organized, if weakly so, and Jomo Kenyatta, the first president, was unwilling to alienate these groups by turning the party to the service of any one of them. Whereas Nkrumah had come to power in Ghana through a coalition that excluded large cocoa planters and felt unbeholden to these agricultural entrepreneurs, Kenyatta understood his own mandate to be far more ambiguous. He was a moderate who believed he required the assistance of both the commercial agricultural elite and the land-poor to maintain his power, both the trade union movement and the smallholders who produced much of the country's grain. Second, Kenyatta realized that all party systems are part of larger strategies for securing order and believed that he could persuade politicians to compromise and limit their claims against the state and against one another by creating auxiliary institutions to facilitate bargaining. It was simply not necessary to freight the party with the task of instilling into the country's population a common set of ideas or a common set of policy positions.

This chapter argues that the success of the early Kenyatta government in securing basic agreement on the "rules of the game," limiting the demands of economic and subnational groups, and promoting compromise rested substantially on the creation of an extra-parliamentary institution to facilitate bargaining among politicians. Like several current understandings of the Kenyatta state,[1] it takes the view that however authoritarian the rulings and amendments to the constitution that made political organization outside of KANU more difficult, the KANU of the Kenyatta era was a weak party. This analysis argues that it was deliberately so and that Kenyatta's refusal to turn it into a strong vehicle for political and social control was made possible by the success of the extra-parliamentary bargaining system he established and the continued power of independent interest groups in the Kenyan economy. The first section of the chapter explores the significance of social structure for the bargaining situation Kenyatta faced at independence. The second section reviews the "stakes" in the competition for government resources during the early Kenyatta period. The third section traces the actions of the main claimants. The fourth section analyzes the character of the party system Kenyatta established as part of his strategy for securing public order. The fifth examines the incentives the harambee system offered claimants to limit their demands and compromise with spokesmen for other economic or subnational groups. The final section looks explicitly at the relationships between the party and the administration in Kenyatta's strategy.

"CIVIL SOCIETY":
CLASS, ETHNICITY, AND CLIENTELISM

At independence, class division and the leaders of class-based organizations held greater power than they did only a few years later. When Jomo Kenyatta took power, the immediate imperative was to achieve the social peace required for the new government to maintain the economic growth necessary to fuel development plans. Stratification within the Kikuyu community had produced the Mau Mau rebellion, a revolt of the Kikuyu *ahoi*, or landless squatters, against both white settlers, who had expropriated land, and many of the chiefs, especially in Kiambu, who also controlled access rights to agricultural plots. Although sympathies and class boundaries within the Kikuyu community and within other communities not directly involved in Mau Mau did not coincide perfectly, it is nonetheless accurate to suggest that during and immediately after the Mau Mau Emergency, the "dispossessed," including landless laborers and squatters, as well as the chiefs in the rich coffee and tea region of Kiambu, both constituted distinct classes, whose members organized to pursue their interests, even if their objective positions and their interests did not correspond exactly with divisions between "capitalists" and "workers," or "peasants" and "petite bourgeoisie," in other parts of the world. Many of the landless or poorer peasants and workers among the Kikuyu continued to try to influence policy by constituting themselves as the Kenya Land Freedom Army (KLFA), under the leadership of former members of the Mau Mau.[2] Most active between 1960 and 1962, the KLFA announced that it would continue to fight an underground movement unless KANU effected a settlement that distributed land to the Kikuyu squatters. The class position of the young agricultural entrepreneurs and the chiefs, both in Central Province and elsewhere, was somewhat more ambiguous, but several of these men exercised sufficient economic and social power that they could credibly threaten to shatter the governing coalition. To prevent that outcome, the nationalist leader J. M. Kariuki cautioned against the consequences of unfettered pursuit of class interests, writing in his memoirs that "leaders must realize that we have put them where they are not to satisfy their ambitions nor so that they can strut about in fine clothes and huge Cadillacs as ambassadors and ministers, but to create a new Kenya in which everyone will have an opportunity to educate himself. . . . Selfish power-seekers will have to go."[3]

Weak, class-based organization rapidly gave way to a society in which vertical, clientelistic ties dominated, partly as a result of the new abundance of resources, such as civil service jobs and money for road construction, at the disposal of the members of the nationalist coalition, and partly through deliberate calculation. The new government moved quickly and successfully to attenuate horizontal divisions, so that by the time it entered its second or third year, patron-client ties had become stronger elements in defining personal identities than incipient classes.

For example, there was a nascent labor movement, formerly one of the bases for the stirrings of nationalist and class sentiment that erupted in the Mau Mau rebellion. The new independence government moved rapidly to limit worker militancy, however, by centralizing union organization and creating new structures for the representation of worker grievances to the government—structures that facilitated co-optation. The Trade Union Amendment Act gave the government the power to register unions, thereby making it more difficult for memberships to oust leaders who were insufficiently activist in their view.[4] Moreover, most workers retained ties to the land and moved into petty trading activities as well. In consequence, a clearly developed understanding of their interest as wage laborers and a willingness to act on such did not materialize. Instead, as scholars as diverse as Gavin Kitching and David Leonard have noted, at independence, Kenya had a class of "workers-and-peasants," not a proletariat on the model of the industrial societies.[5] After the dissipation of the KLFA and the strengthening of government control over unions, these people rarely organized in associations.

The later colonial period had also witnessed the development of a "petite bourgeoisie" in the shape of a class of traders and business entrepreneurs, many of whom secured capital for investment through savings from civil service jobs, and most of whom proceeded to build agricultural enterprises. These men were the organizers of the Kikuyu Central Association, in opposition to many of the chiefs, and constituted part of KANU's underpinning during the independence negotiations at Lancaster House in London. J. M. Kariuki and other nationalist leaders were often frustrated by the unbridled pursuit of economic interest by the members of this class.

Neither of these groups was clearly or exclusively a lobby for the interests of the new entrepreneurs, however, especially after the collapse of effective settler resistance and the end of white domination. The memberships included men and women occupying a variety of economic situations. The early KANU also included the former squatters, the people at the core of the Kikuyu Mau Mau, who pinned their hopes on Kenyatta rather than on the leaders of KADU. Indeed, KADU hoped to grant regional governments control over exchange of land and thus effectively to block the settlement of landless Kikuyu. It was antithetical to the views of the Mau Mau in consequence. Furthermore, in most cases, the new business elites themselves maintained strong ties with relatives who continued to carry on their lives as peasant farmers. The members of the new elite needed to ensure that policies offered resources for these relatives as well.

The availability of land after the Lancaster House agreements also helped diminish the salience of class as an identity in the immediate post-independence period, although the means of distribution later contributed to social stratification. Government purchase of territory in the upper Rift Valley from settlers meant that significant amounts of unoccupied land were suddenly available, and former squatters, smallholders, and new commercial farmers could all expand their holdings without necessarily coming into conflict with one another. Conflicts did emerge, of course, both before and after the Lancaster House negotiations, but for a short period at the beginning of the Kenyatta period, land appeared to be available for all. Moreover, as Christopher Leo has pointed out, "in many cases, members of the bourgeoisie were able to play intermediary roles in the provision of smallholdings for landless people and peasants and to profit personally."[6]

As soon as politicians acquired access to the jobs and material benefits controlled by a new state, horizontal divisions rapidly gave way to vertical, clientelistic ties. By the mid 1960s, political competition took place neither through interest-based associations, the key components of "civil society" in the industrial nations, nor through lineages, clans, or other kinds of ethnic or religious units. Clientelist networks were the primary structures of representation, linking Kenyans to the state through political patrons. Elected officials and senior civil servants competed to secure development projects for communities in their home areas or made monetary contributions to local initiatives in order to secure votes and other elements of political support. One impetus to the formation of clientelist relationships came from farmers' needs to hedge against risk by cultivating ties with those who could supply the resources to tide them over drought, pests or disease, or collapses in producer prices.[7] The other main encouragement was political. With independence, educated and wealthier Kenyans saw the possibility of gaining access to state resources by securing electoral office, but given the difficulty and cost of travel to "press the flesh" in every part of a constituency, a broad, issue-based campaign was scarcely practical. Dispensing patronage was often the most efficient means of building voter support. A notable from a village or location could take home a contribution to the community's school-construction fund and credibly promise to deliver the votes of an entire village.

The expansion of clientelism did not completely supplant class as a form of social identity. It permitted the petite bourgeoisie, Kenya's new and increasingly wealthy entrepreneurs, to protect their accumulated wealth from challenges by workers and farmers by buying the support of the most militant and sowing disarray in the ranks of those who might oppose the disproportionate benefit these elites derived from their positions. It also offered the farmers limited control. If the political elite could divide their ranks by disbursing individual benefits and make it difficult to organize on behalf of a particular set of policies, the farmers could nonetheless extort resources by threatening to vote for alternative candidates and deny an incumbent access to the state, which provided much of the money used to initiate new businesses. As clientelism expanded, action on the basis of a classwide rationality became much more difficult for marginal farmers, but it also meant that politicians had to offer material contributions to their constituents in return for continued ability to accumulate.[8]

If clientelist structures were more common than typical class-based associations, they bore a complex relationship to kinship organization and "ethnicity." Although the official line in Kenya is fervently nationalist and antagonistic to ethnic division, the salience of cultural distinctions of different sorts is reflected in public debate about the problem of "tribalism." Both voters and elites, dissidents and the strongest government supporters have expressed concern about the effects of what Tom Mboya called "negative tribalism."[9] As vice president and as president, Moi has continually stressed the dangers of "tribalism" to the country's stability, denouncing sectionalism of any sort in his public speeches. Joseph Karimi and Philip Ochieng, authors of *The Kenyatta Succession* (1980), captured a popular perspective when they expressed the view that "parochial feelings were only inculcated in the minds of the masses by certain individuals so that those individuals could achieve material ends."[10] Nathan Kahara, a former mayor of Nairobi, did the same when he commented that "the public were not tribal conscious but it was the leaders who divided the people."[11] Organizers of some of the newer technical institutes have also inclined toward that view and have moved to exclude politicians from management of school-development campaigns for this reason.[12] Ethnic division in Kenya is less a reflection of the existence of distinct, well-organized cultural communities than a consequence of the tactics politicians have used in securing public resources for their constituents.

For the Kenyan commentators, politicians act less as spokesmen for well-defined ethnic communities than as propagators of division. To suggest that politicians all make the same general types of claims would be quite wrong, however. In fact, in Kenya, there are significant differences in the character of ethnic claims at the local and national levels and, at the grass roots, both between constituencies and within a single constituency over time. Appeals at the national level are made on behalf of "ethnic blocs," "imagined communities" organized until 1980 through the agency of welfare associations and now managed predominantly through pyramiding patron-client ties, which have remained intact. At the local level, the claims politicians use refer to other types of identity groups, not all of them ethnic. Idioms used by grass-roots politicians are less often "tribal" than they are populist or patronage- or clan-based. Ethnic appeals are used in distinctly different ways at the two levels as well. At the national level, the politicians try to project themselves as spokespersons or to demonstrate that if they do not receive an adequate share of public resources, they can shift the support of their network members to another coalition. Through use of ethnic idiom, the politicians advertise command of or access to networks in which an important criterion for membership is a real or imagined ethnic tie. At the grass roots, the appeals are vehicles for mobilizing electoral support in areas where people from the same lineages and clans live in proximity to one another. They are not the only kinds of appeals politicians make to their constituents, however, and in some cases politicians deliberately avoid them.

In a resource-short polity, patrons have also found ethnic idiom useful as a way of maintaining strained clientelist relationships. Colin Leys has argued this point of view as an explanation of the sharpness of "tribal" distinctions in Kenya. Tribalism "consists in the fact that people identify other exploited people as the source of their insecurity and frustrations, rather than their common exploiters," he writes.[13] Leys explains the increasing frequency of accusations of tribalism in Parliament during the 1960s as the consequence of increases in the number of school-leavers and decreases in the number of white-collar jobs available:

Accusations of tribalism began to be more and more frequently made in parliament, at first mainly in relation to salaried jobs, but gradually extending to jobs in general. What was at stake was the ability of the educated to make good their claims to be benefactors. They discovered that tribal recruitment-patterns built up under colonial rule meant that large areas of patronage—whole departments and firms—were in effect reserved to the patrons of particular tribes.[14]

Ethnic idiom also gave the emerging bourgeois elite in Kikuyu-dominated Central Province the basis for overcoming the fractiousness of those Kikuyu who had not benefited from the transition to independence to the same extent. "So long as enough of the Kikuyu masses believed that [political dominance] was also of prime importance to them, appeals to tribal solidarity would serve the double purpose of reinforcing the Kikuyu leadership's position at the centre, and repelling challenges based on class antagonism within Kikuyu society."

Where elected officials have limited control over policy, and where constituency service is therefore at a premium, more or less overt use of the power of ethnic or regional networks to bargain for state resources occurs on an everyday basis. Lodging other sorts of claims, such as appeals based on class or on a populist platform, generally proves unhelpful to the politician. The benefits to be gained by championing better producer prices for cotton growers or maize producers, for example, are not divisible. To a great degree the gains sought by populist politicians or leaders of class-based movements constitute public goods in the technical sense. Those who do not vote for a candidate nonetheless benefit if the candidate succeeds in winning improvements for producers of cash crops, for instance. The politicians' vote-getting imperatives push them to favor strategies or appeals that will permit them to exclude those who cast their ballots for other candidates from sharing in the benefits, thereby encouraging voters to lend their support in anticipation of a portion of the returns the politicians bring home.[15]

The salience of ethnicity in political competition was also somewhat greater than in many other sub-Saharan countries because of regional differences in standards of living and access to resources. "Region" constituted a third kind of identity, but found its organizational base in ethnic welfare societies because of the coincidence between ethnic and administrative divisions. Access to health care, education, roads and other transportation facilities varied greatly, with Central Province (the Kikuyu heartland) ranking first in all categories. Although most of these regions included some members of the petite bourgeoisie—teachers or civil servants who had acquired farms or businesses—the ability of these individuals to accumulate resources varied according to the regions from which they hailed. Their efforts to secure greater access to the benefits controlled by the state and to defend their own shares put them in competition with the relatively wealthier members of their class from Central Province. Indeed, at independence, KANU held a majority of the seats in fewer than half of the regional assemblies (which Parliament agreed to abolish in 1964).[16]

THE COMPETITION FOR RESOURCES

The pattern of these inequalities meant first that, in the absence of force, the Kenyatta government would have to redistribute some resources to keep politicians from regions that were less well-off as members of the Kiambu-based coalition. Second, to keep the Central Province base from splintering, Kenyatta would have to make some concessions to the landless within his home province, offsetting his close ties with the wealthy Kiambu elite. Further, to maintain the confidence of the industrial countries whose financial assistance Kenya would need to finance rapid growth, Kenyatta also had to ensure that the remaining white settlers' interests were treated judiciously.

This balancing act was a difficult one, made slightly easier by the fact that despite a policy of fiscal conservatism, the resource pie was expanding. Although fights to redress imbalances between Kenya's regions implied reduction in the shares of resources some areas received, the prospect of high rates of economic growth calmed fears that any one group might actually have to accept absolute losses. With an increasing resource base, distributional politics was not a zero-sum game. Economic conditions in the later Moi period would not be so fortuitous.

Good policy and good luck made the new Kenyatta government more fortunate than those of most developing countries in its economic experiences immediately after independence. During the first seven years, average annual real rates of growth in gross domestic product (GDP) were consistently about 6.5 percent. These healthy rates of expansion permitted the then finance minister, James Gichuru, to keep the proportion of total government expenditure to GDP roughly even (to about 30 percent or less) throughout the 1963–70 period, while at the same time making more spending money available in absolute terms. In so doing, he could try to meet some of the competing demands for resources. As leader of a newly independent government seeking to reduce dependence on colonial personnel, Kenyatta had to increase spending on training of Kenyans to reduce foreign technical staff and to reward those who had helped or sacrificed during the struggle and negotiation phases. At the same time, he faced the need to repay loans contracted by the colonial government during the 1940s and 1950s (KSh. 100 million was due foreign banks in 1965, two years after independence),[17] support reimbursement of settlers for expropriation of land, and wean the country away from dependence on the British Treasury, which had supplied 24 percent of government revenues in 1962–63.[18] The flight of foreign capital during the years surrounding independence constrained the revenue-raising options available. High rates of growth, increased direct taxes, and long-term borrowing on domestic capital markets after the imposition of exchange controls in 1965 allowed Gichuru to succeed remarkably well in the tasks confronting him as the first minister of finance.[19]

To many Kenyans, growth was evident in the expansion of local school facilities, roads, and other amenities, as well as in the availability of food, which was produced in abundance and often exported (usually at a loss because of subsidies). Moreover, the purchasing power of the Kenya shilling remained relatively constant. Until the 1970s, inflation averaged only about 2 percent per year—a record low for Kenya and a rate few other rapidly developing nations have ever achieved. Finally, the early decision to tie the Kenya shilling to a bundle of ten currencies (the Special Drawing Right, or SDR) produced a creeping devaluation that kept Kenyan exports competitive and stimulated demand for new production.[20]

Land, nationalization of industry, and education were the stakes that most preoccupied participants in parliamentary debates between 1964 and 1970.[21] Of these three issues, land and education were of utmost importance to all politicians, whose constituents wanted more of both. Floor fights and arguments outside of Parliament focused on which districts would receive how much of the money available for each. Although both assets were finite, for physical or practical reasons, room for expanded use was still abundant.

Kenya also was and remains unusual among African countries in its shortage of arable land to population. Although population-density figures are not high compared to those in some European countries, such as the Netherlands, the poor quality of the soils in much of the country places severe limits on carrying capacity. Nonetheless, population pressure has forced farmers in many arable parts of the country to cultivate even the steepest slopes, denuding hilltops of trees and planting where soil erosion constitutes a major danger. White settlers occupied the most fertile of these lands until the government of Kenya began to buy out their holdings in the early 1960s. Given the constraints on availability of plots and the major role played by the Kikuyu squatters, or *ahoi*, in the Mau Mau rebellion that moved the country toward independence, allocation of acreage formerly controlled by whites was bound to be the center of distributional politics upon Kenyatta's rise to power.

During the 1960s, fights over land took place in the context of a general perception that adequate acreage was available for all if only the government machinery for carrying out title transfers would work effectively. As a result of independence negotiations that provided for government purchase of farms from colonial settlers, using loans provided by the British government and British banks, however, the land was not "free." The new government could make plots available only with the proviso that the recipients repay the cost over several years. The government initiated several different settlement programs, each pitched to a particular economic group. The principal program, the Million Acre Scheme, created three types of settlements: one that placed low-income farmers on high-density holdings of 25 acres; one that placed slightly wealthier, "yeoman" farmers on low-density holdings of 40 acres; and one that offered 260 large plots of 100 acres each to those who could put up substantial amounts of capital of their own or who could provide collateral—usually local politicians, officials, and businessmen. To address the problems of the poor, the government initiated a second scheme (the Haraka Program), which located these farmers on small subsistence plots of 10 acres each, concentrated in 29 different areas.

The programs worked slowly and benefited wealthier Kenyans to a far greater degree than the landless or land-poor. High rates of defaults on loans eventually brought the programs almost to a standstill. Nonetheless, it would be incorrect to say that during the 1960s, these programs were widely perceived as a failure. Although the Land Bank/Agricultural Finance Corporation assistance went principally to large-scale farmers, the Haraka Program succeeded in resettling 13,000 households on 10-acre plots by 1970 (out of a total of 46,000 registered squatters), and the Million Acre Scheme resettled a total of 35,000 households on 1.176 million acres during the same period. Of the approximately 8 million acres of high-potential land under white control at independence, a large amount remained for distribution after 1970.[22]

Although there was much understandable grumbling about the slowness of the transfer process and the favor accorded wealthy farmers, there was not, during this period, the perception that land was unavailable.

The other heavily valued resource during this period was education. By the mid 1970s, Kenya's spending on schools and teachers as a proportion of total government expenditure exceeded that for all but a very few nations in the world. During the first decade of independence, primary school enrollments more than doubled, and secondary school enrollments quintupled. The average annual rate of increase in recurrent government budget expenditures on education was 17 percent.[23]

As in the case of land, education was perceived, during the 1960s, as a resource that need not be rationed and that brought equality—or the chance to secure equality, both in interpersonal terms and between regions. Spending increased with demand, and the government moved in to help staff schools built by communities themselves. Furthermore, communities appeared to accept the government's design of the educational system to stress advancement on merit and allocation of significant resources for higher education, which would be available only to a few who worked hard.[24] Only in the late 1970s did the government put the brakes on spending, and only later still did the greater success of children from wealthier districts belie the claims that an educational system based on equality of opportunity would advance students on the basis of merit and bring about strict equality between social groups and regions.

In sum, bargaining for resources during the period between 1963 and 1970 took place principally over items or benefits that would later carry special significance as arbiters of survival, but that for the time being seemed available to all, if slow in coming. Both land and access to primary and secondary school education were potentially available, and the recognition had not spread that either would become scarce, costly resources, available only to the wealthy. Combined with economic growth that created new income-earning opportunities in formal-sector manufacturing and agriculture, the patterns of resource availability kept popular demands to those negotiable within the political system.

This is not to say that Kenyan political life was a scene of placid discussion over budgets. Far from it. Kenyatta had to draw on his great tactical repertoire to contain a myriad distributional fights and prevent them from splintering the governing coalition.

THE PLAYERS

Historically, Kenyatta had demonstrated little tolerance for the regimentation of union or party platforms. His first political writing appeared in *Muigwithania* ("The Reconciler"), a Kikuyu Central Association (KCA) journal he edited. A literal translation of the Kikuyu title—"He who causes the whole group to understand one another"—captures much of Kenyatta's personal orientation toward politics.[25] His early experiences as a politician built his reputation as a compromiser. Marshall Clough writes that Kenyatta's "reputation was greatest . . . as a persuader, a conciliator, a man who settled quarrels." At a very divisive KCA meeting in 1928, Kenyatta urged members: "Do not break up, for if you break up so will your affairs go to pieces."[26] This advice became one of the hallmarks of Kenyatta's style during the nationalist period, as the new leader sought to draw together the interests of the Kenya Land Freedom Army and at least four Kikuyu political groups (the KCA, the Progressive Kikuyu Party, the Loyal Patriots, and the Kikuyu Land Board Association), as well as the spokesmen for other ethnic communities and labor unions, in the Kenya African Union (KAU), the successor organization to the KCA.[27] J. M. Kariuki noted in his memoirs, published in 1963, that Kenyatta managed to place himself above the fray. "[Kenyatta] does not depend on KADU or KANU, Indian Congress or Indian Freedom Party, New Kenya Party or Coalition, he is more than any political party," Kariuki wrote. "He does not speak of his people as detainees, loyalists, terrorists, Home Guards, 'Mau Mau', Catholics, Protestants, Muslims, Asians, Europeans. Kenyatta is greater than any Kikuyu, he is greater than any Luo or Nandi or Masai or Giriama, he is greater than any Kenyan."[28] During the years before independence, Kenyatta learned that compromise is not always possible, however—that interests are sometimes irreconcilable and that the measure of a leader is not only whether he or she can build successful coalitions when these are required but also how he or she manages tension between groups when it becomes impossible to forge common positions.

Despite his ties with the KCA, Kenyatta worked on behalf of both squatters and the emerging elite of entrepreneurs and civil servants against the settlers in the period leading up to the Emergency. This entente collapsed in the early years of the Mau Mau rebellion, however. Concerned that alliance with urban workers and implicit approval of strike activity could jeopardize KAU's legal standing in the colony, and under government pressure to distance the organization from the more radical elements of the Mau Mau, Kenyatta began to equivocate. Increasingly, Kenyatta's hesitance to come out with a strong show of support for the Mau Mau "Central Committee" lost KAU the backing of urban elements.[29] When Kenyatta was imprisoned by the colonial government as a leader of the uprising, his power in the movement was in fact at very low ebb. Held at Lokitaung and Lodwar for most of the Emergency, Kenyatta acquired a reputation among the younger Mau Mau detainees as a man of an older generation, a member of the elite on better terms with the colonial administration than with the Mau Mau themselves. He proved unable to overcome this perception until his release from prison.

Elevated to the position of "independence leader" more by his political detention under the British than by any role in the shadowy "Central Committee" that planned and carried out the Mau Mau rebellion, Kenyatta emerged onto the political scene as a "moderate," a potential bridge-builder. Faced with both an aggressive group of educated entrepreneurs, some of them reviled as "loyalists" or members of the Home Guard, and with a guerrilla movement, over a thousand of whose militants remained armed and hidden in forest areas that abutted desirable agricultural land, Kenyatta had little choice but to adopt this role if he hoped to oversee a transfer of power to Kenyan Africans. Any violence between these groups would likely result in a quick end to British offers of financial assistance to the new nation. As the Mau Mau Emergency came to a close, Kenyatta at first refused to declare his allegiance to either of the two political parties jockeying for power, KANU and KADU. He later accepted the presidency of KANU on October 28, 1961, but he continued to refuse to define a clear ideological position. Instead, he sought to instill confidence in the new Kenya by meeting with the various parties who made up his diverse constituency. Settler farmers were important, because, as one commentator has written, "they provided a barometer of European confidence in the new Kenya," which was much in need of foreign capital.[30] Kenyatta met with 300 settlers at Nakuru in August 1963 and later with former Mau Mau militants, seeking to draw them out of the forest and into the fold by appearing in public and on newsreel film with a former "Field Marshal" in dreadlocks. The relationship between the Mau Mau detainees and the independence government Kenyatta led remained rocky, but Kenyatta's compromises may well have prevented a descent into violence.

Although Kenyatta's political strategy may have resulted in part from personal predilection, objective conditions favored a strategy of reconciliation and compromise. The character of civil society at the end of the colonial period and the new leader's bargaining position vis-à-vis nascent political groupings both shaped the strategic options available.

At independence, the wealthier Kiambu-based elites had both the money to buy coalition partners and the organization and know-how to pursue their interests. They were the strongest claimants upon the new state. Under Kenyatta's guidance, the membership of the Kenya African Union expanded to include, as one of its main elements, teachers and civil servants, "a group tied to the colonial state both by their current positions and their aspirations to those monopolized by Europeans."[31] Both groups became part of KANU, although some of those from outside Central Province and the Luo areas in the west later walked out of the party to form KADU in protest of Kikuyu-Luo domination. Almost all of those who left returned to the KANU fold later.

The Kiambu group was especially interested in improving infrastructure to facilitate private economic ventures and in securing access to the land up for grabs in the former White Highlands. The possibility of establishing large agricultural estates was particularly inviting. Food grains, as well as coffee and tea for export, looked like good money-making prospects, as did the transport of agricultural commodities between regions. In making both these demands, however, the group faced opposition from other economic and subnational groups, including claimants within it.

The Luo opposition leader Oginga Odinga and the former Mau Mau leader Bildad Kaggia had a common interest in limiting the share of benefits received by the Kiambu community. Kaggia's community included the former squatters and Mau Mau detainees, who also wanted the reward of land in the former White Highlands. These were the people who had fought the battle but who remained landless. With limited education, no knowledge of English or Swahili (the two lingua francas), and few financial resources to use in building an organization or negotiating for support, the former Mau Mau fighters had but a weak bargaining position. The Luo community included a large proportion of the country's formal labor force, as well as many who hoped to benefit from land reform. They too feared that the interests of the Kiambu elite diverged from theirs. They had articulate leadership from two men, Odinga and the more conservative labor leader Tom Mboya, each representing different points of view. But they too lacked the money to forge a strong interest-group organization, despite the beginnings of a political base in the Luo Union. Odinga and Kaggia were to constitute a series of ad hoc alliances throughout the early years of the Kenyatta period. Even before independence, Mboya had sought and obtained legislation to make Kenya a "high wage" country with a small, weakly organized labor force. He pursued a series of separate "deals" with other claimants.

The third locus of power during the Kenyatta period lay with the groups on the edges of the White Highlands, the Kalenjin and the Luhya, who produced much of the country's maize stock. Land was a scarce resource for both of these groups, as it was for both the Kikuyu squatters and the Kiambu business elite. The leaders had coalesced during the Lancaster House negotiations, prior to independence, and formed the Kenya African Democratic Union (KADU) to defend their economic interests against the KANU coalition that included both the Odinga-Kaggia group and the Kiambu community. KADU had differed with KANU most significantly in its stance on regional autonomy and its definition of regional boundaries. Its organizers argued for a federal system with regional legislatures that could each decide how to regulate access to land. They further argued for regional jurisdictions that would effectively preclude a significant Kikuyu voice in the division of the White Highlands. Although the Kalenjin returned solid KADU majorities in the independence elections, the Luhya did not. Factional division among the Luhya weakened the coalition's voice in national politics, as did the limited financial resources the group had at its disposal.

During the 1960s, Kenyatta's task was to manage these competing claims in a way that would prevent the rise of political extremes incapable of negotiating with one another. At least until 1968, continued tenure in the presidency was tied to maintenance of a parliamentary majority. Splintering of the KANU coalition into separate parties or strengthening of existing opposition parties posed a threat to Kenyatta's job. Accordingly, Kenyatta was a staunch supporter of a one-party system. His belief that a single-party system was more appropriate than party competition also stemmed from a crisis in late 1963, when KADU refused to go along with the government's declaration of emergency in the Northern Frontier District on the grounds that it had not been consulted in advance. To the Kenyatta cabinet, KADU's actions appeared to highlight both the potential dangers of regionalism and the clumsiness and immobility that a multi-party system could breed.[32]

In 1964, as KADU's personnel joined KANU, Kenyatta said that
those who were slow in recognizing the virtue of the single-party system
were often the same people who had been "warming their bellies under
imperialist wings" during the struggle against colonialism, and he called
KADU a cabal composed of "self-conceited grasshopper politicians."[33]
What mattered, he argued, was whether the party or parties established
were mass parties. A one-party state with a mass base was just as democratic, in his view, as a state with two mass-based parties. Subsequently, those who threatened that system frequently landed in jail or
suffered the threat of loss of employment or police refusal to license
political meetings. A friend of multi-party democracy Kenyatta was not.
But Kenyatta also feared that unless the spokesmen for important segments of the Kenyan population all believed they had a stake in the
system, the government would become unstable. Inability to facilitate
compromise and "political centrism" seemed likely to invite foreign intervention and exacerbation of centrifugal tendencies. Kenyatta had
every incentive to try to create an "inclusive coalition."

Although economic circumstances were difficult at independence,
Kenyatta had a new array of resources to administer selectively in his
efforts to secure political support among the stronger groups: positions
on the boards of public companies, road construction funds, agricultural services, land. These he used to draw different communities into
the governing coalition and to solidify support among the Kiambu entrepreneurs in particular. He used marriage bonds to build ties, too.
Upon his release from jail, he married into the Koinange and Muhoho
families, both prominent within Kiambu, and cemented ties with three
other landed clan leaders, Charles Njonjo, Arthur Magugu, and Munyua Waiyaki. He built relationships with Kikuyu leaders outside
Kiambu by extending offices to James Gichuru, his former opponent for
control of the pre-independence Kenya African Union, Murang'a District's Julius Kiano, and Nyeri's Mwai Kibaki, a young technocrat with
few Mau Mau credentials to his name who could nonetheless be used to
demonstrate regional representativeness within the Kikuyu home area.
These kinds of patronage relationships do not suffice to maintain order
over the long run, however, and Kenyatta understood that. Those who
receive the benefits of patronage can use their newfound status or
wealth to challenge leadership. Only a head of state who is exceptionally clever in his ability to elevate and demote the "barons" with whom
he allies himself—or keep them guessing—can long maintain power.

POLITICAL STRATEGY AND KANU
AS A CATCHALL PARTY

Under these circumstances, Kenyatta decided to pursue a strategy with three main components. The first was to make sure that KANU remained open to politicians with a wide range of views, in the hope of limiting the tendency of factions to create their own parties—a condition he feared might jeopardize his own tenure in office as well as trigger the kind of splintering that would make it difficult to limit the scope of bargaining and maintain civility in future years. The second was the creation of institutions that would encourage elites to limit the kinds of demands they made on the political system to those that could be met without the total exclusion of other groups. That is, Kenyatta tried to "rig" electoral competition so as to force elites to bargain and compromise with one another. The third was to campaign against those who did not respect his own intentions.

The best strategy of a party leader who wanted to remain as head of government under the electoral rules that then prevailed in Kenya would be to allow as much debate as possible within the party, so as to convince as many aspiring politicians as possible to remain loyal and sustain the party majority in the legislature. At the beginning of the independence period, Kenya's constitution provided for a prime minister to be elected by the members of the lower house of the legislature from among their number. Each member of the legislature had to campaign for a plurality of the votes from a single-member district, except for twelve nominated members of the upper house. To win, a party had to appeal to as many voters as possible, and to do so, it was helpful for the national party to maintain a vague centrist position, while allowing individual party members autonomy to espouse whatever platforms were important to secure votes in particular constituencies. Unity was essential, even if ideological clarity had to be sacrificed. This tactical logic remained compelling even after changes in the constitution first turned the prime minister into a president (without significantly modifying parliamentary arrangements, however) and then, in 1968, made provision for election of the president by direct popular vote.[34] Even after the switch to a presidential system, the individual candidate's need for a plurality in a single-member district maintained the advantage of membership in a loose, centrist party for most, including aspirants to the country's highest office.

To exist as a catchall party, KANU would have to sacrifice the ability to put a strong stamp on legislation, delegating the task of forming legislation to a parliamentary group, which would then balance competing demands. This logic appears to have prevailed. The original KANU coalition included, not only the Kiambu Kikuyu elite and the Luo labor leader Tom Mboya, but also the populist Odinga-Kaggia alliance between the Luo and the Kikuyu squatters. Kenyatta had persuaded the two main coalitions to reason with each other. Within a year of the 1963 election, most of the major figures in KADU also joined the ranks, locating within a single party divergent interests in the future of the White Highlands and in the allocation of the capital budget.

Kenyatta accomplished this result by subtly undercutting efforts to turn the post-independence party into an efficient organization for pursuing the agenda of any particular subgroup. The first major challenge came in 1964–65, when the "radical" wing of the party, the Odinga-Kaggia coalition, sought to "revitalize" the party organization. The plan was to generate discussion of a party platform, then to instill adherence to chosen policies by creating a party "school." With assistance from the Communist bloc, the Odinga-Kaggia group put together a training course at the Lumumba Institute, whose existence Kenyatta announced, with no preliminary fanfare, at the end of December 1964.[35] Although Kenyatta did not object publicly to the creation of the institute, he did nothing to ensure its survival, short of recognizing the need for improving the flow of information among party members and for clarifying of the role of politicians vis-à-vis civil servants. Permission to go ahead with the institute appeared to be a temporary measure to keep the radical wing within the party, possibly with the understanding that the radicals would have to compromise with others if they wished their creation to last.

Kenyatta would not sanction any actions by the Odinga-Kaggia faction that threatened the catchall character of the party, however, and he turned quickly against the Lumumba Institute when the radical wing moved to use the organization to increase its power over other party members. In the actual event, the Odinga-Kaggia coalition saw the institute as a vehicle for developing a clientele and building a soapbox within the party. By April of 1965, the students of the first and only series of classes offered had forged an association of KANU members pledged to the defeat of Kenyatta's "Sessional Paper Number 10 on the Application of Planning to African Socialism," which, name aside, supported a mixed capitalist economic system. They called a national conference of KANU delegates to discuss the party platform.[36] The Kiambu coalition within the party, with Kenyatta's blessing, moved to place the Lumumba Institute under control of the Ministry of Education, where its activities could be monitored and circumscribed. After a parliamentary vote to that effect, the organization died out.

Kenyatta himself called a meeting of delegates at Limuru for March 1966, at which he said he would unveil his own proposals for reorganization of the party, including introduction of a new constitution. Some of the delegates to the conference were handpicked by Daniel arap Moi, who played an important role in managing the affair, presumably to preclude a floor fight between the Kiambu elite and the Odinga-Kaggia radicals.[37] In the actual event, however, the "radicals" saw the party machinery turning against them and created their own political party, the Kenya People's Union (KPU), just before the conference began.

Although the proceedings at Limuru ended in the decision to hold by-elections to test whether the KPU had an electoral mandate, Kenyatta's contributions concentrated on two themes. One common thread running through Kenyatta's proposals at the conference was the need to keep internal party debates from interfering with the operation of the provincial administration, Kenyatta's main vehicle for carrying out policies and maintaining his own ties with the grass roots. In Kenyatta's view, the functions of party and executive ought to be kept distinct and separate. In commenting on the reasons for the March conference, he said that if "the confusion and frustration within the party" were allowed to continue "it could seriously damage the image of the party. . . . In seeking a role for themselves, for example, elected politicians have pressed to take over the executive control of civil servants in the districts."[38] That was as much a warning to the conservatives in KANU as to any who might contemplate siding with the KPU.

Kenyatta proposed creating a paid administration within the party to carry out liaison functions and information exchange. "If civil servants were to become active members of the party, there is a danger that in the division of interest between politics and professionalism the efficiency of the Service would suffer. It would be only too easy for the situation to develop where civil servants are promoted and appointed on the ground of political zeal rather than professional competence."[39] Kenyatta sought to separate the two functions in order to contain division.

The second theme was the need to maintain an inclusive one-party system. As he had made clear on numerous occasions, Kenyatta was no friend of multi-partyism, but it was evident from the speeches at the Limuru conference that he did not favor a strengthened single-party system in which party officials assumed the tasks of the executive either. The president was skeptical of the efforts of politicians in other African countries, especially in neighboring Tanzania, to use the dominant political party as a vehicle for building support for a particular set of policies. "The Government does not intend to submit legislation to Parliament . . . [to make Kenya a one-party State]," he commented. "In other independent States of Africa, there exist a number of other constitutional experiments or practices. We shall continue to watch these developments with brotherly interest and goodwill"[40] . . . but not as potential models. He further cautioned fellow politicians against eliminating dissent within KANU: "Our Party . . . must never come to be manipulated by a few. And while I need not elaborate the point today, the whole strength of our Party must be based on non-alignment."[41]

Maintaining nonalignment was a struggle, however. The leadership of the conservative wing of the party was quite strong, and its members did not all share Kenyatta's faith in a strategy to preserve order that was based on pluralism within KANU's ranks and constant bargaining among groups. Because of their heavy representation on the front bench in Parliament and in the party machinery—and because of their relatively greater wealth and consequent ability to dispense patronage, the conservative faction could more easily secure ascendancy than could other groups. The management of the Limuru conference demonstrated that; maneuvering by Moi and Mboya to handpick delegates had triggered the formation of the KPU, which feared just such a capture of the party's machinery.

Kenyatta also felt pressure from new quarters to prevent the conservative "KANU A" from seizing power now that the KPU had taken some of the "populists" out of the party. The emergence of a multi-ethnic, strengthened backbench opposition to the dominant conservative faction in the aftermath of the conference may have reminded Kenyatta of the difficulty of maintaining unity in a context of diversity, something of which he was already quite aware. Many, although not all, of the KANU A members closest to Kenyatta hailed from the areas right outside of Nairobi: Kiambu, Kiambaa, Gatundu, and Limuru. Mainstream politicians of a less conservative stripe had limited access to the president. The politicians of Nyeri and Murang'a were also underrepresented, and through the leadership of Charles Rubia, a Nairobi MP, and others, some of these MPs constituted their own group within Parliament. This new back bench, along with some junior ministers, most notably Josiah Mwangi Kariuki, moved quickly to attack the ascendancy of the "Gatundu Courtiers," especially when they discovered that frontbenchers were receiving millions of dollars in gratuities from public funds and began to fear for their own ability to dispute those emoluments.[42] Some members of the new backbench group also echoed the themes of the KPU platform, the Wananchi Declaration, and were concerned that they might lose the continued ability to express those. The moment seemed opportune, as the president had said in his Jamhuri Day speech in December 1968 that he would consider primaries for both KANU and the KPU. Nineteen members of the group organized in April 1969 to demand primary elections for party nominations to parliamentary seats, in an effort to deny the conservative faction the ability to choose candidates and screen out those with whom they disagreed.[43] The "Ol Kalou Declaration," as their proposal became known, attracted much support from backbenchers.

The president was attentive to the broad base of the demand for open primaries. Developing tensions within KANU were quite evident. Writing just before the Ol Kalou Declaration, one Kenyan observer remarked that

> For some time now the party machinery has not always been a true reflection of the tempo of the *Wananchi*—a fact which could not have escaped the watchful eye of the President. In such a situation the danger is always that the existing party bureaucracy, having isolated themselves from the people, subsequently use most of their energy, not on the national development effort but in manipulating the party machinery merely to keep themselves in power.[44]

In a manner consistent with his earlier style, Kenyatta decided to go ahead and institute a system of open KANU primaries in May 1969. David Leonard remarks quite correctly that, to Kenyatta's credit, "the president recognized that if he gave the discontented no place to vent their anger they would eventually turn on him. He therefore introduced relatively open KANU primaries and brought electoral competition within the confines of the party. . . . He had brilliantly created a safety valve without diminishing the security of his regime."[45] These steps helped precipitate defections from the KPU to KANU and reduced the outcry when the KPU was banned several months later, in October 1969.

HARAMBEE AND THE BASIS FOR COMPROMISE

Several Kenya scholars have located the source of order during the Kenyatta period in coalition-building strategies that depended on patronage. In this view, Kenyatta constructed a base of support that bound the spokesmen for divergent interests to an overarching loyalty to him as Mzee, the father, and the Kenyan state. He first secured the allegiance of the wealthy Kiambu Kikuyu business elite with offers of farms in the former White Highlands, the relatively fertile swath of land in the high areas around the upper Rift Valley. To prevent fracture of his Kikuyu base, Kenyatta was also compelled to offer land to those who had fought the British in the Mau Mau Rebellion, the squatters of Nyeri, Murang'a, and Nyandarua Districts. With this group of claimants in mind, he negotiated the Million Acre Scheme, mentioned above, which enabled the new government to buy out many of the remaining white settlers, using loans from the British government, and to repay the loans gradually, as squatters purchased plots in the new settlement areas. In practice, the former Mau Mau squatters were slow to receive their bequest, but the publicity surrounding the gesture and Kenyatta's use of Munyua Waiyaki, a member of the elite with well-known, if somewhat overdrawn, ties to the former fighters, as a go-between brought the poorer Kikuyu into the coalition.[46]

In this view, shared here, Kenyatta's use of clientelist ties and his inclusion of representatives of most groups in a broad coalition created a solid base of support and focused the politicians' attention on a struggle for power within KANU instead of on the potential benefits of creating opposition parties or making exceptional demands on state resources. Kenyatta preserved KANU from the effects of competition and rendered it at once an arena where demands might safely be aired and contained and an ineffective instrument for developing a clear program or platform. It was a weak party, regardless of the constitutional amendments and restrictive legislation that appeared, on the face of it, to move Kenya toward a strong single-party-dominant system of government.[47]

The first component of the Kenyatta strategy, the maintenance of a weak party, depended on the second, the creation of a system of bargained exchange in which those who sacrificed resources at the request of the president or a politician from another region could be compensated for doing so. What Kenyatta put in place was far more sophisticated than a simple patronage system, however. Land was not all that Kenyatta traded to fellow politicians for their support. Small-scale "constituency service" projects constituted as harambee, or self-help development, were at least as valuable.

Harambee already existed in an uninstitutionalized form when Kenyatta took power. Residents of an area would join together to provide private, voluntary financial assistance, materials, or labor for a local development project. For example, neighbors each contributed a few shillings toward the construction of a borehole, cattle dip, or other facility from which they all would benefit. At harambee gatherings, the project sponsor provided a gift of funds to supplement those provided by residents. Kenyatta's genius lay in building this institution into a mechanism for ensuring that Kenyans would see some signs of "development" in their home areas, whatever the success of central government efforts; for diverting the attention of politicians from national issues to construction of local infrastructure; for forcing compromise and alliance between spokesmen for different communal groups; and, through personal appearances by the president at harambee gatherings, for rewarding politicians whose constituents lost share in the allocation of public funds. He made harambee a tactic in the pursuit of political order, an essential tool for facilitating compromise and encouraging politicians to limit their bids for control of party offices and platform.

He did so quite deliberately. In 1965, at Kenyatta's request, cabinet minister Tom Mboya drafted a document, entitled "Sessional Paper Number 10 on African Socialism," that outlined a development strategy in which harambee assumed a new and more important role than it had previously occupied. The president initiated the first major self-help project himself, launching a funds drive for a hospital in his Kiambu District constituency, Gatundu. During the next few years, he took every opportunity to encourage voters to judge politicians on their material contributions to their constituencies. "There is no place for leaders who hope to build a nation of slogans," he preached. "If you elect somebody who spends all his time in Nairobi doing nothing, what good is that?"[48] Every political speech he made ended with him chanting, "Harambee! Harambee! Harambee!" and the audience responding with a cheer.

The campaigns reported in the Kenyan press suggested that Kenyatta's promotion of harambee affected voting behavior and the activities of politicians over the long term, as intended. Most campaign speeches pointed to the candidate's contributions at these fund-raisers. In the words of one contestant, "We want a change [of representative] so as to have a person ready to mix freely with people to learn their problems . . . [and at] the same time, a person who can initiate *Harambee* projects to develop the constituency."[49] Two cases were particularly striking as indicators of public expectations of parliamentary representatives. In one instance, the *Daily Nation* reported that three students had announced their candidacies for parliamentary seats. Students might be expected to offer more radical views than most candidates in Kenya and to break with standard campaign rhetoric, but they might also be especially attentive to what "worked" for other politicians in devising their first campaign speeches. All three turned their rhetoric to the importance of harambee participation.

Even after Kenyatta's death, opposition politicians felt compelled to respect the criteria established in 1965. For instance, in his 1979 bid for election to Parliament, the former KPU leader Achieng Oneko stressed his harambee participation in order to make his political comeback. Over a two-year period he made a pointed effort to rest his case on his harambee record. In January 1978, a few months before Kenyatta's death, Oneko made his first speech in his bid for clearance, announcing that since his release in 1975, he had attended 47 harambee meetings and officiated at 20 of them.[50] In a 1979 speech to voters, Oneko stated: "Since I left detention I have contributed more than [KSh.] 80,000/—to *harambee* projects. . . . If clearance is determined by one's participation in nation-building activities, then I am more than cleared."[51] A month later, Odongo Omamo, KANU sub-branch chairman in Bondo, home of both the KPU leaders Oginga Odinga and Oneko, announced: "Bondo KANU sub-branch knows that the two gentlemen have actively participated in several harambee projects in Bondo and, on that score, my sub-branch would find no difficulty in clearing them."[52] National issues ranked second in importance. Indeed, a study by Joel Barkan found that MPs devoted over 70 percent of their time in their constituencies to discussing district matters and no time at all to discussing national issues.[53]

Whether he intended to do so or not, in establishing the harambee system, Kenyatta also provided incentive for members of Parliament from different cultural backgrounds to limit their differences and form alliances. Harambee sponsorship could be very expensive. MPs typically earned about $1,000 a year, including money for travel and expenses. Yet the contributions of individual MPs at a single harambee gathering rarely totaled less than $100. Contributions of $1,000 or more were not uncommon in some constituencies. For an ambitious member of Parliament or a political aspirant, there were two main ways to foot the bill. One was to acquire personal wealth, using the status conferred by political office to gain entry into the business world and parley position into partial ownership of a firm or several firms. The second was to bargain for contributions from senior officials or from spokesmen for other areas or groups.

This need for harambee funds encouraged politicians to limit their demands and to compromise in four different ways. First, it provided senior officials and political leaders with a means of winning cooperation from groups adversely affected by a government action without disrupting the rough proportionality of public allocations. MPs often considered a significant contribution from a senior politician adequate recompense for a reduction in, say, road-construction funds, because the announcement of the project and the contribution had significant electoral impact. Even if the contribution did not make up for funds lost in the development budget, it provided sufficient, closely targeted investment to enable the MP to maintain his electoral edge, particularly if limitations on the mobility of residents reduced the ability of voters to compare levels of local development across the country. Writing on electoral politics in East Africa, Henry Bienen has also remarked on this phenomenon and has argued that "even where the economy is not expanding, the leverage even small amounts of patronage give may be great." [54]

Second, the system also gave politicians a stake in the maintenance of the senior government ministers who were the largest source of harambee funds, creating a convergence of interest between the spokesmen for the different ethnic coalitions and those running the state, as long as the attractiveness of ousting the holders of power to achieve direct access to resources was exceeded by the potential payoffs or benefits through harambee. The need to cultivate potential sources of harambee contributions served to restrain the demands made by spokesmen of different ethnic backgrounds by providing a tangible inducement to agree to a proportional distribution of public resources.

This system differed from the logrolling practiced in state institutions by virtue of its extra-parliamentary character. By creating a "second set of books," a private flow of capital not reflected in the annual development budget, it made it difficult to assess and debate real regional differences in expenditure and welfare. At the same time, it made it possible to accomplish some real redistribution in the short run by boosting a politician's chances of election, while at the same time restraining significant further growth of government-financed infrastructure in the politician's constituency.

Third, this system provided an accepted way of compensating politicians whose constituents suffered a loss of share in the distribution of public development monies. The residents of Central Province had benefited most from the development of infrastructure and educational facilities during the colonial period. After independence, Kenyatta needed to maintain his base of support among the elites of Kiambu, Murang'a, and Nyeri, who dominated Kenya's new business class and whose cooperation was essential to the success of development policy in the early years. He had to do so under difficult conditions, however. First, the demands for revenue and inability to rely on external sources to any great degree led to direct taxes (income tax) being increased from 4 to 6 percent. Few Kenyans earned income taxable under existing legislation, however, and of the roughly 5 percent who did, a large number were members of the Kikuyu elite.[55] Tax evasion among the members of this group was apparently uncommon; proceeds from this and other revenue sources increased sufficiently to move Kenya completely away from dependence on the British Treasury within a short period. Second, it was clearly impossible, or at least very expensive, to govern a country without the electoral support of majorities in at least a few other regions—and it took money to secure that assistance. The share of revenues received by residents outside of Central Province would have to increase.

The pattern of giving at harambee functions during this period reflects Kenyatta's use of the system to compensate the politicians from the Central Province communities that paid taxes. First, Kenyatta and other senior ministers made appearances at local fund-raisers in Central Province, each time contributing substantial sums and thereby elevating the political stature and electoral chances of the sponsor. The higher harambee donation levels for Central Province are a partial reflection of this trend. Second, even if it was not possible to channel more development budget funds to Central Province, it was customary for the government to assume the staffing costs of harambee schools during this period, and in supporting harambee in the province, Kenyatta also indicated that necessary allocations from the recurrent budget for education would be forthcoming.

The money for this use of harambee had to come from somewhere, of course. Some of it came from Kiambu friends, whose incomes from coffee and tea plantations, business ventures, parastatal directorships, participation on the boards of multinationals, and occasional wildlife poaching, generated surpluses that might be donated to the president's favorite "charity," the Gatundu Self-Help Hospital. Foreign visitors and Asian businessmen were also contributors to the hospital.

Fourth, harambee created new links between the state and the farmers that gave the latter a form of restricted, but direct, influence over policy. When residents of an area held a successful harambee meeting and created a school or cattle dip or other agricultural facility, it was often the case that the government had to step in to provide staffing or maintenance. By their choice of projects, then, farmers affected the distribution of resources and policy emphases. As Frank Holmquist has noted in his studies of harambee, self-help took the exclusive right of initiating projects away from ministries.[56] It forced some elements of the farmers' agendas onto the state and prevented the interests of the political elite or the technocrats from dominating fully. According to Holmquist, this pattern did not become widespread until ten or fifteen years after the harambee movement began, however. Ability to exert this kind of influence was at its peak in the mid 1970s. In the early years of the Kenyatta period, it was not one of the significant consequences of this system of extra-parliamentary bargaining. Furthermore, it is important to note that although these arrangements may have given farmers some power of policy initiative, this power was not equivalent to ability to influence agricultural policy more broadly, and neither was it lasting. School construction accounted for about 58 percent of the projects; health facilities, about 10 percent; and churches or mosques, about 8 percent. Projects specifically designed to increase productivity or earnings in agriculture were relatively few.[57] By the late 1970s, the main role in project initiation had shifted from farmers to politicians and KANU officials. Proliferation of harambee projects and underutilization of the facilities created had generated enormous financial burdens for communities, which were increasingly hard-pressed to support the initiatives of politicians.

By institutionalizing harambee, Kenyatta created a tool for managing an inclusive coalition. So successful were his efforts that opposition politicians like Achieng Oneko felt compelled to participate and to use the same idiom in their campaign speeches. In consequence, when Kenyatta died in 1978, the system did not die with him. It was not a tactic all could use equally well, however.

RESTRICTION OF OPPOSITION

Not all politicians felt the urgency of maintaining an inclusive coalition. Backbenchers and senior ministers alike periodically overstepped the bounds Kenyatta had tried to establish. Sometimes they sought to eliminate centers of electoral opposition by framing other candidates for criminal actions—or occasionally by resorting to political violence, including murder. At other times, they tried to change the rules of the game by seizing control of party institutions or by securing passage of laws to restrict the activities of others. The critical difference between the early Kenyatta period and the later years, when Kenyatta was ill, and when Moi took power, was that efforts to pursue these tactics often met with opposition in Parliament, usually from the KANU backbench, which was quite strong. It was only later, as political restrictions mounted, that the party became so factionalized that effective opposition proved difficult, if not impossible.

Some scholars have argued that the real pillar of political order in the early Kenyatta period was repression.[58] The restrictive rules and laws gradually circumscribed the activities of politicians who were at odds with the wealthy Kiambu Kikuyu elite connected to Kenyatta through blood or marriage and predominated over other tactics and rendered them unnecessary, in this view. Certainly, these kinds of tactics were a part of the Kenyan repertoire. The head of state and his key cabinet members were themselves unsure where to draw the line between different kinds of speech and association. Mboya's ambivalence was clear. Much as the Moi government did later, he rested his case on the difference between acceptable "constructive criticism" and unacceptable criticism that simply undermined authority, but he set out no criteria for distinguishing the one from the other. "The judge [is] the Government," Mboya is quoted as having replied when an *East African Standard* reporter asked him to say who would judge which was which.[59] As Susanne Mueller has noted, uncertainty in a new state about "what various regions, factions, and groups would do" if given the chance to support whomever they wished caused the government to disregard civil liberties on occasion, especially because "dominant party leaders were aware that KANU had not built a committed following."[60]

In the immediate post-independence period, the Office of the President moved rapidly to amend the constitution in ways that would insulate Kenyatta from factional feuding and limit the chances that an official opposition party could secure a significant foothold in Parliament. The sixth and tenth amendments to the constitution, passed in 1966 and 1968, respectively, changed the political map. The sixth gave the Office of the President the power to detain Kenyan citizens without trial. The tenth eliminated Kenyatta's dependence on a parliamentary majority by replacing procedures for election of the president by Parliament with procedures for direct, popular election. Accompanying language and legislation terminated provincial councils, restricted independent candidates (candidates without official party affiliations) from running in local or national elections, made the legislature a unicameral assembly, and permitted press censorship.[61] These laws all worked together to insulate the presidency from the battles within KANU and to hamper efforts to challenge the allocation of resources favored by the Kenyatta government.

Kenyatta himself condoned some of these tactics when persuaded that they were necessary to parry efforts by others to disrupt his balancing act. Neither during this period, nor later, does Kenyatta appear to have offered blanket approval for such actions, however, although his control over members of his coalition varied greatly and prevents inference about his real views on the subject. In the early years, Kenyatta appeared sensitive to the possibility that opposition to restriction of political space would bring economic or social pressure to bear on his government.

In the 1963–64 period, for example, members of the KANU backbench, organized as the "Backbenchers' Group," expressed concern that the chief of state and his ministers had chosen too often simply to ignore Parliament. Using their pivotal role in a two-party system as a threat, they announced that unless then Prime Minister Kenyatta returned to consultations with Parliament, they would use their votes to ally with KADU and both block passage of desired legislation and support an alternative candidate. Henry Wariithi, at one time Kenyatta's legal adviser and chief of the Backbenchers' Group explained: "The backbenchers . . . may take a different line from that taken by a Minister. They may criticize the Government. They may vote against the Government: we have an opposition, which can never hope to win a motion unless the backbenchers support them, and this should not be underrated. My group, knowing this, will have to be a kind of watchdog or pressure group to our Government."[62] As Cherry Gertzel has noted, even after KADU disappeared, the Backbenchers' Group retained considerable clout and blocked the passage of several bills whose passage the government sought. So concerned did the government become that it established regular consultations with the group and rejuvenated the KANU Parliamentary Group as a forum for discussing contested bills.[63] The opposition sat on all committees in the assembly until mid 1969, and, as Susanne Mueller notes, Odinga himself continued to chair the Public Accounts Committee as leader of the opposition until that time.[64]

Aside from a five-month period in the aftermath of the abortive 1964 army mutiny, when all political meetings, initially in Nairobi, Ukambani, and Kiambu, and later in the rest of the country, were banned, the first instance in which Kenyatta himself intervened to restrict opposition occurred after Oginga Odinga and Bildad Kaggia decided to pursue the positions they had tried to publicize in the Lumumba Institute by forming a new political party, the Kenya People's Union. Kenyatta first responded that it was necessary to call new elections in districts represented by people who had joined the KPU, on the grounds that people had voted for these men as KANU candidates and now that their KANU affiliation had ended, their electoral mandate had ended too. He then rallied the resources at his disposal—tours by ministers, control of national radio—to campaign in the disputed areas with an intensity that the resource-poor KPU could not match.

Susanne Mueller has focused particularly on the impact that licensing requirements, "rigging" of nomination procedures by district commissioners, and control of "spoils" by the KANU majority had on the ability of Kenyans to formulate and act on demands outside of Kenyatta's own party. By controlling access to government jobs, including teaching posts, and by regulating distribution of licenses for fundraisers, the civil service and KANU branches could deny opposition representatives a livelihood and a soapbox. Using these techniques, they quickly undermined the new KPU in Central Province, the Kikuyu stronghold. Only in the western, Luo areas did the government at first refrain from using the instruments at its disposal to curtail opposition activity, with the consequence that the "radicals" appeared, wrongly, to have a particular ethnic base and to have acted on narrow, sectarian interests.[65] The "rigging" of opposition in this way destroyed the KPU's national electoral appeal and provided the government with the pretext necessary to further curtail its actions.

Kenyatta's understanding of the actions of his former vice president Oginga Odinga reflects a sense of betrayal—of the failure of another independence leader to share in his founding vision and his view of governance. In a speech given shortly after the formation of the KPU, the president sought to comprehend the behavior of politicians to whom he had given freedom and resources and who had tried, inappropriately, to impose their plans on others. "Seldom is there any completely strange element in human behaviour," he said. "In this instance, no new factor has been introduced by the immature behavior of a few frustrated individuals. Their motives were ordinary enough. In some cases, these men had become disappointed in their personal ambitions, or unable to meet their external commitments. They saw no profit for themselves, or for the causes they served, in progress and stability. Some others, among the younger men, were the pitiful victims of flattery allied with purchase." [66]

Once the trust was shattered, however, the president pursued his opponents with a vigor that exceeded the norms of the political civility he had worked so hard to maintain. Since the colonial period, Kenyan law has required registration of all societies, including political "gatherings" of more than seven people, and acquisition of meeting licenses. After the declaration of elections in 1966, the KPU sought to register with local authorities but experienced artificially long delays—delays that severely reduced the candidates' opportunity to campaign for office. In subsequent years, almost half of the KPU requests for registration were rejected—and almost 60 percent in the final year of the party's life.[67] Similarly, the party members were frequently denied licenses to hold meetings and harambee fund-raisers. Finally, as Mueller points out, the heavy dependence of private enterprise on government support meant that KPU supporters had a hard time finding and keeping the jobs they needed to maintain themselves and their families. Employers were not keen to prejudice licenses and contracts by engaging KPU members. Along with the ban on KPU activity in 1969, the attorney general, Charles Njonjo, also de-registered three of the most prominent organizations of former Mau Mau fighters.[68]

THE PROVINCIAL ADMINISTRATION AND THE CIVIL SERVICE

The deliberate effort to maintain a range of views within KANU meant that the party apparatus—at the branch and sub-branch levels, in particular—was never sufficiently cohesive or imbued with sufficient authority to help resolve local conflicts or to serve as reliable conduits for information to and from the central government. Nor was there sufficient coherence in the platform to allow the party to appoint its own administrative officers, who could in turn support the information needs and political demands of cabinet ministers. At both the national and provincial levels, Kenyatta chose to manage affairs of state, win cooperation in the implementation of programs, and resolve disputes, not through his political party, as was the case in many other countries of sub-Saharan Africa, but through the civil service.

The favor shown the civil service, particularly the provincial administration, was evident in presidential statements and actions. Tension between parliamentarians and civil servants emerged shortly after independence and provoked a series of public disputes about the priority of one or the other. Kenyatta sought to draw distinctions between the roles, arguing that the politician was "the instrument through which the people make their voices heard," while the civil servant was a "professional" who was "employed by the government to get things done." [69] He also tried to tell the politicians their place, saying that a civil servant was like a doctor, and asking "who would presume to tell a doctor how and where to operate on a sick person?" The diagnosis, in addition to the prescription, lay in the hands of the professional. All the politicians could do was to indicate that the body was sick. It was perfectly acceptable for a politician to advance the interests of his constituency, but he "should not attempt to use his position of influence to bully civil servants into deviating from national programmes." Kenyatta opposed efforts to require civil servants to become members of the party and sought to repel politicization of civil service ranks. By contrast, after 1964, he met less and less frequently with members of the KANU parliamentary group, first neglecting, then discontinuing the monthly meetings.[70]

The tensions between the civil service and the politicians and pressure to politicize civil service appointments became especially acute as the advantages that accrued to members of the public administration became clear to all. Africanization of the public administration took place in the public sector in Kenya before it began in the private sector. Civil service employment offered a steady salary, a virtual guarantee of lifetime tenure, and, in the early years, the prospect of rapid advancement. Private-sector employment offered fewer opportunities until later, after Africanization became the rule there too. Upper-level civil servants could maintain their families and still have sufficient savings to invest in land back home, in the process known as "straddling." Public-sector jobs would later become the basis for moving into the upper income levels of the petite bourgeoisie and eventually into the ranks of the "wealthy," the matajiri. Between 1963 and 1971, however, investment in private business by civil servants was formally prohibited. The general secretary of KANU, Tom Mboya, bitterly opposed this form of "straddling" on the grounds that it promoted nepotism and "tribalism," and during his lifetime the opportunities formally open to civil servants were strictly limited.[71]

Although the civil service played a stronger role in policy formation and implementation than the politicians under Kenyatta, it is not clear the degree to which Kenyatta was able to preserve the integrity of the civil service as a body removed from the political tug of war. In their studies of Kenya in the 1960s, Goran Hyden and Henry Bienen suggest that there was far more factional division than most scholars have recognized.[72] Certainly, there was significant contact between politicians and civil servants in the districts. A study by Joel Barkan suggests that through the 1970s, a higher proportion of MPs spent time speaking with civil servants in their constituencies rather than with party officials, social leaders, village heads, or businessmen.[73] Barkan suggests that the reason for this pattern was that one of the main voter expectations was that the member of Parliament would intercede on behalf of constituents in local misunderstandings with the administration. At no point, however, did Kenyatta attempt to use KANU to form or implement policies. The administration retained a monopoly over these functions.

PARTY-GOVERNMENT RELATIONS IN POST-INDEPENDENCE KENYA

During the Kenyatta period, one-party dominance did not translate into the creation of the kind of "party-state" Zolberg and others have described as existing in West Africa and in Kenya's neighbor Tanzania, in which the political party served simply as an arm of the office of the president. The Kenya African National Union (KANU) never developed a clear platform during these years, but instead remained a loosely organized catchall party in which candidates championed a wide variety of views. Only when a group of politicians pushed for ideological hegemony within the party were limits on debate drawn. For the most part, Kenyatta sought to keep the party a kind of weak debating society. His few attempts at organizational innovation were designed not to strengthen the party but rather to limit the influence of its members over civil servants and especially over the provincial administration. In this vein, he reduced the role of politicians in the daily management of party affairs and established full-time, paid personnel responsible to a national executive committee, on which he himself wielded great influence. Further, he pushed through legislation to support a system of open primaries to push KANU in the direction of an inclusive, loosely organized party.

Party-government relations in post-independence Kenya were marked by three distinctive features. Unlike leaders of other African countries, Kenyatta perceived that the best way to maintain political order in a society where ethnic or community boundaries usually coincided with economic differences, and where no one community included a majority of the nation's voters, was to eschew central control of political views. Instead, he employed a unique extra-parliamentary bargaining system, harambee, and a loosely defined political party to focus the attention of politicians on local issues and on the formation of alliances across communities, while limiting their power to force agendas on one another.

Second, although there was factional division in KANU, first the existence of an opposition party, KADU, then the rise of the KPU, and, finally, the open primary system helped support the formation of coherent blocs within the ruling party that could sustain debate about issues, including the restriction of political space. During this period, people spoke of two KANUs, a KANU A, or conservative bloc, including both the "Gatundu Courtiers" and a group led by Mboya, and KANU B, the "radical" bloc. When some members of KANU B split away, some of the others remained, by and large as backbenchers. The open primary system came into being partly because of the pressure generated by this group.

Third, during this period, Kenya witnessed a shift from the associational politics of the later Mau Mau Emergency to clientelist politics. The existence of class division in the Kikuyu community at the time of the Mau Mau rebellion strongly shaped Kenyatta's political strategy. The Kenya Land Freedom Army had the power to carry on the Mau Mau struggle. Many militants remained in the Aberdare forest just prior to independence. Kenyatta had to treat their interests seriously in order to maintain stability and the access to Western financial capital that it brought the new government. At the same time, Kenyatta had to take seriously the interests of the chiefs, some of whom had collaborated with the British, and the increasingly powerful agricultural entrepreneurs, who could command popular support and economic clout respectively. As the creation of a new state opened up resources, the new elites of the nationalist coalition sought to assure their own financial prospects and to defend their achievements against a restless class of "dispossessed" people by expanding a system of patronage networks. By the end of the 1960s, the primary basis of politics was not class divi-

sion but competition for resources between patrons and political machines. These groups provided a less favorable medium for issue-based
politics in Parliament, including defense of political space. Nonetheless,
the pressure for open primaries suggests that some of the new political
elite continued to wield sufficient economic or political power to persuade Kenyatta to resist the total takeover of KANU by the Gatundu
Courtiers.

CHAPTER THREE

The Struggle in the Rift Valley, 1970-1975

The early 1970s marked a second stage in the rise of the Kenyan party-state—a stage in which the dominant faction extended its ability to control the "political space" available to others, diminished the power of new opposition factions to assemble enduring bases, and triggered increasing fragmentation. The period from 1970 to 1975 thus saw changes in the way factions arose and competed with one another. It set the stage for the increasing difficulty Kenyans would encounter in resisting later bids by the Office of the President to merge the functions of the party and the administration.

Specifically, the 1970–75 period witnessed the rise of an opposition within the ranks of KANU, followed by the restriction of political life, as members of the dominant faction seized control of key administrative offices and used these to defend themselves against the newcomers. By the end of the 1960s, Kenyatta's close associates had predominated over the remnants of the KANU radicals. As the ranks of the landless and land-poor increased in the early 1970s, however, the demand for redistribution of government resources grew too. Although he was very different in style from Oginga Odinga and the members of the Kenya People's Union, the Kikuyu politician J. M. Kariuki fell heir to the populist cause and began to build a political base among these groups. He became an articulate spokesman for the interests of the "disadvantaged" in Kenya, even if his own private interests were not entirely consonant with theirs, and he used his position as a junior minister in the

TABLE I   KEY MEMBERS OF THE "FAMILY" FACTION
OF KANU'S CONSERVATIVE WING, 1965–1978

Name	Main Political Position	Relationship to Kenyatta
Mbiyu Koinange	MP, Kiambaa, 1963–79 minister of state	brother-in-law
Njoroge Mungai	MP, Dagoretti, 1963– 74	nephew
Peter Muigai Kenyatta	MP, Juja, 1974–79	son
Margaret Kenyatta	Mayor, Nairobi	daughter
George Kamau Muhoho		brother-in-law
Ngengi Muigai		nephew
Bethuel M. Gecaga		brother-in-law
James Gichuru	MP, Limuru minister for finance, minister for defence	
James Njiru	MP Kirinyaga East	
Julius Gikonyo Kiano	MP Mbiri	
Paul Ngei	MP Kangundo	
Jackson Angaine	MP Meru North-West	
Jeremiah Nyagah	MP Embu South	

Kenyatta government to try to change policy. By 1972, some of the Gatundu Courtiers had started to perceive Kariuki as a threat, however,
and members of the group steadily moved to acquire control of administrative positions that would give them greater power to circumscribe
their fellow party member's ability to organize (see Table 1). They split
over this issue, among others, into two groups: the "Family," consisting
of Kenyatta's closest associates and relatives, and a smaller, weaker faction, which included Charles Njonjo, who later helped broker Moi's
accession to the presidency. Although Kenyatta resisted most efforts to
use the party machinery to control the new movement, the Family, or
main conservative faction, eventually succeeded in shattering the populist coalition and increasing the level of fragmentation within KANU.
By the end of 1975, J. M. Kariuki was dead, and the vision of political
competition articulated at the Lancaster House independence negotiations was buried with him.

This chapter outlines the grounds for resurgence of a "populist"
movement within KANU, profiles the bid to organize an opposition,

explores the responses of the dominant faction and the Office of the President, and considers the implications of the actions taken for the long-term character of party-state relations in Kenya.

THE SOURCE OF COMPETITION

Awareness of disproportionate allocation of public funds to Central Province and a few favored constituencies in other areas began to crystallize for Rift Valley residents during the early 1970s. Three issues brought discussion of redistribution into the political arena. The first was the release of the 1972 International Labour Organization (ILO) report *Employment, Incomes, and Equality* and the subsequent debate on the floor of Parliament to determine which, if any, of its recommendations the government should adopt. The ILO team had documented ethno-regional imbalances in level of "development" and advocated measures that would redistribute capital expenditures and recurrent budget allocations for services so as to benefit areas outside of Central Province. The second issue was the termination of several land-distribution programs and concern about the policies and programs that would replace them. Finally, the period 1973–75, in particular, was one in which producers of maize and other cash crops suffered lost income as a result of inappropriate marketing practices on the part of some of the country's agricultural parastatals, sharp increases in the prices of essential inputs, and poor weather conditions. The agricultural crisis sparked further debate about the allocation of government resources to rural areas and to large- as opposed to small-scale farmers.

THE ILO REPORT

In 1970, at the invitation of the Kenyan government, the International Labor Organization initiated an evaluation of the distribution of employment opportunities and other means of income generation. The committee reported to the government in early 1972, and published its analysis and recommendations shortly thereafter. The research depicted regional differences in welfare statistically for the first time, highlighting the privileged position of Central Province. The policy proposals urged a redistribution of public resources to achieve greater equity in levels of "development" and income-earning opportunity between people of different regions and backgrounds. The recommendations included two main lines of action to reduce differences in level of welfare, including

(1) provision of new facilities in neglected regions through "fundamental changes in the pattern of government revenue and expenditure," and (2) implementation of quota systems in vital sectors "to ensure more equitable access to secondary education" and to make access to civil service and military careers more equal.[1]

The government deliberated the evaluations and recommendations for several months without bringing the issues before Parliament, until Elijah Mwangale, MP for Bungoma East, then a backbencher, moved independently to adopt the report and its recommendations. Mwangale feared that Central Province advisors to the president would block an effort to bring the study to the floor and so moved preemptively. In so doing, he observed:

> The reason why I am moving this motion rather than waiting for Government to bring a Sessional Paper to this House is because our experience in the past has been that where there are very strong sectional interests . . . it has been the practice of Government to refuse to bring a Sessional Paper in this House. I want to mention, specifically, the Ndegwa Report. We have had hon. Members clamouring for the Ndegwa Commission Report for almost a year. As you will recall, the Ndegwa Report specifically raised salaries of those well-to-do and ignored the low-paid group to the extent that we, in this House, insist that this particular report be brought here so that we can debate it and, perhaps, have a chance to raise the scales of the low income groups.[2]

Mwangale went on to invoke the ideals of the Mau Mau uprising. "The purposes of Mau Mau activities were based on one thing, namely, imbalance. . . . What is so surprising is that after ten years of independence, these imbalances still exist."[3] The MP envisioned growth but expressed concern about the size of the shares some groups were likely to receive. The emphasis of his statement was not on the mild egalitarianism promoted by the World Bank's philosophy of "redistribution with growth"; instead, it highlighted the need to address more fundamental inequalities, and as such represented a major change from the thinking behind the economic policies of the 1960s. "As you know, today, in this country, we have a lot of disparities in development in that you have certain areas or certain districts which seem to have more services than other districts. You also have certain groups having much more, in terms of wealth, than others, and in order to achieve some economic integration there has to be a complete change in our economic policy," Mwangale noted.[4] He refrained at first from trying to evaluate the political consequences of continued imbalance, but another MP, in a later debate, showed greater temerity, warning, "nobody can fiddle with the members of the public in this country. You may think that the masses are foolish today, but tomorrow you will be having a different opinion about them."[5] Eventually, Mwangale too issued a warning: "If we are going to build a stable society, let us not talk of miracles of economic development when there are no miracles at all. In fact, the miracles are there only for a few people. . . . Government has been bold enough to ask these people [ILO] to come and give us a very good report. If we are going to be of any help, let us accept it."[6]

Support for Mwangale's move and for the ILO report came primarily from members of Parliament representing districts in the Rift Valley. "What the International Labour Organization document has said is, in fact, what many of us in this House have been saying but in a different language," commented J. M. Kariuki, MP for Nyandarua North and assistant minister for tourism and wildlife.[7]

> Have we attempted to do something to combat the pressure and the issues of tribalism? . . . If so, what has the peasant farmer in Kilgoris, Kinangop, Kajiado, Turkana, Machakos, Meru or the pastoral Masai in Narok District gained? Have decisions been made to effect equitable distribution of economic benefits to the various parts of our country and among the various income groups of our community as stated in the KANU manifesto of 1963, and also as repeated by the same people in this House in the years 1969/70?[8]

He echoed Mwangale's dissatisfaction with policies that concentrated on generating absolute gains for all without attention to the size of shares held by particular groups, arguing, "We have, in fact, widened and not bridged the gap between the rich and the poor . . . the planners we have here have looked at what is internationally known as the Gross National Product and because they think that the people living in the urban areas have achieved this, even the people in the rural areas have attained the same."[9] Other representatives raised questions about particular aspects of policy. For example, one MP urged equal sharing in the bid for industrialization. "We should not concentrate all the industries in one place. . . . People in Malindi would like to see an industry there; people in Meru District would like to see an industry and so forth," he observed.

> If we work for the welfare of society and just government of men in Kenya, then our Government should use its influence to ensure that our industrial development is enjoyed in all parts of the country. It does not matter even if the industry would employ only 100, or even 50 people, since these people would benefit . . . we think that it is only our children who would like to

have butter; we must know that even the people in Naivasha would like to have the same.[10]

Mwangale's own efforts to argue on behalf of the motion illuminated the variety of concerns involved. Early in the debate, Mwangale linked attention to the agricultural problems of his district to consideration of the report, requesting that, as a step toward its adoption, restrictions on transport of maize between regions should be dropped. Bungoma and other districts in the central Rift Valley were major maize producers, but it was alleged that the benefits were reduced by inappropriate policies that favored those outside the area. Mwangale equated the system of licensing movement of maize to "black marketeering" and noted that at times "people from Central Province were given licenses to go and transport maize down from Western Province, while [residents] . . . were denied the opportunity of transporting their own produce to market places in Kenya."[11]

Mwangale sought increased educational opportunities for his district as well. "If you look at the admissions to the university in the years 1970, 1971, and 1972, you will see that most of these are from Central Province, not for any reason but just because the teachers in some of these districts are better than those in other districts," he claimed. "So, let us get admissions to the university on a quota basis. We should not only find the Mwangale and Wanyonyi from the Abaluhya community. Let each place have a share."[12] Published at about the same time as the ILO study, the Ndegwa Report, although less concerned about maintaining equality between groups, had nonetheless advocated quotas in university admissions. Mwangale went beyond the earlier report, however, in calling for quotas in the secondary school system as well.

The debate of the ILO report set the stage for revision of the distributive agreements then in effect and for renegotiation of the coalitions supporting and opposing government policy. It made the allocation of services an issue, providing an opportunity to raise questions that just a few years previously had proven much more difficult to bring to the floor of Parliament, on the grounds that such discussions would shatter the overarching loyalty to the nation that all hoped would override undue pursuit of sectional interests.

THE RECURRENT PROBLEM OF LAND

The second issue to rise to new prominence during the early 1970s, and especially in 1974–75, was the "politicization of the land market."[13]

During the first decade of independence, large tracts of land were purchased by the Kenyan government and resold to African settlers. The disposition of the acreage in the Rift Valley had fueled much of the disagreement between KANU and the Kenyan African Democratic Union (KADU) at the Lancaster House Conferences. The KADU bid for a federal system—or "majimboism"—was in large part an effort to keep the land in the former Masai Reserve, Kericho, Nandi, Uasin-Gishu, Trans-Nzoia, and Nyandarua, under the control of the groups living in the Rift, or at least under the control of the local elite. KANU instead urged central control of the region in an effort to forestall local legislation restricting land transfer to those born in the area and to maintain the foothold of the party's Kikuyu supporters in the Rift Valley land market.[14] KANU's victory and the subsequent allocation of plots on subdivided Rift Valley farms to large numbers of Kikuyu settlers provoked resentment among others. The exact proportion of the settlement area held by large farmers or by Kikuyu smallholders is uncertain. Apollo Njonjo's study of landholding in Nakuru District indicates that in 1971, over 50 percent of the acreage under cultivation by individual large-scale farmers was in the hands of Kikuyu owners.[15]

Disaggregated data on migration patterns, which would give some sense of the magnitude of the influx into the Rift, are unfortunately difficult to obtain. A World Bank study based on 1962 and 1969 census data found that nearly half of all out-migrants from Central Province and Western Province settled in the Rift Valley during Kenya's first years of independence.[16] These estimates suggest settlement of about 166,300 former residents of the Kikuyu districts and 100,450 residents of Western Province in the Rift during the seven-year intercensal period.[17] The shortage of acreage for increasing numbers of landless people and the agribusiness interests of Kenyan entrepreneurs also generated concern that foreigners had succeeded in obtaining acreage at the expense of Kenyans. In 1967, the government had disclosed that nearly a million acres of land had been bought by foreigners during the first four years of independence,[18] despite a ban on such transfers.

The 1972–75 period also witnessed a change in government land policy. During Kenya's first decade, three different settlement programs were in effect, as noted in the previous chapter. In 1971, the government introduced a fourth kind of settlement, the Shirika scheme, in which entire farms would be taken over and managed as going concerns on behalf of members, each of whom would be allotted one hectare for private use. The three original programs were phased out during the early 1970s, leaving only the Shirika scheme by 1974. The objective was to permit economies of scale in agricultural production, but one side effect was to constrain access to land; absent participation in a land company, it was difficult for a household to resettle.

With the gradual termination of land distribution programs, save the Shirika schemes, land speculation and land prices increased. One sign of the increased demand for land was a concomitant rise in illegal land transactions. These were reportedly most common in the high tea country of Kericho (a Kalenjin stronghold), where, in only one settlement zone, in 1970, 627 illegal transactions came to government attention.[19]

Kenyan MPs had never displayed reticence in discussions of the land problem. The debate over the ILO report provided yet another occasion for negotiation of claims, however. Waweru Kanja, MP for Nyeri and a former Mau Mau militant, was one who spoke up. After acknowledging that "the land issue is very sensitive," he complained: "Whenever we mention that problem either in this House or outside we are accused of *payukaring* [bickering]. . . . We shall keep on *payukaring* because we were elected to do that."[20]

> Mr. Deputy Speaker, Sir, this country consists of very many tribes and whether or not we like it all the tribes in this country will continue to live in Kenya because they are part and parcel of this country. It is wrong for any tribe to think that it will dominate other tribes for ever. Mr. Deputy Speaker, Sir, we should learn from experience and history, because similar things have happened in other African countries.[21]

Kanja went on to call for a complete change in the system of land allocation, angrily summing up: "We would like to share the national cake, but that is not possible because some of our own people are opposed to such a move."[22]

TROUBLE IN THE MAIZE INDUSTRY

The third problem felt during the 1972–75 period was the consequence of mistaken agricultural policy. Many Rift Valley residents had shifted from subsistence production to smallholder cash-cropping during the preceding years. The minister for finance, Mwai Kibaki, noted a 20 percent increase in marketed agricultural produce during 1972 alone. The dramatic change in the economy of the region was not greeted by adequate extension of services, however. Storage facilities proved too limited to handle increased maize production and farmers found that they were unable to sell all of their surplus. A good maize crop in the latter part of 1972 filled available storage with more than two million bags of surplus grain.

By January 1973, the lack of storage and government refusal to permit export meant that the farmers who had produced so much would not receive payment. No income, no new planting. Unable to purchase seeds and fertilizer, the farmers retreated to subsistence production. A *Daily Nation* editorial urged that the problem receive emergency attention, "for the majority of these farmers have children who will need school fees within the next few weeks."[23] Indeed, by mid January, officials in neighboring Kisii District, in Nyanza Province, suggested that 250 teachers were in danger of losing their jobs because children could not afford to come to school. The local education officer appealed to cooperative societies to help farmers pay the requisite fees.[24] The permanent secretary in the Ministry of Agriculture hurried to assure farmers that the government was trying its best to increase maize storage facilities but acknowledged that the Maize and Produce Board had failed to buy all the maize crop in some areas because of a shortage of space.[25] By February, the board had constructed open shelters in some parts of Eldoret, part of the vice president's home territory. William Saina, MP for Eldoret North, suggested that the government should further consider issuing "a cereal finance" to enable farmers to plant in time for the rains and prevent shortages later in the year.[26]

Agricultural fortunes moved from one extreme to the other. In 1973, the long rains failed and large quantities of imported wheat were required to make up the deficit caused by climatic problems and reduced acreage. "Lack of foresight and bad planning" were also at fault, the minister for cooperatives and social services suggested.[27] Wafule Wabuge, MP for Kitale West, told Parliament later that year that poor access roads and increases in fertilizer costs without corresponding increments in the maize price conspired against greater production and farmers' welfare.[28] Complaints about shortages of essential agricultural inputs continued into 1974. Suppliers of seeds and fertilizer refused credit to customers, in spite of assurances that maize and wheat growers would receive backing from the Agricultural Finance Corporation, and headlines in May that year read: "Cash Crisis Hits Rift Valley Farmers."[29]

Other problems accentuated the perception of a need for change. Delivery of fertilizer was plagued by delay and high price markups. Between 1972 and 1973, before the brunt of the oil-price shock, fertilizer prices climbed by 75 percent.[30] The consumer price index rose sharply, fueled in part by the oil-price increases and in part by abandonment of income taxes for sales taxes. "Kibaki Soaks the Rich"—a reference to heavier levies on luxury goods—was the headline with which the *Daily Nation* prefaced publication of the 1972 budget.[31] In reality, the new lists of taxable items included consumer goods used by the less wealthy, and the budget elicited the opposite reaction from several members of Parliament, one of whom attacked what he saw as government efforts to "keep the *wananchi* [common people] under taxation suppression."[32] The sharp increases in the prices of consumer goods heightened the perception, then widespread, that some Kenyans were profiting at the expense of others. Skyrocketing prices for nearly all commodities sold in the region were attributed to unfair profit margins taken by shopowners after the introduction of a sales tax in June 1972; traders were accused of raising prices 50 to 100 percent, although the tax on local and imported goods was only 10 percent.[33]

As in the case of land, food shortages and increases in the problems faced by maize growers were quick to generate controversy. Unlike land allocation, however, the problems and their consequences made themselves felt swiftly, strongly, and in almost all parts of the country. Shortages of maize could not be disguised, delayed, or justified as necessary for some greater, long-term benefit. They made themselves felt in the marketplaces and ultimately in the physical well-being of citizens. If the ILO report provided an opportunity to renegotiate distributive arrangements, and disputes about land ownership fueled the debate, the maize problems broadened participation and piqued the interest and concern not just of parliamentarians but also of their constituents. The Kitale West MP, Wafula Wabuge, commented in his introduction to a committee's report: "If we have no maize in this country, then it means that we have no government."[34]

ORGANIZING AN OPPOSITION

The perception of inequity in the distribution of public resources quickly generated efforts to lobby for the redistribution of services and re-targeting of development projects. Policy influence requires some sort of sustained organizational base, however—one that can coordinate voting power, help members engage in strategic logrolling, and thereby persuade others to support enforcement of new laws or the implementation of new programs. Without such capacity, an opposition has little hope of being able to represent constituents' broad economic interests and must be content with securing patronage and "constituency service" projects that yield only particularistic benefits. In the context of a one-party-dominant political system, constituting an organizational base can be an extremely difficult enterprise. As the leadership of the Kenya People's Union had discovered earlier, oppositions in single-party-dominant systems must survive a difficult phase in which they have insufficient votes in the party to influence policy or secure access to the party machinery, while at the same time lacking the votes in the legislature to block passage of restrictive election laws, should they decide to break off and form an alternative political association. Even when members of the most powerful faction oppose legislation restricting association, it is difficult to assemble a defense of "political space" if the party contains multiple factions; each faction will attempt to "free ride" on the investment of time and energy and the assumption of risk by the others, and ultimately no defense will materialize.

The period 1970–75 offers a textbook case of the difficulties oppositions face under these circumstances. Those who argued for a "populist" platform sought to organize within KANU. They used the harambee system to build a coalition that posed an increasing threat to policies the Family favored. Before the leaders could assemble a majority within the party or take their positions to the public in the form of an opposition party, however, the dominant faction succeeded in using the positions it held to deny members of the opposition access to soapboxes within KANU and to obtain passage of restrictive legislation. In the period 1972–75, however, the opposition was able to assemble a substantial base of support before it succumbed, because internal party factions had not yet proliferated. Even when some of their constituents had interests at odds with those advanced by the opposition platform, some politicians broke ranks with the dominant group and joined the effort to defend freedoms of association. In later years, as factions proliferated, this form of legislative behavior became less and less common.

THE RISE OF A POPULIST COALITION

The areas affected most strongly by the problems of land distribution and cash-crop production were the districts that included the former White Highlands: Nyandarua, Nakuru, Nandi, parts of Baringo, Uasin-Gishu, Trans-Nzoia, and Elgeyo-Marakwet. Widespread participation in maize production made Bungoma and Kakamega in Western Province potential bases for allies. Parts of Kisii District, near Lake Victoria, also suffered from the vagaries of pyrethrum marketing. Instead of making proportional claims or bids for representation in decision making and administration, group spokesmen moved rapidly to bargain with one another for support.

Two men served as catalysts. In Nyandarua North, on the western edge of Central Province, J. M. Kariuki had won a reputation as an articulate opponent of the Family surrounding Kenyatta. A wealthy member of the Kikuyu elite, Kariuki was in many respects an unlikely leader of "populist" criticism. Born in 1929, he had attended King's College at Budo, in Uganda, and had then gone into the hotel business and quickly made money from enterprises in Nakuru District. Although detained for the duration of the Mau Mau Emergency, "J. M.," as he came to be known, returned to the ranks of the new political elite quite quickly and appears to have developed a strong rapport with Kenyatta. He traveled to England to study briefly at Oxford and then returned to Kenya, where he was elected to Parliament in 1963. He headed the National Youth Service, then a vocational training program for Kenyan secondary school students who were not university-bound, and also became chairman of the Betting and Lotteries Licensing Board, a position he appears to have used to his advantage.[35] He held several positions as a junior minister, including those of assistant minister for agriculture and assistant minister for tourism and wildlife. Even in 1973, two years before his assassination, and several years after increasing state restriction of his activities, he was a guest at the establishment wedding of the son of James Gichuru, minister for defense and a leader of the Family.[36] The residents of Kariuku's constituency, which was host to forty-nine settlement schemes, were predominantly Kikuyu, although not all of them had been landless prior to relocation. Kariuki himself had tried to purchase extensive parcels of land in the area at the expense of those still without acreage but met with opposition from foreign purchasers and Kiambu-based land-buying companies.

At the same time, Kariuki had credentials that set him apart from most of the Kikuyu elite. His parents had moved from Nyeri District to Kabati Forest in the Rift a year before he was born. His heritage therefore resembled that of the Mau Mau militants more than it did that of many of his fellow members of the Kenya African Union. He had participated in the Mau Mau rebellion and been detained by the British, an experience he documented in his autobiographical book *"Mau Mau" Detainee*. He became a leader among the prisoners in the camps where he was interned. After his election to Parliament and his selection as head of the National Youth Service, he developed a strong interest in the condition of the country's "dispossessed." In 1965, he traveled to the United States to study antipoverty programs there and carried some of what he learned back with him. A populist platform was thus consonant with his earlier experiences, his government role, and his personal political interests. Rhetoric and policies that championed the interests of the landless and the rural poor furthered Kariuki's individual interests against those of his competitors in the land market and won him the support of local residents, many of whom produced pyrethrum (used for insecticide), the area's most important cash crop, at a time when government policies discriminated strongly against growers of the chrysanthemums from which it was derived.

The other man who stood most to gain from a change in government policies was John Marie Seroney, deputy speaker of the National Assembly and MP for Tinderet, in Nandi District. Seroney had the reputation of being a stronger advocate of Kalenjin interests than Vice President Daniel arap Moi (a member of the Tugen subgroup), perhaps because of his relative freedom as a backbencher to push for partial interests.[37] The government had charged Seroney with sedition in 1969 after he issued the "Nandi Hills Declaration" laying claim to all settlement land in the district for the Nandi people.[38]

Seroney's father, a teacher, had been a highly respected Kalenjin leader and had in fact served as one of Moi's instructors. The land issue had created a division between the two contemporaries and former friends. Moi succeeded in advancing the interests of his constituents by turning a blind eye to Kikuyu expansion into areas claimed by neighboring Kalenjin subgroups. He secured the settler farms of the Lembus Forest and the Essageri salient for his own small subgroup in the face of competing bids by the Nandi and Elgeyo,[39] who also faced incursions by the Luo and Luhya to the west, and he obtained credit assistance for some Kalenjin interests.[40] To maintain his electoral base and his power within Nandi District organizations, both contested, Seroney had to gain leverage over government land policy and use that bargaining strength to secure remaining settlement areas within the district or in neighboring districts for his own people. To do so, he had to compete with Moi's leadership of the Kalenjin and strike a different set of deals with the State House. Mobilizing a national coalition that could compete with the group surrounding the president was an essential step in gaining leverage.

By 1971–72, cooperation between J.M. and Seroney in the National Assembly was apparent. Throughout the 1972–75 period, the MP employed populist appeals but machine tactics. Harambee contributions from J.M. to potential supporters were the cornerstone of his coalition-building strategy, although full documentation of these is unavailable.[41]

The sources of J.M.'s funds remain unclear. Certainly, he had made a great deal of money himself in land deals and small business enterprises.

A measure both of J.M.'s impact, through harambee, and public recognition of the State House's disapproval came on August 14, 1972, when hundreds of members of the African Independent Pentecostal Church assembled at Kariuki's home, near Gilgil. The church's leader led a ceremony "to pray for the continued strength and willingness of Mr. Kariuki to support *Harambee* projects in the country." The visiting Nyeri MP, Waweru Kanja, speaking of the rationale behind the prayer meeting, is quoted as having said: "Mr. Kariuki had been a very helpful person in respect of self-help projects in the country." [42] Backbenchers from Nyeri, Kiambu, and Murang'a, as well as from Nyandarua, participated, an indication of increasing inroads into the government's Central Province support.

Personally less well-off than Kariuki, and with less capital at his disposal, Seroney was more constrained in his use of harambee to build support, but his doing so was no less controversial. Government objections to Seroney's activities surfaced in the press in February 1973, when the Tinderet MP alleged in Parliament that he had received a threat that the government would "crush" the proposed Samoei Institute for Vocational and Technical Education, for which he had raised harambee funds. Seroney held a news conference in Nairobi and announced that his project had been "obstructed by jealous politicians mainly from outside the District," with the collaboration of civil servants. [43] On February 4, the local administration refused to license further fund-raising for the institute, and five days later, the entire Samoei project was unlicensed. Official sanction was provided instead to a newly registered Samoei Boys and Girls Harambee Boarding School. The *Daily Nation* reported only that "the people of Nandi Hills have thanked Vice-President Daniel arap Moi for his efforts toward raising KSh. 150,000 for construction" and that the school would be managed by a former MP from the district instead of Seroney. [44] The efforts to undermine Seroney continued, with reception of a "Nandi Hills delegation" by the vice president and minister for home affairs at the end of the month. In contravention of standard procedure, the sitting MP was not included. [45] Several members came from outside of Tinderet or even Nandi.

CALLS FOR REDISTRIBUTION

This push for greater equity by the Rift Valley rebels touched several spheres of policy. Land, education, and agricultural services were at the core of the platform, although the demands of coalition members were not always consistent within any one sphere—something the leaders tolerated in an effort to extend their base of support.

The inconsistency of claims was greatest on the subject of land. In order to build a national movement capable of opposing and dislodging the "inner circle," it was necessary to build support within Central Province and the Kikuyu stronghold. The disproportionate benefit received by the Kiambu Kikuyu during the first years of the Kenyatta government meant that making inroads into that district would be difficult. Not all residents of Central Province had benefited to the same degree from the extension of services, however. The former Mau Mau centers of activity had received a disproportionate share of resources compared to other parts of the country, but fewer of their local leaders had acquired positions in government or on the boards of private sector businesses. The division between the largely loyalist business and farming elite on the one hand and the former Mau Mau, the subsistence farmers, and the landless on the other provided an opening. The Rift Valley rebels crafted a strategy that used a populist appeal to create division among the Kikuyu.

Given his role as a moderate during the Mau Mau rebellion and a mediator at independence, Kenyatta could, of course, find support within both Central Province groups. The idea of the J.M. coalition was not to challenge the president's rule but to convince the president that a small group had taken power behind his back and that the way to restore control was to oust that faction in favor of another, or at least to limit the resources the Family sought to aggregate under their control. The strategy was also practical because Kariuki hailed from a Nyeri family originally and could still generate support there. Thus, early in the campaign, the Nyeri politician Wareru Kanja was brought into the periphery of the coalition, calling for a land policy that would give plots to the people who had fought for independence.[46] Other men and women assumed important roles too. Charles Rubia, assistant minister for education, who was originally from Murang'a but had a political base in Nairobi, became a stalwart defender of the right of coalition members to speak freely on the floor of Parliament. Martin Shikuku, MP from Butere, an area of small farms in Western Province, was to become a vocal advocate of the less well-off.

The plea for a land policy that would benefit the landless, although a means of capturing wider Kikuyu support and bolstering J. M. Kariuki's position, stood diametrically opposed to the interests of some of the other parties in the coalition. True, a populist appeal placing ceilings on land ownership would benefit Rift Valley groups by excluding the big Kikuyu landowners from the land market there. But it would not help stem the influx of Central Province settlers into the Rift or enable local machine bosses to reward their supporters with participation in land ventures. A policy to benefit the landless, in general, would operate by formulas that would exclude important local figures whose electoral backing candidates would welcome.

In the actual event, debate over group entitlements gave way to the need to build a coalition broad enough to fracture the Family base. Members of the coalition began to push strongly for populist land policies in mid September 1972.[47] Kariuki introduced the topic repeatedly over a period of several days, calling, at one point, for a change not only in policy but in the policy-making process. Before an audience at Kamusinga, the assistant minister for tourism and wildlife called for "a complete overhaul of the existing social, economic, and political systems in Kenya," claiming that "a small but powerful group of greedy, self-seeking elite in the form of politicians, civil-servants, and businessmen has steadily but very surely monopolised the fruits of independence to the exclusion of the majority of our people. We do not want a Kenya of ten millionaires and ten million beggars."[48] Picking up the refrain, Elijah Mwangale, MP for Bungoma East, warned: "The gap between the 'haves and have nots' in Kenya is widening with only ten percent of the population controlling everything at the expense of others."[49] The period of intense mobilization had started.

Land distribution and land prices remained public issues throughout 1973 and 1974, with the number of critics of government policy steadily growing. A Murang'a District MP, supported by several other backbench Kikuyu politicians, attacked the use of quit notices to eliminate squatting by landless peasants in Central Province and introduced a motion to give those dispossessed plots of their own.[50] When the group later moved that ceilings be placed on land prices,[51] Kariuki announced that the motion was the most important in the history of the House.[52] Resale of land to foreign owners and to large landowners came under fire too, particularly from the Luhya areas, where Martin Shikuku and the MP for the neighboring constituency of Lurambi South had joined forces with J.M.[53]

The leaders of the Rift Valley opposition maintained the pressure for two years, making increasingly concrete calls for change. In July 1974, members of the opposition coalition disclosed evidence of "land rackets" and appropriation of government farms by cabinet ministers. J.M. and Assistant Minister for Education Charles Rubia called for a commission of inquiry. "Cabinet Ministers, Permanent Secretaries, and Provincial Commissioners [are] being allocated land supposed to be set aside for experimental farms in Masailand," Kariuki is quoted as telling the House.[54] John Marie Seroney and a representative from Busia, on the Ugandan border, supported J.M.'s call for an impartial body to deal with land transactions.

The call for equity also extended to provision of educational and economic opportunities, particularly the latter. Members of the Rift Valley coalition made the first bid for local development monies shortly to be made available under the Special Rural Development Program,[55] urging that the Kerio Valley, in the north-central part of the Rift, be the site of the initial project. When Attorney General Charles Njonjo tried to introduce an amendment to make the program nationwide, the backers of the original motion remained firm. They argued that the great potential of the area should long ago have attracted attention from several ministries and tried to force the administration not to follow a strategy that would grant some of the money to portions of Central Province, as Njonjo had proposed.[56] Picking up the refrain, Kitale leaders similarly used the 1973 Kitale agricultural show as a platform to call for location of more industry in the district.[57]

Typical of the exchanges on the floor of Parliament was a debate led by the Kerio South MP, who challenged the government to "embark on a crash program to develop all areas of Kenya which were neglected"[58] and moved:

> That, in view of the fact that Harambee spirit has accelerated and is booming in all advanced parts of the Republic, except in the backward districts which are likely to remain behind for a long time, this House urges Government to assist financially and morally those areas which need crash programmes of development in order to catch up with the rest of the country.[59]

The MP congratulated the government on providing free education in neglected areas but remarked that other districts in need of such opportunities had not been included. He concluded by observing that the gap between haves and have-nots had widened, saying that "in about five years' time [some Kenyans would] be living on top of the Hilton," while the rest would roam the streets. "Equal opportunity for all!" was the resounding finale. Others voiced their approval of the Kerio South MP's motion and called for "equal opportunities for all tribes living in Kenya."[60]

GEMA AND THE BID TO REJUVENATE KANU

The dominant faction moved quickly to preserve its access to the president and its influence over policy, using a variety of political tactics, including the expansion of its financial base to facilitate efforts to lure marginal "rebels" from J.M.'s coalition, capture of critical "gatekeeping" positions in the administration, and a bid to strengthen the party in ways that would potentially decrease the power of rival groups. Its leaders developed these responses with some presidential toleration but not with full presidential support. Kenyatta continued to pursue an independent strategy of accommodation until illness and the growing power of the Family in government removed control from his hands.

The redistribution of resources toward Rift Valley groups did not appeal to Family leaders, who stood to lose benefits and status. The group decided to fight back by strengthening the Kiambu-based ethnic welfare society, the Gikuyu, Embu, and Meru Association (GEMA), mobilizing resources to generate a tighter organization and signal its bargaining power, always under the guise of "cultural preservation." In February 1973, Dr. Njoroge Mungai, the foreign minister and a nephew of Kenyatta's, launched the first GEMA-sponsored social event in Nairobi. Shortly thereafter, GEMA also inaugurated activities in parts of the country where it had never done so before, using its significant and growing financial base as a source of funds for promoting the fortunes of potential supporters throughout the country.

However much GEMA's leaders protested that the organization was not a political body, its actions often crossed into that sphere. For example, in December 1973, GEMA's Nyeri Branch asked the government to divide Nyeri District into eight parliamentary constituencies instead of the four that then existed, some of which were controlled by opponents of the Family. And in 1974, the Family pitted Peter Ndirangu Nderi, a relative of the head of the Criminal Investigation Department, against the Nyeri MP Waweru Kanja and lost by a very narrow margin. Perception that GEMA had become an ethnically based political organization with substantial leverage was reflected in J. M. Kariuki's statement in February 1974 that the "ten years of independence have neither been great nor truly independence. . . . The inauguration and strengthening of such bodies as GEMA, Luo Union, and the New Akamba Union in my view is the most retrogressive step we have ever taken, and constitutes a tragedy in terms of our own advance toward nationhood."[61]

Rejuvenating KANU and its nationalist ideology became one of the main planks in GEMA's strategy. The push for a stronger party started in mid 1972, at the same time that Kariuki and Seroney began to criticize top officials for constraining political association. An assistant minister for works said that Kenya would be "doomed to failure" if KANU did not reorganize to protect the country from those who launched "unwarranted attacks" against the vice president and senior officials.[62] Inaugurating a new recruitment drive in mid 1972, the party's organizing secretary denounced leaders who were "cleverly and cunningly dishing out national seats on a provincial basis and tribal affiliations."[63] William Odongo Omamo, Luo patriarch Oginga Odinga's rival in Siaya, joined the predominantly Kikuyu-inspired push for reorganization in March 1973, in "a determined bid to reawaken the Nyanza people in defence of party democracy."[64] Omamo's support was repaid by the participation of another central Kiambu Family figure, Njoroge Mungai, in a harambee meeting at Ukwala, Siaya, in the Luo country of Nyanza on May 6, 1973.

As 1973 progressed, the KANU reorganization leaders took the first steps toward using the party as a means of political control. In April, Minister of Defence James Gichuru and the Central Province KANU chairman, James Njiru, both GEMA members, violated an unwritten rule in Kenya that during visits by politicians or public officials to constituencies the sitting MP for the area must also be present. The two men held a KANU meeting in Nyandarua, Kariuki's home territory, in his absence. The MP for Laikipia West introduced Gichuru with the words: "The party is much alive and we all know it. Perhaps those who suggest that the party is dead are not politically alive." According to the *Daily Nation,* Njiru boasted: "Just as KANU had managed to crush other parties such as KADU, APP (the African People's Party), and KPU, so it would crush 'any other party these people may be trying to form.'"[65]

A month later, at a KANU meeting in Nakuru District, Gichuru expressed his concern over the attacks of a Rift Valley coalition member, Martin Shikuku, on senior government officials. Those attending the meeting promptly resolved: "Anyone who continues to abuse or level unwarranted charges against President Kenyatta, Mr. Mbiyu Koinange, or Mr. James Gichuru will be dealt with 'mercilessly.'" Gichuru went on to criticize those who preached "sectionalism and regionalism," although, apparently unaware of any inconsistency, he concluded by calling on the wananchi, or common people, to join GEMA, "which he described as a unifying factor among the Kikuyu, Embu, and Meru people."[66]

The bid to strengthen KANU was short-lived and unsuccessful, however, because of suspicion that it was a Kiambu effort to disguise privilege through appeals to nationalism and to meritocratic considerations. Where GEMA's boundaries ended and those of the KANU reorganization group began was unclear. Most of the meetings took place in Central Province, and many of the early speeches urging party reorganization were delivered by Gichuru.[67] Indeed, the first conference to consider reorganization strategy was announced not by national-level party officials but by the KANU executive officer for Central Province. Held in Nyeri township, the meeting was chaired by Gichuru, KANU's vice president in Central Province. Although the 300 delegates and observers came from all parts of Kenya, the choice of speakers was peculiarly unrepresentative. The list, when announced, included Minister for Foreign Affairs Mungai, Minister for State Mbiyu Koinange, and an array of other Kikuyu speakers, including Margaret Kenyatta.[68] Most Luo leaders, save Odongo Omamo, appeared reticent to extend support, despite their relative lack of involvement in the Rift Valley opposition and their historical role as part of the KANU alliance against a "majimboist," federalist system.

Kenyatta did not come out as a public spokesman for party revitalization, although neither did he did express disagreement with those who argued for a stronger, de jure single-party system. In the end, the prospect that Central Province sectional interests would capture the effort to define nationalism made the party a poor vehicle for managing political conflict, as Kenyatta appeared to realize. Eventually, GEMA retreated. In the early months of 1974, the organization's leaders issued frequent protests that they were not involved in party politics, in response to complaints that the reverse was true.

THE PRESIDENT'S STRATEGY

In a style that had brought him success during the independence transition period, Kenyatta initially responded to the "rebellion" in the Rift with increased resources to meet some of the demands for equity and compensation of those who stood to lose. He had paid attention to

J.M.'s demands for greater KANU openness in 1969, when the assistant minister had proposed a system of open primaries. At first, he chose to accommodate again. As oil-price shocks and agricultural problems constrained availability of funds and the demands of both the Rift coalition and the Family escalated, the president would eventually seek to make coalition-building more difficult, placing constraints on speech and association. In the early part of the period, however, maintenance of a loose but broad coalition appeared to be Kenyatta's objective.

The president's first move was to stave off dissatisfaction in the Rift by responding to some of the demands posed by the "rebels." The gestures targeted small numbers of particularly vocal citizens. In April 1973, for example, the president presented land in Nakuru District, to 200 families, 65 of whom were drawn from the landless register. "Kenya Has No Room For Land Bloodsuckers—Mzee" read the *Nation*'s headline the next day. At the ceremony, the provincial commissioner for Rift Valley made a speech thanking the president for his attention to needy families and said that "whenever the President visited the province people knew that a portion of landless people would be provided with *shambas* [plots of land]." [69] Public demonstrations of responsiveness were intended to forestall more politically difficult changes in land-use policy. At the end of the year, the government initiated sugar-growing schemes in Nyanza and Western Province. The first months of 1973 also brought a tour of Eastern Province, announcement of extensive road-building in Meru District, and distribution of 1,600 plots on the edge of the Rift to landless Kikuyu squatters. Finally, in July 1974, the Ministry of Lands and Settlement announced that it was poised to buy around 60,000 acres for redistribution to landless squatters.

Other gestures communicated a sense of greater attention to "neglected areas" in the government's economic decision making. As the agricultural problems of 1973 intensified, Kenyatta embarked on a tour of the districts in the central and northern parts of the Rift, giving away more land at Molo, in Nakuru District,[70] and opening the Kitale, Nakuru, and Eldoret agricultural shows, traditionally important forums for political announcements and coalition-building. In August, he toured the area a second time, and again in September he embarked on a one-week trip. Promises of free primary education, at least in a student's first four years, and announcement of additional road construction in the Rift followed in short order.

In the early years, the president also compensated the leaders of the GEMA elite through harambee contributions and Ministry of Finance purchases of shares in companies they owned, or in which they held part equity. The president himself rarely appeared at these functions, except those in his own constituency. Instead, Vice President Moi, Minister of Finance Kibaki, and Minister of Defence Gichuru, in particular, made public appearances on behalf of the president.

In 1974, as GEMA gathered strength and demanded that the president grant fewer concessions to less privileged regions, the pattern of harambee giving shifted, with much greater flows of funds into Central Province and the Kikuyu areas of Nakuru, presumably as a tactic for staving off still more strident demands by GEMA leaders.[71] The GEMA chief Njenga Karume participated heavily in Central Province harambee in 1974, and Moi often sat on the dais with him. Of particular note was the appearance of the vice president in Gichuru's constituency, Limuru, during the campaign period before the 1974 elections.[72] Given the identification of some of the senior ministers with the Family, it was sometimes difficult to distinguish whether a harambee contribution was an effort to build stronger ties between local members of Parliament and the State House or whether the intention was really to strengthen GEMA's base. It may have been a bit of both, an effort to tame the increasingly strong Family faction within the government and keep its demands limited while at the same time ensuring the predominance of the commercial class over the less well-off.

Harambee was not the only vehicle for dispensing patronage, of course. Government spending on stock purchases skyrocketed in 1973–74. The list of beneficiaries included many companies in which GEMA leaders had a significant stake. Although the primary reason for the increases in purchases may have been economic, the program provided a useful vehicle for political trade as well.

A third form of patronage used to limit disruption was to try to quell the fears of Family members that they would lose access to decision making if their shares of development resources diminished. During the period, none of the Kiambu Kikuyu officials attacked by the opposition lost their appointments to public office. The first cabinet shuffle since 1969 took place in January 1973, its most significant change being the promotion of Eric Bomett, a Family opponent of the Rift Valley coalition, from the portfolio of assistant minister for housing to that of assistant minister for home affairs, where he would have influence in internal security. Another critic of the Rift Valley opposition, William Murgor, MP for Eldoret South, rose to become chairman of the Agricultural Development Corporation, a position that placed him in control of loans to troubled farmers during the 1973–74 agricultural crisis and gave him potentially valuable patronage resources.[73]

In the debate about appointments, J. E. Mbori, MP for the Nyanza constituency of Kasipul Kabondo, confronted Assistant Minister of State, Kamwithi Munyi, arguing that civil service and parastatal employment was inequitably distributed. "Since it is the Government's policy to discourage tribal animosity in this country, what measures has the Minister taken to ensure that in all Ministries and statutory bodies civil servants are equitably mixed?" asked the MP. The assistant minister replied that appointments were based on merit and were blind to tribal origin; therefore, one could not talk of "representative" distribution as "equitable" distribution: "The Member's question is vague and contradictory. He wants officers to be posted regardless of their tribal origin and at the same time he talks of even distribution. You cannot have both. If the member's suggestion was implemented the Government would be acting tribally." [74] The utility of patronage and pork-barrel politics in maintaining habits of competition and compromise between KANU's two main factions diminished over the period, however. J.M. posed a particular kind of challenge. His campaign threatened to divide the country, but particularly the Kikuyu, on class lines. Kenyatta had long worked to avoid such divisions—or their subjective perception. His own health poor, Kenyatta was less and less able to move about the country. Instead, he listened to his closest advisers, many of them tied to GEMA, and perceived a developing threat to stability.

Warnings began to appear in the speeches of government officials as economic problems made Kenyatta's strategy of accommodation more difficult to implement without requiring Central Province to accept losses in development outlays. By May 1973, as rumors of a second political party in the making began to circulate, a change in strategy was put into effect. Vice President Moi attacked a "few troublesome" MPs who were allegedly going behind the scenes to establish another political party. [75] He condemned the "power seekers" again on June 4, at a rally in Nakuru District. A month later, Defence Minister Gichuru also denounced the dissidents who were behind the formation of a new party, arguing that Nakuru Town, in the Rift, "had become the headquarters for a new subversive group of rebel and disgruntled elements." [76] The same day, the president warned the public of saboteurs. "Let me inform you that the Government is watching these developments with both eyes and when the time comes these individuals will be picked up one by one," Kenyatta announced. The next week, a rally in Kiambu denounced the formation of an opposition to KANU, and coupled the attack with the promise of shambas for landless families in the area. Hints continued through the following year, all to the effect that the government would not allow formation of a second party, regardless of what the law permitted.

THE BATTLE FOR POLITICAL SPACE

The Family and the members of the Rift Valley Opposition were quick to recognize that parliamentary and judicial processes were critically important in determining to what degree a group's assets and opportunities, or lack thereof, could affect distributional outcomes. A coalition built on behalf of particular policy changes could only be effective if the members could disseminate their views, and if government officials could be forced to the negotiating table. Kariuki and Seroney thus had a strong interest in preserving their "political space," the ability to assemble and to obtain enforcement of parliamentary decisions through the law. A necessary element of their strategy was therefore a strong defense of freedom of association and the sovereignty of Parliament. The Rift Valley populists were engaged not just in a bid for greater allocation of resources to their areas but also in an effort to negotiate the rules governing discussion of distributive issues.

Parliamentary procedures, consultative processes within the executive, and the strength of the judiciary could affect access to opportunities and the costs of coalition-building, and might thus favor one group over others. Both the Family and the Rift Valley rebels recognized that the procedures could be used to secure or deny "political space" necessary to build bargaining strength. The procedural changes inaugurated during this period were to have further-reaching consequences for the character of party-state relations than the substance of the bargains struck. As many of the politicians realized at the time, the restrictions imposed on political activity by the mid 1970s would make it nearly impossible to organize issue-based political movements, political movements that had change in national-level policies as their end, and to prevent an impending merger between the Office of the President and KANU.

THE RIGHT TO ASSOCIATE UNDER THREAT

The Kenyatta government had challenged freedom of assembly in its proscription of the Kenya People's Union in 1967. Nonetheless, MPs and members of the government, such as J. M. Kariuki, felt able to criticize policy on the floor of Parliament during 1970–71 and to conduct harambee fund-raisers. The protection of these activities was not guaranteed, however. Family allies in Parliament and in government sought almost immediately to constrain the Rift Valley opposition by urging changes in the rules defining "tolerable" behavior. Wherever possible, they sought to replace legal guarantees with procedures allowing administrative discretion.

The right to convene harambee meetings came under attack first, followed by more controversial issues relating to control of Kenya's security apparatus and parliamentary privileges. Harambee sponsorship came under fire in 1972. In April, government restrictions on association became a topic for discussion in Parliament in the aftermath of complaints from Kariuki and others that members of the administration had intervened to stop harambee meetings and gatherings of constituents at which they were present. Attorney General Charles Njonjo stated on the floor that only political meetings needed licenses, but Seroney questioned the extent of the provincial administration's adherence to the rule and the acceptability of having such regulations in any case.

Over the course of the next year, the disputes about the licensing of harambee meetings rapidly evolved into a confrontation between two groups within the government. Controlling the security apparatus and a number of key posts in the administration were members of the Family and associates, led by Minister of State Mbiyu Koinange. Junior ministers and their representatives from areas outside Kiambu found it increasingly difficult, they claimed, to express their views about appropriate policies. The assistant ministers and their allies on the back bench sought to reduce the ability of the Family to determine who could speak and why. Over the objections of Koinange, Njonjo, and other Family members, Seroney introduced a motion to modify the Public Order Act, which had provided the legal grounds for regulating harambee participation. Said Seroney:

> The mischief of this Act lies in the section where the D.C. [district commissioner] has to comply with directives from the Ministry of State, the Commissioner of Police, and the Provincial Commissioner. This means that even if the DC decides to allow a meeting by an MP ... he still has to follow directives from any of those three services. ... The very concept of the Act is wrong. ... We do not need a permit to address the very people who elected us to this parliament.[77]

A Nyanza MP, G. O. Migure, of Mbita constituency, charged that the increasing hindrances to association that emanated from the Office of the President were sponsored by Minister of State Koinange, a key Family member. J.M., too, claimed that a small group of high-ranking officials had entrenched themselves by "belittling and minimising" others.

These comments triggered retaliation. A month later, the district commissioner for Nandi, Seroney's district, banned all meetings—political and harambee—and halted all collection of funds for land purchase.[78] The Western Province commissioner followed suit shortly thereafter and prohibited the Rift Valley opposition member Martin Shikuku, MP from Butere, from addressing meetings in his constituency for an indefinite period.[79] As the debate heated up, the vice president stepped in to clarify the government's position, which, he said, required licensing of all collections of harambee funds, except those conducted by churches, and even then on the condition that no politicians would be among the speakers.[80] The major means available to the opposition for securing a soapbox from which to speak and for cultivating ties with potential allies in other provinces and districts disappeared. Indeed, in the 1974 general elections, the administration canceled all but one of J.M.'s public meetings.[81]

THE CRUMBLING OF PARLIAMENTARY SOVEREIGNTY

The ability to associate was not the only dimension of political space the Family faction sought to restrict. Ability to debate policy in Parliament and the knowledge that decisions taken according to the rules of the assembly would be obeyed were also critical to the capacity to constitute an opposition, and it was precisely these that came under fire during this period as well. Confirmation of parliamentary sovereignty was as important as the ability to convene meetings. MPs, and, indeed, members of the government, could exercise far more bargaining leverage in the formation of government policy if they could air grievances on the floor of Parliament and alert their colleagues and the public to issues they believed important. Likewise they had to have confidence that the civil service and executive would abide by the regulations established by elected officials. The early 1970s brought a steady assault on these parliamentary prerogatives.

The competition to determine the ground rules of political debate in the country began with Kenyatta's request that members of the government critical of current policy choices resign their positions:

> This is a Parliament of Kanu, the national front, and it must function as a primary instrument of our national resolve. To do this properly, there must be certain conventions and rules.

If any Member of my Government feels what is called a crisis of con-
science in regard to any Bill approved by my Cabinet, he should resign as a
Member of the Government, whereupon he will become a backbencher. He
will then be free to oppose the measure under Standing Orders of the House
and his action will be judged by the people within his own constituency.

Mr. Speaker, this is not a question of blocking any parliamentary opposition. The whole business of giving service to the people becomes more complex with each passing year. One of the vital requirements within a stable
Government is discipline, and this discipline must be maintained otherwise
there is betrayal of the people's trust.[82]

Although the request was not entirely unreasonable, as stated, it was
supportable only on the two conditions that members of the government could criticize policy within the cabinet and that backbenchers
could organize their views through a formal opposition party. The latter
option, although not legally proscribed, was de facto prohibited. The
assistant minister for education, Charles Rubia, tried to find a middle
ground between Kenyatta and those members of the government who
had criticized policy by urging that a forum be provided in which assistant ministers would be able to offer their views and suggestions. He
noted that the president's statement appeared to indicate a crisis within
government ranks.[83] Assistant ministers had sought an audience with
the president and vice president, he remarked, and they had been denied. A way to mend the cleavage the president perceived was to take
the comments of assistant ministers seriously.

The focus of the debate shifted to parliamentary sovereignty in May
1972, when Seroney won approval of a motion granting leave for the
introduction of a bill that would amend provisions relating to the election of members of the National Assembly. Both Vice President Moi and
Attorney General Njonjo attempted to block consideration of the proposed bill, which Seroney and Kariuki claimed would make the electoral system more democratic, in part by protecting balloting from government influence. J.M. suggested that Seroney "consult the Attorney
General for ideas and then frame the motion together so that when it is
introduced, the Government will also be part and parcel of this motion." [84]

The Kenyatta cabinet wanted nothing to do with the idea, however.
One week after his remarks, Seroney's passport was held at the airport,
on the grounds that he had no approval for foreign travel from the president or the minister for home affairs.[85] Seroney's fellow MPs quickly
condemned the seizure and ruled that the action was unconstitutional.
One Rift Valley opposition member introduced a motion stating that a

passport held by a "loyal Kenyan citizen is his right and not a privilege" and was given "wild applause," according to reporters at the scene.[86] The motion passed after a stormy debate.

The frontbenchers were divided on a proper response. On June 30, one of Seroney's foes, an assistant minister for housing, alleged that the passport incident was simply a move by some members of the government to "assassinate the character of certain leaders." He echoed previous claims by other MPs that the issue was simply the latest manifestation of a power struggle taking place within the government.[87] The next week Vice President Moi stated that MPs did not have a right to a passport. Seroney stood up in Parliament, waved the edition of the *Nation* that contained the vice president's remarks, and argued that the statement amounted to "a ridicule of the House."

The actions of the minister of state in the Office of the President, Mbiyu Koinange, provoked the next round in the tug-of-war. The minister was responsible for provincial administration, internal security, and a range of related functions, including, at that time, some of the responsibility for land consolidation. Kenyatta's brother-in-law and a member of a prominent loyalist Kiambu family, Koinange had long served as a "palace guard" in the view of several members. One MP insisted that the minister was not "suitable to be in charge of protocol where he could be humiliating Members of Parliament at State functions." [88] He urged Koinange to resign his post, a call echoed by others. The Nairobi MP Charles Rubia again tried to strike a middle ground by reframing the problem as one of accountability. Seroney accepted Rubia's argument but pushed it to its extremes, asking members to redraft the constitution to establish the office of prime minister, so that the chief of the cabinet would serve at the pleasure of Parliament. On that note, the debate ended, at least until year's end.

In the interim, Seroney organized broad support, and when the role of Parliament once again came to the fore, at the end of March 1973, MPs from a number of districts across the country added their voices to the defense of parliamentary sovereignty. For the next three months, the power of the civil service came under periodic scrutiny by members of Parliament allied with the Rift Valley opposition. Seroney chastised parliamentarians who had "surrendered power to civil servants." G. G. Kariuki, MP for Laikipia East, countered, on the side of the government: "We must accept our failure because politicians have surrendered their powers to some people who are executing those same powers very efficiently, powers the politicians were unable to carry out." [89]

The tension within the government heightened during April and May 1973, with the vice president calling for the resignation of those ministers and assistant ministers who "were not ready to support Government policy," a statement to which J.M. responded by asking, publicly, whether he, the MP from Nyandarua North, was the intended reference.[90] Other members of the government entered the conflict on both sides. Assistant Minister for Agriculture Maina Wanjigi told Parliament that "a few individuals calling themselves the 'inner circle' are trying to isolate President Kenyatta from his own people."[91] He urged members of the government to accept criticism in good faith. The government's eventual response was at odds with Wanjigi's suggestion, however. On October 17, 1973, the National Assembly suspended its normal business to debate a special motion tabled by the vice president. The motion read, in part, "that noting the occasion of the twenty-first anniversary of the unjustifiable arrest and subsequent detention of our beloved President and Father of the Nation, Mzee Jomo Kenyatta. . . . This House (1) solemnly reaffirms its confidence and unflinching loyalty and support for His Excellency. . . ."[92] In future months, the motion would give carte blanche to members of the Family in their efforts to circumscribe the activities of the Rift Valley rebels.

RESOLUTION

There was one more act to the drama played out between 1972 and 1975. The manipulation of procedure in which the Family faction engaged jeopardized Kenyatta's search for accommodation through a system of political barter or exchange. The president's ability to secure agreement by facilitating trading of interests depended on his ability to maintain control over the resources used in compensation. Family members had extended their power over those resources during the mid 1970s, however, by maneuvering to win critical positions in the security forces and in business and by using these positions to hamstring parliamentary procedure. Only electoral competition between organized groups, each with a stake in preserving its ability to compete, could make individual seats sufficiently insecure that officeholders would have incentive to observe and maintain the rules of the game and limit their own claims. But the Family had now effectively captured control over the very apparatus responsible for maintaining elections.

No longer content to accept calls for redistribution, the Family coalition, now secure in key governmental posts, obtained the president's support for policies that would further restrict the ability of opponents of government policy to organize. Unable to use the threat of loss of electoral power to keep his subordinates in line and seemingly at the end of his energy, Kenyatta acquiesced. The year 1974 brought increasing attacks on the opposition from the president and vice president, despite Kenyatta's earlier distance from the conflict. At the end of January, the *Daily Nation* reported a speech in which the vice president assailed critics of the government.

> Mr. Moi stated that certain people were going around the country and also issuing statements in the Press which tended to suggest that there was no democracy in Kenya.
>
> The Kenya Government, Mr. Moi added, did not believe in using coercive measures to suppress freedom of expression, individual liberty, or worship. . . .
>
> However, the Government would not entertain destructive criticisms or views which transgressed these freedoms such as claiming that the Government rule was based on dictatorship.[93]

Moi maintained his attack over several months, arguing particularly against proponents of redistribution, who were "envious of other people's achievements."[94] When the restrictions on political participation came to international attention, the vice president and officials, including some members of the National Assembly, lashed out at the messengers, the foreign press, calling, in particular, for the deportation of British Broadcasting Corporation personnel, and on February 26, 1974, the University of Nairobi was closed indefinitely because of disturbances there.

The president entered the debate in June, first urging Kenyans to cultivate a spirit of unity and brotherhood and to discard tribalism and sectionalism.[95] As calls for equitable distribution of development funds throughout the country persisted, Kenyatta's statements became more emphatic, however.[96] At a meeting in Nakuru the day after a parliamentary debate on equity, the president attacked the "disgruntled elements" who sought to undermine the government. These "elements" included "sitting MPs who move around the country, payukaring that the Government has done nothing for *wananchi*," he said—a refrain picked up by many of his subordinates.[97] A week later he made a special appeal to the residents of J.M.'s home area, Nyandarua, to "discard feelings of sectionalism and clanism in order to create a united front capable of advancing economic and social targets in the district."[98]

Despite the government's admonitions, the core members of the Rift Valley opposition retained their seats during the 1974 elections, with J.M. receiving a landslide victory even though unable to hold campaign meetings. Two important Family candidates, Odongo Omamo and Njoroge Mungai, lost their seats, and Minister of Defence Gichuru, won by only a narrow margin against a strong opposition candidate in his constituency, Limuru. Gichuru's son, Gitau Gichuru, lost in Kikuyu constituency. It was not until after the election that the president chose, finally, to act on his words and remove the dissident group from the cabinet, while appointing Omamo and Mungai nominated MPs. At the end of October, J. M. Kariuki, Martin Shikuku, Charles Rubia, and Burudi Nabwera were all dropped from their posts as junior ministers.

Although the gradual redistribution of public monies quietly proceeded, the careers of those who had fought for these policies came to untimely ends (see Table 2). J. M. Kariuki was assassinated in March 1975, last seen in the company of members of the Government Services Unit (GSU) and police. The special investigative committee assembled to handle the case numbered many of J.M.'s friends, including Seroney, Maina Wanjigi, and Rubia, and produced a report suggesting that members of the police force under Family control may have been involved in the murder.

Three assistant ministers, John Keen, Masinde Muliro, and Peter Kibisu, lost their posts after voting against the government on whether to accept the report of the special investigative committee or merely acknowledge it. Seroney and Martin Shikuku were both detained later in 1975, after Shikuku announced to the Assembly that KANU was "dead" and Seroney, then deputy speaker of the House, replied that Shikuku's motion did not need a second as the point was "obvious." Moi protested these comments by leading a walkout by frontbenchers and a significant number of backbenchers. Whenever Seroney was in the chair, thereafter, walkouts occurred. Mark Mwithaga, the Rift Valley opposition leader from Nakuru, was unseated after an election petition. Mwithaga and one of the dismissed assistant ministers went to jail in 1975 on charges of assault and malicious damage to property, most likely the victims of an operation to frame potential successors to J.M. and remove them from the political scene.

Within Nakuru District, GEMA official Kahika Kimani's Kiambu-based Ngwataniro group of land companies became a political force and quickly ousted J.M.'s allies. The Nyeri politician Waweru Kanja moved further toward the periphery of the opposition coalition. Even

TABLE 2   KEY FIGURES IN THE 1974–1975 RIFT
VALLEY OPPOSITION AND THEIR SUBSEQUENT CAREERS

Name	Initial Status	Status after 1975
Joseph Mwangi Kariuki	assistant minister	Assassinated March 1975
John Marie Seroney	MP	Detained 1975–78; defeated in 1979 election; died 1982
Martin Shikuku	MP	Detained 1975–78; assistant minister 1979–85; detained again
Mark Mwithaga	MP	Jailed 1975–77; assistant minister 1979–83; defeated in 1983 election
Waweru Kanja	MP	Assistant minister 1979; jailed 1981–82; defeated in 1983 election
Charles Rubia	minister	Minister 1979–83; MP 1983–88; expelled from KANU 1988; detained 1990–91
George Anyona	MP	Detained 1977–78; barred from candidacy 1979; detained 1982–84
Masinde Muliro	minister	Sacked 1975; defeated in 1979 election; MP from 1984
Peter Kibisu	assistant minister	Sacked 1975; jailed 1975–76; defeated in 1979 election

Seroney lost by a large margin when he ran for Parliament after release from detention. Without J.M.'s assistance and without the prospect of wielding substantial bargaining leverage on behalf of Tinderet in Parliament, Seroney was a less appealing candidate than he had once been. Although a master of patronage politics, Kenyatta had found that repression had its uses. In his own words, "People seem to forget that a hawk is always in the sky ready to swoop on the chickens." [99]

CONCLUSIONS

The period 1970–75 saw important changes in the character of party-state relations in Kenya. KANU provided a framework within which individual MPs could represent the particularistic interests of their constituents; MPs could lobby for projects and question ministers on the performance of tasks within their constituencies. But KANU remained a weak party in several senses. It possessed no internal mechanism for resolving differences between members and forging a common party platform and thus had little role in producing national policies or in aggregating interests—functions parties in multiple-party states often perform. Indeed, the reconfiguration of the electoral rules to eliminate the KPU challenge in the late 1960s removed any electoral pressure to do so, and in the single-party context, such a "rejuvenation" would have meant banishing some views and interests from politics. Moreover, the party exercised little control over policy. Most legislative initiatives originated in the Office of the President, or executive, and appeared on Parliament's agenda for discussion and adoption. The modified republican system of government removed any obligation the chief executive might feel to implement and enforce legislation enacted by the majority party; Kenyatta himself was not dependent on the electoral fortunes of his party. In consequence, the KANU leadership lacked the ability to propose significant new legislation and to control the executive's actions through recourse to a vote of no confidence. As a result of changes in the rules of representation theoretically introduced to reduce "sectionalism," legislative activity became, increasingly, simply a way to divide the spoils.

In two main ways, the period 1970–75 exaggerated KANU's weakness and made it increasingly difficult for members of Parliament to defend their ability to represent the broad economic interests of their constituents. First, the dominant group within KANU, the Family, succeeded in securing legislation that gave the administration and the president greater ability to deny MPs occasion to communicate with their constituents and to build coalitions with other politicians. By the end of the period, the executive had acquired the ability to require licenses for all meetings, including harambee gatherings, and to police church services to ensure that politicians did not use these as political pulpits. It had also gained the power to control the movements of MPs between regions and to proscribe meetings with representatives of foreign countries or international organizations. Finally, by capturing key administrative positions and politicizing some parts of the provincial administration, the Family gave the Office of the President the power to remove MPs whose views appeared especially troublesome. The events of 1975 enlisted the civil service in the business of framing politicians for crimes they had not committed, simply to remove them from the public arena.

Competition between organized and enduring points of view with broad national bases became extremely difficult under these conditions. Party and parliamentary debate degenerated into localism and sectionalism, and coalition-building through exchange of harambee resources lost effectiveness because of the restrictions placed on political involvement in such activity. The kinds of policy positions the Rift Valley opposition leaders had adopted did not bring the promise of special benefit to those who gave their votes to the cause. For the individual voter, casting a ballot for one of the Rift Valley rebels was to throw one's vote away unless the Rift Valley candidate could claim a large number of friends in other constituencies nationwide who promised to support the "populist" national platform in Parliament. J.M. and Seroney could only assemble such a base if they could communicate across district boundaries and build an organization that would endure and permit them to offer credible promises of electoral assistance in future years in return for support of a "rebel" platform in 1974. Although they succeeded in forging such a base and in winning landslides in several districts in the 1974 elections, the events of 1975 cut their aims short and ensured that Kenyan politicians would find it nearly impossible to emulate J.M.'s successes in future years.

Further, in undercutting the ability of politicians to organize, the measures put into effect in the period 1970–75 promoted a new factionalism. Ad hoc groupings replaced organized political association within KANU. These factions came and went depending on the access their leaders had to the Office of the President. This splintering process affected politicians from a number of different regions. The unity of the conservative wing of the party disappeared, as did the coherence of the "populist" coalition J.M. had forged. Ultimately, this fragmentation would make it difficult for any member of Parliament to defend his or her "political space" and to preserve a separate voice within KANU. In future years, members of the Family and the former GEMA leadership would suffer as much from the situation they had helped to create as would the ideological descendants of the Rift Valley rebels.

The Rift Valley rebels were unable to muster sufficient economic clout to block the measures that circumscribed their activities. Although civic associations existed, these were not adequate bases for a nation-wide defense of political space. Large private-sector entrepreneurs, with control over significant numbers of employees or capital and hence bargaining leverage in the president's eyes, were few, and the number of such men and women who found the appeals of J.M. compelling were even fewer. J.M. himself and Charles Rubia were the exceptions, but neither could use his position to threaten economic boycotts or other reprisals in their efforts to prevent further encroachment on speech and association. Smallholders in many locations organized behind J.M., but they lived too close to the margin of survival and were too divided over distribution of patronage to use their economic positions as leverage—for example, by retreating en masse from the market.

CHAPTER FOUR

The Transition Period, 1976-1980

If the period 1970–75 modified the allocation of functions between KANU and the Office of the President and imposed new restrictions on political association, the period 1976–80 witnessed the effects of the accumulated changes on the way politicians mobilized support, as well as further shifts in the allocation of functions between the State House, Parliament, and the party. By 1980, the end of the transition, the ability of citizens to resist the aggregation of functions of representation and maintenance of order in a "party-state" had eroded significantly. The stage was set for the significant changes in Kenyan political life that would take place during the 1980s.

First came change in the endogenous variable described in chapter 1: the degree of faction within the dominant party. There were two dimensions to this phenomenon. The Kiambu Family members in the Gikuyu, Embu, and Meru Association (GEMA), the ethnic welfare society that served Kikuyu interests, had succeeded in ousting their original opposition; the J. M. Kariuki faction disappeared from the ministerial ranks, and from the party leadership, on orders from the State House. But those who had opposed the Rift Valley movement were themselves divided. The signs of fragmentation were apparent during the bid to rejuvenate KANU as a means for controlling dissidence. Although previously allied with the conservative faction in KANU, at least informally, neither Moi nor Attorney General Charles Njonjo appeared at Minister of Defence James Gichuru's Central Province meetings to reorganize the party. Both would have found it difficult to participate in the GEMA-backed effort, Moi because of his own responsibilities to the Kalenjin and to maintenance of his electoral base in Baringo and Njonjo because of the particular features of his own political position. From a Kiambu loyalist family, but without a post as an elected representative, Attorney General Njonjo would have had to subordinate his ambitions to those of Njoroge Mungai, the man best placed for leadership of the Family clique.

Kenyatta's ill health generated psychological insecurity about future opportunities for participation and intensified the struggle for access to policy influence and public resources. By 1975, it was clear that Vice President Moi would be Kenyatta's successor, barring changes to the constitution. Ability to provide well for constituents from his home area was a popular litmus test for assessing the strength of a leader. If he hoped not only to assume the presidency but also to ensure his tenure in office, Moi would have to continue to increase the share of resources going to areas in the west of Kenya. In Moi's imminent accession to the presidency, the Kiambu elite saw a danger to their positions in government and, ultimately, to their ability to hold on to economic power in the country. The leaders of GEMA believed they could supplant the vice president and put their candidate in the presidency, thus maintaining Central Province control over key economic opportunities.

The strategies these two groups used in their struggle for access accelerated the process of fragmentation. After the demise of J.M., few politicians were willing to try to assemble cross-regional coalitions based on common economic interest. Instead, they chose to emulate the Family and establish bases within the ethnic welfare societies then undergoing a resurgence in response to GEMA. These appeared attractive, not only because they provided a response to what looked like "sectionalism" in the Kikuyu community, but also because their status as "cultural organizations" initially made them less vulnerable to state control. The period 1976–79 saw a sharp rise in the formation of ethnic welfare unions—lobbies for sectional interests—in consequence. Success in electoral competition came to mean ability to assemble ad hoc coalitions of these groups, not through promises of future support, for there were no enduring political organizations to help guarantee these, but rather through exchanges of money—harambee funds and private resources. They did not provide stable bases for campaigns and contesting of policy, however, as history would show.

The executive also altered its strategies in this changed political environment. As groupings at KANU meetings divided increasingly along community boundaries and as these groups began to advance unlimited claims for resources against each other, the Office of the President moved to intervene directly in KANU. Provincial commissioners were ordered to extend their control over licensing of harambee meetings to include supervision of party gatherings. This new power was used both before and after Kenyatta's death in 1978 as a way to control GEMA's expanding influence. It constituted a significant alteration in the division of functions between the party and the administration—one that eroded the representative and decision-making powers of the party and constituted another step toward the fusion of functions in a party-state.

This chapter outlines the way the restrictions of political space enacted in the first years of the 1970s altered the incentives politicians faced and made organization of broad-based coalitions with positions on national issues difficult. Through an account of the three major events of the transition period, it documents the increasing factionalization of Kenyan politics. It concludes with a summary of the effects of this process on the relationship between KANU and the executive.

GEMA AND THE CHANGE-THE-CONSTITUTION MOVEMENT

The fragmentation of KANU was evident, first, in the growing visibility of GEMA, the champion of Kiambu interests, and comparable communal organizations in Kenyan politics. With the conclusion of the J.M. affair, the organizational resources of GEMA might have appeared less important to the Family and its efforts to secure influence over policy. After all, the major contender for GEMA's power had been removed from the political scene. That was not the case, however. The Rift Valley period had witnessed increasing restriction of political space. As quasi-cultural organizations, ethnic welfare societies fell less clearly within the State House's sphere of concern than political meetings. The provincial administration and security forces left ethnic welfare societies alone, at least for the time being. GEMA thus retained its raison d'être, inasmuch as it could shelter continued political activity where other organizational forms could not.

The second half of 1975 also saw the first effects of a boom in coffee prices. Earnings were concentrated in the coffee-growing country of Central Province, but most particularly in Kiambu, benefiting the personal bank accounts of many of those allied with the Family—and, of course, the treasury of GEMA, which became an even more powerful vehicle for political activity in consequence. Using these funds and others it had accumulated, the Family faction within KANU's conservative wing moved rapidly to strengthen its political ties in the Rift through land-trading schemes. The GEMA leader Kahika Kimani chaired several land-buying companies with claims in Nakuru District, and these provided the necessary platform. It was from Kahika Kimani's base in the Ngwataniro Companies that Mbiyu Koinange, James Gichuru, and Njoroge Mungai launched yet another effort to seize control over access to the policy process.

In its bid to control resources and policy making, the GEMA group had three options. The first and second of these entailed voting a new president out of office, either by electing someone else to the presidency of the party or by campaigning for a vote of no confidence in Parliament. Neither of these stratagems appeared especially promising. The element of surprise would have to play a major role to prevent Kenyatta's likely successor from marshaling a counterattack, but the need to bargain for support would make that impossible. News of coalition-building efforts would surely leak.

Alternatively, it would be possible to install another Kiambu leader as president, or someone acceptable to the group, by persuading Kenyatta to reshuffle his cabinet and move Moi out of the vice presidency. This Kenyatta did not do—an indication of the disagreement he must have had with Family members, who, it is alleged, did in fact propose such a solution.[1]

The third option was to seek to change the constitutional provisions for succession. These read:

Chapter II, Part I, Section 6
(1) If the office of President becomes vacant by reason of the death or resignation of the President, or by reason of his ceasing to hold office by virtue of Section 10 or Section 12 of this Constitution (qv) an election of a President shall be held within the period of ninety days immediately following the occurrence of that vacancy, and shall be held in a manner prescribed by Section 5 (5) of this Constitution (qv).
(2) While the office of the President is vacant as afore said, the functions of that office shall be exercised—
(a) by the Vice-President; or
(b) if there is no Vice-President, or if the Vice-President considers that he is for any reason unable to discharge the functions of the office of President, by such Minister as may be appointed by the Cabinet."

By changing the constitution to prevent the immediate assumption of power by the vice president, who could, it was feared, use the ninety-day preparation period to rig the elections in his favor, it might be possible to block the formation of a Moi government.

GEMA's plan called for a change in the wording of the constitution. Instead of the temporary appointment of the vice president as acting president for a ninety-day period, in the event of the president's death, the speaker of the National Assembly would take over. The GEMA group apparently thought it could secure the speaker's position, or that Njoroge Mungai, the MP for Dagoretti, a former foreign minister,[2] would win enough votes to be elected president if Moi could be blocked from using the administration to his electoral advantage.

The first steps toward building support for a bid to change the constitution took place in the last month of 1975 and the first half of 1976. The GEMA-backed group pursued a strategy similar to the one it had used in 1974–75, trying to consolidate Kikuyu support while winning Luo and Kamba participation in an alliance. Although KANU's early success over KADU had depended on cooperation between Luo politicians led by Tom Mboya and Kikuyu politicians under Kenyatta, the former partnership between the political elite of the two groups had suffered from Mboya's assassination, allegedly at the hands of Kikuyu, and the proscription of Oginga Odinga's KPU. Ironically, it was the Odinga group, known for its willingness to flaunt Soviet contacts and anti-capitalist points of view, to which the Family business elite now looked for support. Although Odinga's political views departed strongly from those of the Kiambu group, precluding alliance on grounds of common perceptions or style, the Luo politicians agreed to lend support to the movement. The actual provisions of the deal remain obscure, although there is speculation that a combination of financial resources and agreement to modify or terminate the state's detention policies might have captured Odinga's interest.[3] Odinga is alleged to have believed that Attorney General Charles Njonjo, a Moi ally, was behind his detention in 1969 and the continuing refusal to clear his further participation. Although formerly an outspoken enemy of the Kikuyu elite, Odinga suddenly appeared as an honored guest at the wedding of Mbiyu Koinange's daughter. Peter Muigai Kenyatta, the president's son, received similarly cordial treatment when he visited Bondo, Odinga's home, as a guest of honor at a harambee function that included Odinga.[4] The GEMA leader James Gichuru also met with Odinga on a special trip to Nyanza District.

Consolidating Central Province support consumed much of the group's time during the first half of 1976. Gichuru had not been the only member of the Family to encounter troubles in the 1974 election. In some constituencies, Family members had barely held onto their seats. Near Nairobi, in Juja, home to many Luo and Kalenjin migrant workers, Peter Muigai Kenyatta, an outspoken opponent of J. M. Kariuki, had won by fewer than 200 votes, despite the family name and relationship. In Nyeri, the group's candidates faced strong opposition from the followers of J.M.'s ally Waweru Kanja. The Murang'a leader Julius Gikonyo Kiano was in Moi's camp too; GEMA could not automatically carry any of the Kikuyu districts of Central Province.

Throughout the period, GEMA sponsored numerous harambee meetings, at which not only the familiar Family faces but also Peter Muigai Kenyatta and Ngengi Muigai, the president's nephew, appeared. The group waged a struggle for control of the local KANU branches, potentially important bases for generating votes, which were then holding elections.

The Family's supporters clashed with members of the Moi faction. So intense were the rivalries that the provincial commissioner for Central Province, Simeon Nyachae, held meetings of reconciliation in Murang'a and in mid August suspended all KANU branch elections in Kirinyaga.[5] Similarly, confrontations between supporters of different factions at Nairobi KANU rallies led the provincial commissioner for Nairobi to adopt the practice of personally reviewing and licensing every KANU meeting in the area. Commenting on the campaign, the Nairobi leader Charles Rubia, a former ally of the Rift Valley opposition, said:

> You know, Kanu being the only political party in our country, people will claim to be Kanu followers when they really are not observing the rules and regulations of the party. It is common knowledge that people will group together especially at the time of an election and really gang-up. This political ganging up is not something new entirely, but what I condemned is any ganging up against other people and employing thugs to harass political opponents.[6]

Maina Wanjigi, who had played a similar role earlier during the Rift Valley "rebellion," followed suit.

According to press reports, in September 1976, the Family constituted what was later called the Change-the-Constitution Movement. Kahika Kimani, the GEMA leader and Ngwataniro land company chief, was the main speaker at the first public meeting of the Change-the-Constitution group. The purpose of the meeting was to float the proposal that the rules of succession be modified. Over 20 members of Parliament attended, including the former KPU leader and Odinga ally

Achieng Oneko.[7] The group must have assessed the response as largely favorable, because on October 3, the call for amendment of the constitution was repeated by Kimani at a fund-raiser near Limuru, in Kiambu District.

The reaction of the Moi group came quickly. The Mombasa politician Shariff Nassir was first to condemn Kimani's move, followed by the Masai leader Stanley Oloitipitip, who obtained the signatures of 98 MPs opposed to the amendment. The petition suggested that the Moi coalition held a slim majority of the 158 elected members and 12 appointed members of Parliament. It also contradicted Kimani's claim that his group could muster 80 percent of the votes in the Assembly on behalf of the change in the constitution.

Two days later Attorney General Charles Njonjo issued a simple, official-sounding warning: "It is a criminal offence for any person to encompass, imagine, devise, or intend the death or deposition of the President." The editorial page of the *Nation* picked up the theme the next day, chastised Kimani, and pointed to a GEMA effort to disrupt the country. The *Standard* took GEMA's side, however, noting that Njonjo had signed the statement himself, and that the absence of the presidential imprimatur indicated that the announcement was but another volley in the war between the two groups of ministers. Kenyatta himself made no pronouncement. Officials in the provincial administration were quite perplexed about their responsibilities in choosing whether to license meetings of either group. Provincial commissioners separately traveled to see the president and seek guidance in making these new decisions.

One more time, however, GEMA sought to assert the primacy of the Family in the political party and to suggest, by extension, that its effort to change the constitution was totally consonant with the interests of the party and with the intentions expressed at the nation's founding. Kahika Kimani sponsored a large meeting in Meru that attracted thousands of GEMA members. "We are the defenders of this constitution," Kimani told the crowd. "During the J. M. Kariuki affair when the nation faced a crisis we were the people who spoke for the Government because we have the interests of this country at heart."[8] Identifying GEMA with the KANU nationalist cause, he continued:

> We do not want people attacking GEMA and KANU. We do not want KANU to attack GEMA or GEMA to attack KANU. . . . We want all of us to remain under one party. KANU is the Government and GEMA is under them just like young chicks under the wings. KANU should not be opposed

by GEMA at Meru. . . . And KANU should not oppose GEMA. For it was GEMA which was instrumental in laying the foundation of the KANU Government. So if I may ask: Are these unions not the same thing?

Attacking Attorney General Njonjo in particular, Mungai sought to advance the candidacy of Minister of Defence Gichuru, a senior GEMA official:

> We elected Gichuru as chairman of Kanu, and when our leader came from Lodwar,[9] James Gichuru vacated the chairmanship for Kenyatta. . . . Were it other people they would have dug a grave in which to inter Kenyatta. These are the same people who are now claiming that Gichuru is not a genuine supporter of Kenyatta.

The meeting put an end to the bid to change the constitution. The group misread or intentionally failed to heed Kenyatta's wishes. On the day after the meeting, the president moved against GEMA and supported the Njonjo warning with a simple statement reported in the government press: "The Government reiterated its earlier statement by the Attorney General." With those words, Njonjo's warning acquired the presidential imprimatur it had lacked. Unity became the watchword. In a short speech Kenyatta gave a week later, the word *unity* appeared over thirty times. "I want to stress that what is vital in our nation is unity," he told a crowd at Uhuru Park in Nairobi. "Unity has more value than anything else." [10]

Again the Family had failed in its effort to use GEMA as a vehicle for guaranteeing continued influence. The bid to place the party under the control of Family members in the government collapsed in the face of division between members of the Kikuyu elite and Kenyatta's own disapproval of the organization's disproportionate claims. The continued strength of other groups from food-exporting regions of the country within the Office of the President may also have been influential. The western regions of Kenya and the north central part of the Rift Valley produced substantial quantities of maize. Dissatisfaction in those areas could easily cause problems with the country's food supply.

GEMA's prominent role signaled the beginning of a new era in Kenyan politics, in which the effects of the single-party state on civil society became increasingly apparent. Absent ability to convene even small-group political discussions without a license, politicians looked to the reinvigoration of cultural organizations, principally welfare societies, as vehicles for participation and communication. GEMA's flamboyance would rapidly draw other ethnic welfare associations into politics, but the root cause of the sudden proliferation of such societies in the mid 1970s was much deeper. Restrictions on political association between citizens with common economic interests forced those interests to adopt new guises where they could do so. Because most of the country's commercial elite hailed from Central Province, GEMA could claim to act as an organization bent on cultural preservation, while at the same time advancing a distinct set of economic interests. The extent of GEMA's avowed ambitions led other groups to revive the welfare associations that had lain dormant since the colonial period. The pressures these groups generated would shortly bring about the demise of the old KANU nationalism GEMA favored and the rise of KADU-style federalism within the KANU shell.

The changes would also make the Family's political ambitions much more difficult to realize as well. Once parliamentary groupings began to lose their corporate character and rise and fall on their ability to assemble the ad hoc support of welfare associations, it became much more difficult to mount a sustained bid for control of the Office of the President, or the state. Those difficulties made themselves felt in the second event of the transition period—the abortive elections for national posts in KANU.

ETHNIC ARITHMETIC
AND THE PARTY ELECTIONS OF 1977

The year 1977 assured a larger role for ad hoc distributional coalitions in Kenya and sealed the fate of efforts to constitute sustained movements for policy change or reform, even on behalf of a particular set of economic interests, such as those of the Family. Both factional groupings learned firsthand the difficulties of trying to secure the support of party delegates or members of Parliament who had little incentive to cut long-term deals or participate in logrolling that depended on the future reward of concessions. Those with votes traded these to whomever offered the highest price in the days leading up to the balloting, without regard for previous commitments made. There was no reason to do otherwise. Without clear platforms and enduring organizations behind them, faction leaders had no means with which to guarantee either future returns or future sanctions.

GEMA proved tenacious. Having failed in their bid to change the constitution, Mungai, Kimani, Gichuru, and company did not retreat but instead changed strategies. The Kiambu group still believed it could take power from Moi. Some of the spokesmen alleged that Oloitipitip's petition, with its 98 signatures, was not an accurate reflection of sentiment within the Assembly. The members had not understood the statement, and some were coerced into affixing their names the GEMA leaders argued. Mungai may have believed that if he could challenge Moi in an electoral battle, the votes, when cast, would show the old KANU faction victorious.

The prospect of KANU national elections in 1977, the first party elections since 1966, handily offered the Mungai group another way to pursue state power. Electing a slate to the top party positions would enable Mungai to use the party organization, such as it was, to ensure the continued influence of the Family. Although the provincial administration would still maintain some control through its power to license party meetings, a monopoly of the senior party posts would provide the group with a soapbox and ability to initiate clearance of candidates or disciplinary action. Furthermore, because, by law, the president and vice president had to be members of a registered political party, capture of the top party positions would theoretically give GEMA the power to remove the president or vice president.

The contest between the Mungai and Moi factions was waged so openly that as early as January 1977, the *Weekly Review* published maps documenting the progress of each candidate in winning district-level support. The Luo areas received early attention from both camps, with Mungai continuing to pursue a revitalization of the original KANU alliance and Moi seeking to prevent consolidation of the Nyanza vote, by playing on existing divisions in the Luo community. Both men embarked on harambee fund-raising tours of Nyanza in February.

In the month before the elections, the vice president and his backers moved swiftly to build a coalition that would simultaneously capitalize on existing ties in western Kenya and draw attention to Mungai's reliance on a GEMA- or Kiambu-dominated network—forcing Kenyatta's nephew to scramble to include representatives of other groups and expend energy forging alliances he did not have and might not secure in time for the polls. The Moi group had proposed that Minister for Finance Mwai Kibaki, previously unassociated with either camp, run for the national party chairmanship. Although Kikuyu, Kibaki was a technocrat and lacked a strong base in Central Province. His candidacy was acceptable to many Central Province residents left out of the Family network and was therefore useful in undercutting accusations that Moi had blocked the Kikuyu from access to the state.

Packaging a slate was no easy matter, however, as both groups would learn from the troubles they encountered. There were eight party posts under contention: chairman and vice chairman, secretary general and assistant secretary general, organizing secretary and assistant organizing secretary, treasurer and assistant treasurer. The position of party president was not seriously at issue; Kenyatta's authority went unquestioned. The vice presidency was a more complicated matter, inasmuch as vice presidency of the party was generally equated with vice presidency of the republic. The winner of the position would most likely succeed Kenyatta.

The new importance of ethnic welfare societies in Kenyan political life created problems for faction leaders. The existence of eight party posts made comprehensive provincial representation a possibility; Kenya had eight provinces. There were too few seats, however, to permit inclusion of all of the newly organized ethnic groups. Coalition leaders faced a two-part challenge. First, they had to seek cooperation between different communities within the same province. Second, they had to figure out how to prevent defections. In the actual election, posts would be voted for sequentially. Thus, it would be possible for the delegates of a province to lose an intended spot early in the voting and undermine the rest of the slate by switching votes to a candidate from the same province but from a different coalition. The brokers of any slate had to win agreement from delegates to vote as promised or the entire strategy would fail.

Both groups encountered problems in winning enduring support. Swapping of allegiances took place so often in the first weeks that the *Weekly Review* began to speculate that the groupings had disappeared altogether. The protracted negotiations that went on within the Moi coalition provided an example of the difficulties. At first, it appeared that no post would be found for the Akamba, who then insisted on running a candidate against the Masai leader Stanley Oloitipitip, a stalwart Moi supporter, and that the main Luo supporters, William Odongo Omamo and David Okiki Amayo, wanted the position of secretary general, a post earmarked for the incumbent, Robert Matano, a coastal politician and Moi ally. Omamo and Amayo switched their candidacies to the post of treasurer for a time, but that position had just tentatively been allocated to Ngala Mwendwa, the Akamba candidate for whom Oloitipitip had stepped aside in return for the promise of a cabinet appointment. To improve their bargaining positions, delegates could simply hint that they would throw their votes behind the GEMA-backed candidate for secretary general instead of Matano.[11]

In an effort to reduce the time and costs of negotiating a slate, the Moi group convened two meetings, one in Mombasa and one in Nairobi. The Mombasa group was supposed to choose the candidates for the top three posts, which it did, proposing Kibaki as chairman. The Nairobi meeting, whose members became known as the "Kamukunji Group," selected the remaining candidates. Substantial sums of money were rumored to have changed hands during the course of the two meetings, with one source reporting that the Kamukunji group alone had spent almost KSh. 15 million.[12]

In the meantime, the Mungai slate was shaping up, with the Kalenjin MP Taita Toweett to challenge Moi for the vice presidency, Luhya leader Masinde Muliro pitted against Robert Matano for the post of secretary general, and the Masai John Keen, an Oloitipitip rival, nominated for organizing secretary. Nyanza Province Odinga allies received the nominations for treasurer and assistant secretary general. The chairmanship was left to Central Province, as it was in the Moi coalition. Just prior to the election, the slate still had no room for Paul Ngei, an old ally—or for any candidate from the Akamba areas of Eastern Province.

The last-minute scramble was for nought, however. On April 2, the day before the polls, the elections were called off. The constantly shifting allegiances had wrought havoc in the election process and threatened extended court battles over the use of money to purchase support. No outcome was secure from legal challenge, and the existing leadership, working with the State House, canceled the event.

The succeeding months would show just how much the character of the Kenyan political community was changing. Ethnic welfare associations proliferated and grew in strength. The mobilization of the Luo Union in response to GEMA's challenge and the capture of the organization first by Odinga and then by Isaac Omolo Okero showed the growing importance of ethnic welfare societies as political bases at a time when members of Parliament still recalled the treatment J.M. had received when he attempted to forge a broadly based producers' coalition. Kenyans all over the country began to ask whether they, too, might be well served by stronger societies. Luhya leaders publicly queried the "absence of a recognised, acceptable, and respected pressure group."[13] In November 1976, in the aftermath of the Change-the-Constitution bid, Oloitipitip had announced plans to revive the Masai United

Front.[14] The Central Province provincial commissioner, Simeon Ny-achae, subsequently sparked controversy when he urged students from his home area, Kisii, to form a new Abagusii Union.[15] Mulu Mutisya confronted Paul Ngei over the creation of the New Akamba Union.

Having exhausted two options for achieving dominance, GEMA turned to a third. If the party posts could not be secured, then it might be possible to challenge Moi's power in Parliament. A shift in parliamentary seats or alignments might so undermine Moi's base of power that Kenyatta would reshuffle the cabinet. Alternatively, if Kenyatta died, then it might be possible to dislodge Moi by a vote of no confidence.

The major site of activity throughout the remainder of 1977 and 1978 was Nyanza, where both factions continued to seek allies. During the last week of April 1977, a large group of Luo leaders met at Oyugis and resolved, "that for the foreseeable future, Odinga would remain the reference point for political developments among the Luo." The Oyugis Declaration, the document signed at the meeting, called for cooperation with GEMA, a step that would bring greater power to an increasingly divided and peripheral community. In Achieng Oneko's words, the declaration created "an alliance between GEMA and the Luo Union."[16] By June, leaders of the earlier Change-the-Constitution movement began to make regular appearances and contributions at harambee meetings in Bondo, Odinga's stronghold.[17]

To deliver on its commitments, the Odinga faction had to strengthen and extend its hold on the Luo community, rejuvenating the three million-member Luo Union as a vehicle for marshaling electoral support. The reform of the organization, the choice of a "leader of the Luo people," and projection of a unified community image became major news items for the next year and a half.

To strengthen the Luo Union so that it could become "as active as GEMA"[18] was not necessarily to create a Luo Union allied with GEMA or controlled by Odinga, as Mungai and the former KPU leaders were to discover, however. Odinga had competition for leadership of the Luo in the person of his local rival, William Odongo Omamo, whom the Moi coalition had carefully cultivated, and in Isaac Omolo Okero, another Luo politician. Omamo had previously tried to maintain a non-aligned status. In 1977, he broke with that position. Asked what kind of leader the Luo sought, Omamo replied, "We are looking for the kind of leader who does not behave like the legendary banian tree which grows to be a great tree with branches and sub-branches, twigs and plenty of leaves but allows nothing to grow under it." [19] Odinga's presence, he argued, left no room for the range of views so characteristic of the outspoken members of the Luo community. A leader of the Luo would have to be someone who could tolerate many different types of leaders within the various branches and sub-branches of the Luo Union.

Although the GEMA group sought closer ties with Odinga, the Kenyatta State House perceived an Odinga-led Luo community or a possible GEMA–Luo Union alliance as potentially troublesome. It moved to discourage the agreement then under negotiation. The Mungai slate's Luo candidate for KANU assistant secretary general, George Anyona, was detained in May, and at the end of the year, Odinga was denied permission to attend harambee meetings on the grounds that the Luo Union had been accused of trying to raise KSh. 20 million to back Luo candidates in general and local elections.[20]

By a series of maneuvers over the next several months, the government sought to force the Luo Union to detach itself from the Odinga camp and, indeed, to define its activity in provincial rather than ethnic terms. In March 1978, Kenyatta agreed to meet with a delegation led by the Luo Union leader Paul Mbuya. Ngengi Muigai, the president's nephew and a GEMA backer, allegedly arranged the meeting. By the time the audience took place, however, it was no longer a Luo Union affair. Neither Odinga nor Oneko were present, and the function was billed as a Nyanza gathering, including residents of Kisii District, an ecologically and ethnically distinct section of the province. Almost 250,000 walked through the gates of State House Nakuru on the appointed day, led, not by Mbuya, but by the Nyanza provincial commissioner, Isaya Cheluget, a Kalenjin and a sharp critic of the Luo Union, which he had long considered a political organization in the guise of a welfare society.[21] No Luo Union officials spoke, and Mbuya stood on the sidelines, watching.

The effort to take control away from the Odinga faction continued in May and June 1978, through a series of offensives to discourage the Luo from seeking a single leader. "Any attempt to find a super Luo leader has no place in Kenya," Omolo Okero announced. "In any event there is no provision in the Republican constitution for tribal leaders." The Okero group was determined to project the area's parliamentary representatives as the community's only legitimate spokesmen.[22]

On June 30, 1978, William Odongo Omamo, then a nominated MP, moved into the Luo Union headquarters and took control. At a Nairobi press conference, Omamo argued "that the move to suspend union office bearers had been directed by ten branches of the Luo Union after a unanimous decision made at a special general meeting in Kisumu."[23] Mbuya retaliated with the charge that of the 17 people allegedly present at Kisumu, only one was a member of the Luo Union. Although the members of the Luo community were split in their evaluations of the takeover, little was heard from the former union leaders during succeeding weeks, and in an effort to quell dissent, the government inaugurated two large irrigation schemes, one in Kano and the other in the Yala swamp in Bondo, where 10,000 people would be settled on reclaimed land at a cost of over KSh. 1 billion.[24]

The strengthening and proliferation of welfare societies undercut the GEMA nationalist strategy by establishing pressure groups capable of lobbying effectively for group-based concepts of equity instead of settling for a Kikuyu-dominated meritocracy. It was, in some respects, a boon for the Moi coalition. It required GEMA to reveal itself as an ethnic pressure group along with other such groups, abandoning its claims to represent Kenya as a whole.

From the government's perspective, there were drawbacks as well. What if, as in the case of GEMA, the societies fell under the principal control of one of two national coalitions? As powerful instruments for generating resources, the societies could potentially compete with the State House as a base for a national patron. To work, a system of bargained exchange required involvement of multiple parties and fluid alliances. If one group acquired control of local machines, it could block participation of contenders with political bases in other coalitions. This concern was especially strong among senior members of the new government, who did not desire to rid the country of machine organization but did worry about the extent to which control of existing organizations lay in the hands of a potentially strong opposition. The first line of attack was to redefine the memberships of the organizations—especially that of the Luo Union—and to diminish their power.

In January 1978, the government convened a meeting at the Kenya Institute for Administration (KIA) entitled "The Kenya We Want," and high on the list of issues was a review of the role of "tribal organizations." The transformation of the Luo Union audience at State House Nakuru into a Nyanza delegation was partly a response to the agenda set at the KIA conference. GEMA received similar treatment, its scheduled meeting with the president in April being postponed and finally downgraded. Some members of Parliament urged the State House to do away with delegations backed by welfare societies altogether. Merit as the principal criterion for distribution again began to enter public discourse, this time through Moi associates seeking to contain interest-group pressures. Isaac Omolo Okero remarked, for example:

> When we had *uhuru* we came together on the basis of tribal communities. We cannot approach politics in this country the way we did in 1963. The country has changed. Those of us who are of a slightly younger generation are now interested in merit, ability, and the people who can deliver what the electorate want, not merely those who want to see themselves as tribal leaders or spokesmen. We, as leaders, have got to offer our people more than just the claim to tribal loyalty or leadership. It is a different kind of Kenya and it calls for a more national approach to issues rather than what in the past was adequate.[25]

DISTRIBUTIONAL COALITIONS
AND THE 1979 GENERAL ELECTION

The death of President Jomo Kenyatta in August 1978 created a further opportunity to renegotiate the distribution of access. During the ninety-day period after Kenyatta's death, the country prepared for elections. In the interim, Moi was designated acting president by the cabinet. Although the Moi coalition had learned much about the management of ad hoc alliances in the interim, the difficulties of creating a solid electoral base were apparent—and would have been even more so in the absence of patronage to purchase loyalty.

Some of the irregularities the Change-the-Constitution group had envisioned earlier materialized quickly. Only the London *Daily Telegraph* printed the accurate rules for carrying out the transition. Before the local papers could do so, the attorney general announced a slightly different set of arrangements. The government imposed a ban on political meetings between late August and December, the period in which the country would fill the presidential slot. Moreover, the Moi faction quickly seized control of the KANU headquarters and used its influence in the executive committee to limit debate about election sequences and procedures. The party's supreme bodies, the All-Delegates Conference and the National Governing Council, never met.

Njoroge Mungai and his Family supporters proved unable to parry these measures in a sophisticated way. Court challenges were not part of the Mungai group's tactical lexicon. Indeed, some former Family members received an object lesson in the difficulties of containing and reversing encroachment on political space, including some of the same kinds of measures they had used to limit the influence of others in earlier years.

Ethnic welfare societies again provided one of the few available avenues for activity, and their spokesmen quickly voiced their claims. A *Weekly Review* headline summarized parliamentary debates with the words "Equity Issue: Tribalism Becoming a Major Issue in Post-Kenyatta Era."[26] Pressure for redistribution of government and parastatal positions was especially intense, and the State House responded quickly, expanding the size of the cabinet and reshuffling civil service personnel. The creation of new parastatal corporations in the wake of the 1977 collapse of the East African Community conveniently expanded the number of such jobs.

The growth in the number and size of competing welfare associations accelerated as GEMA once again marshaled its forces in a bid to maintain Family influence. Increasing equity meant reducing the proportion of funds spent on development activities in Central Province at a time when recession was limiting growth in the government budget and defense expenditures were taking up an increasingly large share of what was available.[27] The response of those Family members who stood to lose was to try again, cautiously, to construct a coalition for the general elections slated for late October. This time, wary of government reaction, GEMA chose not to push its views openly, however. In September President Moi warned that the police had started to monitor night meetings in Central Province and chastised those who engaged in subversive activities.[28] And after the parliamentary debate about equity in allocation of public revenues, the new president traveled to Nyeri and reminded a gathering there that "traditionally in Africa when a family slaughtered a cow, they did not eat all of it by themselves. They shared with their neighbours, for without their neighbours' vigilance against the cattle rustlers and wild animals like leopards, the owners of the cow may not have managed to keep it."[29]

Again, as in 1977, the Moi-Kibaki group employed a provincial strategy and "ethnic arithmetic" with great success. Replying to his fellow Kikuyu who criticized the approach as an invitation to tribalism, Kibaki commented:

These unfortunately are the realities of Kenya politics. Obviously we would love to have the best man voted into the job irrespective of where he comes from. But in a plural society, talent alone cannot be the determining factor. People feel that equitable representation is just as important in a democratic society. So we thought that we should have every province represented in the national executive of the ruling party. It is only fair.[30]

The Kibaki group had learned several organizational lessons from its previous efforts. In 1977, the Kamukunji leaders had expended substantial time and energy trying to win consensus among the delegates from a province on the choice of an appropriate representative. In many cases, ethnic groups in multi-ethnic provinces put up their own candidates, upon finding that the Kamukunji's choice hailed from a different background. In other cases, the agreement failed to endure even among delegates from the ethnic group represented, the multiplicity of Luo candidates in 1977 being a case in point. In 1978, the Kibaki group decided that the leadership would not try to negotiate with each delegation directly but would ask that the delegations themselves arrive at a consensus by October 28, and that they would agree not to put up anyone else for other national posts.[31] The national-level leaders would decide which provinces would receive which seat. Then a Moi ally in each area would campaign for support of the strategy among local delegates and try to obtain agreement on the particular candidate all Kibaki-aligned delegates would support.

In this political environment, the eventual success of the Moi-Kibaki slate in the 1979 general elections depended on (1) willingness to expend the last-minute energy necessary to keep delegates from defecting to the faction that offered the greatest concessions in the hours before balloting, and (2) expenditure of harambee resources in Central Province to reassure supporters there. To ensure that the agreements worked out at the provincial level would hold, Kibaki organized a group of "envoys" or brokers to assist in ascertaining levels of support and to bargain with uncommitted sub-branch delegates. Commenting on the mechanics behind the strategy, the vice president said:

> The main problem is not so much getting every delegation to support you. The important thing is to go for a number of major blocks, and then work gradually for smaller units. There are areas where, of course, one cannot be terribly sure. Sometimes you get a pledge from a branch chairman and you have to do your own canvassing with the delegates at the sub-branch levels. But for some other branches—people from Taita, for example—once you have got a pledge from the chairman, you can be sure that they will deliver the votes of their different delegates.[32]

The provincial strategists had learned that to prevent defections it was important to lobby supporters right up to the last minute. This time, delegates arrived in Nairobi early and distributed themselves by province among the city's hotels, Central Province commandeering the Jacaranda, a favorite haunt of the Kikuyu political elite. Kibaki and his "brokers," G. G. Kariuki and Stanley Oloitipitip, crisscrossed the town, consolidating their bases of support in the days and nights before the vote. Oloitipitip composed a "pink card" listing the names of those on the Kibaki slate under the heading "Kenya has decided that the following leaders should be elected today 28/10/78" and circulated copies among delegates and members of Parliament.[33] The reaction was not entirely favorable; those opposed to the slate and many of those who supported Kibaki claimed that the naive might assume that the wording implied government indications of the proper way to vote. Whether within the rules or not, the card may have proved an effective reminder to supporters. The Kibaki slate was elected handily.

That Kibaki was able to capture a majority of Central Province delegates was in part a function of the substantial harambee contributions Moi and senior officials poured into the area, both to win support for their candidate and to compensate the Kikuyu politicians for the drubbing they were receiving in Parliament. Harambee from the president and senior officials to Central Province reached an all-time high, with the province taking 84.8 percent of all contributions made that year.

The success of the Kibaki group may also have owed something to the new president's halt on all land allocation. The Kiambu group was well situated to buy and distribute land in its effort to attract support. Kahika Kimani's Ngwataniro companies had already showed themselves powerful brokers in Nakuru. Moi put an end to Kimani's Ngwataniro base and to the use of land as a form of side payment by suspending allocations. The reason given was the need to revise guidelines given to the district land control boards to ensure that transfers of farmland did not produce excessive concentration of ownership and to reduce speculation.

KANU AT THE END OF THE TRANSITION PERIOD

By the end of the transition period in 1980, fragmentation among the KANU parliamentarians increased, putting at risk the ability of members of Parliament to defend their political space from further encroachment. The blocs that Kibaki and Mungai organized for the 1979 general elections were subject to last-minute defections, in large part for one of the reasons outlined in chapter 1. Absent a credible threat to defect to an opposition party, a candidate who debates a party position or takes issue with the most powerful members of the party is likely to find that access to patronage diminishes or that he or she faces sanctions, including possible expulsion from politics. The example of J.M. was ample illustration for many politicians, who began to eschew pledges of allegiance to any one group. Few MPs were willing to accept the costs and risks that sustaining a coherent policy group entailed. Ad hoc coalitions or factions were preferable in this context. Kibaki's frustration with the amount and kind of bargaining involved was symptomatic of these changes.

Factional division increased, too, because the "glue" that had held some of the more enduring blocs together, patronage, suddenly became less readily available. With Moi now president and the Moi-Kibaki slate in control, the patronage and access available to Family members diminished sharply.[34] The electoral success of the Family changed accordingly. The former GEMA leader and Nakuru politician Kahika Kimani lost his parliamentary seat to Koigi wa Wamwere, a detainee and strong populist. A prominent J.M. supporter, Mark Mwithaga, the opponent of the Kimani faction in Nakuru Town, regained his parliamentary seat, while another populist politician who had once worked with Mwithaga as part of the Central Rift Labour Party won in Nakuru East.

Further, in the wake of the restrictions imposed during the Rift Valley struggle, the replacement of the two main cross-regional groupings within KANU by a plethora of rejuvenated ethnic welfare societies made it increasingly difficult to constitute stable bases for policy change or for institutional reform. Fragmentation did not enhance the representation of minority points of view. Instead, it created incentives for political elites to "free ride" on the lobbying efforts of faction leaders and to defect to the faction that offered the most at any given moment. These conditions made it extremely difficult for any one group to forge an organization that could support sustained action.

The transition period also witnessed a change in the allocation of functions between KANU and the executive. For the first time, at the direction of the State House the provincial administration involved itself in the internal affairs of KANU. Hesitatingly at first, provincial commissioners took responsibility for reviewing and clearing party branch meetings and overseeing the selection of speakers. In the first years of the Moi government, the administration would take on even larger roles, eventually obscuring the lines of division between the structures of representation and the structures for maintaining public order. As the party came increasingly under State House control, the ability of members of the political elite to seek institutional reform and to restore their political space to its former dimensions would diminish further.

CHAPTER FIVE

From "Harambee!" to "Nyayo!" 1980-1985

Between 1980 and 1985, the kinds of strategies used to manage competing claims on resources and roles shifted dramatically. There could be no better summary of this change than the difference between the slogans employed by Kenyatta on the one hand and Moi on the other. The celebrated cry of "Harambee!" with which Kenyatta concluded his speeches had encapsulated the late president's approach to politics. At one level harambee bespoke a preference for local-level community action to achieve collective benefits or "development." At another level it embodied a strategy of bargained exchange; Kenyans could "pull together" by compromise—by sacrificing rewards or labor in the knowledge that at some other time or through private means the contribution would be reciprocated—and by refusal to enshrine the interests of one group above all others in the party, or, indeed, in the cabinet. Moi introduced a different slogan and a different conception of appropriate political strategy. "Nyayo!" ("Follow in the footsteps") took the place of "Harambee!" Although the slogan was intended to convey respect for Kenyatta and highlight the need to pursue the course the first president had set for the country, *nyayo* acquired a second interpretation: do what the Office of the President tells you to do. Politics as control began to take the place of politics as exchange.

In December 1978, Moi was hailed internationally when he released all of those held under Kenya's detention laws. The move seemed to herald a "new era of tolerance" in the view of Amnesty International and local observers alike. Although Kenyatta had emphasized that the country's human rights record was far better than that of its neighbors, Amnesty International had decried the detention of politicians associated with the Rift Valley opposition of 1972–75. Moi's action seemed a step toward greater pluralism and greater openness. But that assessment ignored the more likely significance of the release, which had the practical effect not only of demonstrating goodwill but also of reviving the careers of some potential allies against a Kiambu-based coalition.

What the international press did not remark, but the local press quietly noted, was that although the new president had released detainees, he had also reserved the ability to invoke the detention laws whenever he believed necessary, and, further, that the government's first move was to strengthen its control of the police and security forces. Moi shifted the portfolio of the Family member and Minister of State Mbiyu Koinange to Natural Resources, removing the Family from control of internal security and the affairs of the Office of the President. Moi's ally Stanley Oloitipitip took over the Ministry of Home Affairs, but the police force, traditionally part of Home Affairs, moved to the Office of the President. Police Commissioner Bernard Hinga was forced out on charges that his ranks lacked discipline and replaced by the former commander of the Government Services Unit (GSU), Kenya's paramilitary force. Several other senior officers in the police and security forces lost their jobs. The Rift Valley police commissioner, James Mungai, fled the country.[1] On several occasions in November, the government warned that it had started surveillance of subversive activities and that its agents had infiltrated the organizations responsible.[2] The final move of the year was to shuffle personnel in the top ranks of the military, promoting some of the highest-ranking officers and moving others out.

The measures were certainly not unusual, but in this case they presaged further-reaching changes. There were two main alternative strategies for preventing GEMA from gaining additional strength. One was to restrict association. Escalating the risks that political meetings would be discovered by using plainclothes police to monitor activity was one tactic within that strategy. Expanding the scope of licensing restrictions on meetings of any sort was another. The proscription of ethnic welfare societies in 1980 was the major component, however. Between July and December of that year, Moi secured the "voluntary" liquidation of the welfare societies that had proliferated and gained in strength during the 1970s.

The second option, which could be used in conjunction with the first, was to tie KANU more closely to the Office of the President and use it as an instrument for monitoring political splinter groups and controlling political association. Earlier, the Gikuyu, Embu, and Meru Association had sought to rejuvenate and strengthen KANU as a way of projecting Kiambu economic interests and securing the dominance of Family members over the distribution of public resources. During the Kenyatta era, GEMA had consistently failed in this objective. The 1980–85 period saw the Moi government begin to succeed where GEMA had not.

The relationship between KANU and the executive changed markedly as part of this shift. In 1982, the Moi government proposed a constitutional amendment to make Kenya a de jure single-party system. The changes won passage in the Assembly and went into effect during June and July of that year. By the mid 1980s, the party had tightened its disciplinary procedures and invoked rules that permitted the leadership to screen candidates for office and apply a loyalty test. The idea of establishing a party ideological institute and training center resurfaced. Subsequently, the division of functions between party and executive that had prevailed under Kenyatta altered significantly. Under Moi's leadership, KANU began to create youth wings to patrol the country, instill support for the party, and monitor dissent. The party thus acquired a more direct role in law enforcement. The provincial administration became much more active in helping party branches collect dues and membership fees, eventually assuming full responsibility for generating party revenues.[3] Beginning with the 1985 party elections, the Office of the President began to involve itself directly in the selection of the party leadership, arranging that its own candidates for top party offices would run unopposed.

Although not a system in which the party monopolized all association and assumed major powers of law enforcement, along the lines of the Mouvement populaire de la révolution (MPR) in Zaire or even the Convention People's Party in Kwame Nkrumah's Ghana, the Kenyan pattern of governance in the early 1980s was increasingly characterized by the fusion of party and state.[4] What captures the interest of the social scientist is why this transformation occurred in Kenya when it did and in the way it did. Assuming that most politicians, regardless of national origin, follow Plunkitt's adage, "I seen my opportunities and I took 'em," why did those who sought to use KANU as an instrument for controlling political opposition meet less resistance to their pursuit of opportunity than the Family and GEMA had a decade earlier? Why did

Kenyatta feel compelled to permit limited pluralism within the party and to eschew use of the party as a vehicle for controlling dissent, whereas Moi did not?

This chapter proposes an answer to that question. It suggests that although the country's population was becoming more stratified on the basis of wealth, "civil society" remained much the same as it had been earlier. That is, increasing differentials in income between the matajiri (the small group of extremely wealthy Kenyans) and new entrants into the labor market who were unable to find either jobs or land did not translate into changes in associational life. What did alter was the capacity to build enduring organizations to support platforms that focused *either* on broad issues that could be characterized as public goods or on the delivery of pork-barrel benefits for particular localities. It argues that the character of party-state relations altered as factional fragmentation made it increasingly difficult to mount sustained campaigns for national-level policy reform, including resistance to restriction of the political space permitted members of Parliament. The difficulties Kibaki and Mungai encountered in packaging electoral slates and preventing defections by delegates and candidates during the late 1970s became still more pronounced in the 1980s. Furthermore, the expanding powers of the administration to license meetings and associations undermined the use of harambee as a vehicle for constructing cross-regional and cross-ethnic coalitions. By the mid 1980s, it was no longer possible for candidates to venture into areas outside their constituencies with impunity or to hold harambee meetings without the express consent of the Office of the President. These measures heightened the problems associated with forging enduring bases of support for resistance to initiatives from the executive. The chapter outlines the changes that took place in the relationship between the party and the Office of the President and provincial administration during the first part of the 1980s. It then profiles the difficulties members of Parliament encountered in opposing the creation of a party-state in Kenya.

MOI'S ACCESSION TO THE PRESIDENCY

If Kenyatta had enjoyed a reputation as a conciliator before he became chief of state, Daniel arap Moi came to the presidency as a man whose qualities as a leader were largely unknown. Although Moi served as vice president for twelve years, the Kalenjin leader and former KADU chairman had acted primarily as Kenyatta's agent in building bridges between the country's different cultural communities and had had little opportunity, perhaps little inclination, to articulate his own views. He was the nephew of Senior Chief Kiplabat of Baringo and had attended the African Inland Mission school at Karbatonjo, but he had fewer advantages than a chief's relative usually did. His own father had died when Moi was only four. His mother's household was distant from the school he attended, and the family was not well-off. Eventually, he trained as a teacher, partly under the tutelage of the nationalist leader C. M. G. Argwings-Kodhek. Finally, he took up a post as a teacher at the Government African School at Tambach.[5] His early career was marked by a rapid rise through a series of educational posts. He became headmaster at the Kabarnet Intermediate School in 1948, assistant principal at the Tambach Teacher Training College in 1949, and headmaster of the Government African School in Kapsabet from 1954 through 1957.[6]

Moi's first experience in politics came in 1955, when he was appointed to replace the Rift Valley District Council's regional representative to the national Legislative Council, who had decided to step down. He remained as one of seven African members of the national Parliament in 1957. Moi then served as one of the delegates to the Lancaster House independence talks, where he allied himself with KANU. At the time, Odinga described him as "influenced by the missions, overawed by settler power and making a slow adjustment to political trends and the need to make independent judgement."[7] By contrast with the flamboyant Odinga style, however, the same might have been said about most Kenyan politicians. Along with several other politicians, Moi left KANU to form the Kenya African Democratic Union, headed by Ronald Ngala. Concerned that a Kikuyu-Luo coalition had come to dominate, he joined forces with other politicians to create a party that supported a federal system of government in the independence discussions and received a warm reception from some members of the British community, who approved the presentation of this alternative point of view.

Moi held multiple cabinet positions, first as a KADU member, then as a KANU member. In the interim period 1961–63, he served as a minister in Kenyatta's coalition government. Kenyatta appointed him minister of education in 1961, then moved him to the Ministry of Local Government in 1962. Late in 1964, Moi joined other leaders of KADU and agreed to shift his allegiances to KANU. Thus, in the first independence government, Moi received an extremely important portfolio: Kenyatta appointed him his minister for home affairs, a post that had been expected to go to Oginga Odinga, whom Kenyatta designated vice president but gave only limited powers. Moi retained this portfolio even after he became a vice president in 1967, although Mbiyu Koinange long held the ultimate say in the management of the police force, which was part of the ministry.

As minister for home affairs, Moi supervised the police and some of the security forces. At the time, the police outnumbered Kenya's defense forces and played many of the same security roles as the military. Home Affairs oversaw not only regular police activities but also the application of the Public Security Act, which made legal preventive detention of political dissidents perceived to threaten the security of the country. Indeed, no doubt at Kenyatta's direction, it was Moi who oversaw the detention of the eight leaders of the Kenya People's Union. He explained his actions on the grounds that "any government worth its salt must put the preservation of public security above the convenience of a handful of persons who are doing their utmost to undermine it."[8] In spite of this role, Moi appears to have achieved substantial personal popularity with other politicians and with constituents.

What other political lessons Moi acquired from his experience in office are unclear. In his early experiences as an elected representative, Moi developed ties with the politicians from the communities bordering Central Province. These solidarities came largely from a shared interest in expanding employment opportunities in the regions. The neighboring Luhya community and the Kamba community suffered from comparatively high population densities and low earnings levels during the colonial period. Moi joined with the representatives of these areas in the Legislative Council to push for a faster, more comprehensive response to the problem of unemployment.[9] Moi's later "populist" image derived in part from these early stances, in part from Moi's harboring of five Mau Mau rebels on his farm for several weeks of the Emergency (although Moi never articulated a strong nationalist position himself), and from elevation of some former Mau Mau to government positions during the early years of his presidency.

Moi's limited experience in managing the divisions within KANU in post-independence Kenya consisted chiefly in his having run the 1966 conference of party delegates at Limuru that resulted in the withdrawal of the radical faction (see p. 58 above). It was said that Moi had hand-picked some of the delegates to the conference to ensure this outcome. In general, in his dealings with the party and with political associations, Kenyatta relied much more heavily on Tom Mboya both to rout KPU sympathizers from KANU's ranks and then to hold the party together.

After Mboya's death, he carried these negotiations forward himself. In consequence, Moi had relatively little opportunity to learn to manage factional division through bargaining. Indeed, there is some evidence to suggest that he disliked the internal party debates characteristic of KANU in its early years. Odinga recorded in his memoirs that when Moi met Kenyatta while Kenyatta was still in prison at Lodwar, Moi refused to back down from his support of KADU on the grounds that "within KANU there were personality clashes and lack of discipline; KANU had to try to clean up its house before it could expect unity with other groups." [10]

Moi's speeches reflect a continued dislike of debate. In Kenya, as in much of sub-Saharan Africa, the political speech has a ritualized form and is not a good indicator of the actions a leader is likely to pursue. Which kinds of subjects are perceived to require ritual acknowledgment can provide useful clues to a leader's broad attitudes, however. Moi's public utterances are filled with constant allusions to the needs of those less well-off, to his willingness to use a strong hand against politicians who undermine national unity, and to the nyayo "doctrine" of "peace, love, and unity." The populist themes are probably both genuinely felt and politically useful; they remind the public of the need to pay attention to the needs of those whose interests stand most opposed to the disproportionately Kikuyu matajiri. Mixed with these are strong remonstrations against political debate—statements that draw no distinctions between policy debate and "rumor-mongering." For example, in his opening remarks to the KANU Delegates' Conference of April 1980, Moi said:

> This particular conference is an indication of my determination to ensure that the KANU party gives guidance to all the institutions in our republic. . . . You have . . . every right to ask any questions you wish to ask not only on party matters but also on government affairs. But be as positive as possible in your contribution. As a nation . . . we have no time for idle talk or debates. [11]

The threat of police force against those who cross the line between acceptable and unacceptable speech is also a constant theme in Moi's public talks. "I shall not hesitate to take disciplinary action against those Party members of parliament . . . should I find them working against the interest of our nation and our people," Moi reminded the delegates at the 1980 KANU conference. [12]

In his first months in office, Moi won a reputation as a "populist," an advocate of those less well-off. He spoke out often on behalf of the

"little people," the wananchi, and released twenty-six political detainees who were in jail at the end of Kenyatta's presidency, most of them
spokesmen for the interests of the "dispossessed." (Ngugi wa Thiong'o
was among them.) Later he elevated several local politicians who were
longtime opponents of elites allied with the Family or the old KANU A.
These measures won the president some popular support among those
who saw these efforts as attacks on privilege.

These steps were also convenient, however. They gave greater latitude to politicians whose interests were quite opposed to those of the
Kiambu matajiri class. As such, they were part of Moi's efforts to secure
a base of political support at a time when many of the leaders of the civil
service and private commerce were arrayed behind Njoroge Mungai,
the leader of the "shadow cabinet" Moi had defeated during the
Change-the-Constitution Movement. In his Jamhuri Day speech, Moi
announced the release of the detainees, but his next words were: "All
those who have been in detention are now . . . at their homes. However,
I want to warn everyone that my government will not hesitate in taking
immediate and firm action against anyone whose activities threaten our
peace, unity and stability." Three days later, he rushed a bill through
Parliament granting him emergency powers in peacetime.[13]

Moi also sought to secure his base by using the part of the civil service he knew best, the police, to wage an assault against corruption in
the upper reaches of the ministries, undermining the patronage networks of the Kiambu elite who were participants in these. He first
moved to clean up the police, making its leadership more responsive to
his authority. The commissioner, Bernard Hinga, and many senior officers tendered their resignations when the new attorney general, Charles
Njonjo, presented charges of corruption against them. Moi and Njonjo
then turned to the ministries. In a BBC interview, Njonjo explained that
the changes were part of an effort to streamline the lines of command
within the government.[14]

FACTION AND THE PROSCRIPTION
OF ETHNIC WELFARE SOCIETIES

The success of the Njonjo-Kibaki coalition-building efforts in the 1979
elections led not to consolidation of political groupings but to new fragmentation. As René Lemarchand has observed, in authoritarian systems, factions form around those believed to have access to central
decision-making authority and re-form as the fortunes of senior officials

change.[15] The two brokers of the Moi coalition, Charles Njonjo and Mwai Kibaki, were each believed to hold substantial influence with the new president, and politicians clustered around them, forming highly unstable, ad hoc "political splinter groups." In March 1980, public confrontation flared over the flourishing growth of these divisions. One member of Parliament stirred anxiety by saying that Central Province people were in the vanguard of all of the groups.[16] But the president retaliated, saying that he would take disciplinary action against any civil servant, member of Parliament, or party official who sowed disunity.

The president's own actions aggravated fragmentation, however. For a Kenyan head of state from a less powerful community, one of the imperatives for securing authority was to obtain the support of the Kikuyu entrepreneurs, who controlled key parts of the economy, while making sure that Kikuyu in the cabinet were never themselves allowed to build clienteles enabling them to assume power smoothly and quickly in the event of the president's death. It was therefore important that Mwai Kibaki not be allowed to amass legitimacy within the Kikuyu business elite and with other key groups; if Kibaki, the vice president and minister for finance, developed a strong rapport with the Kiambu elite, sponsoring attempts to remove President Moi would be all too attractive to segments of the Central Province community. From Moi's perspective, it was necessary to ensure that Kibaki never won access to such power and that he faced competition for legitimacy as a Kikuyu spokesman from other ministers not in the line of succession.

To carry out this objective, the president began to assemble a number of coalitions, each headed by a competing Central Province politician but including MPs from other regions as well—the better to challenge Kibaki's own "brokered" coalition. These groups not only factionalized support for senior officials such as Kibaki; they also, by their composition, made it difficult for any one Central Province politician to build a solid national base. Indeed, in one of the year's most controversial parliamentary exchanges, Mrs. Wambui Otieno, a Nairobi KANU delegate, accused the government of originating and spreading rumors of political division, thereby encouraging the mushrooming of splinter groups.[17]

Three factions emerged in opposition to the Kibaki group, led respectively by Waweru Kanja (formerly one of J.M.'s allies), by Charles Njonjo, and by the GEMA leader Njenga Karume. Waweru Kanja joined forces with the "Nakuru radicals," the populist successors to

J.M., and with several politicians from the Coast to constitute the most populous of the three factions.[18] The Kanja group sought renewed allocation of public lands to the burgeoning community of squatters in central Kenya and the Rift. On behalf of those who had fought in the Mau Mau rebellion, Kanja pursued claims to land formerly held by white settlers. The Nyeri MP received sharp censure from the president for his stance, however. Recalling the early 1970s, the members of the group realized that they had to guarantee their ability to meet and discuss these issues in public, and the defense of political space assumed a position at the top of their agenda. Conforming to the model established by J.M. and John Marie Seroney, the Nakuru coalition leader Koigi wa Wamwere and others condemned detention without trial. They congratulated Moi for releasing detainees upon his rise to the presidency in 1978, but made a plea for abolition of the detention laws, still on the books and again under consideration. "All the sciences, democracy, and inventions are the result of critical minds," Wamwere said, adding that people should not be punished for being outspoken.[19] "Those who express any views against the leadership should not be viewed as enemies of the country. Instead, they should, all the time, despite the different opinions they express, be considered legitimate citizens of this country and be accorded all their legitimate rights." Subsequently, supporters from other regions supported Wamwere's plea for tolerance.[20]

The movement was short-lived. In his bid to articulate economic demands, Kanja named two high government officials, Charles Njonjo and Ignatius Nderi, as the men behind the detentions of the 1970s and portrayed the two as enemies of the dispossessed. In November 1980, only a few months after the group's formation, the State House relieved Kanja of his post as assistant minister for local government because of his accusations and dealt a definitive blow to the power of the group. Koigi wa Wamwere was later detained.

One of the men against whom Kanja had leveled his accusations, Charles Njonjo, led the second main faction. In April 1980, he quit his post as attorney general, allegedly because he had reached retirement age, and announced that he would run for Parliament in the Kikuyu constituency in Kiambu District, also the site of constituencies held by former "Family" members. The sitting MP, Amos Ng'ang'a, who had won a narrow victory the year before, stepped down in Njonjo's favor. Shortly thereafter, Ng'ang'a became chairman of the Tana River Authority, and the strongest of the candidates he had edged out in the November 1979 election received a prestigious job as chairman of the Kenya Ports Authority.

Speculation about Njonjo's intentions were rife. Reporters immediately hinted that the new MP wanted to create a prime ministerial system that would place the presidency in the hands of a KANU-selected leader.[21] The former attorney general prudently denied this, but rumors and speculation persisted. The *Weekly Review* commented:

> Njonjo's rise in active politics can only be at the expense of Vice-President Mwai Kibaki who comes from Nyeri and who has hitherto been regarded as the undisputed senior politician in Central Province. The issue is seen in some quarters not merely as a struggle for Central Province leadership but for the Number Two spot in the political structure of the country.[22]

Indeed, back in March, two Njonjo allies had accused Kibaki of distorting perceptions and encouraging people to think that a group of Kenyan politicians had their eyes on Kibaki's job and on the presidency. G. G. Kariuki, an ally of Njonjo's from Central Province who was assistant minister in the Office of the President with responsibility for internal security, told the public that the vice president was wrong to suggest that opposition had formed against him and against the president; there were no political groupings in the country. In a direct affront to Kibaki, Kariuki retorted: "We do not have to waste time talking about imaginary issues just because they are spoken of by the leaders of government business [the vice president] and his deputy."[23]

Protestations to the contrary, however, there was substantial evidence that Njonjo associates had assembled to wage war on Kibaki and those around him, and that the president had had a strong hand in Njonjo's elevation. The campaign took two forms. One component was to try to undercut the favor extended the vice president in some parts of Central Province by upstaging Kibaki in local fund-raising appearances. For example, in April 1980, the district commissioner in Murang'a agreed to license a harambee meeting at which the vice president would speak and raise funds for primary schools. A week before the scheduled event, the district commissioner refused an Njonjo ally, Joseph Kamotho, a license to sponsor a harambee gathering to raise funds for a local school on the grounds that he had submitted his request only two days in advance, whereas the law required fourteen days' notice, and that in combination with the vice president's meeting, Kamotho's fund-raiser would place too great a drain on the resources of residents. The gathering would certainly have upstaged Kibaki's visit. Kamotho went ahead anyway and was met at the site by riot police. The story made the papers, and the district commissioner lost his job, in spite of his respect for the letter of the law.

The Njonjo group also sought to persuade the public that Kibaki was responsible for the country's agricultural woes, which had brought maize and milk shortages.[24] The first charges to that effect were aired during March 1980, but the strongest statement of the view came in June, when the *Standard*, a newspaper whose editor was later subject to charges that he had collaborated with Njonjo, started what some called a campaign to place blame on the vice president and on a former minister for agriculture.[25] Shortly thereafter, *Africa Confidential* printed an article suggesting that Kibaki was being encouraged to leave Kenya for a World Bank job. The article received wide circulation in Kenya and necessitated a public refutation by the vice president. At the end of June, Moi bolstered Njonjo's fortunes by making the MP from Kikuyu the new minister for constitutional affairs.

The third faction organized itself through the agency of GEMA. GEMA leaders focused their attacks on the vice president and led business criticism of Kibaki. One GEMA executive remarked, "Kibaki is turning this country into a communist state where the government does everything and leaves no initiative to the private sector."[26] The criticism of the vice president escalated as the organization's strength increased. The assets of the financial operations department of the association, GEMA Holdings, reached KSh. 90 million in May, and in a demonstration of skill in netting benefits for its members, the company announced that it would pay dividends to its shareholders and participate more heavily in charitable activities.

Although President Moi had a hand in creating division among the Central Province politicians who were in the best positions to constitute a challenge to his leadership, the continued involvement of GEMA in national affairs appeared to evoke his fear and ire. Kenyatta had tolerated subgroups within his cabinet, and Moi began by following suit. He expanded the number of cabinet posts from twenty-three to fifty-two, and he left several GEMA leaders in positions of power. The GEMA candidate for the vice presidency, Jeremiah Nyagah, was retained as minister for agriculture. James Gichuru was made one of three ministers of state, along with Nicholas Biwott and G. G. Kariuki. Moi may have believed it possible to lessen the strength of the ties holding the GEMA group together by including some former "opposition" leaders but not others in the cabinet.

Beginning in July 1980, however, the president began a campaign against dissidents and "political splinter groups" of all sorts but with the clear aim of eliminating the financially powerful Kiambu welfare association once and for all. On July 21, the State House announced that all officials of the government would have to demonstrate "100% loyalty or quit" and announced a leaders' conference to discuss the matter. Although it was billed as a sequel to a 1978 conference on "The Kenya We Want," the main outcome of the meeting was a call to wind up all ethnic welfare societies, for so long the rather limited organizational bases of political coalitions. The Kalenjin Union was the first to terminate its affairs, possibly on the understanding that if the president's own ethnic group acted quickly, the residents of Central Province would not view the new policy as an attack on the Kikuyu and would move similarly. In the actual event, GEMA was the last to conclude its operations.

After Moi's July request that ethnic welfare societies wind up their activities, GEMA's chief, Njenga Karume, had initially acceded, then reported that a vote of the membership had urged that the association not be disbanded immediately—an action that bought Karume time to make sure that other societies complied with the directive before GEMA surrendered its power. Arranging for transfer of the organization's extensive business holdings took time, and GEMA had still not disbanded by the end of November. Much of GEMA's portfolio was to be moved to Agricultural and Industrial Holdings, Ltd., an organization led by the former GEMA leader Kahika Kimani. During the first week of December, however, Kimani took a strong stance against this apparent surrender to the president and led a move by four directors of the firm to oust Karume as chairman and to take a stand against disbanding.

Seizing the opportunity, Moi leant his support to Karume, attending a big harambee meeting for primary and secondary schools in Kiambaa, Karume's constituency. By splitting GEMA members between Karume, who could now boast of presidential patronage, and Kimani, Moi undermined the solidarity of the coalition.

Moi's use of harambee funds in this manner represented a significant change over previous strategy. Before, harambee contributions from the president, vice president, or senior officials had been used to compensate those members of Parliament whose constituencies or districts lost resources through changes in public policy (see Table 3). The president's appearance in Kiambaa inaugurated a new period, in which contributions would be used, increasingly, to generate factions by making it in

TABLE 3   DISTRIBUTION OF HARAMBEE CONTRIBUTIONS
FROM THE PRESIDENT, VICE PRESIDENT, OR SENIOR
OFFICIALS, PROPORTION OF TOTAL BY REGION,
1977–1983

	1977	1978	1979	1980	1981	1982	1983
Central Province and central Rift	39.9	84.8	76.1	67.0	74.7	66.1	29.7
Eastern Province	6.9	0	4.6	0.9	2.6	33.3	1.0
Western Province	19.3	7.1	0.9	0	0.3	0	5.2
Rift Valley, excluding Nyandarua and Nakuru	13.2	4.4	14.8	30.5	3.9	0	51.8
Nyanza	7.9	1.5	2.7	1.6	16.2	0	0.1

the interest of members of potential opposition coalitions to turn against their associates and support the Moi government.

THE NEW KANU MONOPOLY

The proscription of ethnic welfare societies did little to reassure Daniel arap Moi that his grasp on the country's highest office was assured. State House had not necessarily undercut the power of GEMA or the Luo Union in his view. The leaders of these societies could salvage the financial resources they had accumulated and seek to advance their interests in other ways, he argued. His mind turned increasingly to fear of underground opposition, rooted, he believed, in the university system but fomented by the former leaders of the welfare unions.

In fact, significant political organization on a scale that could have led to the president's ouster and replacement by a government acceptable to a majority of Kenyans was extremely difficult at this time. Ability to organize sustained backing for cross-regional initiatives was now sharply circumscribed in two ways. First, the presence of multiple factions exacerbated the problem of defections for coalition-builders. Disaffected members of Parliament and local leaders constantly shifted their allegiances to the leader who promised the greatest advantages at any particular moment. Because no one faction chief could offer the prospect of long-term benefits in return for support, opportunism began to run rampant, increasing the negotiating costs associated with promotion of a national platform. Second, restrictions on political space

made it very difficult for local and national leaders to assemble. Because
the government controlled the registration of societies, it could simply
disapprove the papers submitted by an opposition party and refuse to
grant the necessary certification, as had happened in the case of the KPU
in 1966–69.[27] Only a coalition with a very strong parliamentary base
could forcibly have brought the State House's refusal to register a party
to the floor of Parliament for discussion.

Notwithstanding these bars to the effective organization of an opposition, the president appeared increasingly fearful of dissidence in any
form. During the period before and after the measures to eliminate welfare societies, he continually cautioned Kenyans to beware of disgruntled elements and warned that traitors would receive ruthless treatment.[28] Moi employed three tactics to try to secure his grip on power.
First, he tried to expand the scope of restrictions on political activity.
For example, he requested that Parliament contemplate limits on press
freedom as a way to deny potential opposition leaders an audience. The
minister for information and broadcasting announced that Kenya could
no longer afford a free press. "As a young developing country, we cannot afford the luxury of permissive reporting practised by the developed
countries. We must therefore use our mass media systems for nation-
building and in uplifting the standard of living of our people."[29] The
years 1980 and 1981 witnessed implementation of a number of other
measures aimed at safeguarding presidential power, including closure
of the university, harassment of foreign journalists, seizure of lecturers'
passports, warnings of "crackdowns," and a call for the reopening of
detention camps.

Expenditure on police services, especially in rural areas, expanded
greatly. Beginning in 1978 and 1979, the approved budget allocations
for the Office of the President, which in Kenya at this time had responsibility for the police forces, shot up.[30] Disaggregated by type of expenditure, the budget appears to have increased most rapidly in the category
of personal emoluments for the police, Criminal Investigation Department, and Government Services Unit staff, and in the category of GSU
transport (the latter a possible indication of increased activity, as well as
of increased numbers of personnel, although it is not known whether
purchases of trucks and other transport may have been to replace aging
equipment). Because the rates of growth in personal emoluments exceeded the rates of growth in numbers of personnel, it can be assumed
that in addition to enhancing the capability of the police, Moi was seeking to increase their fidelity to him by purchasing their loyalty. By 1985,

the budget of the Office of the President was greater than that of any other ministry or government function, with estimates totaling K£74,932,700.[31]

Simultaneously with the increase in security budgets, evidence of more government surveillance emerged. An unfortunate consequence of strategies that emphasize restriction of political activity and factionalizing opposition in order to maintain stability is the politicization of information. Information "costs" more and becomes something to be bargained and traded because of its scarcity and importance in decision making.

Moi's second tactic was to render illegal any attempt to constitute an opposition to KANU. In June 1982, two months after a statement by the Luo MP George Anyona that he and Oginga Odinga planned to found a new political party, the Office of the President proposed that Kenya be declared a single-party state. Anyona had said that the time was ripe for creation of a second political party, an assertion for which KANU expelled him from its ranks. In May, with Oginga Odinga, he established the Kenya African Socialist Alliance (KASA).[32]

By himself, Odinga did not command sufficient power to warrant such a strong and politically costly reaction on Moi's part. A GEMA-Luo combination, however, could conceivably have rallied sufficient support to force the issue of party registration to the floor of Parliament and Moi's decision most likely reflected an assessment by the president that a party involving Odinga would also involve either the GEMA machine, now underground but not defunct, or the new Rift Valley populists. A Luo-Rift coalition would have wielded less parliamentary power than a GEMA combination but might have elicited substantial popular support during a period when economic difficulties had stirred general unease.

The constitutional amendment to make Kenya a de jure single-party system moved quickly through the legislature, with little overt objection from the honorable members. The difficulty of organizing a parliamentary opposition did not indicate general support for the president's proposal, however. MP Koigi wa Wamwere complained that at a KANU parliamentary group meeting, MPs were threatened with detention without trial if they did not go along with the proposal.[33]

A little more than a month later, Kenyan political life was disrupted by a shadowy coup attempt that startled the country's allies, who had always considered the nation a stable point in an otherwise turbulent continent. The exact character of the "August Disturbances," as they were euphemistically known, has never been clarified and is likely to remain indecipherable. Members of the air force, a youthful and highly educated segment of the military, allegedly combined with university students and disaffected members of the Luo community to dislodge the Moi government. After eleven days of skirmishing in the capital, the rebel group met defeat at the hands of Government Services Unit (GSU) elite forces. The slowness of the army to respond to calls for assistance has led some observers to speculate that the uprising was really two or even three coup attempts launched from different quarters and gone awry. The demands of the coup plotters were never clear, although opposition to the move to a single-party system was widely believed to have been one of the motives.

The Office of the President embarked on a series of moves to try to curtail underground associations. The arrest of a large number of Luo, including Odinga's son, Raila Omolo Odinga, for participation in the August Disturbances, and the detention of the Rift Valley populist and Nakuru North MP Koigi wa Wamwere followed the collapse of the resistance. Surveillance of the university expanded and resulted in periodic questioning and detention of lecturers. The police Special Branch stepped up its monitoring of foreign press organizations and aid agencies, at one point closing the Associated Press offices after AP placed on the wire a story describing food shortages in Meru. The Ford Foundation representative came under fire when a report on the events of 1982 he had prepared for the foundation's New York office was intercepted and passed to the internal security agencies.

State House also moved to limit even more severely the political space available to members of Parliament. One senior minister initiated an inquiry into the funding received by radical MPs for harambee meetings. Next came an end to parliamentary privilege, the provision that enabled members to obtain information from the executive, and on which ability to hold the government responsible for the actions of its officers depended. Finally, on June 4, Parliament voted to reinstate the detention laws, suspended between 1978 and 1982.

Thus, the failure of members of Parliament and extra-parliamentary leaders to resist imposition of restrictions earlier had triggered a poorly planned and coordinated attempt to restore room for political opposition in Kenya. The failure stemmed largely from the difficulty of assembling stable bases of support in a single-party-dominant system with a high degree of fragmentation and from the limitations placed on politicians' ability to use exchange of private harambee funds to secure one

another's support. Over the next three years, resistance to further assumption of party functions by the Office of the President would become more and more challenging. The move to a party-state was almost
assured.

THE NJONJO AFFAIR

Unnerved by the August disturbances and conscious of the effectiveness
of fragmentation as a strategy for controlling opposition, Moi began
again to sow the seeds of division among the Kikuyu representatives in
the cabinet. In December 1982, only four months after the coup attempt, he launched an attack on Charles Njonjo to reduce the power his
former ally had aggregated. The move ended in the former minister's
expulsion from the government and from the party in the summer of
1983. Moi then turned a former Mau Mau Central Committee member,
Kariuki Chotara, into a machine politician, channeling harambee contributions his way in order to create a counterweight to Mwai Kibaki
and to a new faction that had developed around Kenneth Matiba, the
successful Kikuyu businessman who was MP from Murang'a.

Over the years Njonjo had accumulated sufficient political power, as
chief of several branches of the country's internal security operations, to
constitute a threat to the president. The events of August had clarified
the dangers of disloyalty among those who controlled the security apparatus. In December 1982, a group of Luhya MPs spearheaded an attack in Parliament, confronting Njonjo on a series of minor issues. State
House's involvement became clear when, on January 22, Moi became a
member of the Butere Development Fund and promised a personal appearance at a fund-raiser for the Luhya districts, areas previously neglected in the harambee participation of senior ministers. In May, with
the assistance of Martin Shikuku, MP for Butere, the senior Luhya MP,
Elijah Mwangale, launched a full-scale challenge to Njonjo, and Moi
revealed that Kenyans had a traitor in their midst. The president's
speeches never mentioned the traitor by name but dropped clues to his
identity: an MP who wore a three-piece suit and a flower in his lapel—
both well-known characteristics of the minister for constitutional affairs. On June 30, Shikuku also directed remarks against the senior
ministers Stanley Oloitipitip, Joseph Kamotho, Charles Rubia, G. G.
Kariuki, and Robert Matano, most of whom had ties to Njonjo, and
suggested that Parliament was engaged in witch-hunting. The Luhya
MP Fred Omido picked up the attack on Njonjo, and Lawrence Sifuna

made the first request that Njonjo be expelled from Parliament. Mukasa Mango, minister for health and MP for the Luhya constituency Busia East, suggested that expulsion from the cabinet was not enough, and that Njonjo should be brought before a court to face treason charges.

On July 1, 1983, Njonjo resigned his position. Two days later KANU suspended him, along with a less well known figure, the former Butere MP Chief Richard Litunya, a strong rival of Shikuku's. Litunya's suspension came as a result of a meeting called to discuss a telegram he was alleged to have written to Njonjo apologizing for the behavior of the Luhya MPs.

The Shikuku group received its first reward for its alliance with the State House in late July, when Moi visited Butere and raised KSh. 3.1 million for Shikuku's Butere Development Fund. In Vihiga, Moses Mudavadi's constituency, one opposition candidate, Peter Kibisu, was forced out of the race for Parliament, and another, Bahati Semo, fell into disgrace when he refused to follow the bidding of a group of elders who claimed that the people wished Mudavadi unopposed. Vihiga was one of the few sites of possible government interference in an otherwise relatively clean election, by all reports. In the October 1983 cabinet reorganization, the former minister for tourism and wildlife, Elijah Mwangale, was promoted to minister for foreign affairs. Martin Shikuku moved to the Office of the President as an assistant minister for state. Moses Mudavadi maintained his position as minister for local government, and Mukasa Mango exchanged his portfolio as minister for health for that of the minister for cooperative development. Stanley Oloitipitip and G. G. Kariuki were removed from government. Two years later, in 1985, Robert Matano, the third man who had once worked with Njonjo to orchestrate Kibaki's success in the KANU elections, was asked to resign his ministerial portfolio and was defeated in his bid to hold onto his position as secretary general of KANU.

The second attempt to reduce the power of the Kikuyu in the government through a strategy of faction came in the early months of 1985, with the elevation of the former Mau Mau leader from Naivasha, Kariuki Chotara, as an alternative center of power within the Kikuyu community to rival Mwai Kibaki and Kenneth Matiba, the wealthy minister for culture and social services from Mbiri, in Murang'a District. With Njonjo out of the picture, the possibility of unity among the Kikuyu factions presented itself, with Kibaki or Matiba as likely leaders.

In the wake of the Njonjo affair, Moi appointed two leaders of the

Mau Mau rebellion, Kariuki Chotara and Fred Kubai, nominated MPs. With the exception of Bildad Kaggia, leader of the long-banned populist Kenya People's Union, and the former Nyeri MP Waweru Kanja, the leaders of the post-independence Kikuyu community had always come from loyalist backgrounds. Former Mau Mau leaders had played relatively little part in Kenyan politics since 1963. Chotara and Kubai had no connections to the business elite and to "establishment" politics in Kikuyu areas. Indeed, both had opposed Jomo Kenyatta for his moderation; Kenyatta's jailer during the Mau Mau Emergency reported that Chotara had attempted to kill Kenyatta while the two were detained together, and in 1985 Kubai recalled on film for Grenada Television the Mau Mau Central Committee's intention to eliminate Kenyatta had the leader's moderation proved a hindrance.

Chotara established a strong base in Nakuru District, where he replaced Kimani as chief of the local machine and served as KANU branch chairman. The currency he used to establish these relationships was harambee, the funds being provided by the State House. Many of the harambee gatherings he sponsored were held on behalf of the KANU youth wing, which subsequently supported Chotara's ambitions and monitored activities in the district. In spite of an unenforced ban on harambee during the campaign period for the 1985 party elections, Chotara held fund-raisers as often as twice a week without attracting official censure.

In April 1985, Chotara, Kubai, and the Luhya politician who had participated in the ousting of Njonjo, Elijah Mwangale, joined forces to generate opposition to Kibaki within Nyeri District. The group allegedly sought to advance the interests of Mwangale for the vice presidency in an effort to reduce Kibaki's power. In April, Mwangale visited Nyeri District without informing the vice president, a breach of etiquette that generally signals a visitor's strength. Kibaki immediately denounced what he called "political tourism," or unannounced visits between politicians from different districts, and tried, unsuccessfully, to obtain a ruling that members of Parliament not be allowed to enter one another's constituencies except in the company of the incumbent. Chotara was able to influence Nyeri politics, however, through his old Mau Mau ties, one of whom, Samuel Thiberi, had been responsible for the early stages of Kibaki's career and now expressed disenchantment with his performance.[34] At the end of April, Mwangale and Chotara met with the president at State House to discuss the issue further.

NYAYO: FOLLOWING IN THE FOOTSTEPS

One of the central questions that had arisen in the May 1982 debate about the move to a single-party system was whether KANU would continue to remain open to a variety of points of view. At the time, the national executive had just expelled Odinga and Anyona, both of whom were subsequently accused of seeking to establish a competing party. Did these expulsions prefigure a stronger party platform and stricter enforcement of the loyalty pledge that all members signed? Less than a month later, during a speech in western Kenya, the party's organizing secretary, Nathan Munoko, warned that KANU would "not hesitate to throw out of the party people who refused to toe the party line."[35] The August Disturbances put the issue even more clearly at the top of the Kenyan political agenda.

Munoko's remarks heralded a series of changes, most enacted three years later in the course of the 1985 grassroots and national party elections. The conduct of the 1985 party elections and the modifications in party structures and practices that occurred subsequently indicated a shift in party-state relations. There were three elements of the program: (1) an effort to prevent the formation of branch machines with bases of power independent from the national executive committee, (2) extension of the control exerted by the State House over party elections, and (3) introduction of structures that could enable the party to become a stronger instrument of social and political control.

One of the first moves was to require that every party official have won election to a sub-branch before assuming a higher post. MPs who had lost their seats but retained party chairmanships had, in the past, frustrated the efforts of new MPs to promote local development projects.[36] After the conclusion of the 1985 polling, the president declared, "It should be made clear that if you don't get elected at the grassroots, you will not be considered at any other stage, otherwise wananchi will be wondering how you got elected at the national level when they had rejected you."[37] His intention was to prevent the formation of a party machine that could be controlled by a small group of people who remained in office because they had access to resources useful to candidates in elections and could therefore control sections of the party. When the time came for local delegates to elect district officials, these would be the men chosen. Access to resources, not party loyalty, was their mainstay. One way to help ensure that the party bureaucracy did not develop a base of power independent of the executive council was to force all officials to face continual reelection campaigns. "If you are cleaning your cattle, every animal should get into the dip, including their calves," the president noted. "That kind of system will clean the party thoroughly."[38]

Forcing officials to run for election from the sublocation level instead of allowing them to serve whether or not they had campaigned and won in their home areas might enable the government to turn some party members out, but it did not solve the problem permanently. If only elected party members could hold office, then what could prevent incumbent officials from refusing to allow their challengers equal meeting time—or even the necessary clearance papers? It was the obverse of the problem of harassment of new MPs by those they had beaten. During the 1985 elections there were several instances in which registered party members were never given the opportunity to choose among candidates, because incumbent politicians had caucused in advance and agreed to support one candidate unopposed. For example, in Kisii, six of the district's seven MPs (over the objections of the seventh, Zachary Onyonka) agreed to support Lawrence Sagini, a senior politician allied with the powerful chief secretary of the civil service. Although the requirement that officials be reelected at the grass-roots level appeared to undercut the growth of a party machine, given the electoral rules the party followed, the new policy was not likely to have the intended effect.

The problem of choice also arose in connection with the relationships between the civil service, State House, and KANU. The 1985 elections brought three types of changes. One was the incorporation of civil servants into the party, in a major departure from the Westminster model on which Kenya's governmental system was originally based.[39] Whether the measure was adopted as a means of bringing the civil service under the control of the party or simply of raising money from membership fees was unclear. After a series of contradictory exchanges, it was decided that although civil servants would be required to join the party, they would not be allowed to run for party office or involve themselves in debates about party policy. The ruling did represent a significant change in the way people thought about the party and the civil service, however. Traditionally, Kenyatta had used the civil service as a vehicle for exercising control and discerning local opinions.[40] Incorporating the civil service into the party while denying a role for the new members in making policy reversed the relationship.

A second change was less a matter of substance than degree. Previously the civil service had acted on the president's orders to control night meetings, harambee appearances, and political gatherings. During the 1985 KANU electoral period, some officials in the provincial administration abbreviated these steps and simply banned campaign meetings and rallies altogether. The provincial commissioner for Central Province did so on June 18, and his Nyanza counterpart followed suit two days later. Just prior to polling, three Nyanza politicians were arrested and held without charge in Kisumu District.[41]

The third change was in the way State House handled elections for national posts. In 1978, Njonjo, Oloitipitip, and G. G. Kariuki had brokered the slate that won Kibaki the vice presidency. Each candidate they put up was opposed by a candidate from the Mungai slate and several other challengers. At no point did Moi publicly declare himself for or against any contender. In the July 1985 party elections, by contrast, the broker was none other than the State House itself. All candidates ran unopposed, except Burudi Nabwera, who faced a challenge from the incumbent Robert Matano, who refused to step down. The withdrawal of Mwashembu Mwachofi, who had opposed the Moi nominee, Justus ole Tipis, for the treasurer's post, was announced by the president, not the candidate.

The participation of the State House in the conduct of the national elections was only one indication of the increasing control exerted over party affairs by the president. The new requirement that national party officials work at the highest levels of the government meant that either the party would have to choose its managers from among the members of the cabinet or the president would have to appoint elected party officials to senior positions.[42] In either case, the officials were beholden to the State House.

Changes permitted other forms of political control to be exerted by the State House through the party organization as well. The most significant of these was the creation of a disciplinary committee to censure members who deviated from the party's policies. The July 2, 1985, announcement was accompanied by a warning from the president that ministers and other leaders who were "raising their heads" must "sing the song of the government or resign."[43] The first crackdown by the committee came before the end of the month. Describing the campaign, the new KANU chairman, David Okiki Amayo, said that leaders must stop "hankering after power" and "the politics of survival that can only lead to darkness and destruction." The party treasurer, who was also minister for State in charge of security, said that KANU would track and "crush dissidents" and that the country's security personnel would locate subversive elements "even if they go underground."[44] He equated anti-nyayo sentiment with mental illness, saying, "Let those who don't want peace go to Mathare [site of the mental hospital] to have their heads examined."[45] By the end of the year, the disciplinary committee was considering several cases, among them that of Martin Shikuku, one of those who had spearheaded the attack on Njonjo; Shikuku had stepped out of line by accusing the chief secretary of the civil service of owning too much land.

Other practices had the effect of helping the government leaders locate "political groupings" and eliminate them. Although the party constitution called for use of secret ballots, Moi announced that the party would now consistently employ the "queuing system," to which it had often resorted in the past. Under this system, voters line up behind the candidate of their choice. The advantages ascribed to it are that it prevents "stuffing the ballot box" and makes voting simpler for people who are illiterate and cannot read a ballot (the reason Kenya and many other African countries use symbols in addition to names to distinguish candidates). From the administration's point of view, of course, it had the added benefit of exposing which electors cast their votes for which candidate.[46]

There were two other aspects of the use of the party as a vehicle for controlling "tribal groupings," "sectionalism," and "wolves in sheeps' skin acting as an opposition."[47] One was to encourage more people to join the party, where they would be exposed to the nyayo influence—a course of action that also corresponded neatly with the party's financial objectives, which may have been of paramount concern. In March, Minister for Labour Robert Ouko asked local chiefs in his area, Kisumu Rural, to use social gatherings such as funerals, sports meetings, and church services "to preach the need for KANU registration."[48] The South Nyanza district commissioner announced subsequently that wananchi (common people) would not be allowed into markets, shops, or bars without KANU tickets. In parts of Central Province and the Rift Valley, residents were warned that they could be questioned by police on night patrols to determine whether they were party members.[49]

The most visible aspect of the program to use the party as a means of social control was, however, the youth wing. KANU branches had long been allowed to maintain youth groups, which acted as vigilante organizations and rather frequently made news as a result of their abuse of power. The party's former secretary general had been suspicious of the youth wing, warning members not to take the law into their own hands, and most politicians seem to have exhibited similar ambivalence. During the 1985 campaign, the activities of the youth wing were advertised as part of the defense of nyayo. Youth-wingers were celebrated for their anti-crime campaigns in Nakuru and Nairobi and their arrests of suspected thieves. The youth wing played an especially large role under the patronage of the Nakuru boss Kariuki Chotara. In August, KANU announced it would build a college in Machakos that would "aim at making youth-wingers . . . disciplined watchdogs in society." [50] The *Standard* recorded that "until a few months ago the party had, to a large extent, been a monopoly of a few individuals without any meaningful political socialization taking place. There are, however, indications that President Moi wants to take the party to the people—both old and young—and it is hoped the party will play a greater role in providing political education to the youth." [51]

THE PARTY-STATE IN 1985

In early February 1985, Mwai Kibaki, then Kenya's vice president, stood before a crowd of farmers in the dusty center of Karatina Town, a crossroads in densely populated, coffee-growing Nyeri District. Elections for local and national posts in KANU, the country's only legal political party, were shortly to take place, and the Karatina rally was one in a series sponsored by local officeholders throughout the district. A center of Mau Mau resistance activity during the 1950s, Nyeri was Kibaki's home, although the vice president had left his birthplace, first to study for a degree in economics at the University of London and later to represent a constituency in Nairobi. An urbane man who had served as minister of finance under Jomo Kenyatta, Kibaki had subsequently reestablished himself in Nyeri as representative of the rural people of Othaya, a hilly area of small farms, well served, compared to national standards, by a network of schools, health centers, and paved roads. The vice president made the two-and-a-half hour trip between Nairobi and his constituency so routinely that some had accused him of lavishing contributions and attention on local initiatives at the expense of his responsibilities in other areas.

But this visit to Nyeri was strikingly different in tone from earlier tours. The vice president sported his usual business suit and tie, but his characteristic civility had disappeared. Flanked by members of Parliament from local constituencies, the vice president, who was also the second-ranking official in the party, threw off his usually reserved demeanor and warned his listeners not to be duped by "political tourists" from other districts who were out to stir up local animosities. Politicians from other areas were traveling Nyeri's roads at night in "pick-ups full of fat rams" to give to their local "godfathers" so as to convince people of their strength. He alerted his listeners to the activities of "losers" of previous elections who intended to regain political standing by capturing party positions during the upcoming KANU balloting. The opening remarks contrasted sharply with Kibaki's image as a technocrat for whom "politics was probably too dirty a game," a man of measured statements and carefully supported argument.[52] The statesman had turned sharp-tongued politician.

If Kibaki's departure from his previous style and tactics elicited surprise, the reaction of other politicians from the area in which Karatina Town lies brought a still more shocked reaction. At the next gathering, Ngumbu Njururi, a local MP, took issue with the vice president. A relative newcomer to parliamentary politics who had won rapid promotion to the front bench as an assistant minister in the Office of the President, Njururi boldly chastised Kibaki. He said that the man to whom the vice president had elliptically referred as "a godfather," and who had allegedly hosted "political tourists," was his good friend Waweru Kanja, one-time Mau Mau leader. Njururi challenged the vice president to put evidence on the table to support his accusations. His remarks constituted the first public effort by a fellow politician from Nyeri District to take the vice president to task.

Vice President Kibaki was not present to hear Njururi's remarks, but at the next in the series of rallies, held in his own constituency, he heard them elaborated by Kanja himself. More surprising still, he heard Kanja bring greetings to residents from the president, whom the MP had recently met at the official residence in Kabarak. To transmit the president's remarks in such a way was a faux pas in Kenyan political etiquette—or a deliberate slight. By unwritten agreement, delegations to visit the president must include all of the elected officials from an area and especially the senior parliamentary representative, who is always considered the key spokesman. Moreover, it was always the sitting representative from the constituency in which a meeting took place who relayed any messages the president might wish to convey. Kanja's remarks violated these conventions in a manner that implied to some the strong backing of a senior politician outside the district. Kanja had gone so far as to request that the district officer and local KANU sub-branch chairman note in the official record that the people had received the president's greetings and that it was he who had transmitted them.

Kibaki first showed restraint on hearing Kanja's remarks at the Othaya meeting, but later he attacked his former colleague, lashing out once again in uncharacteristic fashion and attacking Kanja's record of participation in local development efforts. Why had Kanja and his allies not helped during the struggle to finance and construct the district's new Standard 8 classrooms? he asked. Why had he failed to participate in school construction in Kieni Division, his home area, during the desperate 1984 drought, when the people could ill afford to build new classrooms? And what was all this about Kanja playing a leading role in the Mau Mau uprising against the British when no one had ever heard who the real leaders were?

Kanja brought the debate back to "political tourism," claiming that the vice president was needlessly upset. It appeared that the vice president worried that he, Kanja, had struck a deal with the Western Province politician Elijah Mwangale. The vice president apparently feared that Mwangale, the minister for foreign affairs, had contacted Kanja in a bid to build opposition to Kibaki's vice presidency. The vice president's fears had no basis, Kanja claimed.

Other politicians and the press quickly adopted the expression "political tourism." The *Daily Nation* columnist Benson Riungu wrote a satire entitled "Sampling the Thrills and Spills of a Political Safari," clothing his political tourists in typical tourist garb and packing them off to various parts of the country in mini-buses labeled "KANU '85 Political Safaris." [53] In place of hotel pamphlets, each "clutched a political map of Kenya," and "all led fat rams on leashes." The tour leader announced to his charges:

> As the leading influence peddlers in Kenya . . . we're duty-bound to ensure that only candidates of our choice get elected to top party posts. This, taking the level of corruption in this country, will obviously mean spreading money around like confetti. And this is the reason why you were chosen—men with the financial means to afford to dish out a million bob [i.e., KSh.] without a qualm, and with no hope of immediate financial gain.
>
> Our mission is to tour the whole country stirring political sentiments as with a stick, to turn brother against brother, location against location. Slipping a couple of thousands into a district party boss' pocket here, a couple of hundreds in the hand of a hoodlum's gang leader there.

Shortly thereafter, President Moi called for an end to such "tourism" and for rules preventing politicians from entering constituencies without the consent of the sitting MP.

Even if the vice president's reaction to politics-as-usual seemed a bit excessive, the press suggested, Kenyan politics had become less a matter of bargaining between the sponsors of coherent platforms than a constant scramble between factions to ensure continued access to state resources. Or, as the *Weekly Review*'s Hilary Ng'weno had observed, personalities and one-on-one negotiation behind closed doors had replaced coherent alliances in support of particular stands on public issues, rendering Kenyan politics completely opaque.

The "political tourism" episode is interesting to the social scientist because it illuminates the ways Kenyan political life had changed during the 1970s and early 1980s, paving the way for the rise of a party-state in a country long famed for its relatively closer adherence to the norms of Westminster parliamentary democracy than most of its sub-Saharan neighbors. It reveals the increasing difficulty politicians faced in building enduring coalitions to support positions on national-level issues—most particularly to oppose the reallocation of functions and privileges between the party and the Office of the President. The event and Kibaki's fears suggest (1) erosion of the effectiveness or usefulness of harambee participation as an essential component both of political success and of coalition-building across political jurisdictions, (2) a high degree of factional fragmentation, inspired or aggravated, to some degree, by direct intervention by the Office of the President in party elections, (3) a high degree of instability in the composition of political groupings, and (4) the absence of well-defined, independent economic interest groups from political debate.

In response to the "political tourism" episode, the *Weekly Review* urged the State House to tolerate the "canvassing for support" entailed in "tourism" of this type. It pointed to the trend toward increasing limitations on political association, which had started to threaten Kenyan stability, and urged a return to greater openness to diverse points of view both within KANU and within Parliament:

> A natural consequence of elections—if they are free and fair—is the creation of alliances, whether of individuals or groups, for the purpose of ensuring victory for those with a common interest. The incumbents, as well as their challengers, will succeed in their respective bids to retain or gain power within the party hierarchy through diverse ways, but the most effective will probably be one that entails bargaining for electoral benefits.
>
> . . . [This] democracy is essential to the public playing out of a struggle between contending interests in accordance with the rules and procedures agreed upon by society. Often the struggle is given most attention, and concern is expressed about the effect of struggles upon the fabric of society. But the greater emphasis ought to be placed on the openness of a democratic

struggle. What would threaten the fabric of society in Kenya is not the open squabbling of leaders in search of votes; what would threaten the fabric of society in Kenya, as indeed in any country, is any process which affects national politics in a fundamental way but is not open to public scrutiny.[54]

The threat to the welfare of Kenyan state and society lay not so much in the maneuvers and invective of the leaders of political coalitions within the party, but rather in the elimination of the linkages between the grass roots and the political elite through restriction of bargaining, the *Weekly Review*'s editor noted. Absent the ability to campaign and to try to secure support through participation in both local development and national policy matters, the fortunes of members of Parliament and party officers would depend on the favor of those in high office, not on accountability to constituents.

Of special concern was the change under way in the relationship between KANU and the Office of the President. Under Kenyatta, KANU had dominated the political scene, to the de facto exclusion of opposition parties. It had remained a weak party, however, with no clear platform and limited political functions. It played relatively little role in articulating and aggregating interests, in formulating legislative proposals, or in socializing young Kenyans into the operation of a parliamentary system. Nor did it assume functions that usually reside with the executive—powers of law enforcement or of policy implementation. In his early years as president, Kenyatta intervened in the affairs of the party principally to prevent "rejuvenation" or capture by a particular set of interests, whether those of the less well-off or of the Kiambu commercial elite. Until the period of his illness, he sought to keep both groups within the party and to encourage compromise between interests and between regions by insisting that people should take participation in local development as an important criterion of a candidate's acceptability. Then the need for funds to contribute to these causes would encourage politicians to bargain with one another and to limit their demands against one another's communities: the slogan "Harambee! Harambee! Harambee!" with which Kenyatta ended his public speeches pointed to an important component of the founder's strategy for keeping disputes within the ruling party.

By 1985, KANU's relationship to the state, to the Office of the President, had changed significantly. The party was increasingly a vehicle for transmitting the views of the president to the grass roots and for controlling the expression of interests within the country and their influence over policy. Party elections had helped organize local interests into coherent platforms to only a very limited degree in the past, but they now ceased to serve that function at all. The intervention of the State House to ensure that its candidates for top party offices ran unopposed, and to reduce the electoral prospects of those whose power the president feared, undercut articulation of interests and aggregation within KANU. The strengthening of party disciplinary committees and screening procedures at the State House's request meant that KANU would become, increasingly, a vehicle for controlling dissent. The on-again-off-again establishment of youth wings further conferred on the party part of the state's surveillance and law-enforcement functions.

The year 1985 saw the rise of a party-state in Kenya, but a distinctively Kenyan party-state nonetheless. Despite severe restriction of political activity by the State House, at no point did KANU acquire the all-inclusive corporatist character or the expanded functions of the Mouvement populaire de la révolution in Zaire, which absorbed all other associations, political and otherwise, and whose cadres operated as official adjuncts of the internal security forces. KANU continued to lack the organizational efficacy to carry out significantly expanded law-enforcement functions, and only later did it seek to absorb economic, sports, cultural, and religious bodies.

Further, the division of functions with the executive varied from year to year. For example, although the youth wings eventually assumed an important place in the party, their members sporting "Moi buttons" to indicate their fidelity to the president, their existence was often barely tolerated. The celebration accorded the KANU youth wing during the 1985 party elections was not unanimously appreciated. Within the ranks of the party were many who disagreed with efforts to use the youth wing for purposes of political or social control, and after the KANU elections, a quiet debate about the role of the organization ensued. Former Secretary General Robert Matano had earlier cautioned against blanket condoning and encouraging of youth-wing activities. The youth wings did not formally have the power of arrest, but several groups in Nairobi, Nakuru, and elsewhere had assumed that right anyway, while others had become bodyguards for local officials.

The new party chairman, David Okiki Amayo, noted in December 1985 that youth-wingers were not provided for in the party structure, and that the idea of a youth wing had developed informally, through pronouncements by party leaders. Vice President Mwai Kibaki also sought to restrain the bid to strengthen the youth wing, saying that it was only in "communist states" that the party acted as a militia too.

Further, he remarked, because "youth-wingers were a creation of party bosses," it was the party leadership's responsibility either to contain the problem the youth wing now posed or disband the organizations.[55] The institutionalization of the party youth wing did not take place until the end of the 1980s, and remained controversial.

Some hesitation also characterized the inauguration of a strengthened disciplinary function. The leadership did constitute a party disciplinary committee, as it had announced earlier, and proceeded to consider the suspension or expulsion of several politicians. Here again, however, the dangers of this step were at least partly acknowledged, although a reversal of policy did not take place. By January 1986, increasing numbers of party members found their names given to the committee for investigation; the committee had provided another vehicle for contending candidates to eliminate opponents. In mid January 1986, the president pardoned the first eighteen people suspended or expelled, however, and said that "misunderstandings among party leaders" had provoked some of the charges and that the "immediate priority" was to ensure unity and happiness in the country.[56] As in the case of the youth wings, however, the disciplinary functions were later restored.

Nonetheless, the relationship between party and state was quite different from what it had been earlier under Kenyatta. At the end of the Kenyatta period, tremendous power was concentrated in the president, but some protections still existed. The judiciary was still independent. Although the government had frustrated formation of opposition parties—indeed, perhaps done away with J. M. Kariuki, the leader of one party in the making—the legal right to constitute an opposition was still on the books. The right to vote was respected. Under Kenyatta, ballot-rigging was the exception rather than the rule. KANU remained quite weak while Kenyatta used the administration to implement policy.

Although not a party-state of the same character as the MPR in Zaire, the Tanzania African National Union (TANU), or Nkrumah's Convention People's Party in Ghana in the early 1960s, in the first years of the Moi period, the Kenyan state nonetheless came to share with these systems a merger of representative and law-enforcement functions, extremely limited pluralism, and concentration of power in the head of state. By the end of the 1980–85 period, most of the key elements in the new relationship between KANU and the Office of the President were in place. The Office of the President controlled the election of candidates to high party office and converted KANU into a vehicle for monitoring opposition at the local level—something the provincial administration and other police forces could do only at the risk of polit-icizing their own ranks. The youth wings and new disciplinary commit-tees were key elements in this system. Their own excesses prompted greater centralization of the party and enforcement of a vague "party line" indistinguishable from the will of senior decision makers at the State House. KANU was no longer an organization for the representa-tion of views and the aggregation of divergent interests into cogent plat-forms. And in that sense Kenya had become what some have called a "no-party state." The use of party structures by the Office of the Presi-dent had distinct consequences for patterns of political behavior, how-ever, and for that reason, the concept of the "party-state" remains use-ful in helping observers understand Kenyan political life. There was increasing pressure to "follow in the footsteps," not of Kenyatta, but of Daniel arap Moi.

CHAPTER SIX

Party, State, and Civil Society, 1985-1990

The late 1980s saw both the consolidation of the changes taking place in Kenya's single-party system and the rise of new forms of resistance that slowed, but did not stop, the processes set in motion earlier. The merger between party and state in 1985 was more permanent than it appeared at the time. KANU declared itself constitutionally superior to Parliament and used its disciplinary powers to bar individuals who criticized policy from electoral politics.[1] Increasingly it absorbed other, formerly separate representative bodies and began to acquire a corporatist character similar to that of Zaire's Mouvement populaire de la révolution (MPR), although not nearly on the same scale. For all that it succeeded in extending its control over the political expression of economic interests among the matajiri, urban groups, and the petite bourgeoisie, at the grass roots in the rural areas, KANU remained weakly organized as a structure of representation, mobilization, and even, in many cases, control. As one farmer told the lawyer Kiraitu Murungi, "only hyenas could prevent him from travelling and in that case, only at night." [2]

As a result of new disciplinary structures within the party, it became difficult to resist further encroachment on political space from within Parliament or the party, and the defense of speech and association became increasingly extra-parliamentary. To the degree that this new pattern of opposition proved effective in limiting some kinds of political restrictions, it succeeded because first law associations, then church groups used their partly protected positions and their international contacts to voice criticisms and influence bilateral aid decisions. Elites have not had sufficient economic power to use boycotts or sectorwide strikes successfully as protection against further encroachment on civil liberties, although two members of the matajiri class, Kenneth Stanley Matiba and Charles Rubia, did mount a campaign for multi-party democracy. Only in the last half of 1990 did segments of Kenya's large informal sector, long considered part of Moi's "populist" base, begin to participate in opposition activities and use the sector's economic position to advantage. By and large, the activities of such elements during the period under study remained diffuse and undirected.

As KANU became more and more a creature of the Office of the President, personal rule began to replace management of demands through institutional mechanisms. The monument built to commemorate the first nyayo decade symbolized this change; it depicted Moi's arm clutching the staff of office and reaching out from Mt. Kenya. So did the 1989 creation of "Moi Day," a new holiday on October 10 of every year. Certainly, the identification of policy with the president did not reach the proportions it did in Zaire or in many other sub-Saharan countries. The provincial administration still handled many functions in accordance with impersonal procedures and criteria. Particularly in Nairobi, however, bureaucrats became increasingly anxious about potential disapproval of their activities by the Office of the President and hesitant to make controversial decisions on their own. The Office of the President became the reference point, slowing the process of institutional development not only in the legislature but also in the bureaucracy itself.

Kenyans and outsiders alike noted the change. At the time of the Njonjo affair (see p. 147 above), the *Weekly Review* had noted that a powerful leader was not a personal ruler but someone who created structures and processes that would help the public manage conflicts of interest over the long term:

> Behind them [the great leaders of the past] these men left nations made up of individuals, but also nations made up of institutions, and in the long run the history of nations is a history of institutions rather than of individuals, and the strength of a nation lies in the strength of its institutions rather than in that of its leading personalities. Indeed, to the extent that powerful individuals stand in the way of the growth of institutions, they contribute to the weakness rather than the strength of their nations.[3]

Outside observers and consultants noted the consequences of the increasing personalization of power. For example, David Leonard remarked that under the prevailing conditions, "permanent secretaries and their equivalents almost never try to build support for the policies they favor with legislators, party personnel, interest groups. . . . Instead, they resolve problems through the use of personal relationships."[4] A study by Joel Barkan suggests that members of Parliament are also reluctant to establish interest-group ties or to represent the interests of groups in the legislature. In a study of members of Parliament in the early 1980s, Barkan found that although a third of Kenyan MPs said speaking in Parliament was their most frequent activity, a higher proportion than the research team found in Korea or Turkey, no Kenyan legislators said they had authored or sponsored bills, worked for a bill in a committee, or offered an amendment. Most significant, only 3.6 percent said they had sought support outside the Assembly, and only 7 percent said they had privately tried to persuade a colleague to vote for or against a measure.[5]

This chapter is not intended to provide an exhaustive account of the 1985–90 period. Its purpose is to demonstrate, first, that the "party-state" was more than a fleeting visitor in Kenya's political history; second, that this system of rule had predictable consequences for forms of political participation; and, third, that although with construction of clever alliances it was possible for disaffected members of the Kenyan community to secure repeal of some measures that threatened their political space, it was difficult to effect significant changes of attitude and strategy in the State House. As the Office of the President used the party as an instrument for securing public order, a means of social and political control, it became increasingly difficult for patronage networks and new associations to operate. Increasingly, those whose interests were threatened by the activities of the government sought bargaining power in alliances with elements of the international community. Others took their opposition underground or participated, quixotically, in street demonstrations and ephemeral displays of disagreement.

THE CONSOLIDATION OF CHANGES
IN PARTY-STATE RELATIONS

The fusion of the party and the Office of the President that started in the mid 1980s continued through the next five years. During this period, the government took several steps to increase the discretion of the president in political affairs. The changes in the relationship between KANU and the State House were but one of these. First, the Office of the President won parliamentary passage of constitutional amendments in 1986 and 1988 that eliminated security of tenure in office for the attorney general, the controller, auditor, and, later, judges of the High Court and Court of Appeal, removing the few remaining judicial checks on the power of the chief executive. These steps met with limited opposition in Parliament but significant objection from the country's legal community, many of whose members argued that the changes would completely undermine the rule of law. Coupled with the absence of a jury system in the country, these changes made judicial processes highly vulnerable to government influence.

Although the effects are still not entirely clear, the government also re-drew the country's political boundaries, creating thirty new constituencies and increasing the number of members of Parliament to 188 elected representatives, 12 nominated members, and two ex officio members.[6] For the most part, the new electoral districts created corresponded to areas that had experienced the greatest population growth. After the changes, the district of Kakamega in Western Province emerged with the greatest number of constituencies, followed by the Kisii and Machakos districts. Many of the changes clearly had political overtones, however. The old Nyeri constituency yielded three new constituencies, whose boundaries split Waweru Kanja's following and forced Kanja to choose where he stood the best chance of sustaining his political career. Butere, the old constituency of the perennial gadfly Martin Shikuku, was divided in half and between provinces, in a move that angered residents and led to protests from the chairman of the local Lwanda-Ooho-Muhaka Progressive Society, who said, "The decision is obviously intended to please a certain politician and not for the benefit of the people."[7]

Third, Moi moved to replace incumbents in key security and governmental "gate-keeping" positions with men of his own choosing and own community. Kalenjin were appointed to the positions of speaker of the National Assembly, head of the Civil Service and cabinet secretary, deputy army commander, deputy air force commander, commandant of the Staff College, chief military intelligence officer, principal staff officer at Army Headquarters, director of the Criminal Investigation Department, commandant of the Government Services Unit, deputy director of intelligence, deputy police commissioner, and presidential escort commander and aide-de-camp to the president, among other posts, including key economic positions.[8]

Fourth, although the State House had temporarily closed some foreign press offices, such as that of the Associated Press, for publishing

food-need statistics ostensibly critical of the government, in 1984, the
real crackdown on journalists began in 1986. The government arrested
and detained several journalists, including Joseph Makoka of the *Nation*. It confiscated editions of foreign and domestic publications containing human rights stories, including *Africa Confidential*, *New African*, the *International Herald Tribune*, the *Economist*, and *Beyond*. It
arrested several foreign reporters and announced that it would review
the work permits of more than one hundred domestic and foreign correspondents.[9] The *Nation* newspaper, owned by the Aga Khan, temporarily lost the ability to cover Parliament when the deputy speaker, Kalonzo Musyoka, who was also national organizing secretary of KANU,
charged that the *Nation* had "scandalized the reputation of members."
Musyoka said that the newspaper had tried to divide Kenyans by saying
that MPs had failed to engage in lively debate of the budget and by
commenting that Kenyans experienced lower standards of living now
than they had at independence. He argued that the company had dismissed journalists and administrators who wanted to be loyal and active KANU members. This behavior he attributed to a program that
permitted an exchange of journalists between the *Nation* and the *Times*
of St. Petersburg, Florida, where, he alleged, journalists were trained to
subvert their nation.[10] Musyoka's charges were partly political and
partly personal, it turned out. The employee dismissed from the *Nation*
staff was a relative, who had been asked to leave for reasons having to
do with job performance. The newspaper lost access to Parliament for
four months. Increasingly the government sought to ban discussion of
certain topics as well, most notably voting procedures.

KANU AS AN ELEMENT OF POLITICAL STRATEGY

A fifth dimension of presidential strategy for controlling conflict was to
further modify the operation of KANU. Although the leadership did
little to improve organization at the local level or to strengthen the party's policy-making capabilities, it did take steps to expand control over
the behavior of the membership. The party took new steps to enforce
loyalty to the president among its members. A new national disciplinary
committee with broad discretion was formed in the early months of
1986. Its powers included the ability to expel party members or otherwise impose sanctions against those who, in its view, committed "any
act which in the opinion of Kanu is not in its interest" or in any way

undermined the party president, the head of state, or the KANU government.[11]

Even members of the government and some KANU stalwarts found this mandate, and its use to manipulate the electoral fortunes of parliamentary candidates, unacceptable. In 1987, Peter Okondo, then minister for labor, raised questions in Parliament about the national disciplinary committee's conduct. Okondo was thereupon hauled before the committee for censure, and quiet outrage grew at the handling of disciplinary proceedings and the violation of the laws guaranteeing protection of views expressed in Parliament.

Elijah Mwangale, a longtime Moi supporter, reassured foreign reporters that Okondo, and anyone else brought before the disciplinary committee, could have refused to respond to the summons, and Moi finally dissolved the committee when it reprimanded Mwangale himself for this statement. It had operated for scarcely more than a year.

Although the organization chart changed after the dissolution of the national disciplinary committee, the party's behavior did not. Presumably with the blessing of the president, KANU branches assumed many of the functions the committee had performed. Disciplinary action by branches expelled a number of senior politicians from the party between 1987 and the end of 1989. These included the former vice president Josephat Karanja, who was installed as Mwai Kibaki's successor, then demoted. Karanja's accusers said that the vice president had sought to murder prominent Kikuyu through staged road accidents, had established ties with malcontents in Uganda, and had ordered KANU members to kneel before him. He never had a chance to respond to the charges. Others expelled included the lawyer Kimani wa Nyoike and two members of Parliament, Kenneth Matiba and Charles Rubia, who were both later detained. Rubia was dismissed in a June 1989 party purge that removed fourteen other politicians. Moi threatened still more expulsions, saying, "The jigger has been removed but many little eggs remain in the wound and they must be killed." [12]

Eventually, panic in the ranks over the power of local branches to expel members and pressure from foreign donors led to temporary suspension of that function under orders from the president. For the decade of the 1980s, however, most politicians lived in fear of losing their positions through a party purge. Indeed, the eventual decision to stop expulsions and replace them with suspensions made little difference. An individual whom the party leadership suspended was barred from participation in future general elections.

Even without the formal instantiation of the disciplinary committee, KANU abrogated parliamentary immunity with increasing frequency. Earlier, members could rest assured that words uttered in Parliament would not open them to prosecution. Without this immunity, argued the framers of the constitution, MPs would not be willing to criticize the activities of ministries, and there would be little meaningful debate. Beginning in 1988, KANU violated this immunity on several occasions, however. For example, one MP voiced concern about the number of murders in his constituency and urged a review of security there. The president criticized the MP, saying that he should not have taken such an issue before the legislature. The MP's local KANU branch suspended him, and a higher party committee upheld the verdict and the penalty. No faction within Parliament was sufficiently stable to mount a successful challenge to the party management on its own.

The party experimented with other ways of controlling competition within its ranks and of ensuring that candidates for elective office would bear the president's stamp of approval. In 1987, KANU sought to implement a system of preliminary elections in which party members selected the three top candidates from among those interested in seeking a parliamentary career; in the event that one candidate secured 70 percent of the vote, that candidate would advance to the general election unopposed. This provision was designed to reduce fragmentation in constituencies and ensure that the candidate eventually elected carried a significant proportion of the votes cast. It limited opportunities for party members critical of existing policies to gain a hearing, however.

The mere ability of KANU branch members to intervene in the licensing and publicity of meetings had significant effects too. The KANU power structure disapproved of Martin Shikuku, often a defender of political space, although a man of unpredictable stances. Shikuku had been part of the investigative committee that looked into J. M. Kariuki's assassination and had faced sanctions for his role. He was tremendously popular in his constituency, Butere, in Kakamega District. In 1988, however, he lost his seat to a virtual unknown. Later, when he won election to the KANU district branch, his election was nullified, and he was sidelined.

Further, beginning in November 1988, the president and KANU mounted a series of "loyalty demonstrations" at which Moi reminded Kenyan citizens of the power he had to destroy the livelihoods of those who criticized the government. Just two months before the staged demonstrations, the wife of the detainee Raila Odinga had filed suit in the

High Court for a writ of habeas corpus on behalf of her husband. Shortly thereafter, she was dismissed from her job as a teacher on the grounds that it was in the public interest to do so.[13] At the loyalty demonstrations, the president announced that he planned more such firings, saying that not only dissidents but those who expressed sympathy with their causes would find themselves without jobs. Moi's New Year's speech of 1989 reiterated the point: citizens should follow the Office of the President if they wanted to keep their jobs.

KANU also began to absorb other bodies that had long performed representative functions. In 1988, the new finance minister, George Saitoti, announced that henceforth lawyers would have to register their practices under the Trade Licensing Act, enabling the Office of the President to put any lawyer of whose activities it disapproved out of business. The Law Society of Kenya (LSK), an independent association set up by an act of Parliament, saw this step as a preliminary to its own absorption into the party. The lawyers' anxiety increased when the president attacked the LSK as "absurd, ridiculous, and obnoxious" and questioned the patriotism of its members, arguing that, "the identity of lawyers is not Kenyan." Vice President Josephat Karanja referred to the legal profession as a "nerve centre for imperialists."[14]

The Kenya Law Society was spared, but other groups were not. In June 1990, KANU made official an association with Maendeleo ya Wanawake, the national women's organization, although it did not merge the organization into its own women's league. It also announced that the national confederation of trade unions would associate with the party, linking the already centrally controlled labor movement still more closely with the regime. In taking these steps, the office of the president and the KANU hierarchy were pursuing a course common to other African party-states. In Zaire, for example, the MPR had absorbed all associations, from youth groups and women's groups to sports clubs. The effect, and probably the intent, was to co-opt political activity by these groups and purchase the support of their leaders with promises of advancement. The ultimate goal was to ensure that there would be no bases for organization and political activity outside the state.[15]

The capture of KANU by the State House was institutionalized in 1988, when a new Ministry for National Guidance and Political Affairs was created to formally attach the party to the state. The mandate of the new ministry included the promotion and mobilization of KANU, projection of the nyayo philosophy, and censorship of print and film media. James Njiru, a longtime proponent of KANU supremacy, became the first to hold the portfolio. Njiru immediately hinted that newspapers and magazines that did not follow the KANU line would find themselves out of business and urged that the queuing system Kenya had adopted should replace the secret ballot all over Africa.[16] Under this new regime, the party grew less tolerant of those who criticized government policies or practices, expanded its ability to intervene in the decisions of other representative bodies, and acquired increasing police functions.

Finally, KANU's police functions expanded during this period. As early as 1987, a KANU leader, the late David Okiki Amayo, announced that the police would receive assistance from the members of the party.[17] Moi's New Year's speech of 1989 empowered KANU to monitor public places, such as bars, hotels, and restaurants, to identify those who opposed the Office of the President. In practice, the country's internal security forces had engaged in such surveillance for many years. Involvement of the general KANU membership greatly increased the scope of operations, however, and introduced an added element of fear that any party member one might have offended, for whatever reason, would be listening for the slightest slip of the tongue. The notice had a chilling effect on political speech, although members of Parliament already felt so constrained by the middle of 1988 that most bills passed with little or no debate, and even the discussion of the usually controversial Foreign Investment Bill took only forty minutes.

The controversial youth wing, once met with resentment by many KANU politicians, resumed its watchdog activities. Youth-wingers were often present at police raids and in marketplaces. In April 1989, it was the youth wing that interrupted a church sermon by the Anglican bishop David Gitari and provoked the party to summon the cleric to appear before the party hierarchy on the grounds that he had waged a press war against KANU and the government.

To fund its expanded activities, KANU either had to increase its dues, increase its membership, or look to other sources of support. In 1985 there was a major campaign to fill the party coffers. Civil servants were told that they would have to join KANU and shell out the money for a membership card but that they could not hold office in the party. This bred resentment, and there was considerable uncertainty at the time about whether the policy would be maintained. It was, and civil servants found that the party was able to deduct the dues directly from their paychecks, before they reached the recipients. In some rural areas, the administration, chartered to help KANU collect dues, prevented people from trading in local markets until they showed proof of membership. This approach had its limits as a revenue-gathering strategy, however. The party leaders turned elsewhere. Usually reliable sources suggest that at least in the late 1980s, funds amounting to $250 million were being diverted from customs to party officials. Whether the end use was for party finances or personal profit is not clear.

CHANGING PATTERNS OF PARTICIPATION

The changes in Kenya's single-party system affected the character of "civil society," or interest-group formation, in several ways. First, it altered the incentives to create organized interests. As David Leonard has noted, where power is concentrated in the hands of a head of state, the ability to secure economic demands derives primarily from personal relationships with the president and his close associates. To gain access to resources, politicians, civil servants, businessmen, and farmers alike seek to cultivate patronage networks, which may increase stratification in the society but confer mixed economic advantages upon their participants. Personalization of power, where that power remains effective, thus attenuates interest-group formation.

Second, the new relationship between KANU and the Office of the President increased the risks of expressing criticism on the floor of Parliament and the difficulty of meeting in privately organized groups, long technically illegal, to talk about policies or about civil liberties. Organized, public opposition by members of Parliament to the expanding role of KANU and the evolving relationship between the party and the Office of the President diminished substantially. Because of the high risk factor, expression of discontent for most who objected to policy decisions or restrictions on political space was likely to take the form of sudden street outbursts or highly symbolic gestures, unless an individual or group thought it could secure special protection.

Third, in an effort both to lower the risks associated with protest and increase bargaining leverage, opponents of the government sought to establish ties with groups in the international community. In the Cold War period, Odinga had tried to sustain his position by turning to the east. The tactic proved unsuccessful. In the post–Cold War period, individuals and groups sought to ally themselves with internationally recognized churches, bar associations, or other movements, or to affect the conditions multilateral and bilateral donors attached to loans and grants to the government of Kenya.

ELITE OPPOSITION

The outspokenness of the former cabinet ministers Charles Rubia and Kenneth Matiba constituted a clear and important exception to the rule and focused an otherwise diffuse opposition during 1989 and 1990. The efforts of Martin Shikuku, Kimani wa Nyoike, and Masinde Muliro also played a role. Rubia and Matiba were the central figures in the main, elite-directed opposition to the Moi government. Rubia had played the role of "moderate" and quiet defender of civil liberties during the 1970s when the Family had urged Kenyatta to move against members of his cabinet with whom they disagreed. During the late 1970s and early 1980s, Rubia's comments rarely appeared in the press, however, and to outside observers he seemed to have disappeared from the scene. Although his interventions in the 1970s and again in the mid 1980s arguably came too late to block the actions of the Office of the President, in both instances, but especially in the second case, he played a key role in defending limited space for public debate, for which he risked much. His record in Nairobi city politics, to which he devoted much of his career, was, on many occasions, less noble.

Rubia intervened first to defend those in the churches who had objected to the president's insistence on abandoning the secret ballot and replacing it with a queuing system. In August 1986, the National Council of Churches of Kenya (NCCK) had issued a statement announcing that its member pastors would not participate in elections that used the queuing system. The Law Society of Kenya joined the NCCK in calling for public debate of the issue. The two organizations had started to work together in the early 1980s, when they constituted the Public Law Institute, a legal aid and civil rights organization. Only three members of Parliament—Masinde Muliro, Kimani wa Nyoike, and Charles Rubia—spoke out on the queuing issue, however.

Rubia intervened again, four months later, during debate of a constitutional amendment bill that eliminated security of tenure in office for the attorney general, controller, and auditor. The bill passed the legislature, with almost no discussion, in only two sittings. The only dissenting voice, this time, was Rubia's, although another MP later joined him. Within a month, the police picked up Rubia for questioning.

A year later, Rubia, who had long been MP for the Nairobi constituency of Starehe, succumbed to the new 70 percent preliminary election rule, which allowed a candidate who won 70 percent or more of the vote in a primary election to advance to the general election unopposed.

In a rigged ballot, Rubia lost to an opponent, 29 percent to 71 percent. Later in 1988, Rubia lost his position on the board of the Commercial Development Corporation, an industrial parastatal. The wealthy businessman, Francis Thuo, the member of the cabinet who defended Rubia at the meeting when the decision was taken, resigned his own position on the board two days later in protest. In 1989, the Nairobi KANU branch suspended Rubia on the grounds that he had participated in anti-government demonstrations and recommended that the national party expel him. The national committee of KANU followed the advice of the party branch and removed Rubia in a purge that included thirteen others. Supporting these decisions, the president issued a statement, saying that he intended to hunt down the advocates of multi-partyism "like rats." [18]

Rubia remained silent for several months, then joined forces with the former cabinet minister Kenneth Matiba to take the defense of "political space" and civil liberties outside the confines of the Parliament and Office of the President, where both were accustomed to fighting their battles. Matiba had entered political life only in 1979, as representative for Mbiri constituency in Murang'a District, Central Province. Like Rubia, he was a wealthy businessman, a member not of the petite bourgeoisie but of the matajiri class. Like many of Kenya's senior civil servants and many of the country's early nationalist leaders, Matiba was a graduate of Alliance High School. Just before independence, he was appointed permanent secretary in the Ministry of Education, where he served as one of the country's first three African permanent secretaries. In the early and mid 1960s, he held posts in the Ministry of Home Affairs and the Ministry of Commerce and Industry. Using the skills and savings he had built as a civil servant, Matiba left government in 1968 and took a job in Kenya Breweries, Ltd. A year later, he moved up to the post of general manager of Kenya Breweries, and then became managing director. By 1977, he had become executive chairman of East African Breweries, Ltd., the parent company. He invested his earnings in the creation of several private companies, including the Alliance Hotel Group. Indeed, later in his career, Matiba is reported to have told the president that to bring chaos upon the country was clearly not his intention in making calls for greater political space; tourism was highly sensitive to political disruption, and he would surely lose a fortune from low occupancy rates in his Mombasa hotels. While holding these business positions, Matiba also took time to help manage the Kenya Football Federation (KFF) and other sports and charitable activities. [19]

Matiba's record of electoral service won him a reputation as a meticulous planner and manager with a flamboyant style. In the months leading to his election in 1979 and later, Matiba applied his business analysis skills to his constituency, developing careful studies of the economic needs of different locations and publishing brochures to attract business to the area. He served as minister for culture and social services, minister for health, and finally, minister for transport and communications. In all of these areas, he made himself a visible public figure, making visits to projects and facilities that were poorly managed and openly discussing both problems and criteria for measuring improvement.

In December 1988, Matiba resigned from the cabinet, on the eve of the arrival of a number of state guests. The reasons for his resignation centered on irregularities in the grass-roots elections for KANU posts in his area, which were later nullified by the district commissioner, and the reluctance of the Murang'a KANU branch chairman to hold fresh elections. In a rigged election, Matiba had failed to carry even his home area. Matiba's objections to the handling of the voting brought censure from the national chairman of KANU, however, and a threat to initiate disciplinary proceedings. The minister for national guidance and political affairs reiterated the KANU chairman's point. Matiba resigned on the grounds that his two colleagues had questioned his integrity and that he was concerned that election irregularities were taking place, not just in the location in question, but in other areas of the country as well.

In May 1990, the two former members of Parliament called a joint press conference to urge legalization of opposition parties. Coincidentally, the U.S. ambassador, Smith Hempstone, had addressed the same call to the members of the Rotary Club over lunch that day, saying it was likely that the U.S. Congress would tie future aid to political performance in all parts of the world. The newspapers associated the two speeches, printing the news of one on the front page and the news of the other on the back. KANU and the Moi government denounced the Matiba-Rubia press conference and its instigators as foreign-inspired.[20] One minister accused Smith Hempstone of "spending his time loitering in slum areas in Nairobi, thus proving beyond reasonable doubt that he was not a true diplomat."[21] The chance association quickly led to greater contacts between the ambassador and the Rubia-Matiba group, but to little more than that. Several days later, Rubia and Matiba issued a thirteen-page discussion of the merits of a multi-party system.

The Matiba-Rubia protest echoed earlier rebellions of propertied citizens in other countries. They attributed the country's increasing economic problems to KANU's "inflexibility and indifference to demands for public accountability."[22] The themes of their campaign included, first and foremost, a vigorous denunciation of the government's inability to contain the spread of corrupt practices. They noted that "while the Government has amply acknowledged this cancerous phenomenon, the Government seems to be helpless in dealing with it."[23] They lamented the "glaring irregularities" that plagued public services such as the Post Office, the Ports Authority, the National Cereals Board, and the General Medical Stores. They condemned "tribal patronage" that supplanted merit as a criterion for advancement. Interference with freedom of association outside the political realm was the main element of their platform, however. They noted the adverse consequences of the abolition of the Kenya Farmers' Association, the thoughtless reorganization of the Coffee Board and the Kenya Tea Development Authority, and the destruction of the Kenya Planters' Cooperative Union (KPCU). "There appeared to be no rational reason for what happened," they said. "What has been the result? Farmers are not paid their due and no reasons are given."[24] Both politicians and their associates stressed that they did not want to bring chaos to their country through their actions. It was simply that politics had interfered with the economic survival of firms and farms and the ability of citizens to live without fear.

Rumor rapidly spread that the two men had already lined up a shadow cabinet that included Rubia as prime minister, the Luo patriarch Oginga Odinga as vice president, Josephat Karanja as minister for foreign affairs, Luhya Masinde Muliro as minister of state in the office of the president, and a number of other critics of the Moi government. The author Ngugi wa Thiong'o was mentioned as a potential minister for universities; Gibson Kamau Kuria, one of the lawyers for Rubia and Matiba, was allegedly the candidate for chief justice; and Bishop Henry Okullu, an important leader of the church-based opposition to political restrictions (see pp. 190–92 below), won a place on the list as minister for culture and religious affairs. The rumored cabinet showed due respect for Kenya's different ethnic and regional communities, allocating a number of the portfolios to non-Kikuyu supporters (both Rubia and Matiba hailed from the Kikuyu community and specifically from the Murang'a group). Those close to the two leaders say there was never such a shadow cabinet, however, and that they were not nearly as well organized as rumor suggested.

The events of June and early July were decisive. In the first week of June, Rubia and Matiba applied to the Nairobi provincial commissioner for a license to hold a public rally and continued their own private meetings with Oginga Odinga and Achieng Oneko to try to get the Luo leaders of the former Kenya People's Union to support their proposals. The provincial commissioner denied the request, and a spokesman for the Moi government warned Kenyan citizens that it had not licensed any meetings on multi-partyism. On Wednesday, July 4, police arrested and detained Rubia and Matiba. Several lawyers and Odinga's son, Raila Odinga, also landed behind bars. Gibson Kamau Kuria and his family took refuge in the U.S. embassy and eventually made their way to the United States. His law partner, Kiraitu Murungi, was abroad at the time and also took refuge in the United States.

The crackdowns on Matiba, Rubia, and other advocates of multi-partyism in Kenya provoked large-scale violence in Nairobi and several Kenyan towns, beginning on July 7, or "Saba Saba Day," as people later referred to it. On that day, Rubia and Matiba were to have sponsored their public rally for multi-party democracy at Nairobi's Kamukunji meeting ground. In the preceding days, residents crowded into the banks and withdrew their savings. Some bought extra food. Rumors of American ships approaching Kenya's shores to support intervention by advocates of a multi-party system circulated in some quarters.[25] Turbulence broke out. Thousands of people poured into the streets in Nairobi, where rioting and looting continued through the weekend in the poorer neighborhoods. Nakuru, Murang'a, Nyeri, Nyandarua, Thika, Narok, and Kiambu, the towns at the center of each of the main Kikuyu strongholds, erupted similarly. In Limuru, the KANU branch headquarters burned to the ground. At least fifteen people died in the disturbances, according to government sources.[26] The rioters offered some political statements, but the events appear to have been largely unorganized, with a large admixture of unfocused popular discontent and a certain amount of purely self-serving activity. The riots caught world attention, however, and brought the plight of the Kenyan advocates of political pluralism under scrutiny.

As members of the business and legal communities began to try to find ways to secure changes in the political system, the heat of government denunciations increased. Minister for Local Government William ole Ntimama heatedly attributed the bid for a multi-party system to the Kikuyu and announced that "a certain ethnic group . . . should be cut down to size in the same manner in which the Ibo of Nigeria were in the sixties."[27] Such statements violated the norms of what most Kenyans, including many clearly in the Moi camp, believed acceptable. It crossed a line recognized by Kenyans in all walks of life: the line between a call for negotiation and a call for the kinds of conflict that ravaged Kenya's neighbors, Uganda and the Sudan, as well as countries such as Liberia and Nigeria. Ntimama's statement generated demands not only for his resignation but also for the dismissal of several other ministers.

MWAKENYA AND DIFFUSE PROTEST

During the 1980s, as political restrictions mounted and members of Parliament became more reticent about speaking out, rumors of a diffuse, usually leaderless underground opposition grew. In a few cases, politicians in exile, such as Koigi wa Wamwere, who had fled to Norway, were alleged to have created parties of their own. The author Ngugi wa Thiong'o founded a London-based association called Umoja, from the Swahili word for "unity," which stood principally for a radical redistribution of land. The members of the group were largely intellectuals.[28] By far the most talked about and least understood of the domestically active groups was Mwakenya, an "opposition" without any clear organization, believed to operate clandestinely and partly through "oaths," as had the Mau Mau in the 1950s, but with a base in Britain.

Mwakenya certainly existed, although the government greatly exaggerated its membership as a pretext for arresting or limiting the activities of critics who held a wide variety of views. In 1986 alone, the Moi government imprisoned over 100 people on charges of belonging to it,[29] and alleged affiliation has provided the pretext for numerous arrests and detentions since. Some critics of the government have suggested that the movement is nevertheless extremely small—a very loose affiliation directed largely by a small group of exiles abroad.

Those who have limited information about Mwakenya suggest that the movement is leaderless, with urban, rural, and exile components. The original impetus allegedly came from university researchers, with whose arrests the government first brought the group to public attention in 1985–86, although it is now believed that many of those detained had no connection to Mwakenya whatsoever. University graduates were allegedly the main people responsible for diffusing the "platform," a vague amalgam of demands for legalization of opposition parties, opposition to foreign military facilities, and a quasi-Marxist analysis of the country's economic and political woes. The "Draft Minimum Programme" of Mwakenya included demands for social justice, which it defined as more efficient public transportation, improved working and living conditions, guaranteed medical care, and free and compulsory secondary education.[30] Rumor suggested that the movement had a rural wing that was heavily Kikuyu in composition. The farmers of the Nakuru and Nyeri districts, the strongholds of the Mau Mau revolt, were supposed to be the bearers of Mwakenya ideas among farmers.[31]

Word about Mwakenya spread through papers that quickly appeared and disappeared, under a variety of names, *Pambana* (The Struggle) and *Mpatanishi* (The Arbiter) being the commonest. Most first appeared in Britain, but because the Moi government made it a high crime to paraphrase or quote from any of the Mwakenya leaflets, few of the statements came to the attention of the broader public. A London-based exile group called Ukenya was allegedly Mwakenya's external affiliate. Founded by Yusuf Hassan, from the Somali areas near Garissa, Ukenya had a parallel platform. Hassan's family disowned their son upon hearing of his involvement, and so powerful was the popular fear of the government's rage that Hassan's home community publicly disassociated itself from any of Ukenya's actions or any criticism of KANU.[32]

Although broad, diffuse opposition of this sort was the government's worst nightmare, because it was impossible to stop it in its tracks by arresting the "leaders," it is also the case that such movements offered no credible replacement in the event the regime fell. There were no politicians practiced in building ties with constituents in open political competition, no elites with experience in managing large organizations, much less a government ministry, and none of the habits of compromise and conciliation essential to the functioning of a multi-party system.

"CIVIL SOCIETY" AND OPPOSITION SUCCESS

The difficulties and the limited successes opposition figures experienced between 1980 and 1981 in preventing further encroachment on space for public contestation were in large part the consequence of new laws and expanded surveillance capacities, but interest-group structure made a difference too. The incentive structure in the single-party system made it very difficult for politicians to organize to protect their ability to speak and to associate. Once implemented, repressive legislation increased the risks associated with opposition, and encroachment on civil liberties accelerated. Under these conditions, only interest-group action that threatened to bring the economy to a standstill or to undermine the remunerativeness of the rental havens those in power had secured for themselves was likely to block further consolidation of the party-state. In the Kenyan case, members of the elite with private business interests had been unable to use the partial protection that independence from a government salary provided to express criticism of the Moi regime effectively. Those who were less well-off found it very difficult to mount collective action. Furthermore, their ranks were divided. Some saw the Moi government's policies, which distributed resources away from the traditionally powerful Kikuyu matajiri, as "populist" and therefore acceptable. Attacks on Charles Njonjo, in particular, conferred on Moi a "populist" label that he did not fully deserve.

THE *MATAJIRI* AND THE LEGAL COMMUNITY

At the end of the 1980s and into 1990, calls for a multi-party system and for a simple loosening of political restrictions came principally from the Kenyan private business community. Few members of this group were publicly vocal in their protests, but discontent grew rapidly. The main concern was that the president was increasingly able to use his expanded powers to intervene in business matters. Appointment of close associates to key economic posts led to use of political criteria in the allocation of critical licenses and even in access to bank loans and foreign exchange. Second, meritocratic personnel policies were difficult to maintain because of interference in the hiring and firing of employees. Third, State House succeeded in manipulating the political process in order to secure new rules that promoted the private business interests of the president and his associates. For example, when Moi acquired bakery businesses, existing bakeries discovered that they faced new rules, quickly legislated, to limit their selling range to Nairobi and to eliminate the competition they would have provided to the president's own enterprises in other areas. Planning business activities, including business expansion, was difficult under these conditions.

Although Rubia had protested restriction of civil liberties on several occasions, his criticism of the Moi government began with his belief that it had done too little to promote the interests of indigenous private-sector entrepreneurs.[33] The government did not interfere with the commercial interests of either Matiba or Rubia, but it did withdraw the passports of the two men in the late 1980s, limiting their ability to work with foreign partners. Furthermore, the president had appointed a disproportionately large number of Kalenjin to key economic posts, creating the specter of increasingly politicized infrastructure services and parastatal sectors. Under Moi, Kalenjin gained control of the governorship of the Central Bank, the Ministry for Cooperative Development, the Ministry of Local Government, and the post of commissioner of cooperatives. The chairs of the Kenya Commercial Bank and Kenya National Insurance were both Kalenjin. Moi's community also gained the directorships of Kenya Posts and Telecommunications, the Agricultural Finance Corporation, the Agricultural Development Corporation, Kenya Industrial Estates, the National Cereals and Produce Board, the Kenya Grain Growers' Cooperative Union, Nyayo Tea Zone, Nyayo Bus Company, and the Kenya Broadcasting Corporation. The government decided to de-register the Kenya Coffee Growers' Union, the representative of smallholder coffee interests, which were predominantly Kikuyu, and sidelined the other body whose officers are elected by coffee growers, the Kenya Planters' Cooperative Union. It also chose to re-shuffle and reorganize the management of the internationally successful Kenya Tea Development Authority.[34] Thus, to the extent that the decision to take a stand on the restriction of political space in 1989–91 was business-related, it was based less on objection to the actual content of policies regarding trade and industry than it was on the long-term prospects for local businessmen in a country where the personal power of the president made greater levels of interference and uncertainty likely.

Class sentiment and class organization remained inchoate, however. On the face of it, commercial and industrial interests in Parliament were stronger than they had ever been. In the years since independence, the social backgrounds of members of Parliament had changed to include many more businessmen than it had originally. In 1963, business was the main occupation or source of income of 6 percent of the members of Parliament; by 1983 the figure had risen to 27 percent.[35] Just over half of the new entrants to Parliament in 1983 were businessmen. Originally, teachers, former civil servants, and professionals (doctors and lawyers) had dominated the ranks of parliamentarians. Although the proportion of professionals remained relatively constant over the years, the proportion of teachers and farmers diminished. Business interests in Parliament were unable to unite in objecting to the president's appointment policy, however. Indeed, by the end of the 1980s, most bills passed with little or no discussion.

Finally, among the majority of businessmen—who could not, after all, count themselves among the matajiri—economic interests were mixed. Most businessmen had other sources of income: small or medium-sized farms, for example. Many had mixed economic heritages, too. At the same time that the occupational backgrounds of members of Parliament had changed, so had the average age, which increased. It is likely that many of the men and women who started as teachers and civil servants launched their own businesses and later acquired the major part of their income from these enterprises. Rapid social mobility and social change may well have attenuated class sentiment. Moreover, the reduction in Kikuyu business fortunes potentially created short-term opportunities for members of other cultural groups to launch businesses. Certainly, the Kalenjin benefited greatly from the difficulties the Kikuyu business-owners experienced.

As both Matiba and Rubia were aware, too, most private-sector businesses were heavily dependent on government capital, contracts, and services. Where appointments to the latter were highly politicized, it was possible for a businessman to face politically motivated and economically devastating cutoffs of electricity, telephone, water, sewer, and transport services or slowdowns in the transfer of bank funds. Shipments could be delayed at truck depots, airports, and harbors. Where these shipments included perishables, such as horticultural exports, the business could easily lose its inventories within a matter of hours. Although the proportion of business equity controlled by Kenyan businessmen had increased markedly since independence, political organization had not expanded concomitantly.[36]

More important, neither Rubia nor Matiba nor any other member of the matajiri class commanded control of a critical sector of the economy, so neither was it possible to initiate a sectorwide strike or slowdown of such potentially devastating proportions that the president would have an incentive to come to the bargaining table. Few other members of the matajiri class openly supported the two men. As noted above, Francis Thuo, a wealthy businessman and founder of the Kenya Stock Exchange, resigned one of his public positions when the government moved to dismiss Rubia from his parastatal posts after his suspension from the party, but few others were able or willing to make similar demonstrations, or could do so without severe repercussions.

The Transport Sector   Moi's greatest fear was that the opposition might acquire bargaining leverage by building contacts and power within the transportation sector. Bus, taxi, or truckers' strikes could easily cripple government business and the Kenyan economy. The sector demonstrated its strength on several occasions before the party and State House took steps to counteract its power. In 1986, the government announced that it would enforce a "no-standing" rule against vehicles and drivers of the Kenya Bus Service, Ltd., a partly British-owned company and the principal provider of bus transportation between the capital and periurban areas. Typically, buses carried as many passengers as could crowd into the aisles. The government argued that standing should not be permitted. The company responded to the ruling by briefly withdrawing bus service from the routes around Nairobi. So great were the resulting disorder and public outcry that the government relented temporarily. It is widely thought that the State House was perturbed by this demonstration of power. Within three months, it began to run "nyayo buses" on many routes, the vehicles often being contributed by European donors and the drivers being drawn from the National Youth Service, a government-run vocational training program. Moi took the decision to launch the service at a KANU parliamentary group meeting shortly after the incident.

Two years later, in 1988, the Nyayo Bus Services Corporation was established to manage the growing fleet of vehicles, which provided increasing competition to Kenya Bus Services, Ltd. KANU retained a hand in its direction. The Nyayo Bus Services Corporation faced a much lower cost structure than Kenya Bus Services, Ltd. All of the vehicles used by Nyayo Bus Services were donated, mostly by the Netherlands and Italy. All of the staff members came from the National Youth Service, effectively subsidizing the firm's labor costs. The Economist Intelligence Unit reported in 1989 that Nyayo Bus was the fastest growing enterprise in Kenya.[37] Kenya Bus Services, which not only faced higher costs but found itself forced to abandon several routes because of the eventual successful enforcement of the no-standing rule, was on its way to ruin.

The main alternative to bus transport was the *matatu* system, a relatively unregulated, low-cost form of travel in converted pickup trucks, whose owners were variously members of the petite bourgeoisie or of the matajiri class, some of whom owned multiple vehicles. This part of the sector also proved to have strong bargaining power. In the late 1980s, owners of matatus belonged to one of two associations, the Matatu Vehicle Owners Association (MVOA) and the much smaller Matatu Association of Kenya. Drivers were often young and vehicles poorly maintained. The incidence of fatal traffic accidents was extremely high.

In the wake of several horrifying accidents, the State House moved to expand safety standards for the sector but met resistance every step of the way. First, in 1986, Moi announced a campaign to remove poorly maintained matatus from the road. The MVOA protested the ensuing police crackdown with a slowdown that left many workers stranded. The police eventually relented. In June 1987, the government announced a requirement that matatus be equipped with speed governors to ensure that vehicles did not exceed acceptable limits. The governors proved extremely expensive—about half the cost of the matatu itself in some cases. Owners and operators protested by going on strike. Again, the State House acceded to the MVOA's demands. Finally, after a crash that killed thirty people in 1988, the government ordered poorly maintained matatus off the road and announced that drivers would have to undergo retesting. It launched sweeps by the police and by members of the National Youth Service. Again, the MVOA initiated a strike, and the authorities caved in.

The content of most of these encounters was not explicitly political. The speed-governor requirement carried some political overtones. Knowledgeable sources have said that several of the president's associates imported the equipment into the country just before and after the ruling, expecting to make money, but that they lost substantial sums as a result of the standoff and policy reversal. In 1990, however, the government moved against owners and drivers it suspected were playing seditious music for the passengers' listening pleasure: songs protesting the razing of shanties in Nairobi; some of Kenyatta's early speeches; "Mathina ma Matiba" ("Matiba's Tribulations"); and the singer Tom Kimani's "Patriotic Contributions," commemorating J. M. Kariuki, and "Big Fish" (*samaki kubwa*, "big fish," is a common term for wealthy or powerful men).[38] Many of these tapes circulated in advance of the Saba Saba riots, and during the Saba Saba demonstrations members of the public burned several vehicles that did not play the tapes. At that point, the State House moved to de-register the associations. Eventually, the government de-registered the Matatu Vehicle Owners Association, making it more difficult for the sector to organize to influence policy.

The Export-Crop Sector   Growers of crops for export could also muster some bargaining power in the Kenyan economy, in large part because of the country's heavy dependence upon the revenues these generated as a source of foreign exchange. Growers thus constituted potential allies for the advocates of political pluralism. Threats to withhold delivery of crops proved only temporarily useful, however. After a protracted struggle and the collapse of coffee prices, farmers in that sector became less vocal in their struggles and representative associations were either disbanded or weakened. In the tea sector, the Moi government succeeded in reorganizing the Kenya Tea Development Authority to give higher prices and higher quotas to farmers from the Rift Valley, particularly from Kalenjin strongholds, at the expense of Central Province communities that cultivated tea that typically commanded higher prices on the international market. The introduction of Nyayo Tea Zones, a new parastatal, also limited the bargaining power of outraged tea farmers by flooding the tea factories with leaves from new, government-controlled plantations and rendering smallholders' tea less valuable.

The Moi government and coffee growers clashed over an extended period, beginning in 1983, when the government decided to turn the Kenya Planters' Cooperative Union (KPCU), the main coffee growers' association, into a parastatal. The coffee cooperatives had long been both a source of substantial income and a site of petty corruption and mismanagement. Certainly, there was a rationale for trying to clean up the cooperatives in an effort to ensure that a higher proportion of coffee receipts went to the farmers who produced the beans. The popular impression of the government's actions in trying to dissolve or reorganize the KPCU, however, was that the State House wanted to reduce the voice of farmers in the management of their affairs and in formation of Coffee Board policies. Specifically, Moi wanted to reduce Kikuyu influence.

The farmers repulsed the first effort to eliminate the KPCU. Then, in October 1986, the government tried to introduce a new method for paying farmers, and the country's lobby for large plantations, the Kenya Coffee Growers' Association (KCGA), joined forces with the smallholders and rebelled. When farmers threatened to stop delivering beans to the Coffee Board, the government relented. In March 1987, the KPCU successfully fought off an effort by the State House to remove the organization's two representatives from the directorship of the Coffee Board, again through the threat of holding up delivery.

Unable to attenuate the power of the coffee growers in this way, the government moved to try to divide the growers on class lines—to sever the link between the small growers and the matajiri. In June 1987, the government announced that it wanted to disband the KPCU and replace it with a National Coffee Cooperative Union (NCCU). The rationales were various. The State House had earlier embarked on a shake-up of personnel in both the Coffee Board and the Kenya Tea Development Authority. These reshufflings had placed a large number of inexperi-

enced managers in high positions, and the reliability of the services both
organizations provided suffered in the view of farmers, who were irate.
Some members of the Moi government suggested that the owners of
large farms (more than fifty acres) had stirred up the trouble and that
this group had benefited disproportionately from the services of the
marketing boards in the past. Indeed, they said, the effort to disband the
KPCU stemmed from a desire to curb the influence of large-scale farmers in that organization and give greater voice to smallholders whose
plots were smaller than fifty acres.[39]

Growers used tried-and-true tactics to repel the government's initiative, and they temporarily persuaded it to back down, but were eventually unsuccessful. When the State House tried the intermediate step of
imposing new voting rules and new directors, farmers gathered to protest these actions and threatened to suspend deliveries of beans to the
Coffee Board. They further called for elimination of the coffee export
tax, and for suspension of the Coffee Board's management to permit
investigation of the alleged disappearance of beans from its warehouses.
Again, the government backed off its demands, but only temporarily.

Shortly after the protests by farmers, the Criminal Investigation Department picked up the KPCU's managing director, Henry Kinyua, for
questioning. Although he was eventually released, Kinyua stepped
down from his position. In 1987, the KPCU itself was first dismantled
and then suspended, its functions being assumed by the Coffee Board.
These changes were interpreted by many as an attack on Kikuyu growers, who generated 70 percent of the country's coffee crop,[40] although
the government may also have taken the measure to reduce the bargaining power of coffee growers who wanted to exceed the country's coffee
quota, set by the International Coffee Organization.

Eventually, the government allowed a reorganized KPCU to register
again, but in a greatly reduced form. Until 1989, the KPCU had been
one of the chief sources of short-term loans for coffee farmers. It was
able to play this role because its assets made it easy for it to obtain
credit, which it then used to extend loans to farmers, and because it
could collect on the loans by recovering the money from the farmers'
coffee receipts.[41] To the degree that the reduced role allowed the union
limited both its assets and its access to farmers' earnings, its credit functions, and consequently the utility of the union to growers, were undermined.

The government was less disposed to bargain with the lobby for large
plantation owners. In early 1989, it dissolved the Kenya Coffee Grow-

ers' Association (KCGA). The *Weekly Review* said this step "marked a decisive stage in recent moves by the state to reduce the influence of mass-based autonomous farmers' organizations in decisions affecting the coffee industry." [42] As had the KCPU, the KCGA had strongly protested the coffee amendment bill of 1987, which proposed many changes in the role of the Coffee Board, including making the chief executive of the board responsible, not to the board's directors, who typically included farmers, but to the minister of agriculture.

Matiba and Rubia had expressed concern that tea farmers, too, were losing their voice in public policy—or at least, tea farmers from the Central Province zones that produced high-grade leaves. The Kenya Tea Development Authority (KTDA) was long recognized as a success story rare among parastatal organizations. During the 1980s, the Moi government took several steps to reorganize the company, replacing the older, more experienced managers with new people more beholden to the president. It also introduced measures that increased the power of tea growers in the west of the country and sowed division among tea farmers, reducing the effectiveness of group action.

The changes in administrative personnel had rapid consequences for the reliability of tea-collection services and for the condition of the country's hundreds of kilometers of tea roads, many of which became increasingly impassable. Farmers in Central Province also began to charge that the KTDA managers or the government were manipulating the level of end-of-season payments, which were supposed to reflect movements in world prices, in contrast to initial payments, which were in proportion to the quantity of tea leaves delivered. In 1989, several hundred farmers in Murang'a District tried to protest deteriorating services and price manipulation by boycotting picking and by burning 2.5 tons of tea leaves already harvested.[43] Matiba, who hailed from Murang'a District, was consequently quite attentive to farmers' demands and incorporated them into his platform.

The Moi government moreover introduced new policies that increased Kenya's tea production but divided the ranks of producers, decreasing the effectiveness of farmers' associations. In 1984, the president launched an effort allegedly both to enhance soil conservation and to increase tea production. The idea was to provide funds for Kenyans to plant narrow strips of tea adjacent to gazetted forests in the multiple expectation of limiting soil erosion when trees were cut, enhancing the capacity of the forest police to observe illegal cutting by creating a space around these forests in which trespassers could be easily seen, and bolstering the country's tea production. In 1987, the president created a new parastatal, Nyayo Tea Zones Development Corporation (NTZDC), to administer the program. By the end of the 1980s, the NTZDC had established zones in fifteen districts, mostly in the Kalenjin and Luhya areas of the western provinces but also alongside the KTDA-run plots in Central Province, encompassing about 15,000 farmers.[44]

The new Nyayo tea zones immediately created problems for smallholders, however, particularly in Central Province and Kericho, where they competed with smallholder production. When the zones were created, the NTZDC decided not to build tea factories but to use existing facilities in nearby smallholder areas instead. That meant, however, that factory capacity was swamped by the new production. Smallholders could not have their tea treated, as they had in the past, because the leaves from the Nyayo zones took precedence. Matiba was right when he noted: "Tea from the Nyayo Tea Zones has completely swamped up the existing capacity."[45] Moreover, the zones interfered with other sources of smallholders' income. Most households were able to obtain permission from the local forest police to graze livestock on gazetted lands during some seasons of the year, or during alternate years. They were restricted to the fringe areas, but they nonetheless had use of them. The Nyayo tea zones interfered with this system, however. In many cases, the government established its zones, not along a narrow strip of already deforested land, but on swaths of land a mile wide cut from existing stands of trees. The forests were placed off limits for grazing in consequence, and farmers were forced to secure pasture elsewhere.

The creation of the tea zones meant that the government received a larger share of the income from tea than it had in the past, and that smallholders lost influence as their share of the proceeds dropped. Withholding or burning tea was no longer the devastating tactic it might once have been. It could no longer be used to force government attention to farmers' concerns. Thus, although growers of coffee and tea, especially in Central Province, were discontented and a potential reserve of followers for an opposition party, they could no longer by themselves lend opposition leaders bargaining power.

The Lawyers Restrictions on political association prevented formation of an opposition party, or even efforts to plan protest. Given the limitations on even small-group discussion of political events, it was extremely difficult for ideas and information to pass between members of the matajiri. There were only two points of indirect contact between individual members of the class and between these men and women and other Kenyans: the lawyers and the clergy. Despite political restrictions, lawyers could still speak with their clients, at least up to a point, and clergy could still speak with members of their congregations or parishes. Through these men and women limited communication could take place, as long as their own positions remained secure. Furthermore, by observing the kinds of cases members of the public asked them to bring, the lawyers, in particular, could see trends in the kinds of problems individuals encountered in their dealings with the government.

Beginning in the 1980s, some members of the legal profession became concerned about the restrictions the Moi government was imposing, and these members sought to organize efforts to challenge laws they believed unconstitutional. They also used their ties to the international legal profession to draw attention to imprisonment of their own members and other Kenyans and to provide a forum for members of other groups to come together. For example, some of the lawyers used the Kenya section of the International Commission of Jurists (ICJ), an organization with consultative status in the U.N. Economic and Social Council (ECOSOC) and in the U.N. Education, Science, and Culture Organization (UNESCO), to facilitate communication. The Kenya section of the ICJ started in 1959. In the 1980s, its organizers urged: "The ICJ Kenya Section should as much as possible take practical and consultative measures to bridge the gap between our aspirations and achievements, . . . identify obstacles to the rule of law, and blocks that retard the enjoyment of human rights . . . ICJ Kenya Section can do this by commissioning research papers, studies, and workshops by lawyers and other social actors."[46] The lawyers created some domestic forums as well. For example, Gitobu Imanyara, later detained, launched the *Nairobi Law Monthly* as a vehicle through which lawyers could exchange ideas and communicate with the outside world.

For the most part, the lawyers were concerned with the same kinds of issues that motivated Rubia and Matiba and prompted the concerns of Kenya's farmers and businessmen. They argued that three government acts in particular had "converted the rights to free expression into concessions granted at the pleasure of government officials," including officials of KANU.[47] These were the Societies Act, which required registration of all associations, the Public Order Act, which allowed preventive detention, and the Film and Stage Plays Act, which limited use of communications media. Some of the most outspoken argued that trespasses on the legal rights of individuals and the decline of the Kenyan economy were the direct consequence of the single-party state, which stifled individual enterprise and initiative.[48] Others examined the problem from an even broader perspective and argued that the extensive role of government in the economies of African countries, including Kenya, was the root of the problem:

> Some African countries which chose socialism as their development model took the view that such freedoms are meaningless to their populations who were half-naked, illiterate, underfed, and diseased. . . . No African country has however been able to achieve any significant economic development through socialism because it is essentially undemocratic. What they have succeeded in doing is increasing repression. . . . Any individual who genuinely criticises a bureaucrat's incompetence, corruption, or mismanagement is accused of sabotage and subversion.[49]

Some lawyers simply demanded greater government accountability. Most concurred, however, that the single-party system had severely restricted the public debate necessary to an efficient economic system. In 1990, a group of fifty-four lawyers urged a loosening of political restrictions and pointed out that KANU was now a minority party with at most five million members, which left twenty million Kenyans without a party affiliation and completely disenfranchised.[50]

Because of the character of their profession and their international ties, the lawyers held greater bargaining leverage in dealings with the Moi government and KANU than did most of the country's economic associations. Even their abilities to achieve repeal of restrictions, to block the implementation of additional measures, and to defend clients were very limited, however. Many of the more outspoken landed in detention for some portion of the 1980s, among them John Khaminwa, Koigi wa Wamwere, George Anyona, Gibson Kamau Kuria, and Gitobu Imanyara. Others went into hiding. Furthermore, although the legal community could facilitate the flow of information between other social actors, it could not provide an organizational base. It could not supply cars to send representatives to speak with farmers in rural areas, for example, or do many of the other things that a coherent opposition would have to do to coordinate economic actors and to use that collective leverage to force the president and his party's leadership to the bargaining table.

Finally, the Office of the President had its own ways of shattering the unity of the legal profession. In January–March 1990, several advocates of a multi-party system among the LSK's membership decided to run their own candidate, Paul Muite, for chairman of the society against the

incumbent, Fred Ojiambo. Muite's supporters, including Gibson Kamau Kuria, Kiraitu Murungi, Dr. Oki Ooko-Ombaka, director of the
Public Law Institute, and others, drafted an explanation of the circumstances that motivated their campaign:

> Deteriorating working conditions, confiscatory taxation, poor remunera-
> tion, decline in standards, rampant corruption, constant vilification of law-
> yers, . . . and the weakening of institutions for the maintenance of rule of law
> and the administration of justice. They are also talking about the Law Soci-
> ety: . . . the Law Society's remoteness from advocates in rural areas. . . . The
> Law Society's failure to lobby against legislation adversely affecting advo-
> cates. . . . The Law Society's indifference to lack of law reports and legal
> literature. . . .
>   . . . Our words are not good enough to remove these complaints. Our
> words must be matched by positive action.[51]

There were other statements against Muite from lawyers who were also
KANU branch chairmen, suggesting that the government had not extended a passport to Muite in the past because he was "not the type of
person who would project the correct image of our beloved Republic to
the international community." [52] The elections themselves were attended
by a variety of irregularities. Ballot papers were not sent to people on
time. Others were handed to lawyers in person, and the recipients were
instructed that they had to indicate their choices then and there and
hand the ballot back to the person who had brought it. Ojiambo was
declared the winner in an election that provoked outrage among many
of the LSK's members. The Muite group sought to carry on its defense
of civil liberties, however, working in large teams, all of whose members
would have to be arrested in the event the government decided to move
against them. For example, when Gitobu Imanyara, editor of the *Nairobi Law Monthly,* was detained on charges of publishing seditious literature, the lawyer John Khaminwa assembled a group of thirty-one
advocates for the defense.[53]

THE CHURCH AND KANU

Church involvement in the protection of civil liberties began in 1986
over objections to replacement of the secret ballot with a queuing system. From the very beginning, there were divisions within the religious
community. Although the National Council of Churches of Kenya
(NCCK) was the first to speak publicly about loss of civil liberties, some
member churches disagreed with the group's position and left the fold.

The NCCK's membership decreased appreciably. In 1986, when the NCCK announced that church leaders and their followers would boycott elections that used the queuing system and published a critique of queuing in *Beyond*, the church publication, at least three member churches broke with the group. The bishop of the African Independent Pentecostal Church said the NCCK was against African culture. The Gospel Church and Association of Baptist Churches of Nyeri announced their support of KANU. The head of the NCCK set the tone for the majority of the churches, however, when he noted: "The question of disloyalty does not arise . . . debate is a healthy exercise. If a country cannot debate an issue of national significance, we shall be denying ourselves the very roots of democracy."[54] Over the next four years, the Anglican Church of the Province of Kenya (CPK) and the Presbyterian Church of East Africa (PCEA) played a major role in sustaining discussion of civil liberties and the restriction of political space when public defender groups, such as the Law Society of Kenya, had succumbed to harassment.

The NCCK and the Reverend Alexander Kipsang Muge of the CPK's Eldoret diocese led the attack on queuing and rapidly attracted fire from KANU and from the Office of the President. Rift Valley political leaders came together at a KANU rally in early 1987 to attack Muge, who had trespassed all the more on the president's patience because his diocese included Moi's home area. Muge replied with fighting words. "I shall not protest against the violation of human rights in South Africa if I am not allowed to protest the violation of human rights in my own country," he declared. The mention of South Africa was, of course, a red flag. Muge persisted, and in a sermon spelled out his understanding of his role, pointing out: "I say things that other people don't want to say simply because they will get into trouble with the politicians."[55]

Muge's remarks won the attention and support of both Anglican and Episcopal leaders around the world, including the archbishop of Canterbury. They created a tactical and stylistic example for other religious communities to follow. The international press responded quickly, alerted to the significance of the church actions by Muge. The BBC broadcast Muge's sermon about the role of the church, allowing Muge to reach many Kenyans who would otherwise not have heard the remarks. The CPK and the NCCK moved quickly to mobilize their international networks and keep the spotlight on the issues raised and on their members, offering a modicum of protection in a dangerous political environment. It also created a new form of political communication, the sermon, which church leaders soon learned to mimeograph and tape for distribution, in the belief that the government was still wary of censoring religious speech.

The churches rapidly broadened their criticisms to include not only queuing but also the detention of political opponents and the obstacles to debate created by a one-party political system. Indeed, a limited and tenuous call for multi-party democracy issued earlier and more clearly from the churches and the legal profession than from any other groups, although Muge himself never made an explicit demand for legalization of opposition parties. Reverend Timothy Njoya of the PCEA was arrested briefly in 1988 for a sermon that proposed the holding of a large *kamukunji*, or council, with amnesty for the country's dissidents, to give all a chance to talk. Bishop Henry Okullu offered the first unequivocal endorsement of a multi-party system in early May 1990, giving a push to Rubia and Matiba. Bishop Okullu had long criticized the KANU leadership and had once referred to some of the leaders as "court poets." [56]

Church activity increased sharply in 1989–90. A New Year's sermon by Reverend Timothy Njoya drew the first public parallels between events in Eastern Europe and the political situation on the African continent, for which he attracted Minister Elijah Mwangale's ire and demands that he be detained without trial. Eighteen Catholic bishops subsequently signed a pastoral letter urging political liberalization and Archbishop Manasses Kuria of the CPK issued a statement calling for overhaul of the electoral system, attacking corruption and forced harambee contributions, and drawing attention to the plight of the poor. Okullu urged a two-term limit on the tenure of any individual in the presidency. Despite virulent government attacks against the churches and KANU claims that Mwakenya had friends among the clerics, the government did not move decisively to stop the activity. (It should be noted, however, that the man who started it all, Bishop Alexander Muge, died in a car crash in Eldoret in mid 1990.)

THE INFORMAL SECTOR, THE OUKO AFFAIR, AND POLITICAL ACTION IN THE SHANTYTOWNS

The other potential domestic source of pressure on the government was action by the members of Kenya's burgeoning informal sector, or *jua kali* (hot sun) enterprises. It would be incorrect to say that the thousands of hawkers, traders, metalworkers, carpenters, and open-air mechanics in this sector, rural and urban, had a single set of economic interests or political objectives. In fact, their interests were extremely varied, as were their relationships with the government and members of the country's business and political elite.[57] If Daniel arap Moi had a strong political base among the members of any single part of the society, however, he had support from some of these small producers and traders, to whom he projected the image of a "populist" opposed to a Kikuyu-dominated business elite.

It is also the case that Moi, like other African leaders, feared the power of this sector. Not only were the traders the "glue" in the Kenyan economy, providing cheap goods and services to a populace less and less able to afford the basic requirements of life, and therefore economically powerful, but they also had political power, which resided in their ability to get out on the streets in numbers and in a form that challenged the capacity of any government to maintain order.

According to some students of the sector, most members remained firmly in the Moi camp.[58] In 1990, two actions of the Moi government began to change the attitudes of some, however. The first was the assassination of Foreign Minister Robert Ouko. A distinguished Luo politician of long standing, Ouko had appeared to be a staunch Moi supporter. He was responsible for negotiating aid arrangements with countries that were bringing increasing pressure on Kenya for political reform—most particularly the United States. Ouko had traveled to America frequently, where senior officials met with him to discuss the linkage between assistance levels and human rights. When Moi announced that he would travel to the United States to meet with the U.S. president, without an invitation from U.S. policy makers, the U.S. ambassador discouraged him from doing so. He traveled to Washington regardless and received no welcome. Among many Kenyans, including some of Moi's supporters, the story goes that upon his return Moi was so furious with Ouko that he ordered his assassination.[59] Whether true or not, the rumor provoked substantial grass-roots outrage, especially in the Luo community, which rioted for several days, cutting Nyanza District off from the rest of the country. Protestors recorded songs about the event, which they circulated to people in other parts of the country on cassettes, traded by members of the informal sector. Among these was "Who Killed Ouko," a song by Sam Muraya. Increasingly, there were reports of two-fingered "salutes" to multi-partyism by hawkers.

In June, after parliamentary discussion of Ouko's death ended, the government took the second action that provoked opposition in the sector. Perhaps fearful of the spread of the subversive cassettes and acting on rumors that anti-Moi forces, allegedly trained in Uganda, were posing as hawkers, the government moved to disrupt the activities of the thousands of entrepreneurs who had operated in the country's legal "gray area." Although it publicly claimed it was only getting rid of some illegal shanties and kiosks on a nearby road, government bulldozers moved in and razed the shanty village of Muoroto, in Nairobi, killing two people, injuring others, and leaving many without places to live. These actions on the part of the Nairobi City Council, acting in concert with KANU, had the effect of opening up real estate for distribution to loyal adherents of the nyayo philosophy. Kenyatta had occasionally bulldozed shanties for that purpose, and the same motive may well originally have been behind the razing of Muoroto, but it came to have a more explicit political rationale under the circumstances that prevailed. When the MP for the area, Maina Wanjigi, expressed outrage and sought restitution, his colleagues in Parliament denounced his actions as divisive and "tribalist." He eventually lost his seat and his position in KANU.[60]

It is likely that these two events influenced the size and style of the riots on July 7, 1990, after the government detained Matiba and Rubia. Reporters observed participants using the characteristic "two-fingered salute" and chanting anti-government slogans. Although the members of the informal sector could not provide an organized forum for discussion, at least some of their number began to lend economic and social weight to the demands for greater openness. For example, foreign observers noted that market women—fruit and vegetable hawkers—lined up in their new locations, pointed to themselves, and chanted, "Human rights!" The government moved against the informal sector a second time in November 1990, razing Kibagare, another shantytown in Nairobi, and leaving 30,000 homeless. KANU members escorted the bulldozers and moved people away from the site. Again, the rumor spread that the government's intention was to stop the circulation of the subversive cassettes, which had rapidly multiplied in number and included a new gospel song entitled "The Poor People of Muoroto." The government stated that the dissident and former detainee Koigi wa Wamwere had incited the residents of the shantytown to oppose KANU and that it would not tolerate such behavior.[61]

It is important to note that the jua kali has itself often been the source of KANU youth-wing members. In recent years, the party has paid its activists, and just as KANU provided income and opportunity to some politicians, it has also provided such for those less well-off. The absence of a single set of economic interests means the sector has brought, and can bring, only limited power to bear to defend political space.

TESTING THE LIMITS

Because of the bargaining structures they create, single-party systems facilitate encroachment on political space and undermine both policy debate and the accountability of state institutions to society. The presence of interest groups angered by government policy stances and able to command control of critical economic sectors may slow these trends and even secure changes in the party system. In most instances, that requires civic associations or interest-group lobbies whose members can continue to provide for their households despite government persecution. That is, members must not be wholly dependent for their economic survival on government-controlled employment. It also requires that members of these groups be able to organize bases for sustained opposition, relationships with one another and with others that permit civic associations to elicit concerted action as long as necessary to force government officials to bargain and to retreat from stances they had earlier assumed. Because single-party systems also shape the character of civil society, favoring cultivation of patron-client ties and communal associations over interest-group organizations, the citizens of most countries of sub-Saharan Africa are likely to find it difficult to halt authoritarianism and to create stable competitive political systems. Although better situated than many nations to broach such a change because of the relatively greater latitude allowed private entrepreneurial activity, Kenya, too, falls into this category.

During the period 1987–90, the combined actions of Matiba, Rubia and other businessmen, members of the legal community, and elements of the church led to the reversal, on paper, of some of the restrictions on civil liberties the Moi government had imposed. The Ministry of National Guidance and Political Affairs endured for only a short time before its dissolution, which was prompted less by the pressure for political reform than by the jurisdictional conflicts it had sown within the government. Many of its functions were assumed by the Ministry of Culture. KANU rescinded its power to expel members and abolished the infamous national disciplinary committee created in 1986. The Kenya Law Society persisted and successfully foiled the threat to subordinate its activities to the party. Weeks after the arrest of Matiba and

Rubia and the flight of lawyers central to the call for multi-party politics, Paul Muite, the earlier opposition candidate for the position of
head of the Law Society, was invited to come out of hiding, and threats
to detain him apparently diminished.

Many of these changes were more cosmetic than real, however. Although the government eventually released Rubia from detention, Matiba long remained incarcerated without trial, as did others, including
Gitobu Imanyara, the editor of the *Nairobi Law Monthly* and a key
legal activist. To a great extent, the suspension rules that replaced the
expulsion rules in KANU represented a change in name only, as they
carried with them the threat of ineligibility to contest all future general
elections. Finally, the party leadership continued to carry out many of
the functions it had allocated to the disciplinary committee long after it
had dismantled the committee itself under pressure.

In late 1991, the Moi government announced the arrest of the former
energy minister Nicholas Biwott and others associated with extensive
high-level corruption and implicated in a Scotland Yard–led investigation of the murder of Robert Ouko. Questioning by a Scotland Yard
official, Malcolm Troon, had revealed that just prior to his murder
Ouko had challenged Biwott over the latter's alleged appropriation of
foreign aid for his own use. Over the succeeding months, foreign donors, friends of Ouko, and high-level officials put information together
that implicated Biwott and a number of the president's associates in the
diversion of aid money (including the entire Swedish assistance package
of the previous year), manipulation of policy to pursue personal business interests, and failure to repay millions of dollars in loans from
Citibank, whose officials were told their lives were in danger unless they
accepted the defaults. When foreign donors met in Paris on November
25, 1991, the representatives agreed to suspend the major part of all
loans and grants to the government of Kenya pending review of efforts
to curb corruption and more tolerance of political pluralism.

On December 3, 1991, the president announced that Kenya would
take the further step of legalizing opposition political parties. Specifically, he noted that parties would be permitted to register with the government and that those who did so could contest future elections. The
rules returned substantially to the form they had taken in the mid
1960s, when the Kenyatta government had manipulated registration to
limit expansion of the Kenya People's Union. The Forum for the Restoration of Democracy (FORD) became an opposition umbrella, first for
two parties, one behind Martin Shikuku and the other behind the law-

yer Paul Muite. Advisers at home and abroad counseled cooperation within FORD, and the two factions rejuvenated their coalition in a tenuous truce. Subsequently the number of internal divisions proliferated, and several ethnic political machines asserted themselves. These included the "House of Mumbi," under the nominal direction of Kenneth Matiba (then very ill), and a Luo counter-group. KANU itself underwent little change in the first weeks following Moi's announcement, provoking the resignation of several cabinet ministers, including Mwai Kibaki, who had hoped to see a greater degree of openness within the ranks. Kibaki constituted an opposition party, the Democratic Party, outside the auspices of FORD.

CHAPTER SEVEN

The Kenyan Party-State in Comparative Perspective

The argument of this book is that the changes in the character of Kenya's single-party system, from one in which the party was loosely organized and possessed limited representative functions to one in which the party became an instrument for political and social control under the guidance of the Office of the President, had three sources. The first was the collapse of the extra-parliamentary bargaining system set up by the harambee program, which had provided an incentive for politicians to limit their claims and negotiate alliances with one another. As the system ceased to perform this function, ethnic welfare associations began to appear more threatening, their revenues used less for deal-making between politicians in different parts of the country and more for the advancement of their members' sectional interests. Second, once adopted, in fact if not in law, the single-party system destroyed incentives for politicians to defend their own political space. It became increasingly difficult to build enduring oppositions in Parliament along the lines of the Backbenchers' Group of the 1960s, and maneuvering between ad hoc factional groupings replaced bargaining between interests. Fragmentation created an incentive for politicians to "free ride" on the labors of others and sell their support at the last minute to the highest bidder. Finally, although the structure of the Kenyan political economy meant that Kenya had a larger and wealthier "private sector" than most countries in Africa, the Moi government was able to make substantial inroads into the bargaining power of groups that could pose a credible opposition. Although the late months of 1990 saw encroachment on political space slow, and under foreign pressure Moi announced the legalization of opposition parties in late 1991, the 1980s would best be remembered as the decade that saw consolidation of the power of the State House to control the political life of the country.

This last chapter tries to place the Kenyan case in comparative perspective. It begins by reviewing the argument made in the preceding chapters. The second section considers whether the variables identified help explain the role of the ruling party in several other, well-studied African cases. The third section focuses on the reasons for "the Kenyan holdout"—that is, for the Moi government's comparatively long resistance to the wave of multi-partyism that swept the continent between 1989 and 1991. The final section briefly relates the findings of the study to the continuing African debate about the relative merits of single-party versus competitive party systems.

THE ARGUMENT IN REVIEW

This study has suggested that three variables are especially important in explaining the course of recent political history in Kenya.

Harambee   Kenyatta had established the harambee system in the 1965 "Sessional Paper Number 10 on the Application of Planning to African Socialism" in part as a way of turning the attention of politicians to the local level and providing them with an incentive to bargain with each other for extra-parliamentary resources. That system worked effectively in most parts of Kenya until the government imposed licensing requirements on harambee meetings in 1974. The licensing requirement provided the State House with a means of controlling the access of candidates to political soapboxes and made it increasingly difficult for some to engage in the cross-regional negotiation that had become the norm in Kenyan parliamentary circles. It undercut the incentive to limit claims against other ethnic or regional communities and to eschew organization on communal lines.

With some notable exceptions, it was not until the Moi government assumed power that the licensing requirement was used to exclude candidates from political office and to manipulate factional divisions, however. Under Kenyatta, the State House had used harambee contributions by senior officials to local self-help efforts to win the support of politicians from districts that would lose under the redistribution of government monies. It had also encouraged members of Parliament and local leaders to participate in one another's fund-raisers.

Under Moi, the harambee system ceased to constitute the extra-parliamentary bargaining system it had once been. By the late Kenyatta years, harambee showed signs of abuse, with the proliferation of expensive projects that often remained half-finished and the expansion of the financial burden the projects placed on poorer residents. Between 1980 and 1984, there were 14,028 harambee projects in the country, more than double the number started in the period 1970 to 1974.[1] The government could not staff the classrooms that represented almost half of these projects and thus intervened to create a "harambee season," which limited communities' abilities to launch these ventures, and to subject the projects to the scrutiny of the district development committees.

Second, it became increasingly difficult for politicians to attend harambee affairs in some areas of the country. Restrictions on "political tourism" sometimes prevented travel by MPs between constituencies. More important, the State House's ability and willingness to use its licensing power to favor some politicians over others severely eroded the bargaining system that had existed and had limited the exclusiveness of the claims politicians made upon the state. Further, and more important, the Office of the President began to use the funds at its disposal to manipulate the political fortunes of members of Parliament. It sought to bolster the position of the former Mau Mau leaders against the more threatening members of the Kikuyu business community. The most notable illustration was the elevation of Kariuki Chotara in Nakuru District as leader of a faction opposed to Mwai Kibaki. Chotara received numerous contributions from the president and from senior officials in order to build support in Nakuru and to constitute a vigorous youth wing there. The State House used the same tactics to pit factions against one another both in the Kikuyu community and in other parts of the country.

Fragmentation in a Single-Party System   If the transformation of the harambee system limited politicians' ability to organize broad bases for the pursuit of changes in national-level policy and the defense of political space, the difficulties coalition-builders faced were compounded by the emergence of multiple factions within KANU. With the gradual collapse, first, of the Backbenchers' Group and then, of the Rift Valley opposition, politicians sought to ally themselves with whichever patron appeared ascendant at the moment, leaving the work of organizing a coalition to others. As these leaders fell with increasing rapidity, most politicians made it a practice to adopt and discard allies quickly and only when absolutely necessary so that they might not themselves experience the reversals of fortune that afflicted those who took stands on policy or politics. When all MPs behaved in the same manner, the credible, enduring "watchdog" function an opposition could provide disappeared and with it the ability to resist the encroachments on political life that would make gradual reform increasingly difficult to secure.

Kibaki was one of the first to discover the challenge that such fragmentation posed for coalition-builders. His experience in brokering coalitions in 1977 and 1979 led him to conclude that the day of enduring organizations that could offer long-term guarantees of contributions or action to supporters were over. Instead, Kenyan politics had become a bidding war between faction leaders who each sought to prevent last-minute defections of adherents and, once in office, let the ad hoc base of his support dissolve.

The proscription of the welfare societies in 1980 and the deliberate efforts of the Moi State House to sow division among the Kikuyu members of the cabinet and Parliament caused factions to multiply and become even more unstable. Under these conditions, it became almost impossible to constitute an organized opposition to the policies proposed or adopted by the Office of the President. Because of the time, expense, and risk associated with coalition-building under these conditions, individual politicians tended to try to "free ride" on one another's organizational efforts. In consequence, opposition to the erosion of parliamentary privilege and the political space formerly accorded Kenyan politicians collapsed.

Independent Interest Groups   To the extent that the party-state did not and has not assumed the range of functions and powers in Kenya that it has in other African countries, it has shown restraint largely because of the existence of interest groups whose economic power independent of government favor or whose international ties have given them leverage over the Office of the President. In conjunction with the legal and church communities, some of the matajiri have sought to reverse the trend toward an increasingly closed political system. Their ability to mobilize opposition through ties to the legal profession gave them limited bargaining power with the Office of the President, but it remained difficult to capture the discontent of farmers and the transport sector because of the intended and unintended consequences of government entry into these parts of the economy.

The role of lawyers and churchmen was critical, even though it did not produce a reversal of the trends. Few others shared the ability of these groups to use attorney-client privilege or the security of clerical relationships to maintain communication between different members of the matajiri class and between Kenyans from other walks of life. Few others possessed the ties to the international community that could cast a spotlight on detentions and harassment and urge donors to suspend aid in protest of human rights violations. Although these groups too have encountered significant obstacles in recent years, they remain stronger in Kenya than in many other sub-Saharan countries, and their activities account in part for the differences in scope and power between the party-state of Zaire, embodied in the Mouvement populaire de la révolution, and that of Kenya. One part of the explanation for the adoption of laws restricting political participation during the Kenyatta period is arguably that the numbers and experience of Kenyan lawyers were extremely limited. The size of the community has grown since that time, but its members are themselves constrained by the laws already enacted.

The international community proved an off-again, on-again ally for those who tried to defend political space. Kenya's comparatively stronger economic record made it a better prospect for assistance than many other African countries. Multilateral donors had only started to discuss the idea of attaching political conditions to loans. Most of these were likely to concern budgetary transparency and reduction of restrictions on the press, and on both of these counts, Kenya could still be said to have performed better than many of its neighbors. In 1987–88, the World Bank and the United States did link release of loans to reinstatement of the secret ballot in the general elections, however, indicating some seriousness of intent.[2]

The bilateral donors had greater flexibility than multilateral institutions, and Britain, the United States, Sweden, and Norway variously brought pressure to bear at first in the cases of individual detainees, then in an effort to produce broader policy changes. The threat of withholding assistance was the usual form of leverage used. The United States and Britain had tried to bring quiet pressure to bear on the Moi government in the early 1980s, principally to trigger the release of political detainees. As the human rights situation in the country worsened, U.S. Congressman Howard Wolpe expressed concern about the concentration of executive power in Kenya, and the State Department placed the issue on the agenda in President Ronald Reagan's talks with Moi. The State Department coordinated its actions with Britain, and Margaret Thatcher's government also raised civil liberties concerns in its negotiations. The differences in the style of the two donor countries' showed in the tone of criticism, however. Britain retained far more cordial relations with the Moi government than did the United States, and both Thatcher and Prince Charles scheduled visits to Nairobi as part of London's efforts. The granting of asylum to Kenyan dissidents also brought verbal clashes between the Kenyan State House and the governments of Norway and Sweden, which offered safe haven, and led to suspension of bilateral aid programs, some of which Finland later assumed.[3]

The degree to which the international community could prove a reliable ally varied, however. The need to maintain a presence in the region even after the Cold War era, debates either about the fate of individual Kenyans who depended on foreign-funded projects or about the best way to produce policy change over the long run, and the need of aid agencies to move money in order to retain their allocations produced tensions on the American side. Finally, the rise of Japan to the position of largest donor also limited the effectiveness of the international community in producing change in the human rights situation, because the Japanese government was unaccustomed to using its aid in this way. Only at the end of November 1991 did the international community organize successfully to challenge the Moi government. At a meeting of donors in Paris, aid providers cooperated with one another to suspend government-to-government assistance to Kenya until Moi could demonstrate improvement in respect for civil liberties and in the honest and efficient conduct of development programs.

Although occupational groups and the international community could cite some successes in slowing encroachment on political space, the Moi government sought new ways to reduce their power and did so successfully in many cases. It reduced the bargaining power of the transport sector and of export-crop producers by de-registering trade associations and reorganizing these markets. It brought new pressure to bear on recalcitrant businessmen by installing relatively unknown Kalenjin backers of the president in critical economic gate-keeping positions. It played a cat-and-mouse game with outspoken members of the legal profession, subjecting a number to detention, then releasing them and inviting those in exile to return home—but without offering guarantees of immunity from future harassment.

Indeed, the long-term effects of factional strategies and restriction of political association arguably are to create the social preconditions for disorder. Requiring licensing of political meetings, invoking detention laws, increasing the power of KANU to discipline members—all raise the risks and expense of forging and maintaining coalitions of any sort. The restrictions on political activity initiated in 1980–85 eliminated the cross-regional coalitions and ethnic machines that group spokesmen had used to channel and control demands and shattered the informal social structures that might have provided substitutes. Under these conditions the "transmission belts" that party representatives provided between average Kenyans and their government have disappeared. Increased "openness" has led, initially, to further political fragmentation in multiple dimensions.

KANU IN COMPARATIVE PERSPECTIVE

The findings in the Kenyan case parallel those of other research on Zaire, Côte d'Ivoire, and Tanzania. In the cases of Zaire and Tanzania, political scientists have observed an evolution of party-state relations similar to that which has taken place in Kenya, although the Tanzanian ruling party most closely resembled the Moi-era KANU earlier in its history. Until recently, the ruling parties in these countries performed minimal representative functions and had little policy initiative, save in conjunction with the president. Instead, they were vehicles heads of state used to gather intelligence and control dissent, with varying degrees of effectiveness in different parts of their respective countries. They shared this character with ruling parties in a few other sub-Saharan countries. In Côte d'Ivoire, however, the ruling party remained weak and heterogeneous, resembling KANU under Kenyatta more than KANU under Moi. It had few functions but permitted some variation in opinion among members. Although it maintained representatives in villages, as did the Tanzanian party, its personnel served mainly to collect dues. Only sporadically were party activists enlisted to maintain political control (as during the country's first multi-party elections in 1990), but the party did maintain tight control of the media. The same variables that are helpful in understanding the Kenyan situation are also helpful in deciphering the patterns observed in these cases.

ZAIRE

Kenya scholars have lamented the increasing ease with which it is possible to make casual comparisons between Kenya and Zaire. As Julius

Nyang'oro has written, "Kenya has generally been regarded as a bastion of political stability and economic progress in a continent where countries have, since independence, deteriorated into political chaos, army rule, and economic basket cases."[4] The closed character of Kenyan politics in recent years has eroded that image and has invited unflattering parallels to a government "with an exceptionally dismal record on human rights."[5]

Certainly, in its organization and functions, KANU has come to resemble a milder form of the Mouvement populaire de la révolution, which was made Zaire's sole legal political party by Mobutu Sese Seko, the head of state, in 1967 and retained that distinction until mid 1990. The N'Sele Manifesto, which outlined the MPR's mandate, conveyed the clear message that the party was an arm of the executive, that it should encompass all political activity in the country, and that it should incorporate other political and social bodies accordingly. The political bureau, equivalent to the KANU executive committee, quickly proceeded to absorb labor federations upon the party's creation in 1967. It took longer to subordinate student groups, but it accomplished that objective, with considerable bloodshed, by 1969, when the Jeunesse du MPR, the party's youth wing, became the sole legal student organization. The independence of the judiciary collapsed somewhat later, in the early 1970s, as judges found that their tenure increasingly depended on the appropriateness of their decisions in the eyes of the party political bureau and the head of state.[6] The political bureau formed committees within private-sector businesses to ensure compliance with state policies. The party pronounced itself the country's supreme political institution.

In function, the MPR and the KANU of the late 1980s shared many characteristics, too. The MPR did not formulate policy or legislation. Policy making was the preserve of the president and his cabinet, or a subset thereof. Since 1974, the party had served primarily to transmit these decisions and to secure compliance with them. This task it accomplished not through its own branches but rather through the Jeunesse. Many branches were so weakly organized that state institutions took over their functions.[7] Party congresses took place infrequently—indeed, only three times between 1967 and 1983. "The MPR became merely another element of the state administrative structure with primarily propaganda functions for the political religion," Thomas Callaghy remarks of the changes in the character of the single-party state in Zaire.[8]

The members of the party elected to the subordinate legislative council came from a list proposed by the party's political bureau. Voting was by acclamation at popular meetings—an arrangement similar to Kenya's now-abandoned queuing system.[9] The candidates represented a limited number of points of view, as Mobutu and the party political bureau were intolerant of differences of opinion among its members on policy matters. The MPR established its own school, the Makanda Kabobi Institute, to train its elites, the leaders of its major component social groups, and the military. It also founded a Study and Research Center on Mobutuism (CEREMO). The party members who were elected legislators also found their roles subordinated to a 121-member party central committee, which Mobutu used to co-opt bases of potential opposition.

There are relatively few analyses of the reasons for the pattern of party-state relations observed in Zaire. In his discussion of state formation in Zaire, Thomas Callaghy suggests that absolutism, including the particular relationship between party and state, has its origins in the challenges of establishing authority or rule over a heterogeneous and particularistic society, a society plagued by intense localism. Like the absolutist rulers of France in an earlier era, Mobutu sought to secure authority by establishing "two kinds of authority at the same time: a direct personal linkage via the legitimating and glorification doctrines of a political religion, and a direct administrative linkage via the new official realm, both of which would bypass intermediary authorities."[10] Party-state relations reflected the strategic choices of rulers as they tried to establish sovereignty in this kind of socioeconomic context.

Callaghy identifies two basic strategies the ruling elite may employ to secure independence from localism and from bureaucratic interests and thereby maintain its position. One is promotion of a bargained exchange of commitments that "reduces uncertainty for both parties," part of a cooperative strategy; and the other is coercion.[11] Cooperative strategies include contracting, co-opting, and coalition-formation. Callaghy reiterates James D. Thompson's observation that where there is little information and great uncertainty, it is generally most efficient and effective to allow those most immediately involved in a policy problem to take responsibility for decision making in order to avert the bottlenecks that referral to a central, higher authority would produce.[12] Cooperative strategies also create difficulties, however. They reduce uncertainty, but they also permit the ruler less latitude; they create arrangements that must be respected. Callaghy notes that most leaders in sub-Saharan Africa use elements of both cooperative and coercive approaches. In contrast to totalitarian political systems, rule is based on a "cover-over strategy" that "uses contracting, coopting, and coalescing tactics plus moderate amounts of coercion and usually a loose, traditionally oriented legitimating mentality."[13]

Leaders use a variety of devices to carry out these combined strategies. Reliance on a prefectural system of administration, which confers a high degree of discretion upon field officers, is one element. In such a system, the prefect "is delegated general authority over all state activity undertaken by other state agencies within his area in order to coordinate and control their activities and adapt them to the general needs of the state and the conditions of the local task environment."[14]

Callaghy is somewhat less clear about the relationship between party and state that arises under these conditions. The party is principally a vehicle for "recentralization" and unification—for keeping participants in political bargains in line, for transmitting the word of the central government to prefects and other local barons, and for projecting the symbols to the inhabitants of remote areas.[15] In this context, the party assumes control functions and becomes an instrument for transmitting the wishes of the ruling elite, monitoring political activity, and controlling association.

Thus Callaghy offers a compelling account of the motivation of a ruler for pursuing subordination of political party affairs to his own office. His explanation is rooted in the organizational demands created by societies in which there are many competing "localisms" or "particularisms" and few common identities. What it does not offer is a way of understanding the limited effective resistance these "particularisms" pose to the consolidation of power in this way, although Callaghy builds a convincing argument that in the case of Zaire the exceptionally effective manipulation of fear was instrumental in keeping opposition to a minimum.

In trying to account for the limited strength of "civil society" in slowing or halting the consolidation of Mobutu's power and the extension of the MPR as an instrument of control, in particular, Michael Schatzberg and Thomas Callaghy both focus on the endogenous effects of a single-party system. That is, once the first elements of the MPR's role were in place, participation in patronage networks, and then in highly unstable political factions unable to organize coherent resistance to encroachment on political space became the norm. As long as government maintained control of resources critical to citizens' lives, the single-party system could shape the character of civil society. "The state deals with any attempt at organization at lower levels of society by either co-optation into the state-party . . . or suppression," Schatzberg notes.[16] There were few incentives for politicians to create a backbenchers' group or to link up with the holders of critical, private gate-keeping positions. Although some illegal opposition parties did form, these were unable until 1990 to gain enough power to exercise bargaining leverage.

By comparison with KANU in Kenya, the MPR of Zaire developed into a party-state very rapidly and more comprehensively. Although the effectiveness of state-sponsored terror played an important part in reducing opposition to the incorporation of social groups, such as labor unions, other factors surely played a role as well. At independence, Zairian society included far fewer people with higher education, including lawyers, than did Kenya. Political parties had no more than three months to organize before the first elections, which, predictably, failed to yield a cohesive government and invited foreign intervention. Interest-group organizations were extremely weak. Years after independence, Zaire continued to display these characteristics, in part because the limited private entrepreneurial activity in key sectors of the economy meant that no group had interests independent of the state and in part because, in a country the size of the United States east of the Mississippi River, there were few passable roads and almost no internal telecommunications to link people with similar interests in different regions. It was simply not possible to constitute the kinds of opposition that existed in the Kenyan case.

TANZANIA

Scholars have drawn frequent comparisons between KANU and the ruling party in Tanzania, Chama Cha Mapinduzi (CCM), the former Tanganyika African National Union (TANU). TANU/CCM developed some of the characteristics of the Moi-era KANU immediately after independence. Every candidate for a parliamentary seat was required to have party approval, and of those who offered their candidacies, the party chose only two per constituency. Beginning in 1968, the party used its powers to expel members of Parliament and others who articulated positions at odds with those of the party leadership, limiting the representative function MPs could play.[17] The membership of the party's national executive committee and central committee was largely determined, not by open elections and politicking in the party ranks, but by the president, as in the case of the Moi-era KANU. Aside from its monitoring functions and responsibility for transmitting information, the party has served as an instrument of social control only sporadically and with often quite limited effectiveness. During the *ujamaa* period, party members worked side by side with the administration to implement Julius Nyerere's villagization program, but its representatives usually found themselves underemployed, collectors of party dues and meeting coordinators.[18]

TANU emerged in 1954, seven years before the country's independence in 1961. President Nyerere declared a one-party state in 1965, and ten years later, in 1975, the party was formally named the supreme political authority in the country. Parliament clearly held a minor position in Nyerere's view. At the time of the declaration of a de jure one-party state, he suggested that Parliament had become so lifeless that it might as well be scrapped altogether, transferring its functions to the party. A presidential commission recommended otherwise, but Parliament remained subordinate to the party and relatively functionless.[19] As in the case of the MPR and, to a much lesser degree, the Moi-era KANU, TANU/CCM incorporated economic interest groups such as labor unions and subordinated them to its authority, absorbing them into the party, where they did not challenge the leadership.[20] Further, the administration or civil service operates under party scrutiny and at the pleasure of the party leadership, which acts as a coordinator or manager of the country's different groups of civil servants and white-collar employees.[21]

The absorption of interest associations and creation of an extensive network of cells came far more rapidly to TANU than to KANU. In 1964, "as the nationalist coalition began to unravel with the confrontation between the state and the Tanganyika Federation of Labour . . . as well as the army mutiny the same year, President Nyerere began to lay the foundation for this new party role in his speeches," John Okumu and Frank Holmquist note.[22] Simultaneously, the presidency was strengthened through creation of a republican form of government and centralization of power in the office, and the party received a mandate to play a larger role in mobilizing support for the president's policies. The party's primary functions developed to include three main tasks: to transmit information and judgments from the central political authorities, the president and his cabinet, to people in rural areas; to build support for the activities of civil servants; and to collect dues.[23] To a far greater degree than KANU, TANU developed an extensive network of rural cells to provide a framework for these activities. Indeed, initially the party was better organized than the civil service, and the help of party cadres in securing local compliance with administrative rulings was critical.[24] Often, district commissioners were drawn from the ranks of the party officialdom instead of the lists of the civil service. In this respect TANU had functions quite different from those of the Kenyatta-era KANU.

The party's role in policy making varied considerably over the years. Early in Tanzania's history, neither the party nor Parliament, the Bunge, had any real authority in policy making, but that changed during the mid 1970s, and TANU/CCM became a locus of policy deliberation to a degree never approached by KANU. Nyerere ensured that in the first years of the party's existence there were regular consultations on policy matters between members of the cabinet and the national executive committee of the party. He met far more frequently and regularly with the party elite than Kenyatta did with the KANU elites. Nonetheless, during the 1960s, policy making was not high on the party's list of priorities. According to Okumu and Holmquist, however, that changed as the president continued consultations with the party elite and secured remuneration for top party members on a par with the salaries received by members of Parliament. Similarly, some outside observers have noted the appearance of sporadic intense interest in policy making at the top levels of the party but suggest that real policy authority continues to reside with the president and small groups of hand-picked advisers.[25] Jeanette Hartmann has suggested these variations were part of a pattern. Specifically, she has argued, there was a presidency-government alliance between 1962 and 1967, and a party-presidency alliance between 1969 and 1974.[26] Throughout, the president exerted strong influence over policy content. After 1974, Nyerere sought to mediate between government and party and assumed substantial central power in the process.

The party's ability to enforce its policy views or those of the president has varied between levels of the organization. Certainly, the leadership took steps to ensure that the party could play such a role. In the early years of the country's independence, TANU had established a training center for personnel, the Kivukoni College, where party officials, members of Parliament, and civil servants received training. The president and party officials monitored elections to ensure that candidates did not "question party policy . . . conduct a private campaign without party supervision, or deviate from official ideology."[27] Finally, the TANU/CCM Youth League was formed to help mobilize farmers in support of government policy. The result, as Naomi Chazan notes, was to ensure that candidates would act as individuals and eschew positions that required organized associational or group support.

The effectiveness of these measures was mixed, however. Although the Kivukoni College may have helped elites hammer out common positions at top levels, it had little effect on the behavior of party members or officials in the rural areas, where the party remained a heterogeneous affair, with very loose standards of ideological conformity. Indeed, many of the party's village representatives were lukewarm supporters of ujamaa and engaged in little active work on behalf of the program. The Youth League was sometimes active but at other times became quiescent when members realized that it was not a quick route to employment. Moreover, although the party is technically superior to Parliament, in recent years MPs have arguably been able to maintain space to criticize the government, although primarily over the quality of administration in the parastatals and civil service.[28]

Although possibly an artifact of scholarship, which has devoted very little attention to institutional structure and relationships, the record suggests that TANU/CCM in its early years resembled the KANU of the Moi era in function, although its elite had a larger policy role. During the 1980s, however, the president was less inclined to use the elaborate network of cells and branches as a vehicle for social and political control than he had been in the past, save during election time. What would account for the differences? By comparison with Kenyatta's Kenya, at independence Nyerere's Tanzania was a more homogeneous society. Once labor unions were incorporated into the party and the army mutiny was suppressed, there were few groups that could pose a credible challenge or countervailing force to the TANU leadership in the short run. Kenyatta faced the armed remnants of a resistance group still hiding in the Aberdare forest, an aggressive group of emerging agricultural entrepreneurs, chiefs eager to preserve the power they had acquired during the colonial period, and settlers whose vociferous objections to policy could easily bring an end to foreign capital flows. Nyerere quickly incorporated representatives of the small petite bourgeoisie into the government, gave the members of the class jobs in the party or the parastatals, and set strict limits on ability to accumulate resources. Those most opposed to the policies of his government—the farmers—were unable to organize effectively and signaled their discontent slowly, although powerfully, by refusing to trade their agricultural surplus on official markets and gradually destroying government finances and urban food supplies. Although their actions effected policy changes over a period of many years, they did not act to open up greater political space or produce guarantees that changes in political institutions would be enacted to prevent repeats of past errors. The lighter touch of recent years has arguably stemmed from Tanzania's heavy reliance on the international community for assistance and the visible failure of past agricultural and industrial policies.

CÔTE D'IVOIRE

In many respects the case of Côte d'Ivoire most closely parallels that of Kenya. Long considered, with Kenya, one of Africa's "success stories," Côte d'Ivoire has displayed some common characteristics. Its economy was and remains heavily based on agriculture and in particular on export-crop production. During the colonial period, it too was a settler colony, and it too both encouraged the development of agricultural enterprises by Africans and discriminated against these in favor of settler production. Its independence was preceded by organization among a new class of indigenous planters, who constituted the base of the country's independence-era political elite. When the government of the country's first president after independence, Félix Houphouët-Boigny, came to power, it too had to contend with a heterogeneous society, although the lines of division were not the same as those drawn in Kenya between Mau Mau militants and squatters on the one hand and the entrepreneurial elite on the other. Instead, the original imperative was to maintain a coalition of ethnic communities, including both chiefs and the new professionals from each area. Although the territorial balancing act introduced some diversity into the party, in more recent times there have been few clear, hard lines of division. Martin Staniland has observed that *faction* is too strong a word to describe the developmentalist perspective that some younger members have brought to party meetings.[29] In 1970, however, many older militants were replaced by younger cadres both in the party and in the National Assembly.[30]

Houphouët's leadership style resembled Kenyatta's in many respects. Even before the Parti démocratique de Côte d'Ivoire (PDCI) assumed the formal mantle of power, it lost most access to policy making and its internal organization and coherence weakened considerably. Just prior to independence, less than half of the party's Bureau politique were able to engage in active party work; many of the key political organizers remained in jail. Ruth Schachter Morgenthau has suggested that there was little resistance in the party to Houphouët's assumption of increasing personal power, because the Bureau politique was unable to muster the clout of the missing "martyrs," whom the membership was unwilling to replace, even as a practical matter.[31] Houphouët often overlooked the disagreement of the Comité directeur, the party's ruling body, and simply acted as he saw fit. He never moved to reestablish the party press and territorial branches, both curtailed in 1951.[32]

Although there was some toleration of a range of views, and despite the fact that there was no clear platform against which to measure party loyalty, direct political competition within the party was impossible for many years. Unlike Kenya, Côte d'Ivoire did not sanction multi-candidate elections, much less multi-party elections, until 1980. In each constituency, députés were elected on a list basis through a simple majority, single-ballot system. As long as there was only one legal political party, there was only one list. The general secretaries of the party submitted the names of potential candidates to the Bureau politique for consideration. Although the Bureau politique held formal responsibility for composing a "national slate," in fact this power was controlled by an inner circle of the president's men.[33] Thus, until 1980, the Ivoirian electoral system was in these respects less open than the Kenyan. There was no political choice.

Beginning in the early 1980s, the party tolerated increasing internal competition. In response to signs of increasing discontent within the country, Houphouët-Boigny created a nine-member executive committee that included five members of the party's younger generation, some of whom had led student movements critical of the government in earlier years.[34] Other younger technocratic elites with "dissident ideas" were given posts in the party or in public corporations and economic ministries. Houphouët also decided to create multi-candidate elections, abandoning the single slate system in which voters merely ratified the party's choice, and to permit candidates not sponsored by the party to compete.

As in Zaire and Tanzania, and Kenya after 1980, the party played a role in transmitting the views and policies of the government, but it was a limited one. Often, party organization at the local level was so dilapidated that the sous-préfet was charged with responsibility for collecting party dues from local residents, as has sometimes happened in the Kenyan case. In practice, the sous-préfets have generally intervened more extensively in local party affairs, protesting poor performance to higher authorities and reporting on local political affairs.[35] The distinction remains between the civil service and the administration, however. Although there is a party-sponsored militia, prior to 1989, the PDCI branches very rarely sought to monitor political activity or act as enforcers of the president's views. Instead, Houphouët has opted to pursue strategies of control similar to those of the early Kenyatta years.

The character of the PDCI and the gradual loosening of the party system to incorporate various interests most likely stemmed initially from the ethnic and economic diversity of the independence coalition and later from the ability of rising elites to command sufficient economic or social power to cause significant disturbances if not accommodated within the system—or if the decisions of the combattants du premier heure appeared to reduce the economic opportunities available to the younger generation. The threat of disturbances in the late 1970s and early 1980s, as economic conditions deteriorated, provided the impetus for the shift to multi-candidate elections and the creation of new bodies within the party to draw younger members of the elite into the PDCI fold. Houphouët's belief that Côte d'Ivoire's future lay with strong ties to France and the need to limit repressive measures in order to sustain that relationship may also have played a role. Finally, in Côte d'Ivoire the cross-ethnic coalitions promoted by the harambee system under Kenyatta were propagated in this instance by extensive internal migration that resulted in substantial mixed settlement in the wealthy cocoa zone. Although occasional outbreaks of resistance on the part of particular ethnic groups have occurred, in recent years patterns of economic change have limited the translation of social identities into political lines of division. Greater internal party pluralism was consequently less threatening to stability.

THE KENYAN HOLDOUT

Factionalism, the personalization of politics, in KANU and among Kenyan parliamentarians during the early 1980s reduced the ability to defend space for criticism of government policies, including the raising of questions about civil liberties. The last half of the decade saw the restrictive measures that had been put in place by the regime render the country's political elite nearly incapable of mounting a sustained opposition. Moi's own private-sector holdings made it difficult for entrepreneurs in any one sector of the economy to use market power as a way of focusing attention on public-sector accountability and on space for debate. In combination, the churches, segments of the informal sector, and a few members of the political establishment tried to take on the Moi government.

Although they succeeded in attracting international attention, persuading donors to participate in limited linkage of aid levels to human rights, and winning a KANU-run review of the party's own affairs, the coalition's efforts to stop encroachment on "political space" met with tough resistance. Throughout March and April 1990, when many other African leaders were announcing transitions to multi-party rule, Moi remained a holdout. He toured the country, denouncing the advocates of a multi-party system as puppets of the West and announcing his intention to defend KANU and the single-party system, for which he won the blessing of the South African ANC leader Nelson Mandela. Moi instructed KANU and the minister for national guidance and political affairs to prepare a defense for the country against Western cultural imperialism. Only when foreign donors withheld aid in late November 1991, pending reduction in high-level corruption and expansion of civil liberties, did the government relax controls and announce that it would permit opposition parties to form.

The purpose of this book is to explain the rise of the party-state in Kenya, not the reasons for its persistence. It offers a way of understanding patterns of authoritarian rule in single-party systems, not a general theory to account for democratic versus undemocratic regimes. Nonetheless, the three propositions set out in chapter 1 help explain the direction Kenya took between 1980 and 1991, as well as the pattern and timing of fast-breaking changes. Specific comparisons to other sub-Saharan countries that legalized opposition parties during the first half of 1990 clarify the significance of the analysis offered.

By the end of 1990, approximately one-third of the forty-seven countries of sub-Saharan Africa had taken limited steps toward political liberalization by legalizing opposition. These countries did not adopt "multi-party democracy"; in most cases, the press remained under government control or public challenge to the regime was limited in other ways. Nonetheless, by the end of July 1991, opposition parties in many countries were enjoying new opportunities to organize and campaign (see Table 4). These cases differed greatly from one another in levels of GDP growth, food production per capita, government spending as a proportion of GDP, defense spending as a proportion of government spending, levels of official development assistance as a percentage of the recipient country's GDP, and the proportion of the labor force involved in agriculture. Although deep skepticism is required in using official

TABLE 4   THE STATUS OF MULTI-PARTY DEBATE IN SUB-SAHARAN AFRICA, JULY 1991, SHOWING PARTICIPANTS IN FIRST WAVE OF CHANGE

Country	Leader	Regime Type
Multi-Party Systems		
Mauritius	Sir Veeransamy Ringadoo	multi-party
Benin	Nicephore Soglo	multi-party
Namibia	Sam Nujoma	multi-party
Cape Verde	Antonio Mascarenhas Monteiro	multi-party
Comoros	Said Mohamed Djohar	multi-Party
Single-Party-Dominant Multi-Party Systems		
Botswana	Quett Masire	multi-party
The Gambia	Dawda Jawara	multi-party
Côte d'Ivoire	Félix Houphouët-Boigny	multi-party
Senegal	Abdou Diouf	multi-party
Zimbabwe	Robert Mugabe	multi-party
Sao Tome and Principe	Miguel Trovoada	multi-party
Opposition Parties Legal		
Mozambique	Joachim Chissano	transition
Cameroon	Paul Biya	transition
Nigeria	Ibrahim Babangida	transition
Madagascar	Didier Ratsiraka	transition
Congo	Denis Sassou-Nguesso	transition
Burkina Faso	Blaise Compaore	transition
Sierra Leone	Joseph Momoh	transition
Angola	José Eduardo Dos Santos	transition
Central African Republic	André Kolingba	single-party
Zaire	Mobutu Sese Seko	transition
Zambia	Kenneth Kaunda	transition
Public Debate Only; No Program		
Tanzania	Ali Hassan Mwinyi	single-party
Togo	Gnassingbé Éyadema	transition

TABLE 4 (CONTINUED)

Country	Leader	Regime Type
Mali	Amadou Toumani Touré	military council
Niger	Ali Saibou	transition
Guinea-Bissau	Joao Bernardo Vieira	transition
Guinea	Lansana Conté	transition
Gabon	Omar Bongo	multi-party
Single-Party Rule		
Equatorial Guinea	Teodoro Obiang Nguema	single-party
Kenya	Daniel arap Moi	single-party
Malawi	Hastings Kamuza Banda	single-party
Chad	Idriss Déby	single-party
Djibouti	Hassan Gouled Aptidon	single-party
Seychelles	France-Albert René	single-party
Rwanda	Juvénal Habyarimana	single-party
No-Party Systems		
Burundi	Pierre Buyoya	military council
Swaziland	Mswati II	monarchy
Lesotho	Justin Metsig Lekhanya	military council
Sudan	Omar Hassan Ahmad al-Bashir	military council
Mauritania	Maouya Ould Sid'Ahmed Taya	military council
Liberia	Amos Sawyer	interim
Uganda	Yoweri Museveni	no party
Ghana	Jerry Rawlings	no party
Ethiopia		unclear
Somalia	Ali Madi Mohammed	unclear

statistics, the absence of any pattern in these figures suggests that the move away from single-party systems has not arisen in any straight-forward way from the economic characteristics of particular coun-tries.[36] It also suggests that aid "windfalls" have not provided a crutch that authoritarian regimes have used to boost their levels of support while at the same time they restrict civil liberties.

Comparison of the cases of Kenya and Côte d'Ivoire permits a better understanding of the impetus for political reform in the latter case and the slowness of Daniel arap Moi to follow the direction of many other sub-Saharan leaders. Both countries have faced international pressure to liberalize their political systems. The two countries share similar eco-nomic bases. They have pursued similar economic strategies over the first twenty-five years of independence, and yet by the end of 1990 they presented very different outcomes. In the case of Côte d'Ivoire, liberali-zation began in 1980. Originally a single-party system, and one of the models for Aristide Zolberg's analysis of the party-state, Côte d'Ivoire instituted municipal elections in 1980, counter to the trend across Af-rica. On May 3, 1990, President Félix Houphouët-Boigny announced the legalization of opposition parties. General elections for president took place in October 1990, and multi-party legislative elections took place on November 25.

What fostered liberalization in the one case and resolute opposition to party competition in the other? In both cases, no single ethnic com-munity included a majority of the population, or even a significant pro-portion. Although economic power was concentrated more strongly than elsewhere among the Baule in Côte d'Ivoire and among some parts of the Kikuyu community in Kenya, in neither country could a single group rule effectively by itself. Before the practices of the 1980s under-cut the system, harambee had facilitated coalition-building between spokesmen for different communities in Kenya. In Côte d'Ivoire, labor shortages in the southern cocoa zone and less productive agriculture in the north, coupled with a surplus of land in relation to available labor, provided incentive for the members of different groups to settle in new villages together and to subordinate community claims to common eco-nomic pursuits. Both existing governments and the underground oppo-sition generally played careful "ethnic arithmetic" and included leaders from other communities. In neither country was fragmentation along ethnic lines a real possibility.

Second, although Zolberg identified Côte d'Ivoire as the model of the party-state in the 1960s, during most of the 1970s and 1980s, Houphouët-Boigny reigned rather than ruled, in a style reminiscent of Kenyatta. Although the PDCI remained the sole legal party until May 1990 and maintained its own representatives in each village of Côte d'Ivoire, it was a loose federation of local leaders with varying interests. Although village PDCI committee presidents helped the *préfet* inform residents of the president's positions on various issues, in very few cases did they perform representative functions themselves or intervene in multi-candidate legislative elections. Their primary function was to collect annual fees for identity cards. Although included in most village decisions, the respect accorded these men usually stemmed, not from fear that the party representative would "inform" the government of disagreements and take action against those with whom the party disagreed, but rather from the personal relationships of these leaders with other village notables. In northern regions, for example, the village party chief was usually related by blood to the chief.[37] The deputies to the national assembly rarely toed a clear party line, and Houphouët-Boigny expended little effort to make them do so, although he did manipulate the political fortunes of cabinet ministers who had acquired too much power in his view. He relied more heavily on the civil service and technocratic class for advice and the implementation of policy.

Moreover, Houphouët-Boigny's strategies for maintaining political control permitted some limited level of debate to exist outside the party and Parliament. Although leaders of the formerly illegal opposition, such as Laurent Gbagbo, landed in detention periodically, as did their counterparts in Kenya, unlike Moi, Houphouët-Boigny generally avoided using the party to police public debate and instead called disputants to the capital for "days of dialogue," after which he would announce that the government had taken steps to address the concerns raised (whether it did or not was another matter). He controlled information, including the newspaper media, much more strongly than did either Kenyatta or Moi, but the political party and the internal security forces in general were far less in evidence on a routine basis, and especially in a "watchdog" or policing role, than were their equivalents in Kenya during the 1980s.

This difference between the systems had three main implications. First, it meant that although there were no large and enduring opposition groups within the national assembly in the Ivoirian case, there was nonetheless greater room for debate and disagreement than within the KANU of the late 1980s. The party did not rid itself of deputies who held divergent views. Indeed, several believed that multi-party competition would improve the functioning of the PDCI and its responsiveness to public concerns. Because the party had so few resources at its disposal and because most deputies did not depend on salaries they received from the party for their livelihoods, there was little incentive for members of the party to defend PDCI hegemony as fiercely as party members defended KANU in Kenya. Any bid to "rejuvenate" the party and impose its supremacy, along the lines of what was done in Kenya, would had to have been introduced into a legislature where criticism had greater legitimacy than it did under Moi.

Second, the looser relationship between party and state in the Ivoirian case meant that criticism of policies outside the National Assembly was more public than it was in the Kenyan case. That is not to say that leaders of the illegal opposition groups did not suffer harassment, jail, and occasional violence. They did. Côte d'Ivoire's political climate permitted formation of a much more coherent and visible opposition than Mwakenya or the rumored "shadow cabinet" of Charles Rubia and Kenneth Matiba. For example, Laurent Gbagbo wrote and published a series of party manifestos available in Côte d'Ivoire long before the move to legalize opposition groups. He was a well-known political figure with recognized allies before the events of 1990.

Third, the strategy Houphouët-Boigny pursued also practically ensured a PDCI victory in the event of a multi-party general election. The grudging tolerance of some kinds of opposition groups meant that even before the legalization of parties in 1990, there were at least six contenders for power. Predictably, the opening up of political life in early 1990 gave rise to extreme fragmentation. Over twenty-one opposition parties declared themselves, effectively splitting the vote and virtually guaranteeing a PDCI victory. Moreover, the PDCI government retained control of significant electoral resources, including the press and building and telephone permits. In a country with some of the highest gasoline prices in the world, the PDCI was the only party to have a preexisting network in the rural areas that it could use to publicize its platform and spread its limited patronage. The high cost of campaigning in rural areas meant that the opposition parties remained largely urban affairs. Houphouët-Boigny thus created a situation where although sharp restrictions of civil liberties met with public outcry, tolerance of some kinds of opposition meant its fragmentation in a general election and certain victory for the president and his party. Elections in 1990 posed no threat.

In the Kenyan case, by way of contrast, the dangers associated with criticism of the government pushed the opposition underground, where it remained diffuse and its strengths were difficult to assess. Other than the shadowy Mwakenya, the only clear opposition most Kenyans heard about was the Rubia-Matiba slate, which attracted more attention than it might have had the government tolerated enough criticism to permit other groups to form and fragment discontent. Further, the use of police powers in preference to patronage and "bargained exchange" limited the kinds of "levers" the party had available to it in a multi-party general election. That is, by shattering regional machines and replacing them with surveillance, the KANU government reduced the kinds of resources it would have at its disposal in a fight to win a competitive election. In a competitive election, KANU stood a good chance of losing.

The third difference between the Kenyan and Ivoirian cases lay in the structure of key interest groups outside of dependence on government. Although the Kenyan transport workers had staged strikes to protest government policies, the fact that Moi had substantial personal business holdings in the sector and that he had attenuated the power of the Nairobi transporters by creating the party-run Nyayo Bus Corporation undermined the effectiveness of the action. In the Ivoirian case, the transport workers—cocoa haulers, other truckers, and taxi drivers— demonstrated their power by striking in the early months of 1990, before the legalization of opposition parties. They called for removal of police- and military-run roadblocks, which were increasing the cost of transportation, and for improvements in the quality of public-sector management. The strike was effective, and the number of roadblocks dropped immediately. As in the case of Gabon and several other of the countries that moved in the direction of multi-party competition during 1990, the transport workers were instrumental in forcibly creating greater "political space," in which criticism of policy could occur, just prior to legalization of opposition parties.

The effects of economic crisis on the interests of political elites, the "organizational bourgeoisie," as Irving Markovitz has called it, also varied between the two countries. In Côte d'Ivoire, the government was heavily dependent on cocoa exports for revenue. When the price of cocoa began to drop, Houphouët-Boigny chose to keep the producer price paid to farmers high. The government stabilization fund thus subsidized farmers, draining the treasury and triggering a liquidity crisis at local banks. By the time the Ministry of Agriculture announced a drop in the producer price, the government was paying out about $1 for each kilogram of cocoa sold. Austerity measures imposed by external donors, combined with the drop in cocoa and coffee prices, and the loss of assets in the banking crisis jeopardized the survival of some members of the Ivoirian elite. The cutbacks eliminated many government jobs (indeed, urbanites felt the pinch before the rural areas), agriculture was no longer very remunerative, and speculative ventures financed through Ivoirian banks collapsed, as did the president's ability to dispense patronage. The crisis affected the incomes and standards of living of a significant proportion of the political elite and lessened willingness to toe a particular ideological line.

In the Kenyan case, the effects of economic crisis were distributed differently. Kenya's efforts to stabilize producer prices differed from those of Côte d'Ivoire. For example, coffee and tea producers received a floor producer price, and then a premium indexed to the world price. The price system therefore relayed more information to farmers about market conditions than in the Ivoirian system. It also limited the drain on government coffers that subsidies constituted. Although the Kenyan economy was already in difficulty, the decline in coffee prices did not affect the livelihoods of the political elite to the extent that it did in the Ivoirian case.

What about the case of Zaire—the African country many political scientists least expected to participate in political liberalization? On April 24, 1990, Mobutu Sese Seko announced a move to a transitional government, with the prospect of two-stage elections in 1991. Opposition parties were legalized. All would compete in the initial legislative elections, and the three parties receiving the largest number of votes would then be able to put up candidates for higher office. The details of this arrangement were not entirely clear, at the time, and were worked out, with many changes and prevarications, over a long period. What was clear was that the MPR would be one of the contesting parties and that Etienne Tshisikedi wa Malumba's Union pour la démocratie et le progrés social (UDPS) would be another.

Press freedom increased. Indeed, new newspapers sprang up for sale in the streets and on the newsstands. Tabloids began to carry political cartoons, which were now legal for the first time. The parties were still cautious, however. Not long after Mobutu's April 24 speech, police had attacked party members at the UDPS office in Tshisikedi's house, injuring the opposition leader and others.

Why did Mobutu decide to liberalize? It would not be entirely correct to see the move to a multi-party system as a completely cynical bid for resumption of foreign loans, which the World Bank and the U.S. Congress had eliminated to protest human rights violations and mismanagement of the public sector. As in Côte d'Ivoire, the political elite in Zaire were facing the prospect of sharply limited opportunities for collecting rents. With World Bank support and IMF involvement sharply reduced, many of the elite were threatened with reductions in their incomes. By various means, some honest, some not, the structural adjustment programs had sustained members of the country's politico-commercial class, either in their posts, through outside consulting, or through occasional diversions into private bank accounts. The collapse of the International Coffee Agreement brought an end to the quota system and eliminated lucrative prebends formerly under the control of regional heads of security and other Mobutu men. Furthermore, the economy had ground to a halt or gone underground to such a degree that it was difficult for members of the political elite to earn foreign exchange, highly valued during periods of exceptional uncertainty, except in the diamond and minerals trade, which were controlled by the Mobutu family, or by consulting for international organizations. With the end of the Cold War came also the prospect of diminished American shipments to UNITA, and of the attendant benefits for the Zairians involved in supply of the Angolan conflict.

Members of the politico-commercial class became extremely concerned. A recurrent theme in conversation was the difficulty of providing for the education of sons and daughters of mistresses, who could not be sent abroad, because of the cost, but who would suffer greatly in the country's nearly defunct educational system. The crisis was so great that even president's advisers quietly argued that a change of government was necessary. Mobutu himself clearly feared the building discontent. He rarely lingered long at any of his homes and constantly moved about the country to stay out of the way of assassination plots.

As in the case of Côte d'Ivoire, some members of the political elite had developed bases that enabled them to confront the president, albeit in an extremely limited number of forums and in a different manner. The Catholic Church had become an important sanctuary for the opposition and exerted highly public moral opposition. Proliferation of security units under the Mobutu government meant that many of the now discontented regional "barons" had arms at their disposal, although Mobutu was still in control of the army and used the different forces to collect intelligence on one another. The bargaining power of the transport sector was not that important because there were no roads in most of the country and foreigners were supplying the means to ship critical exports.

Finally, Mobutu probably believed he could win an election. Caught by surprise when people first expressed discontent, Mobutu nonetheless controlled critical electoral resources and knew that the collapse of the country's road network and telecommunications system would make it very hard for parties to gain broad followings. He encouraged fragmentation among the opposition parties, in some instances providing the means to initiate groups that would absorb votes from the more powerful, better-organized parties.

In sum, Mobutu, like Houphouët, engaged in limited political liberalization partly because he needed to channel discontent among members of the elite and partly because he thought he could retain his position. An election did not imply defeat in his view.

Only with the disappearance of his "populist" base in parts of the informal sector and increasing international pressure did Moi make any attempt to moderate KANU police powers. After the riots of July 1990, the president appointed a KANU panel to review party activities. The exercise resulted in no major changes but did provide a forum for a few critics of the queuing system and the 70 percent rule. The fact that the Office of the President and the KANU leadership felt impelled to call the meeting is significant, however; it suggests that interest-group organization was able to influence further changes in the relationship between party and state, although not directly. More important, during the first week of December, KANU and the president agreed to restore the secret ballot in Kenyan elections. This step marked the first reversal of direction in the restriction of political competition since Moi had come to power, and, indeed, since the last years of the Kenyatta state.

SINGLE-PARTY RULE, "CIVIL SOCIETY," AND PATTERNS OF GOVERNANCE

The current wave of political change in Africa has brought to the fore again an old debate between those who claim single-party democracy is possible and others who say that democracy depends on the existence of multi-party competition. Even in countries where legalization of opposition parties is on the negotiating table—or where opposition groups are already able to compete—leaders, members of the former ruling party, and civil servants often argue behind the scenes that one-party systems are the key to democratic forms of governance in Africa and that multi-partyism is just another World Bank experiment African societies will be forced to endure. The draft document prepared for the May 1991 Conference on Security, Stability, Development and Cooperation in Africa, in Kampala, carefully sidesteps discussion of multi-partyism, saying only: "Every country would ensure that there is no hindrance to alternative ideas, institutions and leaders competing for public support. This principle requires that every participating member should ensure the separation of party from the state." [38]

There is great fear of ethnic schism and its consequences. Advocates of a single-party system invoke the specter of more Liberias, Sudans, and Somalias—more countries whose populations are torn apart by civil strife. In his study of constitutional development in Kenya, J. B. Ojwang observes:

> The main basis of differentiation and of broad-based group solidarity, at least for the time being, is communal, based on 64 or so ethnic groups. . . .
>
> Would this particular mode of diversity serve as a basis for a multi-party system? If so, a major factor of destabilisation would arise, as these tribes would always struggle for domination. . . .
>
> . . . The one-party system appears as an alternative mode of political organisation which accords with the economic and social conditions prevailing in Kenya. [39]

Ironically, given the exclusion of "pro-poor" platforms from the political agendas of most sub-Saharan countries and given the extraordinary wealth accumulated by many heads of state in African single-party systems, there is also fear that political competition will entrench wealthy oligarchs in power. For example, the eminent historian William Ochieng has argued that "candidates who offer themselves for election . . . are . . . the wealthy men who can foot the election bills. While in power, this propertied oligarchy will make laws . . . to the advantage of its own class." [40]

Proponents of single-party systems frequently suggest that political competition will lead to foreign intervention, and that those who lobby for legalization of opposition parties are, indeed, already in the pay of other governments. Heads of state and senior officials fear loss of sovereignty. Although it is certainly the case that sub-Saharan Africa has provided a playing field for various industrial countries, not least the United States and the Soviet Union, and for many of the countries of the Middle East, such as Iraq and Libya, it is far from clear that a one-party system is the best defense against unwanted foreign involvement in a nation's internal affairs. People whose livelihoods are threatened and who fear for their lives or liberty if they protest are likely to seek security in the hot light of foreign scrutiny. In the Kenyan case, it is too simple to say that pressure for increased political openness is a Western imposition, another World Bank experiment. Lawyers, clergy, and environmentalists—and, to a much lesser degree, academics—have used partnerships, not with foreign governments, but with transnational organizations to try to draw attention to their plight and give them some ability to bargain for their own safety. In most cases, the assistance has not taken the form of financial support. Instead, it has delivered something more important and more dangerous in the view of heads of state. It has brought international criticism and the threat of political conditions being attached to badly needed loans.

It is not within the scope of this study to evaluate all of the arguments and evidence pertaining to these larger themes. Nonetheless, the Kenyan case does provide a vantage point from which to assess some of the component issues. It is well to begin by recapturing the claims that lie behind the debate about party systems and their relationship to democracy. The argument for multi-party systems is not that they necessarily produce "better policy"—policies that are either more efficient, more effective, or more just. Indeed, they may permit the temporary ascendance of interests that favor ideas that do not work to the betterment of material conditions for all in the long run and promote policy about-faces and U-turns, or more minor forms of policy instability. The claim on behalf of multi-partyism is both more limited and more fundamental.

Those who champion multi-party competition argue simply that the system improves the ability of the governed to hold the governors to account for their actions, for their fulfillment of the obligations they acquired in assuming leadership. Its purpose is to lower the costs associated with the exercise of voice, or criticism, and thereby to permit gradual reforms that may obviate more drastic, even violent bids for participation by the disenfranchised later. Its ambition is to improve the quality of public management by providing a protected venue for open discussion of policy choice and public administration. It permits a public assessment of whether the leadership or the machinery of government has lived up to promises to use public funds and public powers in a manner consistent with official pronouncements or with the reasonable expectations of the populace. Whether the party elites who win the ability to participate in a multi-party system are indeed representative of broad social interests, and whether they exercise their power responsibly, depends to some degree on the design of electoral rules and in some measure upon the character of the leaders the system produces, including their ability to sustain civility during debates that touch their own personal interests deeply.

Party competition is thus part of the larger effort to secure accountability that is the aim of democratic systems. Democratic governance entails far more than the legalization of opposition political parties. For a system of governance to be democratic, it must permit broad participation, not just in the form of opportunities to select candidates and to vote in elections, but also in eligibility for public office. It must be inclusive. It must also ensure the ability to contest public policy, not just through ability to compete in elections and secure representation in decision making, but also through a variety of other guarantees, including freedom to associate, to speak out on policy matters, to gather and dispense information subject to libel laws, and so on.[41] Democratic governance is a package of guarantees and institutions to support them. Multi-partyism is only one part of that package, and it does not necessarily yield the results intended unless the other elements of that package exist too. Nor, again, is democratic governance a system for securing perfect justice. As John Lonsdale notes: "Public accountability, or public morality, is the chief end of political freedom. Whether it also guarantees social justice and economic development is an altogether thornier question."[42]

Carefully designed multi-party systems can provide a base from which the constant struggle to secure and preserve the other elements of democratic governance can be waged without resort to violence. Even the limited ability to associate and to discuss policy in public that legalized opposition parties provide can create incentives for ministers to air information about the activities of the organizations they run, if only to counter ill-founded charges. The threat that a governing party may lose at the polls may act as a spur to improved public management—to more timely and more efficient delivery of services. Most important, however, this competition provides a way for concerned politicians to spotlight encroachments on ability to contest policy and to offer a credible threat to the incumbent political elite if such measures are not repealed. Thus, there is a clear link between multi-partyism and the broader achievement of democratic governance.

One of the findings of this Kenya case study is that single-party systems are not likely to sustain the same kinds of behavior that accountability demands. That is, single-party democracy is a myth, as many residents of the American South discovered earlier in the twentieth century, when de facto single-party governments denied the civil liberties of some citizens and showed little interest in economic development.[43] There is nothing uniquely "African" about "single-party democracy"; such claims of cultural appropriateness have surfaced everywhere single-party systems have existed, from the Soviet Union to the Old South in the United States, and everywhere they have had similar consequences. In the Kenyan case, the powers of the significant KANU backbenchers' group that provided a limited check on government actions during the mid 1960s were gradually dismantled over the objections of members. In addition to the rapid passage of constitutional amendments that concentrated power in the hands of the president, the 1960s and 1970s saw implementation of licensing restrictions on political meetings and fund-raisers, bans on press coverage of "opposition" politicians, manipulation of the access of supporters of "populist" members to government employment, and elimination of entitlement to a passport. In the presence of such restrictions, it became impossible to organize an enduring base for even moderate stances partly at odds with the interests of the Office of the President.

As in other single-party systems, factions replaced a "backbenchers' group" in Parliament, and Kenya saw the rapid individualization and personalization of political conflict. Unable to organize, eventually members of Parliament lost most of their capacity to call for information, debate issues, or do anything more than rubberstamp legislation. They were incapable of defending their ability to debate policy against still further encroachment under the Moi government, which increased the costs of exercising voice by turning the sole legal party into a vehicle for surveillance of political elites and for securing compliance with policy implementation.

The second observation one might draw from the Kenya case is that constitutions are easily amended and that the "guarantee" of civil liberties and ability to contest policy in new states lies with what political scientists often call "civil society." More specifically, constitutions and bills of rights last only as long as there are individuals who will dedicate their lives to upholding them and who can command or elicit the support of others who hold economic gate-keeping positions and are willing to bring their bargaining leverage to bear when political incumbents threaten the ability to contest policy. The Kenyan single-party system altered greatly during the first twenty-five years of independence. The country moved far more slowly than many of its neighbors toward the kind of party-state described and analyzed in this study, however. The presence of interest groups that could use control of a critical resource to limit encroachments on political space or draw attention to an issue—and were willing to do so—was important in maintaining openness within KANU under Kenyatta. The existence of members of Parliament, lawyers, and churchmen who overcame fear and called upon the resources of these groups was even more fundamental.

There are three important points buried in this observation. First, many of the economies of sub-Saharan Africa have not been hospitable breeding grounds for interest groups whose members are independent of government contracts, licenses, or critical services that incumbents may manipulate in order to ensure political passivity. In general, the government role in the economy has been extensive and of a form that has created opportunities for exactly such behavior. As the framers of Nigeria's attempted transition to a third republic recognized, for multi-party competition to produce its intended effects, it is critically important to guarantee the impartiality of "procedural institutions": the police, the court system, and other "umpires" in the political community. Further, there must be some way to earn a living outside of a government salary or contract. Individuals must have some ability to secure employment without having to pass muster with incumbent politicians. Albert Hirschman has argued that the framers of contemporary Western liberal democracies urged adoption of competitive capitalism for political reasons. Capitalism did not triumph and bring with it liberal democracy. Rather, the two systems were hammered out together. In the eyes of some, competitive capitalism offered a solution to fears that governments would too easily be able to crush dissent. As Montesquieu wrote of the consequences of opening trade: "The statesman looks about with amazement; he who was wont to consider himself as the first man in the society in every respect, perceives himself eclipsed by the lustre of private wealth, which avoids his grasp when he attempts to seize it. This makes his government more complex and more difficult to be carried on; he must now avail himself of art and address as well as of power and authority." [44] Capitalist economic systems generate their own kinds of abuses, too. Nonetheless, a modified form of competitive, not state-sponsored, capitalism, with impartial regulatory mechanisms, can facilitate the defense of civil liberties. That is, it can promote the existence of groups not wholly dependent on the state who can exercise some bargaining leverage to prevent usurpation of powers by the chief executive and ruling party. Concomitantly, by helping to ensure that incumbents who are not returned to office are able to earn a living and support their households outside of government, it may also lower the costs entailed in losing public office.

Even where countries have given private enterprise greater latitude than it has achieved elsewhere on the African continent, as in the cases of Kenya and Côte d'Ivoire, for example, bargaining leverage depends very much on whether the head of state and senior officials are able to buy into sectors of the economy while in office or reorganize the structure of an industry in which they have or plan to secure personal holdings. Blind trusts, public declaration of assets, and enforceable laws against conflicts of interest become all the more important to the health of the polity where there are only fledgling private sectors and the entry of a head of state or senior official into the market as a "private actor" can drastically alter the distribution of power within an industry.

It is well to recall too that a single interest group with economic clout sufficient to bring state activities to a halt may also exert that power on behalf of extremely parochial interests, and may, indeed, use it at times to limit political competition. Rarely are business interests so monolithic that captains of industry or commerce can exact such responsiveness at the expense of other citizens. Nonetheless, stable multi-party systems may well depend on the existence of at least one other interest group with significant power. Labor is usually one candidate for that task; the farmers are another.

Most non-profit organizations, the "thousand points of light" that have loomed so important in American foreign policy during the 1980s, have only extremely limited economic leverage and are usually highly vulnerable to control by state officials. However significant their contribution to the development of participation skills and whatever opportunities they may provide citizens to share information about the problems they encounter, they are weak partners in efforts to protect civil liberties. In the Kenyan case, they have played an extremely limited role.

Second, the protracted existence of a single-party system and attacks against ability to associate outside the confines of a party can shape interest-group structure and modify the effects of private enterprise Montesquieu envisioned. As Jean-François Bayart has noted, "The social actors who are in a position to reduce state control may, for different reasons, remain outside politics. Some fail to enter politics because they cannot conceive of such a thing." [45] Although the case is often overdrawn, Africa's rural majority, the small-scale farmers, face not only collective action problems but are also often more attuned to parallel systems of authority than they are to the formal systems in place. More important, where political information is difficult to secure, where politicians themselves are greatly divided and act only as individuals, with no links to other members of Parliament, and where the cost of expressing criticism is high, interest-group leaders may not be able to conceive of successful efforts to influence policy. Instead, they may decide that it is simply easier to find a high-ranking patron who can bring selective relief from some of the problems that policies have created and choose to live with other difficulties.

In the Kenyan case, absent ability to engage in political organization, many politicians, farmers, and members of the commercial elite formed ethnic welfare societies to permit them to exchange views and bolster the campaigns of favored sons for elective office. In no instance did any of these groups make exceptional bids for control of the state; all of the attempts to build significant opposition parties or movements in Kenya's post-independence history have taken the form of multi-ethnic coalitions, although it is true that GEMA wielded disproportionate (but not exclusive) influence in the years of Kenyatta's illness. The heightened salience of ethnicity in politics was not the straightforward consequence of political competition; rather, it was the consequence of single-party monopoly and increasing political repression. When the Moi government proscribed these groups, patron-client ties acquired increased attractiveness to those who sought control over policy. When these, too, were shattered, opposition went underground.

Third, it is not only groups but individuals who are vitally important in upholding the tenets of a constitution. Certainly, knowing that one wields economic clout grants some confidence to a critic, as it may bring some protection from poor treatment at the hands of the authorities. Where a country is small enough that the head of state can monitor the behavior of most members of the elite, and where press coverage is controlled, however, even the *samaki kubwa*, the big man, may fear the consequences of dissent. The Kenyan case suggests that those likely to take a stand, to assume responsibility for organizing others, and to maintain civility and discipline are those who have a professional calling that accords special importance to these actions. Some of the clergy are in this category. More important, the members of the legal profession have both a professional and material incentive to assume the dangers of the critic's role. This group occupies a special position under these circumstances and is most likely to be able to spearhead change. It is also vitally important in developing the interpersonal skills, attitudes toward authority, and historical memory necessary to restrain demands and foster the habits of compromise party competition requires and to persuade others of the need to maintain a multi-party system even when the bargaining power of the interest groups that helped bring it into being alters. The legal profession is thus an important agent for institutionalizing party competition.

Appendix:
The Uses of Evidence

Because of political restrictions on research and journalism, Africa specialists rarely obtain the kind of systematic data on government actions and the behavior of elites a scholar would ideally have. In the case of this analysis, clearance restrictions and government nervousness engendered by the 1985 party elections circumscribed the data and interviews the author could pursue. For example, within a day of the author's arrival, records of harambee meetings, which are licensed by the government, were placed under the sole control of the head of internal security. Suspension of clearances for foreign political scientists then in the country meant that on-site interviews threatened the careers of those whose lives are chronicled in the text.

The analysis presented in this book therefore rests heavily on interviews conducted with Kenyans traveling outside of Kenya and on archival sources, although not exclusively on these. Even where the information presented came originally from an interview, the author has included citations of public sources, to facilitate the work of other scholars who may later wish to delve into parts of the historical record in greater depth. Because Kenyans interviewed in the United States planned to return to their country at some date, their names are protected.

The archival data are of three types. First, the analysis of flows of harambee funds comes from newspaper notices of harambee meetings. Although no doubt imperfect records, the *Daily Nation* and the *Stan-*

dard newspapers do carry brief notices of the travels of *senior* political figures and of their presence at meetings in rural districts. Although the newspapers rarely report the content of speeches and cannot be relied on to convey accurate transcriptions of political statements, they can be used effectively to note the number and location of harambee gatherings attended by senior officials and the amount of money pledged at these.

Second, from time to time the text makes reference to budgetary outlays for various governmental functions. Again, budget figures are notoriously inaccurate in African settings in general. The Kenyan figures for some kinds of functions, where reporting for purposes of meeting IMF conditionality agreements is necessary and where technical advisers oversee the budget process, are more reliable than they are in most comparable settings. These figures should be approached with caution, but the general direction of change and the approximate magnitude are likely to be correct.

Third, the account relies heavily on newspaper identification of the timing of meetings and the lists of participants. The *Daily Nation* and the *Weekly Review* are the primary sources of this material. Although both operate under some constraints on subject matter the government considers appropriate, neither source was closely controlled until the late 1980s. For reporting of the mere fact of a meeting between leaders and of statements made on the floor of Parliament (which can be verified by visiting foreign officials and guests), these sources are reliable. Again, one would want to use caution in drawing on accounts these sources offer of popular political activity. In all cases, the author has avoided use of the party-controlled newspaper, the *Kenya Times*. Where appropriate, she has also noted skepticism about events reported by individuals who later acquired careers with the government and may have benefited from reports they wrote while on the staff of a newspaper.

The editorial policies of the *Weekly Review* and its chief, Hilary Ng'weno, may have undergone changes that affected the kinds of stories featured since the mid 1980s, although the evidence is mixed. Several knowledgeable Kenyans have argued that the newsweekly predicted events and "set the stage" for things to come more often than would be possible without inside information. They hint that the Moi State House may control reportage and have noted rumors that the president has actually bought controlling equity in the magazine. Whether the *Weekly Review*'s ability to predict changes and shifts in political fortunes stems from good reporting, well-placed sources, and editorial prescience or from the exercise of government control is difficult to say. In 1983, KANU bought the Ng'weno-owned Stellascope publishing house, but The Weekly Review, Ltd. is not part of that company. The author has no hard evidence of additional exchanges.

It is this author's view that political savvy and a sometimes too-great desire to forestall a government crackdown have produced the kind of reporting readers have seen in the past few years. The magazine contains more feature articles on the economic attractiveness of the western provinces and towns than it did earlier. Those have little real effect on the balance of coverage, however. Of greater concern is that the magazine's word choice sometimes connotes acceptance of State House positions and interpretations of events as truth. Oddly enough, many of the articles that correspond most strongly with the vocabulary and message of the State House are articles on the role of the press. Ng'weno has increasingly taken the line that foreign correspondents are under the control of other governments and cannot be trusted, and that the kind of press suited to African settings is not the kind of elite press characterized by the major U.S. papers, which, he argues, are not read by most Americans, who can neither afford them nor understand the kinds of articles they offer.[1]

Although the frequency with which the publication carries editorials, comments, or reportage openly critical of government policies and practices has diminished since restrictions on freedom of the press have increased, Ng'weno continues to publish occasional statements or accounts that present alternative points of view, in the forms of observations buried in the text, which are far more nuanced than the material that State House usually disseminates. What the *Weekly Review* does not do is assume the role of a partisan press on the European model. Nor does it engage in arguably much-needed muckraking.

A second criticism of the *Weekly Review*'s reportage is that it overemphasizes the salience of ethnicity in Kenyan politics. This criticism appears to be at least partly justified. The magazine only rarely carries articles on the concerns of businessmen, smallholders, workers, or informal-sector entrepreneurs. If the interviews the author carried out offer any gauge of the kinds of the individual motivations for political activity, then the publication underreports economic or "class" issues and overemphasizes the importance of clan distinctions.

The author interviewed a number of Kenyans inside and outside of the borders of the country. Those interviewed outside the country include three members of Parliament, six civil servants, and thirteen Kenyan lawyers and academics involved in the activities described. The identities of these individuals must remain anonymous under the current political restrictions that affect the country. The author thanks these respondents for their willingness to be interviewed and regrets that she had so little opportunity to pursue additional conversations.

Notes

CHAPTER 1

1. Jane Perlez, "Kenya's Plan for Tower Annoys Aid Donors," *New York Times*, December 29, 1989.

2. René Lemarchand has argued that factions are "non-corporate, highly personalized and intensely competitive social aggregates" based on access to highly valued political resources rather than common fundamental economic interests. They are ad hoc in his view, compared to interest groups, which possess both shared long-term interests and a higher level of internal organization. The argument articulated later in this chapter suggests that within single-party systems, corporate groups in the dominant party tend to give way to multiple factions, except in the case that the corporate groups have strong independent financial backing or control critical functions in the economy. For more on the distinction between factions and corporate groups, see René Lemarchand, "The State, the Parallel Economy, and the Changing Structure of Patronage Systems," in *The Precarious Balance: State and Society in Africa*, ed. Donald Rothchild and Naomi Chazan (Boulder, Colo.: Westview Press, 1988), pp. 149–70.

3. See Nelson Kasfir, *The Shrinking Political Arena: Participation and Ethnicity in African Politics, with a Case Study of Uganda* (Berkeley: University of California Press, 1976).

4. Joel D. Barkan and Frank Holmquist, "Peasant-State Relations and the Social Base of Self-Help in Kenya," *World Politics* 41, 3 (April 1989): 359.

5. Dirk Berg-Schlosser, "Modes and Meaning of Political Participation in Kenya," *Comparative Politics* 14 (July 1982): 410.

6. See,e.g., Henry Bienen, *Armies and Parties in Africa* (New York: Holmes & Meier, 1978).

7. See Martin Kilson, "Authoritarian and Single-Party Tendencies in African Politics," *World Politics* 15 (January 1963): 262–94.

8. Immanuel Wallerstein, "The Decline of the Party in Single-Party African States," in *Political Parties and Political Development*, ed. Joseph LaPalombara and Myron Weiner (Princeton: Princeton University Press, 1966), pp. 201–16.

9. Samuel Huntington, "Social and Institutional Dynamics of One-Party Systems," in *Authoritarian Politics in Modern Society: The Dynamics of Established One-Party Systems*, ed. Samuel Huntington and Clement Moore (New York: Basic Books, 1970), p. 11.

10. Ibid., p. 9.

11. Aristide Zolberg, *Creating Political Order: The Party-States of West Africa* (Chicago: University of Chicago Press, 1966), pp. 90–91.

12. Ibid., p. 7.

13. Robert Jackson and Carl Rosberg, *Personal Rule in Black Africa* (Berkeley: University of California Press, 1982), pp. 19 and 23.

14. This literature is now extensive. Some of the more helpful general discussions include: Goran Hyden, *No Shortcuts to Progress: African Development Management in Perspective* (Berkeley: University of California Press, 1983); Joel S. Migdal, "Strong States, Weak States: Power and Accommodation," in *Understanding Political Development*, ed. Myron Weiner and Samuel Huntington (Boston: Little, Brown, 1987); id., *Strong Societies and Weak States: State-Society Relations and State Capacity in the Third World* (Princeton: Princeton University Press, 1988).

15. Crawford Young and Thomas Turner, *The Rise and Decline of the Zairian State* (Madison: University of Wisconsin Press, 1985), p. 20.

16. Thomas Callaghy, *The State-Society Struggle: Zaire in Comparative Perspective* (New York: Columbia University Press, 1984), p. 32.

17. Hyden, *No Shortcuts to Progress*, p. 41.

18. Ibid., p. 48.

19. See, e.g., Goran Hyden, *Beyond Ujamaa in Tanzania* (Berkeley: University of California Press, 1981).

20. Rafael Kaplinsky, "Capitalist Accumulation in the Periphery—The Kenyan Case Re-examined," *Review of African Political Economy* 17 (1980): 97.

21. Colin Leys, *Underdevelopment in Kenya: The Political Economy of Neo-Colonialism* (London: Heinemann, 1977), p. 207.

22. Ibid., p. 210.

23. See, e.g., Peter Anyang' Nyong'o, "Introduction," in *Popular Struggles for Democracy in Africa*, ed. Peter Anyang' Nyong'o (London: United Nations University / Zed Press, 1987), p. 21.

24. Peter Anyang' Nyong'o, "The Decline of Democracy and the Rise of Authoritarian and Factionalist Politics in Kenya," *Horn of Africa* 6, 3 (1983): 32.

25. Nicola Swainson, "State and Economy in Post-Colonial Kenya, 1963–1978," *Canadian Journal of African Studies* 12, 2 (1978): 363.

26. See Colin Leys, "Capital Accumulation, Class Formation, and Depen-

dency: The Significance of the Kenyan Case," in *The Socialist Register, 1978*, ed. Ralph Miliband and John Saville (London: Merlin Press, 1978), p. 247.

27. Colin Leys, "Kenya: What Does 'Dependency' Explain?" *Review of African Political Economy* 17 (1980): 109.

28. Ibid., p. 111.

29. Michael Chege, "The African Economic Crisis and the Fate of Democracy in Sub-Saharan Africa," in *Democratic Theory and Practice in Africa*, ed. Walter Oyugi (Portsmouth, N.H.: Heinemann, 1988), p. 201.

30. Based on the author's calculations and data drawn from International Bank for Reconstruction and Development, Africa Technical Department, "Draft Data Document" (Autumn 1991), and United Nations Development Programme, *African Economic and Financial Data* (Washington, D.C.: World Bank, 1989).

31. The U.S. Congress banned military loans to Kenya in 1990 in order to protest human rights abuses. Prior to that period, the United States had taken an increasingly outspoken position in support of civil liberties and against the restriction of political opposition then occurring in the country. The Bush administration permitted the release of the last $5 million of an earlier military assistance loan in the spring of 1991 in an effort to persuade Kenya to accept anti-Quaddafi Libyan commandos the United States had trained in Chad, then rescued when a pro-Libyan government took power in a coup d'état there. The congressional limitation on future assistance remained in place, however.

32. Sholto Cross, "L'Etat c'est moi: Political Transition and the Kenya General Election of 1979" (University of East Anglia, Discussion Paper No. 66, April 1983), p. 12.

33. This analytic perspective is articulated in part in the works of African writers such as Chinua Achebe and in part in Richard Sandbrook, *The Politics of Africa's Economic Stagnation* (Cambridge: Cambridge University Press, 1985).

34. Sandbrook, *Politics of Africa's Economic Stagnation*, and Irving Leonard Markovitz, *Power and Class in Africa: Introduction to Change and Conflict in African Politics* (Englewood Cliffs, N.J.: Prentice-Hall, 1977).

35. Fernando Henrique Cardoso, "On the Characterization of Authoritarian Regimes in Latin America," in *The New Authoritarianism in Latin America*, ed. David Collier (Princeton: Princeton University Press, 1979), p. 37.

36. Guillermo A. O'Donnell, *Modernization and Bureaucratic-Authoritarianism* (Berkeley: Institute of International Studies, University of California, 1979), p. 55.

37. For a detailed explication of this sequence, see David Collier, "Overview of the Bureaucratic-Authoritarian Model," in *New Authoritarianism in Latin America*, ed. Collier, pp. 19–32.

38. Cardoso, "On the Characterization of Authoritarian Regimes," pp. 33–67.

39. David Collier, "The Bureaucratic Authoritarian Model: Synthesis and Priorities for Future Research," in *New Authoritarianism in Latin America*, ed. Collier, pp. 396–97.

40. Young and Turner, *Rise and Decline of the Zairian State*, p. 27.

41. See Henry Bienen and Mark Gersovitz, "Consumer Subsidy Cuts, Violence, and Political Stability," *Comparative Politics* 19 (October 1986): 25–44.

42. Peter Anyang' Nyong'o, "State and Society in Kenya: The Disintegration of the Nationalist Coalitions and the Rise of Presidential Authoritarianism, 1963–78," *African Affairs* 88, 351 (April 1989): 231, 232.

43. Colin Leys offers an insightful account of this kind of appeal in his book *Underdevelopment in Kenya*.

44. The analysis offered here focuses on the incentives facing political elites. It draws on the work of political scientists who have studied parts of the world other than Africa, especially that of Mancur Olson, *The Rise and Decline of Nations* (New Haven: Yale University Press, 1982), and Albert Hirschman, *Exit, Voice, and Loyalty* (Cambridge, Mass.: Harvard University Press, 1970). Other Africa scholars, such as Robert Bates, have argued that party systems affect the utility calculations of individual voters:

> Under a competitive party system, it makes sense for citizens to pay attention to a candidate's stand on those issues affecting the entire national political system. For if a candidate is committed to a party, then her success could conceivably affect national policy; her performance at the polls would combine with the performance of other candidates from her party and their joint performance would help to define which team would subsequently control the government. . . . [Under a single-party, multiple-candidate system] if successful, a candidate will become but one of over 100 members of Parliament; the candidate's success would therefore have little impact upon national policies. In the absence of a competitive party system, voters, behaving rationally, should therefore tend to pay more attention to the ability of candidates to do things of immediate, local value than to their stands on national issues.

(Robert Bates, *Beyond the Miracle of the Market: The Political Economy of Agrarian Development in Kenya* [Cambridge: Cambridge University Press, 1989], p. 92 and n. 54)

45. For a discussion of the way party systems affected political outcomes in the "one-party states" of the American South, and specifically of the way they contributed to localism, see V. O. Key, Jr., *Southern Politics* (New York: Knopf, 1949), pp. 302–3.

46. "Political departicipation appears to . . . [increase] the weight of local issues, lessens the salience of ethnicity and enhances the stature of strategically connected local notables. . . . 'Access' is indeed a key resource in conditions of political departicipation, and thus much of the dynamics of factionalism appear[s] to revolve around the structures and personalities through which access can be gained or denied," René Lemarchand argues in "The State, the Parallel Economy, and the Changing Structure of Patronage," pp. 158–59.

47. On the party as political machine, see Henry Bienen, "Political Parties and Political Machines in Africa," in id., *Armies and Parties in Africa*, pp. 62–77.

48. V. O. Key, Jr., noted that in the American South, between 1869 and the 1950s, one-party systems differed from one another in structure and in the character of political debate. At one end of the spectrum, Virginia and Tennessee displayed limited fragmentation and tight control by dominant machines. At the

other end of the spectrum, Mississippi and Florida offered cases of extreme fragmentation and, in the case of Florida, a high degree of mutability in the definition of factional boundaries. Key located the source of these differences partly in the distribution of different kinds of economic activities within each state, patterns of migration, and the size of the public coffers. See his discussions of these cases in Key, *Southern Politics*.

49. For an analysis of the American South in this same vein, see ibid. "The lack of continuing groups of 'ins' and 'outs' profoundly influences the nature of political leadership," Key writes. "Free and easy movement from loose faction to loose faction results in there being in reality no group of 'outs' with any sort of corporate spirit to serve as critic of the 'ins' or as a rallying point around which can be organized all those discontented with the current conduct of public affairs" (ibid., p. 304). For a formalization, see Hirschman, *Exit, Voice, and Loyalty*.

50. Again, the case of the American South between the late 1800s and the 1950s is informative. See V. O. Key, Jr., "Southern Suffrage Restrictions: Bourbon Coup d'état?" in *Southern Politics*, pp. 533–54.

51. Thomas Callaghy, "Lost between State and Market: The Politics of Economic Adjustment in Ghana, Zambia, and Nigeria," in *Economic Crisis and Policy Choice*, ed. Joan M. Nelson (Princeton: Princeton University Press, 1990), p. 37.

52. This observation defines democratic political structures as those required for public contestation of policy, as outlined in Robert Dahl, *Polyarchy: Participation and Opposition* (New Haven: Yale University Press, 1971, 1985).

53. See Barrington Moore, Jr., *The Social Origins of Dictatorship and Democracy: Lord and Peasant in the Making of the Modern World* (Boston: Beacon Press, 1966).

54. Henry Bienen, *Kenya: The Politics of Participation and Control* (Princeton: Princeton University Press, 1974).

55. See John Okumu with Frank Holmquist, "Party and Party-State Relations," in Joel Barkan, *Politics and Public Policy in Kenya and Tanzania* (New York: Praeger, 1984).

56. I borrow the distinction between "reign" and "rule" from Chalmers Johnson and Thomas Callaghy, who use it in their work on Japan and Zaire respectively.

57. For a detailed analysis of these policies, see Susanne Mueller, "Political Parties in Kenya: The Politics of Opposition and Dissent, 1919–1969" (Ph.D. diss., Department of Politics, Princeton University, 1972).

58. Callaghy, *State-Society Struggle;* Young and Turner, *Rise and Decline of the Zairean State*; and Michael Schatzberg, *The Dialectics of Oppression in Zaire* (Bloomington: Indiana University Press, 1988).

59. Although this study uses some analysis of aggregate data, most of the evidence comes from review of the timing of meetings and legislation. My attempt to provide a more systematic account of the use of harambee resources in electoral politics was circumscribed by events. A few days after my arrival in Kenya in 1985, the government placed its records of harambee meetings (which must be licensed) under the sole control of the head of internal security. Ner-

vousness engendered by the 1982 coup attempt and the widespread belief that the 1985 party elections might bring additional trouble resulted in the suspension of research clearances for most political scientists and made direct interviews with politicians impossible. Subsequently, I was able to interview a number of politicians and administrative officials while they were outside the country. The analysis reflects their contribution, although individual attribution is withheld to protect those who spoke.

CHAPTER 2

1. See esp. David Throup, "The Construction and Deconstruction of the Kenyatta State," in *The Political Economy of Kenya*, ed. Michael Schatzberg (Praeger: New York, 1987), and Henry Bienen, *Kenya: The Politics of Participation and Control* (Princeton: Princeton University Press, 1974).

2. The fullest discussion of the KLFA is contained in Tabitha Kanogo, *Squatters and the Roots of Mau Mau* (Athens, Ohio: Ohio University Press, 1989), pp. 164–69.

3. Josiah Mwangi Kariuki, *"Mau Mau" Detainee: The Account by a Kenya African of His Experiences in Detention Camps, 1953–1960* (London: Oxford University Press, 1963), p. 181.

4. For a fuller discussion, see David Goldsworthy, *Tom Mboya: The Man Kenya Wanted to Forget* (New York: Africana Publishing Co., 1982). p. 229.

5. See Gavin Kitching, *Class and Economic Change in Kenya* (New Haven: Yale University Press, 1980); David Leonard, *African Successes: Four Public Managers of Kenyan Rural Development* (Berkeley: University of California Press, 1991).

6. Christopher Leo, *Land and Class in Kenya* (Toronto: University of Toronto Press, 1984), p. 177.

7. Leonard, *African Successes*, pp. 80–81.

8. For extensive discussions of the differences between class or associational politics and the politics of patron-client relationships, see ibid. and Robert Bates, "The Nature and Origins of Agricultural Policies in Africa," in id., *Essays on the Political Economy of Rural Africa* (Berkeley: University of California Press, 1983).

9. Tom Mboya, *Freedom and After* (London: André Deutsch, 1963), p. 28.

10. Joseph Karimi and Philip Ochieng, *The Kenyatta Succession* (Nairobi: Transafrica Press, 1980), p. ix.

11. *Daily Nation*, December 1, 1975.

12. *Daily Nation*, August 18, 1980.

13. Colin Leys, *Underdevelopment in Kenya: The Political Economy of Neo-Colonialism* (London: Heinemann, 1977), p. 199.

14. Ibid., pp. 203–4.

15. For an extended discussion of this argument, see Bates, " Nature and Origins of Agricultural Policies."

16. Leonard, *African Successes*, p. 104.

17. J. R. King, *Stabilization Policy in an African Setting: Kenya, 1963–1973* (London: Heinemann Educational Books, 1979), p. 61.

18. A. T. Brough and T. R. C. Curtin, "Growth and Stability: An Account of Fiscal and Monetary Policy," in *Papers on the Kenyan Economy*, ed. Tony Killick (London: Heinemann Educational Books, 1981), p. 41.

19. King, *Stabilization Policy*, p. 61.

20. Brough and Curtin, "Growth and Stability," p. 45.

21. Cherry Gertzel, *The Politics of Independent Kenya, 1963–1968* (Nairobi: East African Publishing House, 1970), pp. 136–37.

22. H. W. O. Okoth-Ogendo, "Land Ownership and Land Distribution in Kenya's Large-Farm Areas," in *Papers on the Kenyan Economy*, ed. Killick, p. 329.

23. Tony Killick, *Papers on the Kenyan Economy*, ed. id., p. 265.

24. David Court, "The Education System as a Response to Inequality," in *Papers on the Kenyan Economy*, ed. Killick, passim, pp. 287–90.

25. Jeremy Murray-Brown, *Kenyatta* (London: George Allen & Unwin, 1979), p. 109.

26. Marshall Clough, *Fighting Two Sides: Kenyan Chiefs and Politicians, 1918–1940* (Niwot, Colo.: University Press of Colorado, 1990), pp. 127, 130.

27. George Bennett, "The Development of Political Organizations in Kenya," *Political Studies* 5, 2 (1957): 125.

28. Kariuki, *"Mau Mau" Detainee*, pp. 178–79.

29. Bruce Berman, *Control and Crisis in Colonial Kenya: The Dialectic of Domination* (Athens, Ohio: Ohio University Press, 1990), p. 338.

30. Murray-Brown, *Kenyatta*, pp. 304, 309.

31. Berman, *Control and Crisis in Colonial Kenya*, p. 324.

32. H. W. O. Okoth-Ogendo, "The Politics of Constitutional Change in Kenya since Independence, 1963–1969," *African Affairs* 71, 282 (January 1972): 19.

33. Jomo Kenyatta, "A One-Party System," in Jomo Kenyatta, *Suffering without Bitterness* (Nairobi: East African Publishing House, 1968), p. 228.

34. The shift to a republican system in 1964 abolished regional assemblies established during the independence negotiations at Lancaster House but turned the prime minister into a president in name only. The president remained bound to an elected legislature of which he had to be a member and the lower house retained the right to issue a vote of no confidence. Kenya moved to a true presidential system only after the tenth amendment to the constitution in 1968, at which time Kenya had become a de facto single-party system. For an excellent discussion of the changes in electoral rules, see Gertzel, *Politics of Independent Kenya*.

35. Ibid., p. 63.

36. Ibid.

37. *Current Biography, 1979*, s.v. "Moi, Daniel arap" (New York: H. W. Wilson Co., 1979).

38. Kenyatta, address at the Limuru Conference, March 13, 1966, in Kenyatta, *Suffering without Bitterness*, p. 298.

39. Kenyatta, address at the Limuru Conference of March 13, 1966, as it appears in Kenyatta, *Suffering without Bitterness,* p. 300.

40. Kenyatta, address at the opening of Parliament, November 2, 1965, as it appears in Kenyatta, *Suffering without Bitterness,* p. 286.

41. Kenyatta, address at the opening of Parliament, November 2, 1965, as it appears in Kenyatta, *Suffering without Bitterness,* p. 286.

42. *Africa Contemporary Record, 1969–70,* p. B125.

43. Leys, *Underdevelopment in Kenya,* p. 235.

44. C. A. Kamundia,"Primaries in Kenya," *East Africa Journal* 6 (May 1969): 9.

45. Leonard, *African Successes,* pp. 105–6.

46. Throup, "Construction and Deconstruction of the Kenyatta State," p. 40.

47. Henry Bienen has argued that (1) the absence of strong competition reduced the incentive for party discipline and fostered debate within the ranks, and (2) the perception of weakness discouraged politicians from investing in the party. See "Party Politics in Kenya," in Bienen, *Armies and Parties in Africa* (New York: Holmes & Meier, 1978), p. 87.

48. Njuguna Ng'eth'e, "Harambee and Development Participation in Kenya: The Politics of Peasants and Elites Interaction with Particular Reference to Harambee Projects in Kiambu" (Ph.D. diss., Carleton University, Ottawa, July 1979), pp. 135, 131.

49. Ibid., p. 131.

50. *Weekly Review,* January 23, 1978, p. 5.

51. *Daily Nation,* June 16, 1979.

52. *Weekly Review,* July 6, 1979, p. 9.

53. Chong Lim Kim, Joel D. Barkan, Ilter Turan, and Malcom Jewell, eds., *The Legislative Connection: The Politics of Representation in Kenya, Korea, and Turkey* (Durham, N.C.: Duke University Press, 1984), p. 83.

54. Bienen, *Armies and Parties in Africa,* p. 68.

55. Brough and Curtin, "Growth and Stability," p. 45

56. Frank Holmquist, "Self-Help: The State and Peasant Leverage in Kenya," *Africa* 54, 3 (1984): 81.

57. Peter M. Ngau, "Tensions in Empowerment: The Experience of the *Harambee* (Self-Help) Movement in Kenya," *Economic Development and Cultural Change* 35, 3 (April 1987): 525.

58. This view is argued most forcefully in Susanne Mueller, "Government and Opposition in Kenya, 1966–1969," *Journal of Modern African Studies* 22, 3 (1984): 399–427.

59. *East African Standard,* quoted in Susanne Mueller, "Political Parties in Kenya: The Politics of Opposition and Dissent 1919–1969" (Ph.D. diss., Department of Politics, Princeton University, 1972), p. 80.

60. Mueller, "Political Parties in Kenya," p. 497.

61. The legal history of the period is best documented in Gertzel, *Politics of Independent Kenya.*

62. Henry Wariithi as quoted in Gertzel, *Politics of Independent Kenya,* p. 40.

63. Ibid.

64. Mueller, "Political Parties in Kenya," p. 413.

65. Mueller, "Government and Opposition in Kenya," p. 424.

66. Kenyatta, broadcast of April 26, 1966, in the wake of the formation of the KPU, as it appears in Kenyatta, *Suffering without Bitterness*, p. 303.

67. Mueller, "Government and Opposition in Kenya," p. 410.

68. Robert Buijtenhuis, *Mau Mau Twenty Years After* (Paris: Mouton, 1973), p. 131.

69. "Speech by His Excellency the President at the Kenya Institute of Administration, December 15, 1965," Kenya News Agency Handout No. 768, as quoted in Gertzel, *Politics of Independent Kenya*, pp. 168–69.

70. John Okumu and Frank Holmquist, "Party and Party-State Relations," in *Politics and Public Policy in Kenya and Tanzania*, ed. Joel Barkan (New York: Praeger, 1984), pp. 53–54.

71. Peter Anyang' Nyong'o, "State and Society in Kenya: The Disintegration of the Nationalist Coalitions and the Rise of Presidential Authoritarianism, 1963–78" *African Affairs* 88, 351 (April 1989): 241.

72. Goran Hyden, "Administration and Public Policy," in *Politics and Public Policy*, ed. Barkan, p. 115; Bienen, *Kenya*, pp. 58–65.

73. Chong Lim Kim et al., *Legislative Connection*, p. 82.

CHAPTER 3

1. International Labour Organization, *Employment, Incomes and Equality* (Geneva: ILO, 1972).

2. Kenya, National Assembly, *Official Report*, April 26, 1973, p. 878.

3. Ibid., p. 879.

4. Ibid.

5. Kenya, National Assembly, *Official Report*, May 3, 1973, p. 1033.

6. Kenya, National Assembly, *Official Report*, June 13, 1973, p. 108.

7. Kenya, National Assembly, *Official Report*, May 8, 1973, p. 1154.

8. Ibid.

9. Ibid., p. 1156.

10. Kenya, National Assembly, *Official Report*, May 3, 1973, p. 1034.

11. *East African Standard*, April 27, 1973.

12. Kenya, National Assembly, *Official Report*, June 13, 1973, p. 108.

13. Apollo Njonjo, "The Africanization of the 'White Highlands': A Study in Agrarian Class Struggles in Kenya, 1950–1974" (Ph.D. diss., Department of Politics, Princeton University, 1977).

14. "The KADU argument ran simply and consistently as follows. It was 'unthinkable' that the Nandi and the Kipsigis should be separate. . . . Hence the demand for the creation of the present huge Rift Valley Province. . . . as soon as pre-colonial territories in the White Highlands were recognised, then such spheres would be legally codified and sanctified by vesting them in regional governments. Much more crucial, however, was the KADU demand that transactions in settler estates within a region be controlled by the Regional Assembly" (ibid., 40–46).

15. Ibid.

16. International Bank for Reconstruction and Development, *Kenya: Population and Development* (Washington, D.C.:IBRD, 1980), p. 30.

17. Compiled from ibid., p. 29.

18. Njonjo, "Africanization of the 'White Highlands,'" p. 465.

19. Ibid.

20. Kenya, National Assembly, *Official Report,* June 13, 1973, p. 101.

21. Ibid.

22. Kenya, National Assembly, *Official Report,* June 13, 1973, p. 102.

23. *Daily Nation,* January 3, 1973.

24. *Daily Nation,* January 19, 1973.

25. *Daily Nation,* January 20, 1973.

26. *Daily Nation,* February 27, 1973.

27. *Daily Nation,* December 5, 1973.

28. *Daily Nation,* November 23, 1973.

29. *Daily Nation,* May 2, 1974.

30. Kenya, National Assembly, *On the Current Economic Situation in Kenya,* Sessional Paper No. 1 of 1974 (Nairobi: Government Printer, 1974), p. 2.

31. *Daily Nation,* June 16, 1972.

32. *Daily Nation,* June 24, 1972.

33. *Daily Nation,* August 3, 1973.

34. Njonjo, "Africanization of the 'White Highlands,'" p. 496.

35. The parliamentary investigation of Kariuki's death notes that as chairman of the Betting and Lotteries Licensing Board, he "helped many wananchi to acquire betting machines" and "contributed significantly to various Harambee projects in the country" (Kenya, National Assembly, Report of the Select Committee on the Disappearance and Murder of the Late Member for Nyandarua North, The Hon. J.M. Kariuki, M.P., June 3, 1975).

36. *Daily Nation,* May 4, 1973.

37. *Weekly Review,* June 5, 1979, p. 11.

38. Colin Leys, *Underdevelopment in Kenya: The Political Economy of Neo-Colonialism* (London: Heinemann, 1975), pp. 228–29.

39. David Throup, "The Construction and Destruction of the Kenyatta State" (paper presented at the Johns Hopkins School for Advanced International Studies Conference on Kenya, Washington, D.C., April 11–12, 1986), p. 17.

40. Leys, *Underdevelopment in Kenya,* pp. 228–29.

41. Early in 1972, the government allegedly banned the Voice of Kenya from covering Kariuki's harambee appearances, and newspapers appear to have taken their cue from this. The *Daily Nation* reported a National Assembly debate about these allegations on July 6, 1972. The MP for South Tetu, Mwai Koigi, asked: "Why have instructions been issued against the Assistant Minister for Tourism and Wildlife that when he donated for *harambee* projects the news cannot be broadcast over the Voice of Kenya radio?" Koigi added that Kariuki had recently given a hospital in South Tetu a hundred bags of cement, but that Koigi's request to J. Z. Kase, assistant minister for information and broadcast-

ing, that the meeting be publicized had been turned down on the grounds that there were instructions not to give coverage to Kariuki. In Parliament, Kase denied that any such instructions had been issued. Carla Heath of the University of Illinois, Urbana-Champaign, has, however, reported statements by VOK employees that such a ban was in effect (letter to the author, May 1986).

42. *Daily Nation,* August 15, 1972.

43. *Daily Nation,* February 5, 1973.

44. *Daily Nation,* February 10, 1973.

45. The delegation included Baringo South MP Eric Bomett, Belgut MP W. K. Rono, and Mosop MP G. N. Kalya, as well as two representatives defeated in the 1969 elections, former Kerio Central MP W. C. Murgor and former Aldai MP J. K. Cheruiyot. See *Daily Nation,* March 3, 1973.

46. *Daily Nation,* March 25, 1972.

47. *Daily Nation,* September 21, 1972.

48. *Daily Nation,* September 25, 1972.

49. *Daily Nation,* September 28, 1972.

50. Pharis Wachira of Makuyu led the attack and others joined in, including B. M. Karangaru of Embakasi, Mark Mwithaga of Nakuru Town, and George Mwicigi of Kandara. Kitui Central MP James Kitonga added his support, the first from the Akamba districts.

51. Kuria Kinyanjui of Lari led the effort. G. G. W. Nthenge of Iveti South, Henry Cheboiwo of Baringo North, B. M. Karungaru, and J. M. Kariuki contributed.

52. *Daily Nation,* December 1, 1973.

53. *Daily Nation,* May 16, 1974.

54. *Daily Nation,* July 4, 1974.

55. The Special Rural Development Program (SRDP) was a project designed to spur development in outlying areas. It was funded by a six-country consortium, in which the U.S. Agency for International Development was one partner.

56. *Daily Nation,* April 6, 1972.

57. *Daily Nation,* May 6, 1972.

58. *Daily Nation,* November 3, 1973.

59. *Daily Nation,* December 1, 1973.

60. Ibid.

61. *Daily Nation,* February 13, 1974.

62. *Daily Nation,* July 1, 1972.

63. *Daily Nation,* July 5, 1972.

64. *Daily Nation,* March 7, 1973.

65. *Daily Nation,* April 16, 1973.

66. *Daily Nation,* May 7, 1973.

67. *Daily Nation,* March 7, 1973.

68. *Daily Nation,* February 27, 1973. Others were Mbiri MP Julius Gikonyo Kiano, Mwai Kibaki, and three long-time friends of the group leaders, Kangundo MP Paul Ngei, Meru North-West MP Jackson Angaine, and Embu South MP Jeremiah Nyagah.

69. *Daily Nation,* April 7, 1973.

70. *Daily Nation,* June 27, 1973.

71. Based on calculations drawn from newspaper accounts of harambee meetings attended by senior ministers and government officials. Official data on the amount of money collected and disbursed are currently under the control of the Office of the President.

72. *Daily Nation,* March 11, 1974.

73. Apollo Njonjo notes that Murgor was the most outspoken KADU critic of Kikuyu acquisition of land in the Rift Valley at independence. The change in his views may have resulted from high levels of development spending in and around Eldoret township, which is only a few kilometers from Moi's birthplace near Kabarnet. See Njonjo, "Africanization of the 'White Highlands,'" p. 409.

74. *Daily Nation,* April 13, 1973.

75. *Daily Nation,* May 14, 1973.

76. *Daily Nation,* June 11, 1973.

77. *East African Standard,* April 23, 1973.

78. *Daily Nation,* May 17, 1973.

79. *Daily Nation,* June 28, 1973.

80. *Daily Nation,* June 4, 1973.

81. Kenya, National Assembly, "Report . . . on the Disappearance and Murder of . . . J. M. Kariuki," p. 12.

82. *Daily Nation,* March 22, 1972.

83. *Daily Nation,* March 30, 1972.

84. *Daily Nation,* June 15, 1972.

85. *Daily Nation,* June 26, 1972.

86. *Daily Nation,* June 29, 1972.

87. *Daily Nation,* June 30, 1972.

88. *Daily Nation,* July 12, 1972.

89. *Daily Nation,* April 19, 1973.

90. *Daily Nation,* May 16, 1973.

91. *Daily Nation,* July 18, 1973.

92. *Daily Nation,* October 17, 1973.

93. *Daily Nation,* January 23, 1974.

94. *Daily Nation,* March 11, 1974.

95. *Daily Nation,* June 4, 1974.

96. *Daily Nation,* June 14, 1974.

97. *Daily Nation,* June 15, 1974.

98. *Daily Nation,* June 24, 1974.

99. Kenyatta as quoted in E.S. Atieno-Odhiambo, "Democracy and the Ideology of Order in Kenya," in *The Political Economy of Kenya,* ed. Michael Schatzberg (New York: Praeger, 1987), p. 177.

CHAPTER 4

1. Joseph Karimi and Philip Ochieng, *The Kenyatta Succession* (Nairobi: Transafrica Press, 1980), p. 17.

2. Mungai, Kenyatta's nephew, lost the 1974 election, but was appointed a member of Parliament thereafter and placed on the board of the Kenya Pipeline Company, in which the government purchased shares.

3. Karimi and Ochieng, *Kenyatta Succession*, pp. 18–19.

4. The meeting also included Odinga's future arch-rival, William Odongo Omamo. *Weekly Review,* October 11, 1976, p. 9, and September 27, 1976, p. 5.

5. *Weekly Review,* August 30, 1976, pp. 4–6.

6. Ibid., p. 7.

7. Karimi and Ochieng, *Kenyatta Succession*, p. 19.

8. Ibid., p. 28.

9. Kenyatta was detained by the colonial government at Lodwar, in the north of Kenya, during the Mau Mau uprising.

10. *Weekly Review,* October 25, 1976, p. 3.

11. *Weekly Review,* March 14, 1977.

12. *Weekly Review,* April 4, 1977, p. 10.

13. *Weekly Review,* August 1, 1978, p. 13.

14. *Weekly Review,* November 15, 1976.

15. *Weekly Review,* February 14, 1977, p. 10.

16. *Weekly Review,* January 23, 1978, p. 9.

17. See, e.g., the record of the meeting between Mungai and Oneko. *Daily Nation,* June 13, 1977.

18. Oloo Aringo as quoted in *Weekly Review,* January 23, 1978, p. 9.

19. *Weekly Review,* July 4, 1977.

20. *Weekly Review,* December 26, 1977.

21. *Weekly Review,* April 21, 1978, p. 3.

22. *Weekly Review,* May 26, 1978, p. 4.

23. *Weekly Review,* June 30, 1978, p. 7.

24. *Weekly Review,* August 18, 1978, p. 45.

25. *Weekly Review,* May 26, 1978, p. 4.

26. *Weekly Review,* December 2, 1978, p. 6.

27. The government was increasingly concerned about Somali incursions in the northeastern part of the country.

28. *Weekly Review,* September 29, 1978, p. 6.

29. *Weekly Review,* October 27, 1978, p. 6.

30. *Weekly Review,* October 13, 1978, p. 13.

31. Ibid., p. 9.

32. Ibid., p. 13.

33. *Weekly Review,* November 3, 1978, p. 4.

34. David Throup, Magdalene College, Cambridge, letter to the author, 1986.

CHAPTER 5

1. Police commissioner James Mungai's flight was allegedly in response to discovery of a plot by members of the Nakuru Stock Theft Unit, GEMA, and GEMA's allies in the Rift to assassinate Moi, Kibaki, and Njonjo. In their book *The Kenyatta Succession* (Nairobi: Transafrica Press, 1980), Joseph Karimi and Philip Ochieng relate the story behind the "Ngoroko Affair" in some detail, based on documentation provided by the Attorney General's Office. Absent evi-

dence to corroborate the documents provided by that office, then headed by Charles Njonjo, the veracity of the story must remain in question, however. While possibly true, the account was highly convenient to the new president, providing grounds for strengthening surveillance of local and national politicians. Ochieng subsequently became editor of the *Kenya Times*, the KANU party newspaper. The appointment may or may not have been related to this episode and may or may not provide an indication of the reliability of the reports.

2. *Weekly Review*, November 10, 1978, p. 12.

3. Based on interviews carried out with a member of the provincial administration and with members of Parliament, 1990.

4. See, esp., Thomas Callaghy, *The State-Society Struggle: Zaire in Comparative Perspective* (New York: Columbia University Press, 1984); Michael Schatzberg, *The Dialectics of Oppression in Zaire* (Bloomington: Indiana University Press, 1988); and Naomi Chazan and Deborah Pellow, *Ghana: Coping with Uncertainty* (Boulder, Colo.: Westview Press, 1986).

5. *Weekly Review*, September 8, 1978, pp. 6–7.

6. *Current Biography, 1979* (New York: H.W. Wilson Co.), p. 261.

7. Oginga Odinga, *Not Yet Uhuru* (London: Heinemann, 1967), p. 143.

8. *Current Biography, 1979*, p. 262.

9. John Harbeson, *Nation-Building in Kenya: The Role of Land Reform* (Evanston, Ill.: Northwestern University Press, 1973). p. 67.

10. Odinga, *Not Yet Uhuru*, p. 208.

11. Daniel arap Moi, *Continuity and Consolidation in Kenya: Selected Speeches, December 1979–July 1981* (Nairobi: East African Publishing House, 1982), p. 11.

12. Ibid., pp. 5–6.

13. *Weekly Review*, December 15, 1978, p. 7; Kiraitu Murungi, "Forms and Illusions of Democracy in Africa's One-Party States: The Struggle for the Right to Political Participation in Kenya" (paper presented at Seminar on Human Rights Research, Harvard Law School, Cambridge, Mass., May 1991), p. 49.

14. *Weekly Review*, December 29, 1978, p. 7.

15. René Lemarchand, "The State, the Parallel Economy, and the Changing Structure of Patronage Systems," in *The Precarious Balance: State and Society in Africa*, ed. Donald Rothchild and Naomi Chazan (Boulder, Colo.: Westview Press, 1988), pp. 149–70.

16. *Weekly Review*, March 21, 1980, p. 4.

17. *Weekly Review*, March 28, 1980, p. 6.

18. *Daily Nation*, May 29, 1980. Koigi wa Wamwere was the spokesman. The group also included Martin Shikuku and Mwacharo Kubo.

19. *Daily Nation*, June 5, 1980.

20. *Weekly Review*, June 13, 1980, p. 14. Among those who joined in support were Kimani wa Nyoike, Eric Khasakhala, Peter Anyieni, and Jeremiah Nyagah.

21. *Weekly Review*, April 25, 1980, p. 5.

22. *Weekly Review*, June 6, 1980, p. 5.

23. *Weekly Review,* March 28, 1980, p. 5.

24. The 1979–80 fiscal year saw significant food shortages. The government erected police barricades against the smuggling of maize, rice, and wheat between districts. By February 1980, Kenya had started to dip into its strategic maize reserves, and the government raised prices for staples, only to drop them a week later in the face of overwhelming public protest. Producer and consumer price hikes for some commodities were later reinstated. To make matters worse, the price of coffee collapsed, bringing an end to the "beverage boom" of the late 1970s and an end, as well, to construction projects and business ventures launched in anticipation of continued high returns for coffee and tea. The cash crunch many farmers experienced as a result of financial overextension sharpened the impact of the increase in food prices on the average family budget.

25. *Weekly Review,* October 24, 1980, p. 9.

26. Ibid.

27. Susanne Mueller, "Government and Opposition in Kenya, 1966–1969," *Journal of Modern African Studies* 22, 3 (1984): 399–427.

28. *Daily Nation,* July 5, 1980.

29. *Daily Nation,* July 10, 1980.

30. The Office of the President includes the Provincial Administration, Special Branch, the Presidential Press Unit, the Inspectorate of Statutory Boards, the National Registration of Persons Bureau, the Cabinet Office, the Government Press, the police departments, the National Youth Service, the Government Chemist, and the Presidential Commission on Soil Conservation and Afforestation.

31. This figure comes from the author's own analysis of the Kenyan budgets between 1970 and 1985.

32. See George M. Anyona, "How Kenya Became One Party-State by Law," *Nairobi Law Monthly* (April/May 1990): 32–34.

33. Murungi, "Forms and Illusions of Democracy in Africa's One-Party States," paper presented at Seminar on Human Rights Research, Harvard Law School, Cambridge, Mass., May 1991, p. 49.

34. David Throup, Magdelene College, Cambridge, letter to the author, 1986.

35. *Weekly Review,* June 18, 1982, p. 5.

36. *Daily Nation,* March 27, 1985.

37. *Daily Nation,* July 2, 1985.

38. *Daily Nation,* July 2, 1985.

39. *Daily Nation,* March 2, 1985.

40. John Okumu, "Party-State Relations in Kenya and Tanzania," in *Politics and Public Policy in Kenya and Tanzania,* ed. Joel Barkan (New York: Praeger, 1979, 1984).

41. *Weekly Review,* July 5, 1985, p. 20.

42. *Weekly Review,* February 1, 1985, p. 13.

43. *Standard,* July 2, 1985.

44. *Daily Nation,* July 23, 1985.

45. *Standard,* July 23, 1985.

46. The *Weekly Review* came out in strong opposition to the queuing sys-

tem three weeks before the president announced its adoption. See the issue of June 7, 1985, pp. 3–4. Subsequently, this issue has served as a rallying point for opposition, with increasing participation from churches.

47. *Daily Nation,* March 28, 1985. Speech by Julius Muthamia.

48. *Standard,* April 9, 1985.

49. *Daily Nation,* April 13, 1985.

50. *Daily Nation,* August 19, 1985.

51. *Standard,* May 11, 1985.

52. *Weekly Review,* February 22, 1985, p. 6.

53. *Daily Nation,* February 24, 1985, p. 8.

54. *Weekly Review,* March 8, 1985.

55. *Weekly Review,* December 13, 1985, p. 8.

56. *Weekly Review,* January 24, 1986, pp. 14–15.

CHAPTER 6

1. Neither Parliament nor KANU has ever taken this decision formally, although some politicians have pushed for a constitutional amendment. Instead, the supremacy of the party emerged through a series of decisions in which KANU disciplined MPs for criticisms they had raised on the floor of Parliament—statements technically protected from prosecution by the Powers and Privileges Act. For one account, see *Weekly Review,* November 7, 1986, pp. 4–6.

2. Kiraitu Murungi, "The Role of the International Commission of Jurists (Kenya Section) in Promoting the Rule of Law and Protecting the Enjoyment of Human Rights," *Nairobi Law Monthly* 12–13 (December 1988–January 1989): 51.

3. *Weekly Review,* July 22, 1983, p. 4.

4. David Leonard, *African Successes: Four Public Managers of Kenyan Rural Development* (Berkeley: University of California Press, 1991), p. 258.

5. Chong Lim Kim et al., eds., *The Legislative Connection: The Politics of Representation in Kenya, Korea, and Turkey* (Durham, N.C.: Duke University Press, 1984), p. 137.

6. These changes have received relatively little attention and analysis. They were introduced in the *Kenya Gazette,* Supplement No. 92, December 24, 1986. The *Daily Nation* reported the changes in its December 27, 1986 edition. The *Weekly Review* carried a brief analysis in its January 9, 1987 edition.

7. *Daily Nation,* January 2, 1987.

8. *Africa Confidential,* October 26, 1990.

9. This information was widely reported in the press. The most comprehensive summary through 1987 appears in a luridly titled, but nevertheless fairly accurate, publication of the United Movement for Democracy in Kenya, *Moi's Reign of Terror: A Decade of Nyayo Crimes against the People of Kenya* (London: Umoja Secretariat, 1989).

10. *Nairobi Law Monthly* 20 (December 1989–January 1990): 27.

11. The *Weekly Review,* September 18, 1987, pp. 4–14, gives an extended

discussion of the terms of reference for this committee and the cases pending when the committee was disbanded in September 1987.

12. Daniel arap Moi as quoted in *Weekly Review*, May 11, 1989.

13. *Weekly Review*, September 30, 1988.

14. *Africa Confidential*, January 26, 1990, p. 4.

15. For a detailed analysis of the Zairian case, see Crawford Young and Thomas Turner, *The Rise and Decline of the Zairian State* (Madison: Wisconsin University Press, 1985), pp. 193–201.

16. *Weekly Review*, April 22, 1988, pp. 4–5.

17. *Weekly Review*, May 3, 1987, p. 7.

18. *Africa Events*, August–September 1990, p. 25.

19. Biographical information comes from *Weekly Review*, December 16, 1988.

20. In fact, the United States had clearly indicated its support of public defender groups and advocates of expanded civil liberties for several years prior to this encounter, earning the Kenyan president's wrath. The suspicion of foreign involvement predated the specific event, and the ambassador's words merely drew public attention to a potential linkage between economic assistance and political liberalization.

21. Economist Intelligence Unit, *Country Report: Kenya*, fourth quarter, 1990, p. 7.

22. *Nairobi Law Monthly* 25 (September 1990): 3.

23. Kenneth Matiba and Charles Rubia, "Statement on Multi-Partyism," *Nairobi Law Monthly* 23 (April–May 1990): 36.

24. Ibid., p. 37.

25. *Africa Events*, August–September 1990, p. 22.

26. *Weekly Review*, July 13, 1990, p. 4.

27. Economist Intelligence Unit, *Country Report: Kenya*, fourth quarter, 1990, p. 9.

28. Ibid., p. 6.

29. *Africa Confidential*, January 7, 1987.

30. "The Draft Minimum Programme of Mwakenya," as reproduced in Umoja, *Struggle for Democracy in Kenya: Special Report on the 1988 General Elections in Kenya* (London: Umoja Secretariat, 1988), p. 96.

31. *Africa Confidential*, January 7, 1987.

32. Colin Legum and Marian E. Doro, eds., *Africa Contemporary Record: Annual Survey and Documents, 1986–1987* (New York: Africana Publishing Co., 1989), p. B332.

33. *Weekly Review*, December 12, 1986, p. 3.

34. *Africa Confidential*, October 26, 1990.

35. Charles Hornsby, "Kenya's National Assembly," *Journal of Modern African Studies* 27, 2 (1989): 290–91.

36. See the debate over the figures and their significance in the *Review of African Political Economy* 17 (January–April 1980): 83–105.

37. Economist Intelligence Unit, *Country Report: Kenya*, third quarter, 1989, p. 17.

38. *New African*, September 1990, p. 18.

39. See the discussion in the *Weekly Review*, June 5, 1987. It was the case that farmers holding less than fifty acres had no vote at the association's annual meeting, despite the fact that they held 59 percent of the equity. Most of the directors of the KPCU were smallholders, however.

40. Economist Intelligence Unit, *Country Report: Kenya*, first quarter, 1988, p. 10.

41. *Weekly Review*, January 20, 1989, p. 24.

42. *Weekly Review*, April 7, 1989, p. 24.

43. Economist Intelligence Unit, *Country Report: Kenya*, first quarter, 1988, p. 12.

44. *Weekly Review*, January 20, 1989, p. 42.

45. Matiba and Rubia, "Statement on Multi-Partyism," p. 37.

46. Murungi, "Role of the International Commission of Jurists," p. 50.

47. Ibid.

48. See, e.g., J. R. Otieno, "Has the System of a One-Party State Outlived Its Usefulness in Africa?" *Nairobi Law Monthly* 17 (July–August, 1989): 7.

49. Murungi, "Role of the International Commission of Jurists," p. 50.

50. Economist Intelligence Unit, *Country Report: Kenya*, fourth quarter, 1990, p. 8.

51. *Nairobi Law Monthly* 21 (February 1990), pp. 7–8.

52. Ibid., p. 13.

53. *New African*, May 1991, p. 17.

54. *Weekly Review*, August 29, 1986, p. 5.

55. *Weekly Review*, April 24, 1987.

56. *Weekly Review*, January 12, 1990, p. 4.

57. See Jennifer Widner, "Interest-Formation in the Informal Sector: Cultural Despair or a Politics of Multiple Allegiances?" *Comparative Political Studies* 24, 1 (1991): 31–55.

58. See, e.g., the unpublished work of Kinuthia Macharia, Department of Sociology, Harvard University.

59. From interviews conducted in the United States with Kenyan MPs. On the floor of Parliament, Waruru Kanja spoke openly about an assassination in the style of the assassination of J. M. Kariuki.

60. For one account, see *Weekly Review*, June 8, 1990, pp. 4–8. This account is based on the *Weekly Review* and on interviews with observers, conducted in the United States.

61. Jane Perlez, "A Shantytown of 30,000 Bulldozed in Nairobi," *New York Times*, December 2, 1990.

CHAPTER 7

1. Peter M. Ngau, "Tensions in Empowerment: The Experience of the *Harambee* (Self-Help) Movement in Kenya," *Economic Development and Cultural Change* 35, 3 (April 1987): 526.

2. Colin Legum and Marian E. Doro, eds., *Africa Contemporary Record:*

Annual Survey and Documents, 1986–1987 (New York: Africana Publishing Co., 1989), p. B334.

3. Ibid., 1987–1988, p. B318.

4. Julius E. Nyang'oro, "The Quest for Pluralist Democracy in Kenya," *Transafrica Forum* 7, 3 (Fall 1990): 74.

5. Ibid.: 77.

6. Michael Schatzberg, *The Dialectics of Oppression in Zaire* (Bloomington: Indiana University Press, 1988), p. 105.

7. Thomas Callaghy, *The State-Society Struggle: Zaire in Comparative Perspective* (New York: Columbia University Press, 1984), p. 173.

8. Ibid., p. 67.

9. Ibid., p. 175.

10. Ibid., p. 115.

11. Ibid., pp. 93–94.

12. Ibid., p. 102.

13. Ibid., p. 96.

14. Ibid., p. 105.

15. See the discussion in ibid., pp. 171–75.

16. Schatzberg, *Dialectics of Oppression in Zaire*, p. 141.

17. Party-government relations in Tanzania remain largely undocumented. For references, see William Tordoff, "Residual Legislatures: The Cases of Tanzania and Zambia," *Journal of Commonwealth and Comparative Politics* 15, 3 (November 1977): 235–49, and Zaki Ergas, "The State and Economic Deterioration: The Tanzanian Case," *Journal of Commonwealth and Comparative Politics* 20, 3 (November 1982): 286–308.

18. Michaela von Freyhold, *Ujamaa Villages in Tanzania: Analysis of a Social Experiment* (New York: Monthly Review Press, 1979), pp. 40–41.

19. Helge Kjekshus, "Parliament in a One-Party State: The Bunge of Tanzania, 1965–70," *Journal of Modern African Studies* 12, 1 (March 1974): 19–20.

20. Henry Bienen, *Tanzania: Party Transformation and Economic Development* (Princeton: Princeton University Press, 1967), p. 12.

21. Von Freyhold, *Ujamaa Villages in Tanzania*, p. 118.

22. John Okumu and Frank Holmquist, "Party and Party-State Relations," in *Politics and Public Policy in Kenya and Tanzania*, ed. Joel Barkan and John Okumu (New York: Praeger, 1984), p. 49.

23. Bienen, *Tanzania*, pp. 334–36.

24. Okumu and Holmquist, "Party and Party-State Relations," p. 49.

25. Jan Kees van Donge and Athumani J. Liviga, "Tanzanian Political Culture and the Cabinet," *Journal of Modern African Studies* 24, 4 (1986): 633, 636.

26. Jeanette Hartmann, "President Nyerere and the State," in *Tanzania after Nyerere*, ed. Michael Hodd (London: Pinter Publishers, 1988), p. 166.

27. Naomi Chazan, "African Voters at the Polls: A Re-examination of the Role of Elections in Politics," *Journal of Commonwealth and Comparative Politics* 16, 2 (July 1979): 138.

28. There is considerable debate about the extent of this ability. See Jan Kees

van Donge and Athumani J. Liviga, "The 1985 Tanzanian Parliamentary Elections: A Conservative Election," *African Affairs* 38, 350 (January 1989): 47–61; Tordoff, "Residual Legislatures"; and Ergas, "State and Economic Deterioration."

29. Martin Staniland, "Single-Party Regimes and Political Change: The PDCI and Ivory Coast Politics," in *Politics and Change in Developing Countries,* ed. Colin Leys (Cambridge; Cambridge University Press, 1969), p. 173.

30. Michael A. Cohen, *Urban Policy and Political Conflict in Africa: A Case Study of the Ivory Coast* (Chicago: University of Chicago Press, 1974), p. 141.

31. Ruth Schachter Morgenthau, *Political Parties in French-Speaking West Africa* (Oxford: Clarendon Press, 1964), p. 210.

32. Aristide Zolberg, *One-Party Government in the Ivory Coast* (Princeton: Princeton University Press, 1964), pp. 185–86.

33. Ibid., p. 273.

34. Howard French, "One-Party State at a Crossroads," *Africa Report* 30, 4 (July–August 1985): 17.

35. Staniland, "Single-Party Regimes and Political Change," p. 168, as well as the author's own research in the 1980s.

36. See the similar conclusion of John Wiseman, *Democracy in Black Africa: Survival and Revival* (New York: Paragon House, 1990), p. 182.

37. Based on the author's own research in Côte d'Ivoire, 1987–90.

38. Conference on Security, Stability, Development and Cooperation in Africa, Draft Document, Kampala, Uganda, May 22, 1991 (unedited version).

39. Jackton B. Ojwang, *Constitutional Development in Kenya: Institutional Adaptation and Social Change* (Nairobi: African Centre for Technology Studies (Acts) Press, 1990), p. 65.

40. *Weekly Review,* April 26, 1991, pp. 20–21.

41. For a fuller discussion of the approach used here, see Robert Dahl, *Polyarchy: Participation and Opposition* (New Haven: Yale University Press, 1971, 1985).

42. John Lonsdale, "Political Accountability in African History," in *Political Domination in Africa: Reflections on the Limits of Power,* ed. Patrick Chabal (Cambridge: Cambridge University Press, 1986), p. 128.

43. V. O. Key, Jr., *Southern Politics* (New York: Knopf, 1949).

44. Albert O. Hirschman, *The Passions and the Interests: Political Arguments for Capitalism before Its Triumph* (Princeton: Princeton University Press, 1977), p. 82.

45. Jean-François Bayart, "Civil Society in Africa," in *Political Domination in Africa: Reflections on the Limits of Power,* ed. Patrick Chabal (Cambridge: Cambridge University Press, 1986), p. 121.

APPENDIX

1. See Ng'weno's statement to UNESCO as reprinted in the *Weekly Review,* May 24, 1991.

Bibliography

Alila, Patrick O. "Luo Ethnic Factor in the 1979 and 1983 Elections in Bondo and Gem." Institute for Development Studies, University of Nairobi, Working Paper No. 408, June 1985.

Amnesty International. *Kenya: Torture, Political Detention, and Unfair Trials.* London: Amnesty International Publications, 1987.

Anker, Richard, and John Knowles. *Population Growth, Employment, and Economic-Demographic Interactions in Kenya—Bachue Kenya.* New York: Gower (ILO) 1983.

Anyang' Nyong'o, Peter. "The Decline of Democracy and the Rise of Authoritarian and Factionalist Politics in Kenya." *Horn of Africa* 6, 3 (1983): 25–34.

———. "State and Society in Kenya: The Disintegration of the Nationalist Coalitions and the Rise of Presidential Authoritarianism, 1963–78." *African Affairs* 88, 351 (April 1989): 229–51.

———, ed., *Popular Struggles for Democracy in Africa.* London: United Nations University Press / Zed Books, 1987.

Anyona, George. "Supremacy of Parliament in Kenya: A Review of The Nation Debate." *Nairobi Law Monthly* 20 (December 1989-January 1990): 18–24.

Arnold, Guy. *Kenyatta and the Politics of Kenya.* London: J. M. Dent and Sons, 1974.

Ashford, Douglas. *The Elusiveness of Power: The African Single Party State.* Cornell Research Papers in International Studies, No. 3. Ithaca, N.Y.: Center for International Studies, Cornell University, 1965.

Banton, Michael. *Racial and Ethnic Competition.* Cambridge: Cambridge University Press, 1983.

Barkan, Joel D. "Bringing Home the Pork: Legislator Behavior and Political Change in East Africa." In *Legislatures in Development: Dynamics of*

Change in New and Old States, edited by Joel Smith and Lloyd Musolf, pp. 265–88. Durham, N.C.: Duke University Press, 1978.

———. "The Electoral Process and Peasant-State Relations in Kenya." In *Elections in Independent Africa,* edited by Fred Hayward, pp. 213–37. Boulder, Colo., 1987.

———. "Political Linkage in Kenya: Citizens, Local Elites, and Legislators." Occasional Paper, Center for Comparative Legislative Research, University of Iowa, September 1974.

———, ed. *Politics and Public Policy in Kenya and Tanzania.* New York: Praeger, 1979, 1984.

Barkan, Joel D., and Michael Chege. "Decentralizing the State: District Focus and the Politics of Reallocation in Kenya." *Journal of Modern African Studies* 27, 3 (1989): 431–53.

Barkan, Joel D., and Frank Holmquist. "Peasant-State Relations and the Social Base of Self-Help in Kenya." *World Politics* 41, 3 (April 1989): 359–80.

Barkan, Joel D., and John Okumu. "Semi-Competitive Elections, Clientelism, and Political Recruitment in a No-Party State: The Kenyan Experience." University of Iowa Center for Comparative Legislative Research, Reprint Series, No. 66, 1979.

Barrows, Walter. "Ethnic Diversity and Political Instability in Black Africa." *Comparative Political Studies* 9, 2 (July 1976): 139–69.

Bates, Robert. "Approaches to the Study of Ethnicity." *Cahiers d'études africaines* 10, 4 (1970): 546–61.

———. *Beyond the Miracle of the Market: The Political Economy of Agrarian Development in Kenya.* Cambridge: Cambridge University Press, 1989.

———, ed. *Essays on the Political Economy of Rural Africa.* Berkeley: University of California Press, 1983.

Bell, C. L. G. "The Political Framework." In *Redistribution With Growth,* edited by Hollis Chenery et al., pp. 52–72. IBRD/Institute for Development Studies, Sussex; New York: Oxford University Press, 1974.

Bennett, George. "The Development of Political Organizations in Kenya." *Political Studies* 5, 2 (1957): 113–30.

Bennett, George, and Carl Rosberg. *The Kenyatta Election.* London: Oxford University Press, 1971.

Berg-Schlosser, Dirk. "Consociationalism in Kenya." *European Journal of Political Research* 13, 1 (1985): 95–110.

———. "Modes and Meaning of Political Participation in Kenya." *Comparative Politics* 14 (July 1982): 397–414.

———. *Tradition and Change in Kenya.* Paderborn, Ger.: Ferdinand Schoningh, 1984.

Berg-Schlosser, Dirk, and Rainer Siegler. *Political Stability and Development: A Comparative Analysis of Kenya, Tanzania, and Uganda.* Boulder, Colo.: Lynne Rienner, 1990.

Berman, Bruce. *Control and Crisis in Colonial Kenya: The Dialectic of Domination.* Athens, Ohio: Ohio University Press, 1990.

Bienen, Henry. *Armies and Parties in Africa.* New York: Holmes & Meier, 1978.

———. *Kenya: The Politics of Participation and Control.* Princeton: Princeton University Press, 1974.

———. "The Party and the No-Party State: Tanganyika and the Soviet Union." *Transition* 111 (March–April 1964): 25–32.

———. *Tanzania: Party Transformation and Economic Development.* Princeton: Princeton University Press, 1967.

Bienen, Henry, and Mark Gersovitz. "Consumer Subsidy Cuts, Violence, and Political Stability." *Comparative Politics* 19 (October 1986): 25–44.

Bonner, Raymond. "African Democracy." *New Yorker*, September 3, 1990, pp. 93–105.

Brokensha, David, and John Nellis. "Administration in Mbere: Portrait of a Rural Kenyan Division." Institute for Development Studies, University of Nairobi, Discussion Paper No. 114, June 1971.

Buijtenhuis, Robert. *Mau Mau Twenty Years After: The Myth and the Survivors.* Paris: Mouton, 1973.

Callaghy, Thomas. "Lost between State and Market: The Politics of Economic Adjustment in Ghana, Zambia, and Nigeria." In *Economic Crisis and Policy Choice*, edited by Joan M. Nelson, pp. 257–319. Princeton: Princeton University Press, 1990.

———. *The State-Society Struggle: Zaire in Comparative Perspective.* New York: Columbia University Press, 1984.

Cardoso, Fernando Henrique. "On the Characterization of Authoritarian Regimes in Latin America." In *The New Authoritarianism in Latin America*, edited by David Collier, pp. 33–57. Princeton: Princeton University Press, 1979.

Carter, Gwendolyn M., ed. *African One-Party States.* Ithaca, N.Y.: Cornell University Press, 1962.

Chabal, Patrick, ed. *Political Domination in Africa: Reflections on the Limits of Power.* Cambridge: Cambridge University Press, 1986.

Chazan, Naomi. "African Voters at the Polls: A Re-examination of the Role of Elections in Politics." *Journal of Commonwealth and Comparative Politics* 16, 2 (July 1979): 136–56.

Chazan, Naomi, and Deborah Pellow. *Ghana: Coping with Uncertainty.* Boulder, Colo.: Westview Press, 1986.

Chege, Michael. "The African Economic Crisis and the Fate of Democracy in Sub-Saharan Africa." In *Democratic Theory and Practice in Africa*, edited by Walter Oyugi, pp. 191–205. Portsmouth, N.H.: Heinemann, 1988.

Clough, Marshall. *Fighting Two Sides: Kenyan Chiefs and Politicians, 1918–1940.* Niwot, Colo.: University Press of Colorado, 1990.

Cohen, Michael A. *Urban Policy and Political Conflict in Africa: A Case Study of the Ivory Coast* . Chicago: University of Chicago Press, 1974.

Coleman, James, and Carl Rosberg. *Political Parties and National Integration in Tropical Africa.* Berkeley: University of California Press, 1966.

Collier, David. "Overview of the Bureaucratic-Authoritarian Model." In *The New Authoritarianism in Latin America*, edited by David Collier, pp. 19–32. Princeton: Princeton University Press, 1979.

Collier, Ruth Berins. *Regimes in Tropical Africa: Changing Forms of Supremacy, 1945–1975.* Berkeley: University of California Press, 1982.

Conference on Security, Stability, Development and Cooperation in Africa. Draft Document. Kampala, Uganda, May 22, 1991. Unedited version.

Court, David, and Kenneth C. Prewitt. "Nation versus Region in Kenya: A Note on Political Learning." *British Journal of Political Science* 4 (January 1974): 109–15.

Cross, Sholto. "L'Etat c'est moi: Political Transition and the Kenya General Election of 1979." University of East Anglia, Discussion Paper No. 66, April 1983.

Currie, Kate, and Larry Ray. "State and Class in Kenya: Notes on the Cohesion of the Ruling Class." *Journal of Modern African Studies* 22, 4 (1984): 559–93.

Daalder, Hans. "Government and Opposition in the New States." *Government and Opposition* 1, 2 (February 1966): 205–26.

Dahl, Robert. *Polyarchy: Participation and Opposition.* New Haven: Yale University Press, 1971, 1985.

de Wolf, Jan J. *Differentiation and Integration in Western Kenya.* The Hague: Mouton, 1977.

Eisenstadt, S. N., and Lewis Kroniger. "Patron-Client Relationships as a Model of Structuring Social Change." *Comparative Study of Society and History* 22, 1 (January 1980): 42–77.

Elkan, Walter. "Is a Proletariat Emerging in Kenya?" *Economic Development and Cultural Change* 24 (1976): 695–706.

Ergas, Zaki. "The State and Economic Deterioration: The Tanzanian Case." *Journal of Commonwealth and Comparative Politics* 20, 3 (November 1982): 286–308.

Fatton, Robert. "Liberal Democracy in Africa." *Political Science Quarterly* 105, 3 (1990): 455–73.

Ferraro, Gary P. "Kikuyu Kinship Interaction in Nairobi and Rural Kiambu." Institute for Development Studies, University of Nairobi, Discussion Paper No. 12, August 1970.

Foltz, William J. "Ethnicity, Status, and Conflict." In *Ethnicity, Status, and Nation-Building,* edited by Wendell Bell and Walter Freeman, pp. 103–16. Beverly Hills, Calif.: Sage Publications, 1974.

———. "Political Opposition in Single-Party States of Tropical Africa." In *Regimes and Oppositions,* edited by Robert Dahl, pp. 143–70. New Haven: Yale University Press, 1973.

French, Howard. "One-Party State at a Crossroads." *Africa Report* 30, 4 (July–August 1985): 14–18.

Furedi, Frank. "The African Crowd in Nairobi: Popular Movements and Elite Politics." *Journal of African History* 14, 2 (1973): 275–90.

Gertzel, Cherry. "The Constitutional Position of the Opposition in Kenya: The Appeal for Efficiency." *East Africa Journal* 4, 6 (October 1967): 9–11.

———. "Kenya's Constitutional Changes." *East Africa Journal* 3, 9 (December 1966): 19–31.

———. *The Politics of Independent Kenya, 1963–1968.* Nairobi: East African Publishing House, 1970.

————, ed., *The Dynamics of the One-Party State in Zambia*. Manchester: Manchester University Press, 1984.

Ghai, Y. P., and J. P. W. B. McAuslan. *Public Law and Political Change in Kenya*. Nairobi: Oxford University Press, 1970.

Gitonga, Afrifa K. "The Dialectics of Cultural Syncretism and Material Realism: Meru Central Constituency, 1983." Paper presented at Seminar on Electoral Politics in Kenya, Department of Government, University of Nairobi, August 1984.

Godfrey, E. Martin. *Kenya: Economic Prospects to 1985*. Economist Intelligence Unit (London), Special Report No. 99, 1981.

Godfrey, E. Martin, and Gideon Mutiso. "The Political Economy of Self-Help." *Canadian Journal of African Studies* 8, 1 (1974): 109–133.

Godia, George. *Understanding Nyayo: Principles and Policies in Contemporary Kenya*. Nairobi: Transafrica Press, 1984.

Goldsworthy, David. "Ethnicity and Leadership in Africa: The 'Untypical' Case of Tom Mboya." *Journal of Modern African Studies* 20, 1 (1982): 107–26.

————. *Tom Mboya: The Man Kenya Wanted to Forget*. New York: Africana Publishing Co., 1982.

Good, Kenneth. "Kenyatta and the Organization of KANU." *Canadian Journal of African Studies* 2 (1968): 115–36.

Gordon, David F. *Decolonization and the State in Kenya*. Boulder, Colo.: Westview Press, 1986.

Greene, David. *Kenya: Growth and Structural Change*. Washington, D.C.: International Bank for Reconstruction and Development, 1980.

Grosch, Barbara. "Agricultural Parastatals Since Independence: How Have They Performed?" Institute for Development Studies, University of Nairobi, Working Paper No. 435, January 1986.

Hakes, Jay E., and John Helgerson. "Bargaining and Parliamentary Behavior in Africa: A Comparative Study of Zambia and Kenya." In *Legislatures in Comparative Perspective*, edited by Alan Kornberg, pp. 335–62. New York: David McKay, 1973.

Harbeson, John W. "Land Reforms and Politics in Kenya, 1954–70." *Journal of Modern African Studies* 9, 2 (August 1971): 231–52.

————. *Nation-Building in Kenya*. Evanston, Ill.: Northwestern University Press, 1973.

Hartmann, Jeanette. "President Nyerere and the State." In *Tanzania after Nyerere*, edited by Michael Hodd, pp. 165–74. London: Pinter Publishers, 1988.

Hayward, Fred, ed. *Elections in Independent Africa*. Boulder, Colo.: Westview Press, 1987.

Hirschman, Albert. *Exit, Voice, and Loyalty*. Cambridge, Mass.: Harvard University Press, 1970.

————. *The Passions and the Interests: Political Arguments for Capitalism before Its Triumph*. Princeton: Princeton University Press, 1977.

————. "The Changing Tolerance for Income Inequality in the Course of Economic Development." *World Development* 1, 12 (December 1973).

———. "The Turn to Authoritarianism in Latin America and the Search for Its Economic Determinants." In *The New Authoritarianism in Latin America*, edited by David Collier, pp. 61–98. Princeton: Princeton University Press, 1979.

Hodgkin, Thomas. *African Political Parties*. Harmondsworth, Eng.: Penguin Books, 1961.

Holmquist, Frank. "Peasant Organization, Clientelism and Dependency: A Case Study of an Agricultural Producer's Cooperative in Kenya." Ph.D. diss., Indiana University, April 1975.

———. "Self-help: The State and Peasant Leverage in Kenya." *Africa* 54, 3 (1984): 72–91.

Hopkins, Raymond F. "The Influence of the Legislature on Development Strategy: The Case of Kenya and Tanzania." In *Legislatures and Development: Dynamics of Change in New and Old States*, edited by Joel Smith and Lloyd Muslof, pp. 155–86. Durham, N.C.: Duke University Press, 1978.

———. "The Kenyan Legislature: Political Functions and Citizen Perceptions." In *Legislative Systems in Developing Countries*, edited by G. R. Boynton and Chong Lim Kim, 207–31. Durham, N.C.: Duke University Press, 1975.

———. *Political Roles in a New State: Tanzania's First Decade*. New Haven: Yale University Press, 1971.

Hornsby, Charles P. W. "The Member of Parliament in Kenya, 1969–1983: The Election, Background, and Position of the Representative and Its Implications for His Role in the One-Party State." M. Phil. thesis, St. Anthony's College, Oxford, 1985.

———. "The Social Structure of the National Assembly in Kenya, 1963–83." *Journal of Modern African Studies* 27, 2 (1989): 275–96.

Horowitz, Donald L. *Ethnic Groups in Conflict*. Berkeley: University of California Press, 1985.

Huntington, Samuel, and Clement Moore. *Authoritarian Politics in Modern Society: The Dynamics of Established One-Party Systems*. New York: Basic Books, 1970.

Hyden, Goran. *Beyond Ujamaa in Tanzania*. Berkeley: University of California Press, 1981.

———. *No Shortcuts to Progress: African Development Management in Perspective*. Berkeley: University of California Press, 1983.

Hyden, Goran, and Colin Leys. "Elections and Politics in Single Party Systems: The Case of Kenya and Tanzania." *British Journal of Political Science* 2, 4 (October 1972): 389–420.

Independent Kenya. London: Zed Press, 1982.

International Bank for Reconstruction and Development. Africa Technical Department. "Draft Data Documents." Autumn 1991.

———. *Kenya: Population and Development*. Washington, D.C.: IBRD, 1980.

International Commission of Jurists (Kenya Section). *Law and Society: Selected Papers from a Seminar, November 24–26, 1988*. Nairobi: English Press, 1989.

International Labour Organization. *Employment, Incomes, and Equality*. Geneva: ILO, 1972.

Jackson, Robert, and Carl Rosberg. *Personal Rule in Black Africa*. Berkeley: University of California Press, 1982.

Kamundia, C. A. "Primaries in Kenya." *East Africa Journal* 6, 5 (May 1969): 9–14.

Kanogo, Tabitha. *Squatters and the Roots of Mau Mau*. Athens, Ohio: Ohio University Press, 1989.

Kaplinsky, Rafael. "Capitalist Accumulation in the Periphery—The Kenyan Case Re-examined." *Review of African Political Economy* 17 (January– April 1980): 83–105.

Karimi, Joseph, and Philip Ochieng. *The Kenyatta Succession*. Nairobi: Transafrica Press, 1980.

Karioki, James N. "University of Nairobi and the Demise of Democracy in Kenya." *Transafrica Forum* 7, 3 (Fall 1990): 83–93.

Kariuki, Josiah Mwangi. *"Mau Mau" Detainee: The Account by a Kenya African of His Experiences in Detention Camps, 1953–1960*. London: Oxford University Press, 1963, 1975.

Kasfir, Nelson. "Explaining Ethnic Political Participation." *World Politics* 31 (April 1979): 365–88.

———. *The Shrinking Political Arena: Participation and Ethnicity in African Politics, with a Case Study of Uganda*. Berkeley: University of California Press, 1976.

Keller, Edmond J. "Education, Ethnicity, and Political Socialization in Kenya." *Comparative Political Studies* 12, 4 (January 1980): 442–69.

Kenya. Institute of Administration. *A Guide to the Constitutional Development of Kenya*. Nairobi: Government Printer, 1970.

Kenya. National Assembly. Report of the Select Committee on the Disappearance and Murder of the Late Member for Nyandarua North, The Hon. J.M. Kariuki, M.P., June 3, 1975. Typescript.

Kenyatta, Jomo. *The Challenge of Uhuru: The Progress of Kenya, 1968 to 1970*. Nairobi: East African Publishing House, 1971.

———. *Harambee! The Prime Minister of Kenya's Speeches, 1963–64*. London: Oxford University Press, 1964.

———. *Suffering without Bitterness*. Nairobi: East African Publishing House, 1968.

Kenyatta University. "The President Speaks: An Index of Speeches by His Excellency President Daniel arap Moi, August 1978–December 1984, 1985.

Key, Vladimir Orlando. *Southern Politics*. New York: Knopf, 1949.

Khapoya, Vincent B. "Kenya under Moi: Continuity or Change?" *Africa Today* 27, 1 (1980): 17–32.

Kibaki, J. B. "Transtribal Politics in Kenya and the Little General Elections." Diss., University College, Dar es Salaam, March 1968.

Killick, Tony, ed. *Papers on the Kenyan Economy*. London: Heinemann Educational Books, 1981.

Kilson, Martin. "Authoritarian and Single-Party Tendencies in African Politics." *World Politics* 15, 2 (January 1963): 262–94.

Kim, Chang Hwan. "The Concept and Social Position of 'Managerial Elite' in Contemporary Kenya: With Special Reference to Africanization." Institute for Development Studies, University of Nairobi, Working Paper No. 431, October 1985.

Kim, Chong Lim, Joel Barkan, Ilter Turan, and Malcolm Jewell, eds. *The Legislative Connection: The Politics of Representation in Kenya, Korea, and Turkey.* Durham, N.C.: Duke University Press, 1984.

King, J. R. *Stabilization Policy in an African Setting: Kenya, 1963–1973.* London: Heinemann Educational Books, 1979.

Kitching, Gavin. *Class and Economic Change in Kenya.* New Haven: Yale University Press, 1980.

Kjekshus, Helge. "Parliament in a One-Party State: The Bunge of Tanzania, 1965–70." *Journal of Modern African Studies* 12, 1 (March 1974): 19–43.

Kuria, Gibson Kamau. "The Independence of the Legal Profession and the Judiciary." In International Commission of Jurists (Kenya Section), *Law and Society: Selected Papers from a Seminar, November 24–26, 1988,* pp. 37–47. Nairobi: English Press, 1989.

Lamb, Geoff. *Peasant Politics.* New York: St. Martin's Press, 1974.

LaPalombara, Joseph, and Myron Weiner, eds. *Political Parties and Political Development.* Princeton: Princeton University Press, 1966.

Lemarchand, René. "Political Clientelism and Ethnicity in Tropical Africa: Competing Solidarities in Nation-Building." *American Political Science Review* 66 (1972): 68–90.

———. "The State, the Parallel Economy, and the Changing Structure of Patronage Systems." In *The Precarious Balance: State and Society in Africa,* edited by Donald Rothchild and Naomi Chazan, pp. 149–70. Boulder, Colo.: Westview Press, 1988.

Leo, Christopher. *Land and Class in Kenya.* Toronto: University of Toronto Press, 1984.

Leonard, David. *African Successes: Four Public Managers of Kenyan Rural Development.* Berkeley: University of California Press, 1991.

Leys, Colin. "Capital Accumulation, Class Formation and Dependency: The Significance of the Kenyan Case." In *The Socialist Register, 1978,* edited by Ralph Miliband and John Saville, pp. 241–66. London: Merlin Press, 1978.

———. "Kenya: What Does 'Dependency' Explain?" *Review of African Political Economy* 17 (January–April 1980): 83–105.

———. "Politics in Kenya: The Development of a Peasant Society." *British Journal of Political Science* 1, 3 (1971): 313–43.

———. *Underdevelopment in Kenya: The Political Economy of Neo-Colonialism.* London: Heinemann, 1975, 1977.

Lofchie, Michael F. *The State of the Nations: Constraints on Development in Independent Africa.* Berkeley: University of California Press, 1971.

Makokha, Joseph. *The District Focus: Conceptual and Management Problems.* Nairobi: Africa Press Research Bureau, 1985.

Mamdani, Mahmood. "The Social Basis of Constitutionalism in Africa." *Journal of Modern African Studies* 28, 3 (1990): 359–74.

Mans, Rowland. "Kenyatta's Middle Road." *Conflict Studies* 85 (1977): whole issue.

Markovitz, Irving Leonard. *Power and Class in Africa: An Introduction to*

Change and Conflict in African Politics. Englewood Cliffs, N.J.: Prentice-Hall, 1977.

Matiba, Kenneth, and Charles Rubia. "Statement on Multi-Partyism." *Nairobi Law Monthly* 23 (April–May 1990): 35–37.

Maxon, Robert M. *Conflict and Accommodation in Western Kenya: The Gusii and the British, 1907–1963.* London: Associated University Presses, 1989.

Mboya, Tom. *Freedom and After.* London: André Deutsch, 1963.

McKown, Roberta E., and Robert E. Kaufman, "Party System as a Comparative Analytic Concept in African Politics." *Comparative Politics* 6 (October 1973): 47–72.

Médard, Jean François. "The Underdeveloped State in Tropical Africa: Political Clientelism or Neo-Patrimonialism?" In *Private Patronage and Public Power,* edited by Christopher Clapham, pp. 162–92. New York: St. Martin's Press, 1982.

Migdal, Joel S. *Strong Societies and Weak States: State-Society Relations and State Capacity in the Third World.* Princeton: Princeton University Press, 1988.

———. "Strong States, Weak States: Power and Accommodation." In *Understanding Political Development,* edited by Myron Weiner and Samuel Huntington, pp. 391–434. Boston: Little, Brown, 1987.

Miller, Norman. *Kenya: The Quest for Prosperity.* Boulder, Colo.: Westview Press, 1984.

Moi, Daniel arap. *Continuity and Consolidation in Kenya.* Selected speeches. Nairobi: East African Publishing House, 1982.

———. *Transition and Continuity in Kenya.* Selected speeches. Nairobi: East African Publishing House, 1979.

Moore, Barrington, Jr. *The Social Origins of Dictatorship and Democracy: Lord and Peasant in the Making of the Modern World.* Boston: Beacon Press, 1966.

Morgenthau, Ruth Schachter. *Political Parties in French-Speaking West Africa.* Oxford: Clarendon Press, 1964.

Mueller, Susanne. "Government and Opposition in Kenya, 1966–1969." *Journal of Modern African Studies* 22, 3 (1984).

———. "Political Parties in Kenya: The Politics of Opposition and Dissent, 1919–1969." Ph.D. diss., Department of Politics, Princeton University, 1972.

Muriuki, Godfrey. "Central Kenya in the Nyayo Era." *Africa Today* 26, 3 (1979): 39–42. Special Issue on Post-Kenyatta Kenya.

Murray-Brown, Jeremy. *Kenyatta.* London: George Allen & Unwin, 1979.

Murungi, Kiraitu. "Forms and Illusions of Democracy in Africa's One-Party States: The Struggle for the Right to Political Participation in Kenya." Paper presented at Seminar on Human Rights Research, Harvard Law School, Cambridge, Mass., May 1991.

———. "The Role of the International Commission of Jurists (Kenya Section) in Promoting the Rule of Law and Protecting the Enjoyment of Human Rights." *Nairobi Law Monthly* 12–13 (December 1988–January 1989): 48–51.

National Council of Churches of Kenya. *Who Controls Industry in Kenya?* Report of a Working Party. Nairobi: East African Publishing, 1968.

Nellis, John. "The Ethnic Composition of Leading Kenyan Government Positions." Uppsala: Scandinavian Institute for African Studies (Nordiska Afrikainstitutet), 1974.

Ngau, Peter M. "Tensions in Empowerment: The Experience of the *Harambee* (Self-Help) Movement in Kenya." *Economic Development and Cultural Change* 35, 3 (April 1987): 523–38.

Ng'eth'e, Njuguna. "Harambee and Development Participation in Kenya: The Politics of Peasants and Elites Interaction with Particular Reference to Harambee Projects in Kiambu." Ph.D. diss., Carleton University, Ottawa, July 1979.

Ngugi wa Thiong'o. *Detained: A Writer's Prison Diary.* London: Heinemann, 1981.

Njonjo, Apollo. "The Africanization of the 'White Highlands': A Study in Agrarian Class Struggles in Kenya, 1950–1974." Ph.D. diss., Department of Politics, Princeton University, 1977.

Nordlinger, Eric. *Conflict Regulation in Divided Societies.* Cambridge, Mass.: Harvard University Press, 1972.

Nyang'oro, Julius E. "The Quest for Pluralist Democracy in Kenya." *Transafrica Forum* 7, 3 (Fall 1990): 73–83.

Ochieng', William R. "Tribalism and National Unity: The Kenyan Case." In *Politics and Leadership in Africa,* edited by Aloo Ojuka and William R. Ochieng', pp. 254–71. Nairobi: East African Literature Bureau, 1975.

Odinga, Oginga. *Not Yet Uhuru.* London: Heinemann, 1967.

O'Donnell, Guillermo A. *Modernization and Bureaucratic-Authoritarianism.* Berkeley: Institute of International Studies, University of California, 1979.

Ojwang, Jackton B. *Constitutional Development in Kenya: Institutional Adaptation and Social Change.* Nairobi: African Centre for Technology Studies (Acts) Press, 1990.

Ojwang, Jackton B., and Janet W. Kabebei. "Law and the Public Interest: Proceedings of a Seminar at Kisumu, Kenya, 2–7 March 1986." Institute for Development Studies and the Faculty of Law, University of Nairobi, 1988.

Okoth-Ogendo, H. W. O. "The Politics of Constitutional Change in Kenya since Independence, 1963–1969," *African Affairs* 71, 282 (January 1972): 9–34.

Okumu, John. "Party and Party-State Relations." In *Politics and Public Policy in Kenya and Tanzania,* edited by Joel Barkan and John Okumu, pp. 43–63. New York: Praeger, 1979.

Olson, Mancur. *The Rise and Decline of Nations.* New Haven: Yale University Press, 1982.

Oyugi, Walter. *Democratic Theory and Practice in Africa.* Portsmouth, N.H.: Heinemann, 1988.

Rothchild, Donald. "Ethnic Inequalities in Kenya." *Journal of Modern African Studies* 7, 4 (December 1969): 689–711.

———. "Middle Africa Hegemonial Exchange and Resource Allocation." In *Comparative Resource Allocation,* edited by Alexander J. Groth and Larry L. Wade, pp. 151–80. Beverly Hills, Calif.: Sage Publications, 1984.

———. "Progress and the One-Party State." *Transition* 111, 10 (September 1963): 31–36.

———. *Racial Bargaining in Independent Kenya: A Study of Minorities and Decolonization.* London: Oxford University Press, 1973.

Rothchild, Donald, and Victor Olorunsola. *The State versus Ethnic Claims: African Policy Dilemmas.* Boulder, Colo.: Westview Press, 1983.

Rothchild, Donald, and Naomi Chazan, eds. *The Precarious Balance: State and Society in Africa.* Boulder, Colo.: Westview Press, 1988.

Sandbrook, Richard. "Patrons, Clients, and Unions: The Labour Movement and Political Conflict in Kenya." *Journal of Commonwealth Political Studies* 10, 1 (March 1972): 3–27.

———. *The Politics of Africa's Economic Stagnation.* Cambridge: Cambridge University Press, 1985.

Schatzberg, Michael. *The Dialectics of Oppression in Zaire.* Bloomington: Indiana University Press, 1988.

———, ed. *The Political Economy of Kenya.* New York: Praeger, 1987.

Schmidt, Steffan, James Scott, Carl Lande, and Laura Gusti, eds. *Friends, Followers and Factions.* Berkeley: University of California Press, 1977.

Shils, Edward. "Opposition in the New States of Asia and Africa." *Government and Opposition* 1, 2 (February 1966): 175–204.

Southall, Aidan. "From Segmentary Lineage to Ethnic Association—Luo, Luhya, Ibo, and Others." In *Colonialism and Change,* edited by Maxwell Owusu, pp. 203–29. The Hague: Mouton, 1975.

Spenser, John. *The Kenya African Union.* London: KPI, 1985.

Staniland, Martin. "Single-Party Regimes and Political Change: The PDCI and Ivory Coast Politics." In *Politics and Change in Developing Countries,* edited by Colin Leys, pp. 135–75. Cambridge: Cambridge University Press, 1969.

Staudt, Kathleen A. "Administrative Resources, Political Patrons, and Redressing Inequities: A Case from Western Kenya." *Journal of Developing Areas* 12, 4 (July 1978): 399–414.

Swainson, Nicola. *The Development of Corporate Capitalism in Kenya.* London: Heinemann Educational Books, 1980.

———. "The Rise of a National Bourgeoisie in Kenya." *Review of African Political Economy* 8 (January–April 1977): 339–60.

———. "State and Economy in Post-Colonial Kenya, 1963–1978." *Canadian Journal of African Studies* 12, 2 (1978): 357–81.

Tamarkin, Mordechai. "From Kenyatta to Moi—The Anatomy of a Peaceful Transition of Power." *Africa Today* 26, 3 (1979): 21–38. Special Issue on Kenya after Kenyatta.

Thomas, Barbara. *Politics, Participation, and Poverty.* Boulder, Colo.: Westview Press, 1985.

Throup, David. "The Construction and Destruction of the Kenyatta State." In *The Political Economy of Kenya,* edited by Michael Schatzberg, pp. 33–74. New York: Praeger, 1987.

Tordoff, William. "Residual Legislatures: The Cases of Tanzania and Zambia." *Journal of Commonwealth and Comparative Politics* 15, 3 (November 1977): 235–49.

Toulabor, Comi M. *Le Togo sous Eyadéma*. Paris: Editions Karthala, 1986.

Umoja [Umoja wa Kupigania Demokrasia Kenya/United Movement for Democracy in Kenya]. *Moi's Reign of Terror: A Decade of Nyayo Crimes against the People of Kenya*. London: Umoja Secretariat, 1989.

————. *Struggle for Democracy in Kenya: Special Report on the 1988 General Elections in Kenya*. London: Umoja Secretariat, 1988.

United Nations Development Programme. *African Economic and Financial Data*. Washington, D.C.: World Bank, 1989.

van Donge, Jan Kees, and Athumani J. Liviga. "The 1985 Tanzanian Parliamentary Elections: A Conservative Election." *African Affairs* 38, 350 (January 1989): 47–62.

————. "Tanzanian Political Culture and the Cabinet." *Journal of Modern African Studies* 24, 4 (1986): 619–40.

Von Freyhold, Michaela. *Ujamaa Villages in Tanzania: Analysis of a Social Experiment*. New York: Monthly Review Press, 1979.

Wallerstein, Immanuel. "The Decline of the Party in Single-Party African States." In *Political Parties and Political Development*, edited by Joseph LaPalombara and Myron Weiner, pp. 201–16. Princeton: Princeton University Press, 1966.

Wallis, M. A. *Bureaucrats, Politicians, and Harambee*. Manchester Papers on Development, No. 4. Manchester: University of Manchester, 1980.

Wassermann, Gary. *Politics of Decolonization: Kenya Europeans and the Land Issue, 1960–1965*. Cambridge: Cambridge University Press, 1976.

Weiner , Myron, and Samuel Huntington, eds. *Understanding Political Development*. Boston: Little, Brown, 1987.

Widner, Jennifer. "Interest-Formation in the Informal Sector: Cultural Despair or a Politics of Multiple Allegiances?" *Comparative Political Studies* 24, 1 (1991): 31–55.

Wiseman, John. *Democracy in Black Africa: Survival and Revival*. New York: Paragon House, 1990.

Young, Crawford. "Class, Ethnicity, and Nationalism." Social Science Research Council, 1986.

————. "Patterns of Social Conflict: State, Class, and Ethnicity." *Dædalus* 111, 2 (Spring 1982): 71–98.

Young, Crawford, and Thomas Turner. *The Rise and Decline of the Zairean State*. Madison: University of Wisconsin Press, 1985.

Zolberg, Aristide. *Creating Political Order: The Party-States of West Africa*. Chicago: University of Chicago Press, 1966.

————. *One-Party Government in the Ivory Coast*. Princeton: Princeton University Press, 1964.

PERIODICALS

Africa Confidential (London)
Africa Contemporary Record (New York)
Amnesty International Reports (London)
[Economist Intelligence Unit] *Country Report: Kenya* (London)

Current Biography (New York)
The Daily Nation (Nairobi)
The East African Standard (Nairobi)
Kenya Times (Nairobi)
Nairobi Law Monthly (Nairobi)
The Standard (Nairobi)
The Weekly Review (Nairobi)

GOVERNMENT DOCUMENTS

Kenya. Ministry of Finance and Economic Planning. Central Bureau of Statistics. *Statistical Abstract.* Nairobi: Government Printer, various dates.
Kenya. Ministry of Finance and Economic Planning. Central Bureau of Statistics. *Development Plan.* 1970–74. Nairobi: Government Printer, 1970.
Kenya. Ministry of Finance and Economic Planning. *Kilifi District Development Plan.* Nairobi: Government Printer, 1984.
Kenya. Ministry of Finance and Planning. Central Bureau of Statistics. *Economic Survey.* Nairobi: Government Printer, various dates.
Kenya. National Assembly. *Official Report.* Nairobi: Government Printer, various dates.
Kenya. National Assembly. *On the Current Economic Situation in Kenya.* Sessional Paper No. 1 of 1974. Nairobi: Government Printer, 1974.
Kenya. Working Party on Government Expenditures (Philip Ndegwa, chairman). *Report and Recommendations.* Nairobi: Government Printer, 1982.

Index

Abagusii Union, 122
Abaluhya. *See* Luhya community
Africa, sub-Saharan: evolution of multi-party systems in, 215–18; single-party system in, 4–7, 215–18; Soviet Union intervenes in, 225; U.S. intervenes in, 225
Africa Confidential (newspaper), 141, 166
African Independent Pentecostal Church, 88, 191
African National Congress (ANC), 215
African People's Party (APP), 93
Aga Khan, 166
Agricultural and Industrial Holdings, Ltd., 35, 142
Agricultural Development Corporation, 96, 180
Agricultural Finance Corporation, 49, 83, 180
Agriculture, Ministry of, 83
Akamba community: in 1977 elections, 120–21
Alliance High School, 173
Alliance Hotel Group, 173
Amayo, David Okiki, 170; as chairman of KANU, 152, 159; in 1977 elections, 120
Amnesty International, 130–31
Angola, 223
Anyona, George, 145; arrested and detained, 189; expelled from party, 150; in 1977 elections, 123

Argwings-Kodhek, C. M. G., 134
Army mutiny (coup attempt, 1964), 69
Associated Press (AP): offices closed, 146, 165
Association, freedom of. *See* Freedom of assembly and association
Association of Baptist Churches of Nyeri, 191
"August disturbances" (unsuccessful coup attempt, 1982), 2, 145–47, 150

Baringo district, 85, 111, 134
Barkan, Joel, 4, 63, 72, 164
Bayart, Jean-François, 230
Berg-Schlosser, Dirk, 4
Betting and Lotteries Licensing Board, 86
Beyond (periodical), 166, 191
Bienen, Henry, 21, 64, 72
"Big Fish" (song), 183
Biwott, Nicholas, 141; arrested, 196
Bomett, Eric, 96
Bondo district, 63, 114, 122, 124
Bourgeoisie. *See* Entrepreneurs
Brazil, 16–17, 21
British Broadcasting Corporation (BBC), 104, 137, 191
Bungoma district, 80, 85
Bungoma East constituency, 78, 90
Bureaucracy. *See* Civil service
Bush, George: and military assistance to Kenya, 239n
Busia district, 91
Busia East constituency, 148

Businessmen. *See* Economic elites
Butere constituency, 165, 168
Butere Development Fund, 147–48
Butere district, 89, 100, 147–48

Callaghy, Thomas, 13, 28, 205–7
Cardoso, Fernando, 20
Central Bank, 180
Central Province, 41, 46–47, 53, 65, 69,
    81, 86, 89, 94, 118–19, 121–22, 126–
    28, 135, 138, 140, 152, 153, 173, 184,
    186–87; and resource allocation, 77–
    78, 88, 96–97, 110–12
Central Rift Labor Party, 129
Chama Cha Mapinduzi (CCM; Tanza-
    nia): compared to KANU, 208–11;
    Nyerere's relationship with, 210
Change-the-Constitution Movement,
    115, 121, 125, 137
Charles, Prince, 203
Chazan, Naomi, 210
Chege, Michael, 16
Cheluget, Isaya, 123
Chotara, Kariuki, 147–49, 200; and
    KANU youth wing, 154, 200; opposes
    Kenyatta, 149
Churches. *See* Clergy
Church of the Province of Kenya (CPK;
    Anglican), 191–92; KANU attacks,
    191
Citibank, 196
Civil liberties. *See* Freedom of assembly
    and association; Freedom of speech;
    Freedom of the press; Political parties,
    opposition
Civil service, 51, 58; economic role of,
    71; forced to join KANU, 170; Ken-
    yatta favors, 70–72; under Moi, 137,
    151–52, 163, 165, 179; in party-state,
    12–14, 108, 151; and "straddling," 71
Civil society, 41–47, 109, 133, 171–78,
    195, 201–4, 224–32; and opposition
    political parties, 178–97; and pace of
    shift to party-state, 28–30, 36–37;
    single-party system's effects on, 117–
    18, 159, 168–71, 195, 207–8, 228–
    29; in "weak states–strong societies"
    argument, 11–14
Clergy: Mwakenya movement and, 192;
    oppose single-party system, 188, 190–
    92, 195, 202, 214, 229, 231; political
    divisions among, 190–91; use sermons
    as political communication, 191–92
Clientelism, 33–34, 46, 125, 207, 231;
    GEMA and, 95–97; Kenyatta and, 55,
    61; matajiri class protests, 175; Moi
    and, 139–40, 200–201; in party-state,

164, 198, 200–201; political conse-
    quences of, 42–46
Clough, Marshall, 51
Cocoa zone (Côte d'Ivoire), 214, 218
Coffee Amendment Bill (1987), 186
Coffee Board, 175, 184–86
Coffee industry: Moi government and,
    184–86
Collier, David, 20
Colombia, 20
Commerce and Industry, Ministry of,
    173
Commercial Development Corporation,
    173
Conference on Security, Stability, Devel-
    opment and Cooperation in Africa
    (Kampala, 1991), 225
Convention People's Party (Ghana), 132,
    160
Cooperative Development, Ministry for,
    180
Côte d'Ivoire, 3, 14; closed electoral sys-
    tem of, 212–13, 220; compared to
    Kenya, 204, 212–14, 218–20, 222;
    economic crises in, 221–22; economic
    development in, 218–19; fragmented
    political opposition in, 220; historical
    background of, 212; limited political
    criticism allowed in, 219; local admin-
    istration in, 213; as party-state, 204,
    212–14, 218–19; private economic
    sector in, 230; transportation sector's
    political power in, 220
Coup attempts, 2, 69
*Creating Political Order: The Party-States
    of West Africa* (Zolberg), 6
Cross, Sholto, 17
Culture, Ministry of, 195

Dagoretti constituency, 114
Daily Nation (newspaper), 63, 83–84,
    88, 95, 102, 104, 116, 156, 233–34
Daily Telegraph (London newspaper),
    125
Democracy: possibility of, in single-party
    system, 224–25, 227–28
Democratic Party, 197

East African Breweries, Ltd., 173
East African Community: collapses
    (1977), 126
East African Standard (newspaper), 67,
    116
Eastern Province, 95, 121
Economic elites, 53–55, 57–58, 61, 65,
    86, 90, 137, 172–77, 179–81. *See also*
    Matajiri class

Economic growth and development: under Kenyatta administration, 41–43, 47–48; and inequality and distribution, 49, 77–84, 89–92; lack of, under Moi, 179–81

Economist Intelligence Unit, 182

Economist (magazine), 166

Education, Ministry of, 58, 173

Education reforms, 48, 50, 95; in Rift Valley Province, 81–82, 89, 91

Eldoret district, 95

Eldoret North constituency, 83

Eldoret South constituency, 96

Elections (1977), 118–27; canceled, 121

Elections (1979), 125–28, 174

Elections (1983), 3

Elections (1985), 2, 132, 150–52, 154–56, 233; campaign meetings banned, 152; Moi controls, 152

Elgeyo community, 87

Elgeyo-Marakwet district, 85

Embu community, 94

Employment, Incomes, and Equality (ILO report), 77–80, 82, 84

Entrepreneurial power: concentrated in party-state, 17–19, 29

Entrepreneurs: and political power, 42–43, 46, 51, 73, 86, 90, 137, 172–77, 179–81

Ethiopia, 2

Ethnicity, and politics, 44–46, 64, 69, 71, 92–94, 112–25, 126, 134, 147–49, 225

Ethnic welfare societies: increased importance as pressure groups, 92–94, 110, 112–18, 120–21, 124–26, 198, 231; Moi suppresses, 131, 142–44, 201, 231. *See also* names of individual organizations

Export-crop sector: Moi attempts to control, 183–87, 203

Factionalism: nature of, 237n

"Family" faction (KANU), 76, 85–86, 89, 92–93, 95–96, 98–100, 103, 105, 107–8, 111–13, 129, 131–32, 139, 172; attempts to change constitution, 113–18; in 1977 elections, 118–19; in 1979 elections, 125–26; takes control of party, 110

Film and Stage Plays Act, 188

Finance, Ministry of, 95

Financial policies: in Kenyatta administration, 47–48

Finland, 203

Ford Foundation, 146

Foreign aid: political conditions attached to, 174, 193, 202–3; suspended (1991), 196, 203, 215, 239n; suspended to Zaire, 223

Foreign Investment Bill (1988), 170

Forum for the Restoration of Democracy (FORD), 196

France, 206, 214

Freedom of assembly and association, 110, 178, 227; KANU restricts, 168, 171; Kenyatta restricts, 98–100, 107, 112, 117–18; Moi restricts, 131–33, 143–44, 162, 187–88, 199–200, 204, 228

Freedom of the press, 233–35; Moi restricts, 144, 165–66, 188, 231; in Zaire, 222

Freedom of speech, 178, 227; Moi restricts, 162

"Free-riding," 25–26

Gabon, 221

Garissa, 178

"Gatundu Courtiers," 59, 73–74, 76

Gatundu Self-Help Hospital, 65

Gbagbo, Laurent, 219–20

General Medical Stores, 175

Gertzel, Cherry, 68

Ghana, 3, 5–6, 40, 132, 160

Gichuru, Gitau, 105

Gichuru, James, 35–36, 47, 55, 86, 93–94, 96–97, 105, 110, 113, 114, 117, 141; in 1977 elections, 118

Gikuyu, Embu, and Meru Association (GEMA), 108, 138, 231; attacks Kibaki, 141; attempts to change constitution, 113–18; challenges Moi in Parliament, 122–23; and clientelism, 95–97; government attempts to undercut, 124; Moi eliminates, 142–43; in 1979 elections, 126, 129; in 1977 elections, 118–19, 121–24; power struggle with Moi, 111–12; proscribed, 35; strengthens KANU, 92–94, 110, 116–17, 132; supports Kiambu interests, 110–13, 132; weakened under Moi, 131–32

Gilgil, 88

Giriama, 51

Gitari, David, 170

Gospel Church, 191

Government African School (Kapsabet), 134

Government African School (Tambach), 134

Great Britain, 15, 177, 202–3

Grenada Television, 149

Guinea, 5

Harambee system, 34–35, 39, 70, 85, 91, 93, 95–96, 99–100, 108, 111–12, 192, 233; failure of, 200; and formation of political alliances, 63–65, 114, 119, 123, 127–28, 140, 142, 146–48, 198–200, 218; Kariuki uses, 87–88; Kenyatta establishes, 60–66, 130, 199–200, 214; Moi restricts, 133, 199–200; origins of, 61–62; political impact of, 62–63, 66, 73, 149, 199–200, 241n; supports schools, 65–66, 140, 142, 200
Hartmann, Jeanette, 210
Hassan, Yusuf, 178
Hempstone, Smith: association with Moi's political opponents, 174, 253n
Hinga, Bernard, 131, 137
Hirschman, Albert, 20, 229
Holmquist, Frank, 4, 66, 209–10
Home Affairs, Ministry for, 131, 135, 173
Houphouët-Boigny, Félix: compared to Kenyatta, 212, 219; legalizes opposition political parties, 218; political strategy of, 212–14, 218–21
Human rights. See Freedom of assembly and association; Freedom of speech; Freedom of the press
Hyden, Goran, 11, 13–14, 72

Ibo community (Nigeria), 176
Imanyara, Gitobu, 188; arrested and detained, 189–90, 196
Indian Congress Party, 51
Indian Freedom Party, 51
Industry, nationalism of, 48
Informal sector: potential political power of, 193–95, 214; as source of youth-wing members, 194–95; as strong base for Moi, 193
Interest groups. See Civil society
International Coffee Agreement: collapses, 223
International Coffee Organization, 185
International Commission of Jurists (ICJ): as means of outside communication, 188
International community: dissidents maintain ties to, 171, 188, 202–3, 226; Tanzania and, 212
International Herald Tribune (newspaper), 166
International Labor Organization (ILO): Employment, Incomes, and Equality, 77–80, 82, 84
International Monetary Fund (IMF), 1, 223, 234

Iraq: intervenes in sub-Saharan Africa, 225
Israel, 15
Italy, 182
Ivory Coast. See Côte d'Ivoire

Jackson, Robert, 11
Japan: and Kenyan foreign aid, 203
Jeunesse du MPR (youth wing; Zaire), 205
Journalists: Moi arrests and detains, 166
Jua kali. See Informal sector
Judicial system: Moi weakens, 164–65
Juja, 115

Kabarak, 155
Kabati Forest, 86
Kaggia, Bildad, 31, 53–54, 57–58, 69, 149
Kahara, Nathan, 44
Kajiado district, 79
Kakamega district, 85, 165, 168
Kalenjin community, 54, 82, 87, 111, 115, 123, 133, 165, 179–81, 184, 187, 203; in 1977 elections, 121
Kamau, Gibson Kuria, 175, 190; arrested and detained, 189; seeks asylum in U.S., 176, 203
Kamba community, 114, 135
Kamotho, Joseph, 140, 147
Kamukunji Group: in 1979 elections, 127; in 1977 elections, 121
Kamukunji meeting ground (Nairobi), 176
Kamusinga, 90
Kanja, Waweru, 88–89, 92, 105, 115, 165; as faction leader, 138–39, 149; in 1985 elections, 155–56
Kano district, 124
Kaplinsky, Rafael, 15
Karanja, Josephat, 167, 169, 175
Karatina Town, 154–55
Karbanet Intermediate School, 134
Karimi, Joseph: The Kenyatta Succession, 44
Karioki, James, 14
Kariuki, G. G., 102, 127, 140–41, 147; in 1979 elections, 152; removed from government, 148
Kariuki, Josiah Mwangi, 36, 41–42, 59, 110, 121, 128–29, 183; assassinated, 76, 86, 105, 111, 160, 168, 246n; background of, 86–87; on ethnic divisions, 79; and Kenyatta, 86; on Kenyatta, 51; "Mau Mau" Detainee, 86; as spokesman for populist faction, 75–76, 86–94, 98, 100–101, 103–6, 108–

9, 115–16, 138–39; and use of harambee system, 87–88, 246n
Karume, Njenga, 96; as faction leader, 138–39, 142
Kasipul Kabondo constituency, 97
Keen, John, 105; in 1977 elections, 121
Kenya: Bush and military assistance to, 239n; coalition politics in, 40; compared to Côte d'Ivoire, 204, 212–14, 218–20, 222; compared to Tanzania, 204, 208–11; compared to Zaire, 204–5, 208; economic crises in, 222; human rights record of, 130–31; nationalist coalition disintegrates, 22; restrictions on research in, 233–35; single-party system constitutionally established in, 39–40, 132, 145, 150, 162, 188–90, 198, 243n; unified political opposition in, 220–21; U.S. military interests in, 15–17
Kenya African Democratic Union (KADU), 31, 43, 51–54, 68, 73, 93, 114, 118, 133–34, 245n; absorbed by KANU, 55, 57; and land reform programs, 81
Kenya African National Union (KANU), 37, 47, 51–54, 74, 134, 166, 189–90, 194, 204; absorbs KADU, 55, 57; absorbs Maendeleo ya Wanawake, 169; All-Delegates Conference, 125; attacks CPK, 191; Backbenchers' Group, 68, 198, 200, 228; branches assume disciplinary functions, 167; branch headquarters burned (1990), 176; centralizes electoral process, 150, 158–59; civil service forced to join, 170; compared to MPR (Zaire), 205, 208; compared to TANU and CCM, 208–11; consolidation of power within, 2–3, 32–33, 37–38, 75–77, 85, 162–64; constitutionally superior to Parliament, 162–65, 252n; controls police and security forces, 170; Delegates' Conference (1980), 136; disciplinary committee of, 152–53, 159–61, 162, 166, 174, 204; disciplinary committee dissolved, 167–68, 195; discontinues secret ballot, 153, 170, 172; diverts foreign aid to public officials, 196; diverts public funds to party officials, 171, 200; expells Wanjigi, 194; factionalism and pluralism in, 1–3, 31–32, 35–36, 39–40, 54, 58–60, 70, 73, 75–77, 85, 108, 110–12, 118, 128–29, 157–58, 168, 198, 200–201; "Family" faction of, 76, 85–86, 89, 92–93, 95–96, 98–100, 103, 105, 107–8, 111–13, 129,

131–32, 139, 172; "Family" faction takes control of, 110; fear of Mwakenya movement, 178, 220–21; financial objectives, 153; GEMA strengthens, 92–94, 110, 116–17, 132; increased social control by, 150, 159–61; institutes preliminary elections, 168, 172–73; internal disagreement on enhanced functions, 159–61; Kenyatta restructures, 56–60; Kenyatta's relationship with, 210, 229; makeup of early membership, 42–43; matajiri class protests poor performance of, 174–75, 195, 201; Moi liberalizes, 224; National Governing Council, 125; new headquarters, 1; nonalignment of, 59; and Office of the President, 110, 112, 132–33, 143–47, 150–54, 157–61, 163–66, 168–71, 198; and open primary elections, 60; opposition faction develops within, 75–77, 84–85; opposition to Moi within, 172–77; organizes loyalty demonstrations, 168–69; Parliamentary Group, 68, 71; party conference at Limuru (1966), 58–59; and "political space," 98, 112, 128–29, 162, 168, 173; popular fear of, 178; populist faction in, 75–76, 85–108; populist faction ousted from, 110; purge within, 32; radical wing of, 57–58, 69, 75, 135; requires party membership by all citizens, 153, 170–71; restricts freedom of assembly and association, 168, 171; revenue-gathering activities, 170–71; Review Committee, 4; suppresses parliamentary sovereignty, 100–103, 158; takes over law enforcement functions, 132, 158, 160; violates parliamentary immunity, 168; weak structure of, 39–40, 56–58, 61, 72–73, 107, 158, 160, 162, 166, 198, 244n; youth wing, see Youth wing (KANU)
Kenya African Socialist Alliance (KASA): established to oppose Moi, 145
Kenya African Union (KAU), 51–53, 55
Kenya Breweries, Ltd., 173
Kenya Broadcasting Corporation, 180
Kenya Bus Service, Ltd., 182
Kenya Coffee Growers' Association (KCGA), 180; dissolved, 185–86; opposes Moi, 184
Kenya Commercial Bank, 180
Kenya Farmers' Association, 175
Kenya Football Federation (KFF), 173
Kenya Grain Growers' Cooperative Union, 180

Kenya Industrial Estates, 180
Kenya Institute for Administration (KIA), 124
Kenya Land Freedom Army (KLFA), 41–42, 51, 73
Kenya National Insurance, 180
Kenyan Public Law Institute, 17
Kenya People's Union (KPU), 63, 73, 75, 93, 107, 115, 122, 176, 196; established, 58–59, 69; suppressed, 3, 60, 69–70, 85, 98, 114, 135, 144, 149
Kenya Planters' Cooperative Union (KPCU), 175, 180; Moi reorganizes, 185; opposes Moi, 184
Kenya Ports Authority, 140, 175
Kenya Posts and Telecommunications, 180
Kenya Stock Exchange, 181
Kenya Tea Development Authority (KTDA), 175, 180; Moi reorganizes, 184–86
Kenya Times (party newspaper), 234
Kenyatta, Jomo, 11, 43, 93, 122, 133–34, 154, 172, 183, 194, 204, 211, 224, 231; and clientelism, 55, 61; and constitutional changes, 56–58, 61, 67; death of, 36, 63, 66, 125, 137; disputed succession to, 111, 113–18, 120; establishes harambee system, 60–66, 130, 158, 199–200, 214; and "Family" faction of KANU, 76; favors civil service and provincial administration, 70–72; on his political rivals, 69–70; Houphouët-Boigny compared to, 212, 219; imprisoned, 52, 136; J. M. Kariuki and, 86; in 1977 elections, 120; Parliament supports, 103; political repression by, 67, 97–100, 103–4, 106, 131, 219; political strategy and personality of, 1–4, 19, 31–35, 37, 40, 51–66, 72–74, 97–98, 103, 130–31, 133, 141, 151, 158, 214, 219; and populist faction, 89, 92, 94–95, 97, 103–4; relationship with KANU, 210, 229; relations with Mau Mau organization, 51–52; and resource allocation, 47–50, 68, 74, 104; restricts freedom of assembly and association, 98–100, 107, 112, 117–18; restricts political opposition, 66–67, 75–76, 202; restructures KANU, 56–60; rise to power, 52; strategic marriage ties, 55; supports open primary elections, 60, 69, 72, 74, 94–95; supports single-party system, 54–58, 61, 94, 158; suppresses attempt to change constitution, 117; suppresses parliamentary sovereignty, 100–101

Kenyatta, Margaret, 94
Kenyatta, Peter Muigai, 114–15
Kenyatta Succession, The (Karimi & Ochieng), 44
Kericho district, 81, 187
Kerio South constituency, 91
Kerio Valley, 91
Key, V. O., 26
Khaminwa, John, 190; arrested and detained, 189
Kiambaa constituency, 59
Kiambu district, 41, 47, 59, 62, 86, 88–89, 92–94, 96, 99, 102, 105, 118–19, 128, 131, 139, 176; coffee boom's effect on, 112; economic elite in, 53–55, 57–58, 61, 65, 67, 132, 137–38; GEMA supports interests of, 110–13, 116, 132
Kiano, Julius Gikonyo, 55, 115
Kibagare (shanty village): government razes, 194
Kibaki, Mwai, 55, 82, 84, 96, 159–60, 167, 197; background of, 154; as faction leader, 137–38, 140–41, 148, 200–201; GEMA attacks, 141; in 1977 elections, 119, 121; in 1979 elections, 126–29, 133, 137; in 1985 elections, 154–57
Kibisu, Peter, 105, 148
Kieni division, 156
Kikuyu Central Association (KCA), 42, 51
Kikuyu community, 73, 75, 86, 89, 93–97, 105, 110, 119, 134, 136, 167, 175–76, 178, 180–81; as dominant political force, 51, 55, 61, 114, 117, 148; as economic force, 34–35, 46, 138, 147, 185, 200, 218, 248n; and Mau Mau uprising, 41, 43, 49; in 1979 elections, 126, 127–28; reduced power in government, 147–49, 201; and resource allocation, 81, 87
Kikuyu constituency, 141
Kikuyu Land Board Association, 51
Kilgoris, 79
Kimani, Kahika, 105, 113, 115–16, 128, 142, 149; in 1977 elections, 118
Kimani, Tom, 183
Kinangop district, 79
King's College (Uganda), 86
Kinyua, Henry, 185
Kiplabat, 134
Kirinyaga district, 115
Kisii district, 83, 85, 122–23, 151, 165
Kisumu district, 124, 152
Kisumu Rural constituency, 153
Kitale district, 91, 95
Kitale West constituency, 83–84

Kitching, Gavin, 42
Kivukoni College (Tanzania), 210–11
Koinange, Mbiyu, 93–94, 99–100, 102, 113–14, 131, 135
Korea, 164
Kubai, Fred: opposes Kenyatta, 149
Kuria, Manasses, 192

Labor movement, 42, 53, 57
Laikipia East constituency, 102
Laikipia West constituency, 93
Lake Victoria, 85
Lancaster House independence negotiations, 42–43, 76, 134
Land Bank, 49
Land reform programs, 41, 48–50, 53–54, 75, 81, 84–85, 139, 177; and expropriation, 49; Haraka Program, 49; Million Acre Scheme, 49, 61; Moi halts, 128; in Rift Valley Province, 81–82, 89–91, 113; Shirika scheme, 81–82
Lands and Settlement, Ministry of, 95
Law Society of Kenya (LSK), 189–91, 195–96; Office of the President threatens, 169; opposes abandonment of secret ballot, 172
Lawyers: Moi attempts to repress, 189–90, 203; oppose single-party system, 169, 172, 187–90, 192, 195, 201–2, 229, 231–32
Lemarchand, René, 137, 237n
Leo, Christopher, 43
Leonard, David, 42, 60, 163, 171
Leys, Colin, 14, 45–46; *Underdevelopment in Kenya*, 15–16
Liberia, 177; ethnic divisions in, 225
Libya, 239n; intervenes in sub-Saharan Africa, 225
Limuru constituency, 116, 176; party conference in (1966), 58–59, 135
Litunya, Richard, 148
Local Government, Ministry of, 134, 176, 180
Lodwar, 136
Lonsdale, John, 227
Loyal Patriots, 51
Luhya community, 54, 80, 87, 90, 135, 147–48, 187; in 1977 elections, 121
Lumumba Institute, 31, 35, 57–58, 69
Luo community, 51, 53–54, 57, 69, 87, 93–94, 114, 115, 134, 145–46, 175–76, 193; in 1977 elections, 119–20
Luo Union, 54, 92, 143; government attempts to undercut, 122–24
Lurambi South constituency, 90
Lwanda-Ooho-Muhaka Progressive Society, 165

Maathai, Wangari, 1
Machakos district, 79, 165
Maendeleo ya Wanawake: KANU absorbs, 169
Magugu, Arthur, 55
Maize and Produce Board, 83
Maize crisis: in Rift Valley Province, 80, 82–84, 117
Makanda Kabobi Institute (Zaire), 206
Malindi district, 79
Malumba, Etienne Tshisikedi wa, 222
Mandela, Nelson, 215
Mango, Mukasa, 148
Markovitz, Irving Leonard, 18, 221
Masai community, 51, 79, 116; in 1977 elections, 120–21
Masailand, 91
Masai Reserve, 81
Masai United Front, 121
Matajiri class, 23, 71, 133, 136, 162–63, 173, 180, 184, 187; protests clientelism, 175; protests KANU's poor performance, 174–75, 195, 201
Matano, Robert, 147–48, 159; in 1985 elections, 152; in 1977 elections, 121
Matatu Association of Kenya, 182
Matatu Vehicle Owners Association (MVOA): opposes government regulation, 182–83
Matatus (public transport vehicles): poor safety records of, 182–83
Mathare, 153
"Mathina ma Matiba" (song), 183
Mathira constituency, 155
Matiba, Kenneth Stanley, 147–48, 163, 183, 197; arrested and detained, 176, 194–96; background of, 173; loses in rigged election, 174; in 1979 elections, 174; opposes Moi, 172, 174–76, 179, 181, 188, 220–21; purged from KANU, 167; and tea industry, 186–87; urges formation of opposition parties, 174, 192
"Mau Mau" Detainee (Kariuki), 86
Mau Mau organization: Central Committee, 52, 147, 149; Kenyatta's relations with, 51–52
Mau Mau uprising, 55, 61, 70, 73, 78, 86, 89, 139, 148–49, 154, 177–78, 200, 212; Kikuyu and, 41, 43, 49; Moi and, 135
Mbiri constituency, 148, 173
Mbita constituency, 99
Mbori, J. E., 97
Mboya, Tom, 44, 53, 57, 59, 135; assassinated, 114, 136; and political repression, 67; "Sessional Paper Number 10 on the Application of Planning to Afri-

Mboya, Tom (*continued*)
can Socialism," 57, 62, 199; on "straddling," 71
Mbuya, Paul, 123–24
Meru community, 94
Meru district, 79, 95, 116, 146
Migdal, Joel, 11
Migure, G. O., 99
Mobutu Sese Seko, 205–7; legalizes opposition political parties, 222; political
strategy of, 206, 223–24; relationships
with the Zairian military, 223
Moi, Daniel arap, 4, 15, 17, 31–32, 37,
47, 58–59, 76, 87, 88, 96–97, 204;
abolishes parliamentary privilege, 146;
arrests and detains journalists, 166; attacks Njonjo, 147–48; attempts to
control export-crop sector, 183–87,
203; attempts to control pressure
groups, 125; attempts to control transportation sector, 181–83, 201, 203,
221; attempts to repress lawyers, 189–
90, 203; background of, 134–35; civil
service under, 137, 151–52, 163, 165,
179; and clientelism, 139–40, 200–
201; and coffee industry, 184–86; creates division among his competition,
141; defends single-party system, 215;
designated acting president, 125; dis-
likes debate, 136; dissolves KANU disciplinary committee, 167; eliminates
GEMA, 142–43; and evolution of
party-state, 129, 162–63; and GEMA,
110–11; GEMA challenges in Parliament, 122–23; given emergency powers in peacetime, 137; governmental
strategy of, 1–2, 19, 33, 35–37, 131–
32, 198–99; halts land reform programs, 128; as head of police and security forces, 135; helps form KADU,
134; informal economic sector as
strong base for, 193; joins KANU,
134; KCGA opposes, 184; as Kenyatta's successor, 111, 128–29; KPCU opposes, 184; lack of economic growth
and development under, 179–81; legalizes opposition political parties,
196–97, 199, 215; liberalized KANU,
224; and Mau Mau uprising, 135; as
minister for home affairs, 134–35;
New Year's speech (1989), 169–70; in
1977 elections, 119–22, 124–25; in
1979 elections, 125–28, 152; in 1985
elections, 156; opposes resource allocation, 104–5; opposition to, 172–77;
and personalization of power, 163–64,
166–68, 171, 214, 228; political fears

of, 143–44; political repression by, 67,
101–2, 104, 143–45, 162–63, 219;
political strategy and personality of,
130–34, 141, 218; power struggle
with GEMA, 111–12, 114–16; preference for police force, 136–37; protects
his private business interests, 179, 214;
reinstates detention laws, 146, 204; re-
leases political detainees, 130–31, 137,
139; reopens detention camps, 144; reorganizes KPCU, 185; reorganizes
KTDA, 184–86; represents Rift Valley
Province on Legislative Council, 134;
reputation as populist, 135–37, 163,
193, 224; restricts freedom of assembly and association, 131–33, 143–
44, 162, 187–88, 199–200, 204, 228;
restricts freedom of speech, 162; restricts freedom of the press, 144, 165–
66, 188, 231; restricts harambee system, 133, 199–200; restricts political
opposition, 67, 125–26, 204; restricts
"political space," 143, 146, 162, 164,
191, 203; restructures electoral system,
150–51, 161; strengthens police and
security forces, 131, 144–45, 165;
suppresses ethnic welfare societies,
131, 142–44, 201, 231; suppresses political opposition, 141–47, 161; and
surveillance of opposition, 131–32,
145, 221, 228; and tea industry, 184–
87; weakens GEMA, 131–32; weakens
judicial system, 164–65
Moi Day, 163
Mombasa, 116, 121, 173
Montesquieu, Baron de la Brede de la,
229–30
Moore, Barrington, 30
Morgenthau, Ruth Schachter, 212
Mouvement populaire de la révolution
(MPR; Zaire), 132, 159–60, 162, 169,
202, 207, 209, 222; compared to
KANU, 205, 208; opposition to, 205;
political manifesto of, 205; youth
wing, 205
Mpatanishi (newspaper), 178
Mudavadi, Moses, 148
Mueller, Susanne, 67–70
Muge, Alexander Kipsang: protests vio-
lations of human rights, 191
Muigai, Ngengi, 115, 123
Muigwithania (journal), 51
Muite, Paul, 189, 196; as opposition
leader, 197
Muliro, Masinde, 105; in 1977 elections,
121; opposes Moi, 172
Multi-party systems: arguments in favor

of, 226–27; evolution of in sub-
Saharan Africa, 215–18; vs. single-
party systems, 224–27, 232
Mungai, James, 131, 248n, 249n
Mungai, Njoroge, 92–94, 105, 111,
113–14, 117, 122, 137; in 1979 elec-
tions, 125, 128, 133, 152; in 1977
elections, 118–19, 121, 123
Munoko, Nathan, 150
Munyi, Kamwithi, 97
Muoroto (shanty village): government
razes, 194
Murang'a district, 55, 59, 61, 65, 88–90,
115, 140, 147–48, 173–76, 186
Muraya, Sam, 193
Murgor, William, 96
Murungi, Kiraitu, 162, 190; seeks asy-
lum in U.S., 176, 203
Musyoka, Kalonzo, 166
Mutisya, Mulu, 122
Mwachofi, Mwashembu: in 1985 elec-
tions, 152
Mwakenya movement: and the clergy,
192; as government pretext for har-
rassment, 177–78; KANU's fear of,
178, 220–21; purported program of,
177–78
Mwangale, Elijah, 147–49, 192; disci-
plined by KANU committee, 167; in
1985 elections, 156; on resource allocation, 78–80, 90
Mwangale community, 80
Mwendwa, Ngala: in 1977 elections,
120
Mwithaga, Mark, 105, 129

Nabwera, Burudi, 105, 152
Nairobi, 44, 59, 62, 88–89, 92, 102,
115, 117, 121, 123, 127, 138, 154,
159, 163, 172–74, 179, 182–83, 203;
antigovernment riots in (1990), 176;
City Council, 194
Nairobi Law Monthly, 188, 190, 196
Naivasha district, 80, 148
Nakuru district, 81, 85–86, 93, 95, 97,
104–5, 113, 123–24, 138, 149, 154,
159, 176, 178, 200
Nakuru East constituency, 129
Nakuru North constituency, 146
Nakuru Town, 97, 129
Nandi community, 87
Nandi district, 51, 81, 85, 87, 100
Nandi Hills, 88
"Nandi Hills Declaration," 87
Narok district, 79, 176
Nassir, Shariff, 116

National Cereals and Produce Board,
175, 180
National Coffee Cooperative Union
(NCCU), 184
National Council of Churches of Kenya
(NCCK): opposes abandonment of se-
cret ballot, 172, 191–92; opposes
single- party system, 190–92
National Guidance and Political Affairs,
Ministry for, 169, 195
National Youth Service, 86, 182–83
Nation (newspaper), 166
Ndegwa Commission Report, 78, 80
Nderi, Ignatius, 139
Nderi, Peter Ndirangu, 92
Netherlands, 48, 182
New African (newspaper), 166
New Akamba Union, 92–93, 122
New Kenya Coalition, 51
New Kenya Party, 51
Ngala, Ronald, 134
Ng'ang'a, Amos, 139
Ngei, Paul, 122; in 1977 elections, 121
Ngwataniro community, 105
Ngwataniro land companies, 113, 115,
128
Ng'weno, Hilary, 2–3, 157, 234–35
Nigeria, 16, 176–77, 229
Njiru, James, 93, 169
Njonjo, Apollo, 81
Njonjo, Charles, 55, 70, 76, 91, 99, 101,
114, 153, 163; expelled from govern-
ment and party, 147–49; as faction
leader, 137–41; and GEMA, 110–11;
Moi attacks, 147–48; in 1979 elec-
tions, 137, 152; warns against chang-
ing the constitution, 116–17
Njoya, Timothy, 192
Njururi, Ngumbu: in 1985 elections, 155
Nkrumah, Kwame, 40, 132, 150
Nkrumah Ideological Institute (Ghana), 6
Non-profit organizations, 230
Northern Frontier district, 54
Norway, 177, 202–3
N'Sele Manifesto (Zaire), 205
Ntimama, William ole, 176–77
Nyachae, Simeon, 115, 122
Nyagah, Jeremiah, 141
Nyandarua district, 61, 81, 85, 88, 93,
176
Nyandarua North constituency, 79, 86,
103
Nyang'oro, Julius, 204–5
Nyanza district, 153, 193
Nyanza Province, 83, 93, 95, 97, 99,
114, 119, 121–24, 152
Nyayo Bus Company, 180

Nyayo Bus Services Corporation, 182, 221
Nyayo Tea Zones, 180, 184
Nyayo Tea Zones Development Corporation (NTZDC), 187
Nyerere, Julius, 211; declares Tanzania a one-party state, 209; relationship with TANU and CCM, 210
Nyeri constituency, 165
Nyeri district, 55, 59, 61, 65, 86, 88–89, 92, 105, 139, 149, 154–55, 176, 178
Nyoike, Kimani wa, 167; opposes Moi, 172
Nyong'o, Peter Anyang', 14–15, 22–23

Ochieng, Philip: *The Kenyatta Succession*, 44
Ochieng, William, 225
Odinga, Oginga, 15, 31, 35, 53–54, 57–58, 63, 68–69, 75, 93, 114–15, 121–23, 134, 145–46, 175–76; attempts ties to international community, 171; expelled from party, 150; on Moi, 134, 136
Odinga, Raila Omolo: arrested and detained, 146, 168, 176
O'Donnell, Guillermo, 20
Ojiambo, Fred, 190
Ojwang, J. B., 225
Okero, Isaac Omolo, 121–23, 125
Okondo, Peter: disciplined by KANU committee, 167
Okullu, Henry, 175; urges formation of opposition parties, 192
Okumu, John, 209–10
Oligarchy: single-party system and, 225
Ol Kalou Declaration, 60
Oloitipitip, Stanley, 116, 131, 147; in 1979 elections, 127–28, 152; in 1977 elections, 119–21; removed from government, 148
Omamo, William Odongo, 63, 93–94, 105, 122–24; in 1977 elections, 120
Omido, Fred, 147
Oneko, Achieng, 63, 66, 115–16, 122–23, 176
Onyonka, Zachary, 151
Ooko-Ombaka, Oki, 190
Othaya constituency, 154
Otieno, Wambui, 138
Ouko, Robert, 153; assassinated, 193, 196
Oxford University, 86
Oyugis Declaration (1977), 122

Pambana (newspaper), 178
Parliament: economic makeup of, 180–

81; KANU constitutionally superior to, 162–65, 252n; Public Accounts Committee, 68
Parliamentary system: in Kenyatta administration, 30–32
Parti démocratique de Côte d'Ivoire (PDCI), 5, 212–14, 219–20
Party-state: and bureaucratic authoritarianism, 19–21; civil service in, 12–14, 108, 151; clientelism in, 164, 198, 200–201; concentration of entrepreneurial power in, 17–19, 29; constitutional modification in, 29; control of financial resources in, 12–13, 75, 77; Côte d'Ivoire as, 204, 212–14; defined, 5; and economic underdevelopment, 14–17; effect on social structure, 11–14, 117–18; and electoral monopoly, 9–10, 12, 22; ethnic and religious divisions in, 23–24; and external economic dependence, 14–15; and lack of economic development, 10–12; Moi and evolution of, 129; nature of, 7–10; opposition to rise of, 36–38; policy issues in, 24–25; political elites in, 24–26, 30, 178–79; political participation in, 164; political repression in, 3–4, 7–8, 13, 21, 28–30, 33, 36; rise of, 5–7, 8–22, 23–25, 36–37; shifting personal factions in, 137–38; Tanzania as, 204, 208–13; and weak opposition factions, 24–26, 75–76; Zaire as, 204–8, 213
"Patriotic Contributions" (song), 183
Patronage. *See* Clientelism
Police and security forces: Criminal Investigation Department, 92, 144, 165, 185; Government Services Unit (GSU), 105, 131, 144, 146, 165; increased budgets, 144–45; under KANU control, 170; Moi strengthens, 131, 144–45, 160, 165; Special Branch, 146; threaten to crush opposition, 152–53
Policy issues: in party-state, 24–25
Political elites: economic threats to in Zaire, 223; nature of, 23; in party-state, 24–26, 30, 178–79; strategies of, 44
Political meetings, licensing of. *See* Freedom of assembly and association
Political parties, opposition: arguments in favor of, 227; civil society and, 178–97; Kenyatta restricts, 66–67, 75–76, 202; Moi legalizes, 196–97, 199, 215; proscribed, 36, 132
Political repression: in party-state, 3–4, 7–8, 13, 21, 28–30, 33, 36
"Political space": KANU and, 98, 112,

128–29, 162, 168, 173; Moi restricts, 143, 146, 162, 164, 191, 203; populist faction and, 98, 109; single-party system and, 195, 198, 221
"Political tourism," 154–57
"Poor People of Muoroto, The" (song), 194
Populist faction (KANU), 75–76, 85–108; Kariuki as spokesman for, 75–76, 86–94, 98, 100–101, 103–6, 108–9, 115–16; Kenyatta and, 89, 92, 94–95, 97, 103–4; ousted from party, 110; and "political space," 98, 109
Post Office, 175
Presbyterian Church of East Africa (PCEA), 191–92
President, Office of the, 39, 77, 98, 102, 107–8, 117–18, 148, 172–73, 200–201, 234; assumes media censorship powers, 169–70; controls 1985 elections, 152, 157; increased power under Moi, 130–31, 144–45, 251n; KANU and, 110, 112; and political repression, 67–68, 140; redraws constituency boundaries, 165; selects candidates for elections, 132, 157, 160; suppresses parliamentary sovereignty, 171; takes control of KANU, 132–33, 143–47, 150–54, 157–61, 163–66, 168–71, 198; threatens LSK, 169; traditional political role, 2–4, 32–33, 36
Private sector: in Côte d'Ivoire, 230; and single-party system, 229–31
Progressive Kikuyu Party, 51
Protest songs, 183, 193–94
Public Law Institute (PLI), 172, 190
Public Order Act, 99, 188
Public Security Act, 135
Pyrethrum production, 87

Queuing system of voting: opposition to, 153, 170, 172, 191–92, 224

Reagan, Ronald, 203
Regional assemblies, 47
Religion. See Clergy
Resource allocation: in Central Province, 77–78, 88, 96–97; Central Province controls, 110–12; Kenyatta and, 47–50, 68, 74, 154; Kikuyu and, 81; Moi opposes, 104–5; Mwangale on, 78–80, 90; in Rift Valley Province, 77, 88–91, 110; in Western Province, 80
Rift Valley Province: agricultural crisis in (1979–80), 77, 96, 251n; demands for economic development in, 91–92; education reforms in, 81–82, 89, 91; land

reform programs in, 81–82, 89–91; maize crisis in, 80, 82–84; political opposition in, 108–10, 113–16, 117–18, 131, 184, 200; resettlement in, 81; resource allocation in, 77, 88–91
Riungu, Benson, 156
Roman Catholic Church: as political force in Zaire, 223; urges political liberalization, 192
Rosberg, Carl, 11
Rotary Club, 174
Rubia, Charles, 59, 89, 91, 101–2, 105, 109, 115, 147, 163; arrested and detained, 172, 176, 194–96; loses in rigged election, 173; opposes Moi, 172–73, 175–76, 179, 181, 188, 220–21; purged from KANU, 167, 173; urges formation of opposition parties, 174, 192

Saba Saba Day (1990): antigovernment riots on, 176, 183, 194, 224
Sagini, Lawrence, 151
Saina, William, 83
Saitoti, George, 169
Samoei Boys and Girls Harambee Boarding School, 88
Samoei Institute for Vocational and Technical Education, 88
Sandbrook, Richard, 18
Schatzberg, Michael, 207–8
Schools: supported by harambee system, 65–66
Scotland Yard, 196
Security agencies. See Police and security forces
Semo, Bahati, 148
Seroney, John Marie: background of, 87; as spokesman for populist faction, 87–88, 91, 93, 98–102, 105–6, 108, 139
"Sessional Paper Number 10 on the Application of Planning to African Socialism" (Mboya), 57, 62, 199
Shikuku, Martin, 89, 93, 100, 105, 147–48, 153, 165, 168; opposes Moi, 172; as opposition leader, 196
Siaya district, 93
Sifuna, Lawrence, 147
Single-party system, 240n; clergy oppose, 188, 190–92, 195, 202, 214, 229, 231; constitutional changes establish in Kenya, 39–40, 132, 145, 150, 162, 188–90, 198, 243n; difficulty of political opposition in, 85; effects on civil society, 117–18, 159, 168–71, 195, 207–8, 228–29; factionalism in, 27, 146; and fear of foreign intervention,

Single-party system (*continued*)
225–26; Kenyatta supports, 54–58,
61, 94, 159; lawyers oppose, 169, 172,
187–90, 192, 195, 201–2, 229, 231–
32; Moi defends, 215; NCCK opposes,
190–92; and oligarchy, 225; and "political space," 195, 198, 221; possibility of democracy in, 224–225, 227–
28; private economic sector and, 229–
30; in sub-Saharan Africa, 4–7, 215–
18; vs. multi-party system, 224–27,
232
Societies Act, 188
Somalia, 2, 16; ethnic divisions in, 225
Somali ethnic group, 178
South Africa, 3, 191, 215
Soviet Union, 114; intervenes in sub-
Saharan Africa, 225; single-party sys-
tem in, 228
Special Rural Development Program
(SRDP), 91, 247n
Squatters (*ahoi*), 41, 43, 49, 51, 53, 57,
81, 95, 139, 212
Standard (newspaper), 141, 154, 233
Staniland, Martin, 212
Starehe constituency, 172
State House. *See* President, Office of the
Stellascope (publishing house), 234
Study and Research Center on Mobutu-
ism (CEREMO; Zaire), 206
Sudan, 2, 177; ethnic divisions in, 225
Swainson, Nicola, 16
Sweden, 196, 202–3

Tambach Teacher Training College, 134
Tana River Authority, 139
Tanganyika African National Union
(TANU): compared to KANU, 208–
11; Nyerere's relationship with, 210
Tanganyika Federation of Labour, 209
Tanzania, 3, 5, 11, 72; compared to
Kenya, 204, 208–11; homogeneous so-
ciety in, 211; and international com-
munity, 212; local administration in,
209, 211; as party-state, 204, 208–13;
relationship between party and state
in, 208–12
Tanzania African National Union
(TANU), 160
Tax system, 65
Tea industry: Matiba and, 186–87; Moi
government and, 184–87
Thatcher, Margaret, 203
Thiberi, Samuel, 149
Thika, 176
Thiong'o, Ngugi wa, 14, 137, 175, 177
Thompson, James D., 206

Thuo, Francis, 173, 181
Times (St. Petersburg, Florida), 166
Tinderet constituency, 87, 88, 106
Tipis, Justus ole: in 1985 elections, 152
Toweett, Taita: in 1977 elections, 121
Trade Licensing Act, 169
Trade Union Agreement Act, 42
Trans-Nzoia district, 81, 85
Transportation sector: Moi attempts to
control, 181–83, 201, 203, 221; politi-
cal power of in Côte d'Ivoire, 221; in
Zaire, 223–24
Tribalism. *See* Ethnicity, and politics
Troon, Malcolm, 196
Tugen people, 87
Turkana district, 79
Turkey, 164

Uasin-Gishu district, 81–85
Uganda, 2, 86, 91, 167, 177, 194
Ujamaa movement (Tanzania), 209, 211
Ukenya group, 178
Umoja association, 177
Underdevelopment in Kenya (Leys),
15–16
Union pour la démocratie et le progrés
social (UDPS; Zaire), 222
UNITA (Angolan political movement),
223
United Nations: Economic and Social
Council (ECOSOC), 188; Education,
Science, and Culture Organization
(UNESCO), 188
United States, 208; foreign aid from,
174, 193, 202, 223, 239n; grants asy-
lum to Kenyan politicians, 176, 203,
233; intervenes in sub-Saharan Africa,
225; military interests in Kenya, 15–
17; single-party system in, 228, 240n,
241n; State Department, 203
University of London, 154
University of Nairobi: closed (1974),
104, 144; increased surveillance at,
146

Vihiga constituency, 148

Wabuge, Wafule, 83–84
Waiyaki, Munyua, 55, 61
Wallerstein, Immanuel, 7, 9
Wamwere, Koigi wa, 129, 139, 145, 177;
arrested and detained, 146, 189, 194
Wananchi Declaration, 60
Wanjigi, Maina, 103, 105, 115; expelled
from KANU, 194
Wanyonyi community, 80
Wariithi, Henry, 68

Warren, Bill, 16
Weekly Review (newspaper), 2, 119–20, 126, 140, 157–58, 162, 186, 234–35
Western Province, 81, 85, 89, 95, 100, 156, 165; and resource allocation, 80
White Highlands, 53–54, 57, 61, 85, 245n
"Who Killed Ouko" (song), 193
Wolpe, Howard, 202–3
World Bank, 1, 78, 81, 141, 202, 223, 225–26

Young, Crawford, 12, 21
Youth League (TANU & CCM; Tanzania), 210–11
Youth wing (KANU): in 1985 elections, 154, 159; recruited from informal economic sector, 194–95; resumes vigilante activities under Moi, 170; as vigilante group, 132, 149, 153–54, 159–60, 200

Zaire, 3, 5, 14, 22, 37, 132, 159–60, 162–63, 169, 202; compared to Kenya, 204–5, 208; economic threats to political elite in, 223; foreign aid suspended, 223; fragmented political opposition in, 224; freedom of the press in, 222; as party-state, 204–8, 213; relationship between party and state in, 206–7; Roman Catholic Church as political force in, 223; transportation sector in, 223–24
Zimbabwe, 3, 14
Zolberg, Aristide, 5, 7, 9–11, 13, 18, 23, 72, 218; *Creating Political Order: The Party-States of West Africa*, 6

Compositor: Graphic Composition, Inc.
Text: 10/13 Sabon
Display: Sabon
Printer and Binder: BookCrafters, Inc.